Competition Law in China

Jingyuan Ma

Competition Law in China

A Law and Economics Perspective

Springer

Jingyuan Ma
School of Law
Central University of Finance
and Economics
Beijing, China

ISBN 978-981-15-5104-8 ISBN 978-981-15-5105-5 (eBook)
https://doi.org/10.1007/978-981-15-5105-5

This Springer imprint is published by the registered company Springer Nature Singapore Pte Ltd.
The registered company address is: 152 Beach Road, #21-01/04 Gateway East, Singapore 189721, Singapore

Preface: Competition Law in China—A Law and Economics Perspective

This book provides a comprehensive overview on competition law and policy in China. By adopting a law and economics methodology, the book analyses the political, economic and legal environment of the competition system in China, and examines the substances of the Anti-monopoly Law from both a positive and normative approach. It explains the mixes of competition and industrial policies, the predominant pattern of administrative enforcement and the role of competition regulatory agencies. It also compares the antitrust practices in monopoly agreement, abuse of dominant positions and concentrations with those in the US and EU when law and economics criteria are taken as the benchmark. The book will be valuable for academics, researchers, and students who are interested in comparative competition law, as well as for business practitioners with experiences of doing business in China.

This book is supported by Humanities and Social Sciences Fund of the Ministry of Education (Regulation on Data Monopolies 教育部人文社科青年基金项目"数据垄断的法律规制研究" Project No. 18YJC820047), Program for Innovation Research (Legal Regulations of the Sharing Economy 共享经济的法律规制研究 Project No. QL18014), and Research on the Rule of Law of Data Opening and Trading in the Digital Era (智能时代数据开放与交易的法治研究) at Central University of Finance and Economics.

Beijing, China Jingyuan Ma

Acknowledgements

I am grateful to Prof. Niels Philipsen at Maastricht Institute for Transnational Legal Research (METRO) for his help and guidance on publishing this book. My sincere gratitude also goes to Prof. Michael Faure, Prof. Wu Tao, Prof. Stefan Weishaar, Prof. Roger van den Bergh and Prof. Mel Marquis for their insightful comments and suggestions. I owe special thanks to Dr. Caspar Schwalbe for his continuous support and encouragement. Profound thanks also to my competition law class students from 2014 till 2019 at Central University of Finance and Economics. I am grateful to Lydia Wang, Arulmurugan Venkatasalam, Muruga Prashanth Rajendran and the production team at SpringerNature for their kind and professional assistance in the publication process, and to Graham Sedgley for reviewing and proofreading all chapters of this book.

Contents

About the Author

Jingyuan Ma is an Assistant Professor at Central University of Finance and Economics in Beijing. Jingyuan holds an LLM in Law and Economics from the University of Hamburg and the University of Ghent (2010), and a BA in Economics from Beijing Foreign Studies University (2009). She obtained her Ph.D. from the University of Hamburg, Erasmus University Rotterdam and the University of Bologna, taking part in the European Doctorate in Law and Economics programme (EDLE). She teaches comparative competition law and economics, economic law, and market regulatory law. She has authored a monograph and several articles on comparative perspectives of competition policy in the US, the EU and China.

Abbreviations

ACCC	Australian Competition and Consumer Commission
AIC	Local Branches of SAIC
AMC	The Anti-monopoly Commission
AML	The Anti-monopoly Law of China
AUCL	Anti-Unfair Competition Law
BIS	Department for Business, Innovation and Skills (UK)
CA	Competition Authority
CBRC	China Banking Regulatory Commission
CFI	Court of First Instance
CIRC	China Insurance Regulatory Commission
CLPC	Competition Law and Policy Committee
CMA	Competition and Markets Authority
CPC	Communist Party of China
CSRC	China Securities Regulatory Commission
DOJ	Department of Justice
EC	European Community
ECN	European Competition Network
EU	European Union
FTC	Federal Trade Commission
GATT	General Agreement on Tariffs and Trade
ICN	International Competition Network
ITO	International Trade Organization
JFTC	Japanese Federal Trade Commission
KFTC	Korean Fair Trade Commission
MIIT	Ministry of Industry and Information Technology
MOFCOM	Ministry of Commerce
MPHPT	Ministry of Public Management, Home Affairs, Posts and Telecommunications
NDRC	National Development and Reform Commission
NPC	National People's Congress

OECD	Organization for Economic Cooperation and Development
OFT	Office of Fair Trading
OTC	Office of the Trade Commission
RPM	Resale Price Maintenance
SAIC	State Administration of Industry and Commerce
SAMR	State Administration for Market Regulation
SETC	State Economic and Trade Commission
SIPO	State Intellectual Property Office
SOE	State-owned Enterprises
SSNIP	Small but Significant and Non-transitory Increase in Price
TCC	Trade of Competition Commission
UK	United Kingdom
UNCTAD	United National Conference on Trade and Development
US	United States
WTO	World Trade Organization

List of Charts

Chapter 1
Introduction

Abstract After a thirteen year' legislative debate, the Anti-monopoly Law of China was enacted in August 2007 and came into force in August 2008. The first decade enforcement experience has shown that the AML has three main characteristics: incorporating non-economic goals into the purpose of the law; the predominant influence of administrative power in the practices of monopoly agreement, abuse of dominant position and concentrations; and the prevailing pattern of administrative enforcement. This book aims to explore the underlying political, economic and legal environment of those characteristics and to understand the advantages and limitations of the Chinese competition law and policy when a law and economics analytical framework is adopted. The introductory chapter provides an overview of the research question, structure of the book, and the methodology of law and economics, comparative legal studies and behavioural economics. It also discusses the academic and social relevance of this book.

1.1 Introduction

China's competition Law (the Anti-monopoly Law of the People's Republic of China, hereafter, the AML) was promulgated in August 2007 and came into force in August 2008. Three administrative agencies—the National Development and Reform Commission (NDRC), the State Administration and Industry and Commerce (SAIC), and the Anti-monopoly Bureau of the Ministry of Commerce (MOFCOM) comprised the regulatory institutions for competition in China. In May 2018, the three enforcement agencies merged into one under the State Administration for Market Regulation (SAMR). Since September 2017, the AML has been under revision and on January 2, 2020, the SAMR published a draft version of the revised AML for public comment (hereafter, the 2020 draft revision of the AML).[1]

[1] Shichang Jianguan Zongju Jiu Fanlongduan Fa Xiuding Caoan (Gongkai Zhengqiu Yijian Gao) Gongkai Zhengqiu Yijian De Gonggao (市场监管总局就《<反垄断法>修订草案（公开征求意见稿）》公开征求意见的公告) (Announcement of the SAMR on the Draft Revision of Anti-Monopoly Law [Draft for Public Comment]) January 2, 2020, available at http://www.samr.gov.cn/hd/zjdc/202001/t20200102_310120.html. Accessed 8 March 2020.

J. Ma, *Competition Law in China*,
https://doi.org/10.1007/978-981-15-5105-5_1

The AML has experienced a thirteen year legislative debate—the longest among market regulatory laws in China since the reform and opening up policy in 1978. Although the structure of the law has clearly followed the EU model, and monopoly agreements, abuse of dominant position and concentrations are the three main regulatory fields, the first decade of enforcement experience has shown that the AML has its distinct characteristics. First, the AML has made it explicit that industrial policy considerations are not excluded from competition law. The goals of developing a socialist market economy and protecting public interests are both included in the main goals of the AML under Article 1.[2] Second, the substantive law of the AML has followed the model of the EU competition law by dividing into three pillars: the prohibition of monopoly agreements (Chap. 2), abuse of dominant position (Chap. 3), and concentrations (Chap. 4). Whereas more attention has been paid to merger control after the enactment of the AML, SAIC, NDRC and courts have taken positive action on investigating the other two types of anti-competitive conduct in recent years. Private cartel type price fixing agreements are influenced with monopolistic behaviour by public and administrative entities, in particular trade associations; a dominant position is often obtained through governmental authorization and charging excessive prices is possible because the business operator is the exclusive business provider in the given market. Merger review has to go through a strict ex-ante administrative procedure. The AML provides lenient treatment for administrative monopolies, and the fair competition review was only adopted in 2016 to improve the enforcement of administrative monopolies. Third, administrative enforcement prevails for private or criminal enforcement, and the competition agency plays a dominant role in the implementation of the law, and administrative fines have been frequently imposed on cases related to cartels, vertical restrictions, abuse of dominance and concentrations. In merger control, behavioural remedies have been extensively applied.

To follow the discussions of the legislative debate and main contents of the AML in the past years,[3] this book aims at examining the developments of the AML and to provide an up-to-date overview on the competition law and policy in China. It particularly provides an in-depth analysis of the three characteristics mentioned above from a law and economics perspective. In the first part, it discusses the interacting relationship between competition law and industrial policies in the legislative debate of the AML and reviews the main arguments of incorporating non-economic goals in Article 1 of the AML. In the second part, particular attention is given to the substantive law by studying the cases on monopoly agreements, abuse of dominant position and concentrations. It studies the substances of competition laws and regulations in China, including the contents of AML and provisional rules issued by SAIC, NDRC, MOFCOM and SAMR. It reviews the prevailing influence of administrative power in

[2]Article 1 of the AML reads that the law is enacted for preventing and restraining monopolistic conduct, protecting fair competition in the market, enhancing economic efficiency, safeguarding the interests of consumers and social public interest, and promoting the healthy development of a socialist market economy.

[3]Wang and Su (2014), Wei (2013), Zheng (2010), Wang (2008), Huang (2008), Owen et al. (2008), Gerber (2008), Jung and Hao (2003), Van den Bergh and Faure (2011).

facilitating monopoly agreements, strengthening the dominant position of the business operators, and the administrative procedure in merger review. It also discusses the problem of administrative monopoly, and the recent progress of fair competition review in combating administrative monopolies. In the third part, it studies the role of administrative agencies and the choices of sanctions on the enforcement of AML. From a law and economics perspective, it discusses the economic reasons and advantages for relying on administrative control, and how a balanced enforcement system could be built when behavioural economics evidence is taken into account. The last part of the book also includes the internationalization of competition law and the extraterritorial effects of the AML. It shows that the international cooperation of the AML has been managed through competition agencies, and a cooperation between regulators is needed for an effective enforcement of the law.

As a positive study, the book shows how a competition law regime has been developed through an administrative top-down hierarchy and while administrative competition authorities are the main enforcers of the law, at the same time monopolistic behaviour used to be arranged by other administrative agencies. It discusses the legislative debate, recent cases, fair competition review system, and recent institutional reforms. It explains the contents of the law and the interpretations of the provisions by summarizing the case decisions. By taking a normative view, the book adopts law and economics theories to examine how economic analysis could be applied in the context of competition law in China. It studies the criteria on the mixes of regulatory instruments, the choices of sanctions, the role of courts and experts, and behavioural biases of different enforcers, and discusses the advantages and challenges for relying on an administrative enforcement system. The third part of the book discusses whether the current enforcement is aligned with economic analysis, and in particular how the competition practice in China could be compared with the US and the EU.

1.2 Structure of the Book

The book has three main parts: the overview of the AML, the substantive law of the AML, and the enforcement of the AML, and each part takes both a positive and a normative view. Part I (Chaps. 2 and 3) provides an overview of the AML on the legislative background, the substances, the enforcement structure and the procedural law. It explains why industrial policy has been incorporated as one of the five main goals of the AML. Part 2 (Chaps. 4–7) describes the contents of the law, including the interpretation of the law, the provisions issued by the competition agencies, and the landmark cases of horizontal and vertical restrictions, abuse of dominance position, merger review and administrative monopolies. Part 3 (Chaps. 9–12) analyses the enforcement agency, the choice of sanctions, role of courts and experts, and how current enforcement institutions could be explained from a behavioural economics perspective. It studies how competition agency functions in China, and discusses why administrative fines have been extensively applied while criminal sanctions have not been in place. From a normative aspect, this part will discuss how competition agencies should be structured to improve enforcement, how the key values of independence, accountability, transparency, capacity building in the regulatory performance assessment could be fulfilled, and when comparing with the criteria of the 'smart mix' of public and private enforcement, how private and criminal enforcement should be incentivized. Specifically, recent developments of behavioural economics should also be taken into account to design a more effective and efficient competition regime.

1.3 Methodology

The research methods in this book include law and economics, comparative legal studies, institutional economics and behavioural law and economics. Theories on competition law and the enforcement of law will be studied in detail. Law and economics theories will serve as the foundation for the normative criteria of competition law and its enforcement.

1.3.1 Law and Economics

Competition law has deep roots in classical and neo-classical economics. In the context of competition law, economic concepts are frequently applied and a close interaction between economic and legal theory has been observed. Law and economics theory will be used as the benchmark in this book when examining the characteristics of Chinese competition law, and it will also be taken as the criteria when discussing the normative questions of whether the current enforcement system could be improved. Empirical methods have been applied to analyze the monopolistic agreements were given administrative fines imposed by SAIC, NDRC, Price Bureau and their local branches between 2008 and 2018. The empirical results are discussed in Chap. 4 (horizontal agreements), Chap. 9 (Enforcement of Competition Law: Public Enforcement and Competition Agencies) and Chap. 10 (Enforcement of Competition Law: Economic Analysis of Antitrust Sanctions).

1.3.2 Institutional Economics

Following Douglas North's central claim that institutions matter for improving the performance of the market and to facility economic growth,[4] the design of competition institutions, in particular the function of competition enforcement authorities,

---

[4]North (1990).

is relevant to explain the effectiveness of the competition law, and to affect outcomes as part of the function of a market economy.[5] Competition agencies may have different policy priorities at a particular stage of industrialization, and the reform of competition agency is closely interrelated with the economic and institutional reform. Theoretical discussions in institutional economics and political economy may explain the role that the competition agency aims to play, and to understand the legal framework of the competition policy from a broader view.

1.3.3 Behavioural Law and Economics

In recent decades, behavioural psychologists,[6] economists[7] and social scientists[8] have devoted significant efforts to study the heuristic biases in individual decision-making process, and has provided new explanations to situations where public and private actors may deviate from the rational choice model that classic law and economics literature rely on. Behavioural economists and cognitive psychologists have argued that people have limited brainpower to calculate the utility pay-off of their conduct; rather, they often engage in a process of "satisficing", in which process a target is chosen to meet their aspiration. Herbert Simon defined it as "bounded rationality".[9] The cognitive biases were discovered by a series of experiments conducted by both psychologists and economists, including anchoring effects, prospect theory, loss aversion, framing, endowment effect, hindsight bias, representative effects, egocentric bias, availability heuristic, status quo bias, and aversion to extremes.

Research on the behaviour of public actors indicates that government failure may occur when public actors are biased. In particular, introducing debiasing strategies, such as learning effect, to correct irrational decisions is more difficult for public actors than private actors. Chapter 12 of this book will introduce the most updated research on behavioural law and economics, behavioural political economy, and behavioural administration theory, to discuss why a competition agency may perform sub-optimally due to the behavioural bias of agency staff and bureaucrats. It will provide additional explanations for the deficiencies of the organization design of the agency, and for discussing the possible solutions for developing debiasing mechanisms to improve the quality of the decisions of competition agencies.

[5]Sokol (2010).

[6]Tversky and Kahneman (1982), Kahneman (2003), Kahneman et al. (1982), Evans (1984).

[7]Babcock and Loewenstein (1997), Benartzi and Thaler (1995), Camerer and Hogarth (1999).

[8]Fiske and Taylor (1991), Weinstein (1980).

[9]Simon (1979).

1.3.4 Comparative Legal Studies

Chinese competition law has clearly incorporated the main structures of the EU Competition Law, and the recent trend of 'a more economic approach' has also triggered the debate of moving towards more economic analysis in Chinese law. When comparing the economic criteria that have been taken as the benchmark for the choice of enforcement instruments, it will be valuable to compare practices in China with the US and EU. The methodology of comparative legal studies will be applied mainly in the third part of this book in order to discuss the characteristics and recent developments on the enforcement patterns in the US, EU and China (choices on administrative, civil and criminal enforcement, choices on sanctions and the mixes of regulatory instruments).

1.4 Academic Relevance and Limitations

Since the enactment of the Sherman Act over a century ago, competition law has experienced dramatic shifts in its goals, functions, and institutional designs. Although the subject itself is a clear integration between micro-economic concepts and deep roots in legal history, the debate between economists, lawyers, behaviouralists, political scientists and philosophers never ends.

In the 12th year of the AML, this book provides a comprehensive review of the competition law and policy system in China. In addition to providing the most-updated information on legislation, cases and enforcement systems, it is built up on a solid theoretical foundation of institutional economics and comparative competition law and economics. Starting from the legislative debate on competition goals, the book argues that although competition goals have been narrowed down to economic welfare analysis in the US and EU, non-economic goals in particular industrial policy concerns are clearly included in the AML in China. When comparing the substantive law in the US, EU and China, monopolistic behaviour conducted by private businesses and those facilitated by administrative organs have both been observed, and administrative monopolies are one of the main targets of the AML. In the aspect of enforcement system, economic theory and a law and economics analytical framework has been incorporated to discuss the current enforcement regime in China.

The book will contribute to the recent debate on comparative competition law. Studying the particular characteristics of the Chinese competition law would be relevant to understand the success and limitations of antitrust legal transplantation, to study the global trend of antitrust internationalization and to provide suggestions for how the Chinese competition enforcement could be improved. The institutional function of competition agencies, the role that they should play, and their internal and external organizations have been changed during the past decades, and the changes will continue in the coming years. Thus, this book serves as a theoretical baseline, and the review of competition agencies will have to be updated when new changes are made, and when more disciplines are incorporated into competition law.

References

Babcock, L., & Loewenstein, G. (1997). Explaining bargaining impasse: The role of self-serving biases. *Journal of Economic Perspective, 11,* 109–126.

Benartzi, S., & Thaler, R. H. (1995). Myopic loss aversion and the equity premium puzzle. *Quarterly Journal of Economics, 110*(1), 73–92.

Camerer, C. F., & Hogarth, R. M. (1999). The effect of financial incentives. *Journal of Risk and Uncertainty, 19,* 7–42.

Evans, J. St. B. T. (1984). Heuristic and analytic processes in reasoning. *British Journal of Psychology, 75,* 451–468.

Fiske, S. T., & Taylor, S. E. (1991). *Social cognition* (2nd ed.). New York: McGraw-Hill.

Gerber, D. J. (2008). Economics, law and institutions: The shaping of Chinese competition law. *Journal of Law and Policy, 26,* 271–299.

Huang, Y. (2008). Pursuing the second best: The history, momentum and remaining issues of China's anti-monopoly law. *Antitrust Law Journal, 75,* 117–132.

Jung, Y. J., & Hao, Q. (2003). The new economic constitution in China: A third way for competition regime? *Northwestern Journal of International Law & Business, 24,* 107–142.

Kahneman, D. (2003). Maps of bounded rationality: Psychology for behavioral economics. *The American Economic Review, 93*(5), 1449–1475.

Kahneman, D., Slovic, P., & Tversky, A. (Eds.). (1982). *Judgment under uncertainty: Heuristics and biases*. New York and Cambridge: Cambridge University Press.

North, D. C. (1990). *Institutions, Institutional change and economic performance*. Cambridge: Cambridge University Press.

Owen, B. M., Sun, S., & Zheng, W. (2008). China's competition policy reforms: The anti-monopoly law and beyond. *Antitrust Law Journal, 75,* 231–266.

Simon, H. A. (1979). Rational decision-making in business organizations. *The American Economic Review, 69*(4), 493–513.

Sokol, D. D. (2010). Antitrust, institutions, and merger control. *George Mason Law Review, 17,* 1055–1148.

Tversky, A., & Kahneman, D. (1982). Judgements of and by representatives. In D. Kahneman, P. Slovic, & A. Tversky (Eds.), *Judgement under uncertainty: Heuristics and biases* (pp. 84–98). Cambridge: Cambridge University Press.

Van den Bergh, R., & Faure, M. (2011). Critical issues in the enforcement of the anti-monopoly law in China: A law and economics perspective. In M. Faure, & X. Zhang (Eds.), *Competition policy and regulation, recent developments in China, the US and Europe* (pp. 54–72). Cheltenham: Edward Elgar.

Wang, X. (2008). Highlights of China's new anti-monopoly law. *Antitrust Law Journal, 75,* 133–150.

Wang, X., & Su, J. (2014). *Competition law in China* (2nd ed.). The Netherlands: Kluwer Law International.

Wei, D. (2013). Antitrust in China: An overview of recent implementation of Anti-Monopoly law. *European Business Organization Law Review, 14*(1), 119–139.

Weinstein, N. D. (1980). Unrealistic optimism about future life events. *Journal of Personality and Social Psychology, 39*(5), 806–820.

Zheng, W. (2010). Transplanting antitrust in China: Economic transition, market structure and state control. *University of Pennsylvania Journal of International Law, 32*(2), 643–721.

Part I
Overview of the Anti-monopoly Law

Chapter 2
Competition Law in China: An Overview

Abstract The Anti-monopoly Law of China (the AML) was promulgated in 2007 and came into force in August 2008. The AML has incorporated both economic and non-economic goals, and industrial policy concerns are considered to be predominant. The role of State-owned enterprises and the issue of administrative monopolies has to be understood in the context of market reform and the developments of national industrial policy. The AML followed clear bureaucratic enforcement, and since August 2018, the State Administration for Market Regulation (SAMR) has become the enforcement agency of the AML. The AML is composed of 57 articles in 8 chapters. Chapter 1 provides general provisions, and Chap. 2 (Articles 13–16) deals with monopoly agreements. Chapter 3 (Articles 17–19) covers the abuse of dominant position, and Chap. 4 (Articles 20–31) focuses on concentrations. Chapter 5 (Articles 32–37) deals with administrative monopolies. Chapter 6 is about investigative procedure (Articles 38–45). Chapter 7 (Articles 46–54) is on legal liabilities and the last chapter is supplementary provisions. In addition, provisions issued by the SAIC, NDRC, MOFCOM and SAMR are relevant to understand the procedural rules of the AML.

2.1 Introduction

On 30 August 2007, after thirteen years of discussion, the Anti-Monopoly Law of the People's Republic of China (the AML) was promulgated by the 29th session of the 10th Standing Committee of China's National People's Congress, and it entered into force in August 2008. In 2020, the AML has marked its twelfth anniversary. The formulation of the AML has followed the EU competition Law,[1] with three main chapters dealing with monopolistic agreements, abuse of dominant position, and concentrations. However, the first decade's enforcement experience has shown its particular pattern. For example, the five different goals mentioned in Article 1 of the AML included both economic and non-economic goals, and industrial policy concerns which are considered to be predominant. The legislative process of this

[1] Wei (2011), Gerber (2008), Jung and Hao (2003), Samuels (2007), Zheng (2010).

J. Ma, *Competition Law in China*,
https://doi.org/10.1007/978-981-15-5105-5_2

law coincided with the market reform in China, which aims at establishing a market economy.[2] Therefore, the AML not only establishes the legal foundations for a competitive market, but also fulfills several social goals, such as the protection of the public interest and the pursuit of a socialist market economy. The role of state-owned enterprises and the issue of administrative monopolies has to be understood in the context of market reform and the developments of national industrial policy. The tension between different policy goals makes the enforcement of the AML more difficult. Since its enactment, there has been a considerable debate over how this law could be effectively implemented.[3]

The AML in China has followed a clear bureaucratic enforcement style, and enforcement agencies may exercise their power on competition issues in a similar way to that of other administrative duties. Administrative enforcement has predominated in all three main areas, and private enforcement and criminal enforcement has been underdeveloped. State Administration for Industry and Commerce (SAIC), National Development and Reform Commission (NDRC) and the Anti-monopoly Bureau of the Ministry of Commerce (MOFCOM) are the three enforcement agencies in charge of non price-related conduct, price-related monopolistic conduct, and merger review respectively. After experiencing the advantages as well as limitations of the three-headed enforcement structure, the three enforcement agencies were restructured and unified into one, the State Administration for Market Regulation (SAMR) in August 2018.

2.2 Competition Rules Before the AML

On October 17, 1980 the State Council adopted the Provisional Rules on the Development and Protection of Socialist Competition.[4] The administrative regulation acknowledged that competition has been developed since the adjustment and reform made after the market reform, and it specified that competition in socialist economies should be carried out under the guidance of the state plan on the basis of the public ownership, and competition is promoted to ensure all production and business units will complete the national production and marketing plan, improve product quality, management, labour efficiency and reduce costs. This regulation for the first time acknowledged that product prices, designated by the state under the planned economy, should be permitted in order to make adjustments to stimulate competition, and enterprises have the right to lower the price, whereas the price increases have to be approved by the price management division. In the 1980s, the State Council and the

[2] Wei (2013).

[3] Van den Bergh and Faure (2011).

[4] Guanyu Kaizhan He Baohu Shehui Zhuyi Jingzheng De Zanxing Guiding (关于开展和保护社会主义竞争的暂行规定) [Provisional Rules on the Development and Protection of Socialist Competition] (promulgated by the State Council on 17 October 1980, effective on 17 October 1980, and repealed on 6 October 2001).

ministries of transportation, import and export management,[5] foreign commerce, and construction[6] have adopted competition rules for preventing regional blocks on the circulation of products. In September 1987, the State Council enacted the administrative regulation on price control,[7] and in Article 3 it stipulates that the State adopts the principle of "combining direct price administration and indirect price control", and three types of prices for commodities and rates of service fees will be implemented: state stipulated price, state guided price and the market adjusted price.

Since the early 1990s, several laws and administrative regulations which aimed at preventing anti-competitive practices were implemented. The Anti-unfair Competition Law was adopted at the 3rd Session of the Standing Committee of the Eighth National People's Congress on September 2, 1993, and it was revised at the 30th Session of the Standing Committee of the Twelfth National People's Congress on November 4, 2017. As stated in Article 1, the law is enacted for the purposes of promoting a socialist market economy, protecting competition, preventing unfair competition, and safeguarding the lawful rights and interests of businesses and consumers. This law outlines the basic framework for competition policy before the AML. The law before amendment prohibits predatory pricing which will restrict competition (Article 11), or forced tying and bundling (Article 12), and the law prohibits public utilities or other enterprises from holding monopoly positions that restrict competition by forcing others to purchase specific commodities (Article 6). Article 7 of this law also deals with administrative monopoly. It states that government organs should not abuse administrative power to restrict competition by forcing others to purchase products. The other issues that this law addresses, such as bribery, false advertisement, prohibition of fraudulent practices, and coercive sales, made some commentators believe that this law is more like a consumer protection law, not an antitrust law.[8] After the enactment of the AML, the provisions on competition issues have been removed. The Anti-unfair Competition Law empowered SAIC as the enforcement agency. This law was amended on November 4, 2017, and provisions

---

[5]Guojia Jingji Weiyuanhui, Jinchukou Guanli Weiyuanhui, Jiaotongbu, Duiwai Maoyi Bu, Guanyu Gaige Waimao Yunshu Guanli Tizhi Huiyi Jiyao (国家经济委员会、进出口管理委员会、交通部、对外贸易部关于改革外贸运输管理体制会议纪要 1981) [Minutes of the Meeting on Reforming the Management System of Foreign Trade Transportation, promulgated by State Economic Commission, Import and Export Management Committee, Ministry of Transportation, and Ministry of Foreign Trade] (effective in 1981); Guowuyuan Guanyu Zai Gongyepin Gouxiao Zhong Jinzhi Fengsuo De Tongzhi (国务院关于在工业品购销中禁止封锁的通知) [Notice of the State Council on the Prohibition of Blockade in the Purchase and Sale of Industrial Products] (promulgated by the State Council on April 10, 1982, effective on April 10, 1982).

[6]Guowuyuan Guanyu Gaige Jianzhuye He Jiben Jianshe Guanli Tizhi Ruogan Wenti De Zanxing Guiding (国务院关于改革建筑业和基本建设管理体制若干问题的暂行规定) [Provisions of the State Council on the Reform of the Management System of the Construction Industry] (promulgated by the State Council on September 18, 1984, effective on September 18, 1984).

[7]Zhonghua Renmin Gongheguo Jiage Guanli Tiaoli (中华人民共和国价格管理条例) [Regulations of the People's Republic of China on Price Control] (promulgated by the State Council on September 11, 1987, effective on September 11, 1987).

[8]Owen et al. (2008).

on competition issues such as exclusive dealing (Article 6), abuse of administrative power (Article 7), below-cost sales (Article 11) and tie-in sales (Article 12) have been removed to ensure the conciliation of the Anti-Unfair Competition Law and the AML.[9]

In December 1997, the 29th meeting of the Standing Committee of the Eighth National People's Congress adopted the Price Law and it became effective on May 1, 1998. The Price law provides the legal framework for the mechanism of price regulations, and clarifies that prices are mainly made through market force and fixed independently by business operators through market competition, and only a few commodities are fixed by business operators in accordance to the benchmark or ranges of the price set by the government departments in charge of prices. Article 14 of the Price Law prohibits business operators from manipulating market prices through collusion that harms the interest of consumers or other business operators, or engaging in dumping sales below costs in order to obtain market dominance and impede market order, or conducting price discrimination for the same merchandise or services under the same trading conditions. Article 17 of the Price Law requires industrial associations to comply with laws and regulations on prices, and to act with self-discipline in accordance with guidance from government price departments.

To facilitate the implementation of the Price Law, the enforcement agency of the Price Law,[10] the NDRC, which became another enforcement agency of the AML in later years, issued the Interim Provisions on Preventing the Acts of Price Monopoly in June 2003.[11] Article 3 of this regulation states that market predominance should be determined by three elements: the market share in the relevant market, the product substitutability and the difficulty of market entry. Article 4 of the provision prohibits business operators from conducting price monopolistic behaviour including uniformly determining, maintaining or changing prices, controlling prices by limiting supply or production, controlling prices in bidding, tendering or auction. Articles 5–8 refer to provisions for prohibiting market dominance. Article 5 prohibits business operators from abusing market dominance by setting resale prices and Article 7 prohibits anti-competitive conduct including dumping at prices below costs or by means of rebates, subsidies and gifts in order to squeeze out competitors. Article 8 stipulates that no business operator is allowed to rely on its market dominance to charge discriminatory prices for the same transaction objects.

---

[9]For an overview of the comparison between the 1993 and the 2017 Anti-unfair Competition Law in the English language, see China Amends Anti-unfair Competition Law: What are the Changes and What to Expect, Linklaters, January 2018, available at https://www.linklaters.com/en-us/insights/publications/asia-news/china-update/2018/china-amends-anti-unfair-competition-law (accessed 28 March 2020).

[10]Zhonghua Renmin Gongheguo Jiagefa 中华人民共和国价格法 [Price Law of the People's Republic of China] (issued by the Standing Committee of the National People's Congress on December 29, 1997 and effective on May 1, 1998).

[11]Zhizhi Jiage Longduan Xingwei Zanxing Guiding (制止价格垄断行为暂行规定) [Interim Provisions on Preventing the Acts of Price Monopoly] (promulgated by the State Development and Reform Commission, June 18, 2003, effective on November 1, 2003).

The Ministry of Commerce established their antitrust office in 2004, showing their interest in investigating antitrust cases and in drafting legislation, especially in the field of merger and acquisitions. The office was named as the Ministry of Commerce Anti-Monopoly Bureau (MOFCOM). This office is responsible for the implementation of the Interim Provisions for Foreign Investors to Merge Domestic Enterprises, an administrative regulation on merger and acquisitions issued by six administrations in March 2003.[12] This provision stipulates that foreign investor when merging a domestic enterprise must apply for approval and make registration of modification or establishment. Article 15 of the provision listed the documents submitted to the approval agency, and Article 17 states that the approval agency shall make decisions on whether the approval is to be granted within 30 days as of the receipt of the documents submitted. The provision was amended and replaced by Interim Provisions on the Takeover of Domestic Enterprises by Foreign Investors in 2006.[13] Article 3 of the 2006 provision stipulates that the takeover of domestic enterprise by a foreign investor must not cause excessive concentration in order to exclude or limit competition, and must not impede social economic order, harm public interest or cause loss of state-owned assets. Chapter 5 (Articles 51–54) of the 2006 Provision is the antitrust review, and has specified the thresholds and requirements on merger review. During 2007 (one year before the AML came into force) the MOFCOM had already conducted over 220 reviews of merger cases.[14] These practices made the MOFCOM more experienced in investigating antitrust cases and implementing other merger control guidelines after the enactment of the AML. In 2009, to ensure that the 2006 provision was consistent with the AML, MOFCOM issued the Decision of the Ministry of Commerce on Amending the Provisions on the Merger or Acquisition of Domestic Enterprises by Foreign Investors,[15] and Chap. 5 of the 2006 Provision had been removed, and a supplementary provision was added in Article 51 to clarify that the declaration standards will be specified by the Provisions of the State Council on the Standards for the Declaration of Business Concentration, a merger review provision issued in accordance with AML.

---

[12] Waiguo Touzizhe Binggou Jingnei Qiye Zanxing Guiding (外国投资者并购境内企业暂行规定) [Interim Provisions for Foreign Investors to Merge Domestic Enterprises] (promulgated by Ministry of Foreign Trade & Economic Cooperation, State Taxation Administration, State Administration for Industry & Commerce, State Administration of Foreign Exchange, issued on July 3, 2003 and effective on December 4, 2003).

[13] Guanyu Waiguo Touzi Zhe Binggou Jingnei Qiye De Guiding (关于外国投资者并购境内企业的规定) [Interim Provisions on the Takeover of Domestic Enterprises by Foreign Investors (2006 Revision)](promulgated by Ministry of Commerce, State-owned Asset Supervision & Administration Commission of the State Council, State Taxation Administration, State Administration for Industry & Commerce, China Securities Regulatory Commission, State Administration of Foreign Exchange, issued on August 8, 2006, effective on September 8, 2006).

[14] Wu (2008).

[15] Shangwubu Guanyu Xiugai Waiguo Touzi Zhe Binggou Jingnei Qiye de Guiding de Jueding (商务部关于修改《关于外国投资者并购境内企业的规定》的决定) [Decision of the Ministry of Commerce on Amending the Provisions on the Merger or Acquisition of Domestic Enterprises by Foreign Investors] (issued on June 22, 2009, effective on June 22, 2009).

Anti-monopoly policies have also been reflected in other laws. Article 16 of the Law on the Protection of Consumer Rights and Interests prohibits business operators from setting unfair or unreasonable trading conditions, or forcing consumers into transactions.[16] Article 32 of the Foreign Trade Law stipulates that no business operators shall conduct monopolization in foreign trade business activities. Article 33 of the Foreign Trade Law[17] prohibits business operators from conducting unfair competition acts such as selling commodities at unjustified low prices, collusion in bidding and tendering and other unfair competition acts including disseminating false advertisements or offering commercial bribes in business activities of foreign trade. Article 9 of the Law on Commercial Banks stipulates that commercial banks must conduct business according to the principle of fair competition.[18] Article 32 of the Bidding Law[19] prohibits tenders from engaging in collusion when setting bidding prices, or excluding other tenders from participating in fair competition. Article 115 of the Insurance Law[20] stipulates that insurance companies must operate in accordance with the principle of fair competition.

2.3 Drafting Process of the AML

In 1987, an antitrust law drafting team was established under the Legislative Affairs Office of the State Council.[21] The task of drafting the AML was allocated to a group in 1994, whose members were selected from the SAIC and the State Economic and Trade Commission (SETC).[22] This group drafted the competition law for China by examining antitrust laws in other jurisdictions, including the antitrust laws in the United States, Germany, Japan, Australia, and South Korea.[23]

---

[16] Zhonghua Renmin Gongheguo Xiaofeizhe Quanyi Baohu Fa (中华人民共和国消费者权益保护法) [Law of the People's Republic of China on Protection of Consumer Rights and Interests] (issued on 31 October 1993, effective on 1 January 1994, revised on 27 August 2009, amended on October 25, 2013).

[17] Zhonghua Renmin Gongheguo Duiwai Maoyi Fa (中华人民共和国对外贸易法) [Foreign Trade Law of the People's Republic of China] (issued on 12 May 1994, effective on 1 July 1994, revised on 6 April 2004, amended in 7 November 2016).

[18] Zhonghua Renmin Gongheguo Shangye Yinhang Fa (中华人民共和国商业银行法) [Law of the People's Republic of China on Commercial Banks] (issued on 10 May 1995, effective on 1 July 1995, amended on 27 December 2003, amended on October 1, 2015).

[19] Zhonghua Renmin Gongheguo Zhaobiao Toubiao Fa (中华人民共和国招标投标法) [The Bidding Law of the People's Republic of China] (issued on 30 August 1999, effective on 1 January 2000, amended on December 27, 2017).

[20] Zhonghua Renmin Gongheguo Baoxian Fa (中华人民共和国保险法) [Insurance Law of the People's Republic of China] (issued on April 24, 2015, effective on April 24, 2015).

[21] Neumann, The Slow Boat to Antitrust Law in China, *Faegre Baker Daniels*, 23 December 2003, available at https://www.faegredrinker.com/en/insights/publications/2003/12/the-slow-boat-to-antitrust-law-in-china (accessed 30 March 2020).

[22] Huang (2008).

[23] Hittinger and Huh (2007, p. 249).

After the SETC was abolished during the government agency reform in 2003, MOFCOM took its place.[24] The standing committee of the National People's Congress included the Chinese Competition Law in the eighth (in 1994), the ninth (in 1998) and the tenth (in 2003) legislative schedule. The drafting process, however, took nearly a decade. The first finished draft was distributed among business professionals and legal scholars in 2002. During the drafting process, foreign experts and officials from the competition authorities in the US, Germany, Japan, Australia, and Korea, as well as officials from international organizations were consulted.[25] The draft law was reviewed by experts from both public and private sectors in the EU, Japan, and Korea.[26] In October 2004, another draft was submitted by the MOFCOM to the Legislative Affairs Office of the State Council.[27] In June 2006, the Legislative Affairs Office of the State Council submitted the finished draft to the Standing Committee of the National People's Congress (NPC). When Mr Cao Kangtai, the Director of the Legislative Office under the State Council, submitted this draft to the NPC for the legislative review, he mentioned three reasons why this AML should be enacted[28]: first, monopolistic agreements should be prohibited for the reason that both consumers and other competitors will be harmed; monopolistic agreements will also be obstacles to establishing an integrated national market; second, a law has to be established to mitigate the negative effects created by mergers and concentrations; third, a competition framework needs to be established in China, which will form an open and transparent legal environment for business.

In June 2006, Premier Minister Wen Jiabao chaired the State Council executive meeting, during which the AML (draft) was discussed and passed. The draft was revised and further reviewed by the Standing Committee of the National People's Congress in June 2007.[29] On 30 August 2007, the twenty-ninth session of the Tenth National People's Congress passed the AML and this law took effect on 1 August 2008.

2.4 Overview of the AML

The AML is composed of 57 articles in 8 chapters. Chapter 1 provides general provisions. Chapter 2 (Articles 13–16) deals with monopoly agreements,[30] including the prohibited horizontal monopoly agreements (Article 13), the prohibited vertical monopoly agreements (Article 14) and a list of exemptions that may be granted

---

[24]Shang (2005), The Development and Legislation of Competition Policy in China (发展中的中国竞争政策与立法, April 27, 2005; see also Owen et al. (2008, p. 236).

[25]Howell et al. (2009).

[26]Howell et al. (2009, p. 56).

[27]Berry (2005, p. 140).

[28]Huang (2008, p. 119).

[29]Owen et al. (2008).

[30]AML Chap. 2, Articles 13–16.

(Article 15). The prohibited monopoly agreements include fixing or changing prices of commodities; restricting the level of output or sales; dividing the market of sales or raw material procurement; limiting the purchase of new technology or new facilities; involvement in boycott transactions; fixing the price of commodities for resale to a third party; and restricting the minimum price for resale to a third party. Article 15 provides the seven circumstances that can be exempted from these prohibitions, including monopoly agreements that for the purpose of improving technologies, developing new products, improving product quality, enhancing efficiency and the public interest, promoting competition for small and medium-sized businesses, or mitigating sales loss in economic recessions, preserve justifiable interests engaging in international trade and cooperation.[31]

Chapter 3 (Articles 17–19) covers the abuse of dominant market position.[32] Article 17 first lists the actions that should be considered as an abuse of a dominant position. These actions are selling or buying products at unfairly high or low prices, and, without justification, selling products at prices below cost, refusing to trade, exclusive dealing, tying, or applying dissimilar prices or terms.[33] Article 18 specifies the determining variables for defining dominant market status, including the market share in the relevant market, the competitiveness of the relevant market, the capacity of controlling the sales or raw material procurement market, the undertaking's financial and technical condition, and the difficulty of market entry.[34] Article 19 further clarifies the criteria for calculating market dominance. A business operator will be considered to hold a dominant market position when its market share in the relevant market is at least 50%; or two undertakings' joint market share accounts for two thirds of the relevant market; or three undertakings' joint market share is three quarters or above. Specifically, in the latter two circumstances, the business operator with a market share of less than ten percent should not be taken into account.[35]

Chapter 4 (Articles 20–31) of the AML focuses on concentrations.[36] This chapter lays the legal foundation for the merger control policy, followed by three layers of administrative rules enacted after the AML. This chapter includes the definition of concentration, the circumstances under which a concentration must not be declared to the anti-monopoly authority under the State Council, the documents to be submitted for a declaration of a concentration, the procedure of declared concentration review, the relevant elements that should be considered in concentration examination, the exemptions of prohibition regarding public interests, restrictive conditions, publication of decisions and considerations of national security.

---

[31] AML Chap. 2.

[32] AML Chap. 3, Articles 17–19.

[33] AML Article 17.

[34] AML Article 18.

[35] AML Article 19.

[36] AML Chap. 4, Articles 20–31.

The last four chapters of the AML deal with administrative monopoly,[37] the investigatory procedure,[38] legal liabilities[39] and supplementary provisions,[40] and the provisions will be discussed in detail in Chaps. 8 and 10 of this book, and also in Sect.2.4.2 of this chapter.

2.4.1 *Overview of the AML Enforcement Agencies*

According to Articles 9 and 10 of the AML, the competence of organizing, coordinating and guiding the anti-monopoly work is granted to the Anti-Monopoly Commission (AMC), a central antitrust authority responsible to the State Council. This Commission is responsible for policy formulation and co-ordination. The AMC may authorize local governments in provinces, autonomous regions and municipalities to take responsibility for enforcement. According to Article 9 of the AML, the five functions that this commission plays are (1) studying and drafting relevant competition policies; (2) organizing the investigation and assessment of overall competition situations in the market, and issuing assessment reports; (3) constituting and issuing anti-monopoly guidelines; (4) coordinating anti-monopoly administrative law enforcement; (5) other functions as assigned by the State Council.

On July 28, 2008, the General Office of the State Council published the Notice of the General Office of the State Council on the Main Functions and Members of the Anti-Monopoly Commission of the State Council[41] and stated that the main functions of the AMC include researching and drafting competition policies, organizing the investigation and assessment of the competition status in the market, issuing reports of the evaluation and guidelines, coordinating and assisting the enforcement. The AMC office consists of one director, Wang Qishan, the Vice Premier of the State Council, four vice-directors, including Chen Deming, the Minister of Commerce, Zhang Ping, Chairman of the NDRC, Zhou Bohua, Director-General of the SAIC, and Bi Jingquan, Deputy Secretary-General of the State Council, and 14 commissioners from ministries and institutions including NDRC, Ministry of Industry and Information Technology (MIIT), the Ministry of Supervision, the Ministry of Finance, the Ministry of Transport, MOFCOM, the State-owned Assets Supervision and Administration Commission (SASAC), SAIC, the State Intellectual Property

[37] AML Chap. 5, Articles 32–37.

[38] AML Chap. 6, Articles 38–45.

[39] AML Chap. 7, Articles 46–54.

[40] AML Chap. 8, Articles 55–57.

[41] Guowuyuan Bangongting Guanyu Guowuyuan Fan Longduan Weiyuanhui Zhuyao Zhize He Zucheng Renyuan De Tongzhi (国务院办公厅关于国务院反垄断委员会主要职责和组成人员的通知) [Notice of the General Office of the State Council on the Main Functions and Members of the Anti-Monopoly Commission of the State Council] (issued by the General Office of the State Council on July 28 2008, effective on 28 July 2008).

Office (SIPO), the Legal Affairs Office of the State Council, the China Banking Regulatory Commission (CBRC), the China Securities Regulatory Commission (CSRC), the China Insurance Regulatory Commission (CIRC), the State Electricity Regulatory Commission (SERC). On 17 June 2011, the MOFCOM announced the formal establishment of an AMC office, which would operate within the MOFCOM.

In October 2008, the Ministry of Commerce released a report which assigns responsibility for the enforcement of the AML to three administrative authorities. First, the NDRC is responsible for enforcing the rules of the AML on anticompetitive agreements and abuse of dominance that are price-related. Second, the SAIC is responsible for investigating non-price-related anti-competitive behaviour, including monopolistic agreements, abuse of dominant position and abuse of administrative power to restrict competition. SAIC and its local branches used to be responsible for enforcing the Law for Countering Unfair Competition. Third, the Anti-monopoly Bureau of the Ministry of Commerce (MOFCOM), established in August 2008, deals with pre-merger and acquisition notifications, investigations and assessments, as well as competition issues in international trade. The SAIC, the NDRC and the Ministry of Commerce are three State-level authorities under the direct supervision of the State Council. The SAIC and the NDRC have government departments at provincial levels. The power of antitrust enforcement and these new antitrust responsibilities have to be combined with other existing administrative duties, such as drafting industrial and commercial policies, formulating national plans for industry, and facilitating domestic and international trade.

In March 17, 2018, according to the Decision of the First Session of the Thirteenth National People's Congress on the State Council Institutional Reform Proposal[42] issued by the National People's Congress, the duties of the SAIC, the General Administration of Quality Supervision, Inspection and Quarantine, the China Food and Drug Administration, the anti-monopoly bureau of the NDRC and MOFCOM, and the AMC are consolidated into the newly established State Administration for Market Regulation (SAMR). In July 2018, the State Council issued the Provisions on the Functions, Structure and Staffing of the State Administration for Market Regulation,[43] which specifies the structure and responsibilities of the SAMR. Article 3 states that the SAMR must implement the guidelines, decisions and arrangements of the CPC Central Committee in supervision and administration of the market, and the responsibilities of the SAMR including drafting legislative laws, regulations,

---

[42] Di Shisanjie Quanguo Renmin Daibiao Dahui Diyici Huiyi Guanyu Guowuyuan Jigou Gaige Fangan De Jueding (第十三届全国人民代表大会第一次会议关于国务院机构改革方案的决定) [Decision of the First Session of the Thirteenth National People's Congress on the State Council Institutional Reform Proposal] (issued on March 17, 2018, effective on March 17, 2018).

[43] Guojia Shichang Jiandu Guanli Zongju Zhineng Peizhi, Neishe Jigou He Renyuan Bianzhi Guiding (国家市场监督管理总局职能配置、内设机构和人员编制规定) [Provisions on the Functions, Structure and Staffing of the State Administration for Market Regulation] (issued by the General Office of the Central Committee of the Communist Party of China, General Office of the State Council on July 30, 2018, effective on July 30, 2018).

policies, standards of market supervision and administration, in charge of the registration of business enterprises, organizing and guiding market regulatory law enforcement, coordinating the enforcement of the AML, unfair competition, infringement of trademarks, patents and intellectual property rights and administrating advertising activities, quality control, product quality, equipment and food safety regulation, the administration of measurement, standardization, inspection and testing, and in charge of a national administrative system of certification and accreditation. The SAMR is composed of 29 departments and since March 2018, the SAMR has integrated the administrative functions of the State Administration for Industry and Commerce, China Food and Drug Administration, the General Administration of Quality Supervision, Inspection, and Quarantine, and has supervisory responsibilities for the National Medical Product Administration and the China National Intellectual Property Administration.[44] On December 28, 2018, the SAMR issued the Notice of the State Administration for Market Regulation on the Empowerment of Anti-monopoly Law Enforcement.[45] The Notice clarified that the SAMR directly empowers market regulatory departments in provinces, autonomous regions and municipalities to be responsible for cases of monopoly agreements, abuse of market dominance, administrative monopolies within their administrative regions, and the enforcement criterion and standards should be unified. The SAMR will strengthen the coordination of antitrust enforcement nationwide. The market regulatory department at provincial level will report the case filing to the SAMR within ten working days after placing the case on file. SAMR and their local branches will regularly organize expert lectures, exchange seminars and case analysis to train professional personnel and to enhance the capabilities and standards of competition enforcement. Article 2 of the Interim Provisions on Prohibiting Monopoly Agreements issued by the SAMR on June 26, 2019[46] made it clear that anti-monopoly enforcement institutions include SAMR and market regulation departments at the provincial level. Market regulation departments at the level of province, autonomous regions and municipalities are authorized to enforce monopoly agreements in their respective regions. A critical assessment of the competition agencies will be dealt with in detail in Chap. 9 of this book.

[44]SAMR official website http://www.samr.gov.cn/jg/.

[45]Shichang Jianguan Zongju Guanyu Fan Longduan Zhifa Shouquan De Tongzhi (市场监管总局关于反垄断执法授权的通知) [Notice of the State Administration for Market Regulation on the Empowerment of Anti-monopoly Law Enforcement] (issued by the State Administration for Market Regulation on December 28, 2018 and effective on December 28, 2018).

[46]Jinzhi Longduan Xieyi Zanxing Guiding (禁止垄断协议暂行规定) [Interim Provisions on Prohibiting Monopoly Agreements] (issued by the State Administration for Market Regulation on June 26, 2019, effective on September 1, 2019).

2.4.2 *Overview of the Procedural Law*

2.4.2.1 The AML

The competition procedural rules in China are composed of Chap. 6 of the AML on the investigation of suspicious monopolistic conduct, and the internal procedural provisions issued by SAIC, NDRC, MOFCOM and SAMR. Chapter 6 (Articles 38–45) specifies procedural rules in case filing (Article 38), investigation (Articles 39–41), respondent obligations (Articles 42 and 43), publication of the case decision (Article 44), and the termination and suspension of the investigation (Article 45).

To file an antitrust case, any entities or individuals may report suspicious monopolistic conduct to the enforcement agency. The agency must ensure the confidentiality for the reporter, and when the tip-off is supported by relevant evidence, the agency should initiate an investigation.[47] Once the investigation is initiated, the enforcement agency can take measures which include[48]: (1) enter the business operator offices or any relevant place for investigation purpose; (2) require business operators under investigation, or any relevant individual, entities, or interested parties to disclose relevant information; (3) review and duplicate relevant business documents, agreements, accounting books, business correspondences, electronic data, or other related files and documents of the business operator under investigation, or any relevant individuals, entities or interested parties; (4) seize and detain the relevant evidence; (5) inquire about the bank accounts of the business operators under investigation. All of the above-mentioned measures can only be taken after a written report is submitted to the principal officials of the enforcement agency and an approval has been issued. During the investigation, the agency should send at least two officials and their working licences should be presented. When the official is conducting the inquiry, a transcript should be written and the person under investigation should sign the transcript.[49] The agency and the investigatory staff have the responsibility to keep business secrets confidential.[50]

Articles 42 and 43 specify the procedural obligations for parties under investigation. The respondents must cooperate with and assist the enforcement agency to conduct the inquiry, and should not refuse or obstruct the investigation.[51] Business operators or interested parties under inquiry are entitled to make statements. The agency should verify the facts, reasons, and evidence provided by the respondents.[52] After the investigation, the agency should make a decision on whether the suspicious conduct is to be filed as a monopoly case, and the decision should be publicized.[53] Article 44 also mentions the transparency requirement, that after the investigation

[47] Article 38, AML.

[48] Article 39, AML.

[49] Article 40, AML.

[50] Article 41, AML.

[51] Article 42, AML.

[52] Article 43, AML.

[53] Article 44, AML.

and verification of the suspected monopolistic conduct, the authority should make an official decision in accordance to law and such decision may make known to the public.[54]

Article 45 stipulates the termination and suspension of the investigation. Once the investigation is initiated, if the business operator under investigation promised to take measures within the time limit accepted by the agency to eliminate the anti-competitive effects, a suspension of the investigation may be considered by the agency. The decision on suspension should state explicitly the contents of the measures that are promised by the business operator under investigation. After the decision on suspension is issued, the agency should monitor the implementation process. If the business operator implements the promise, the agency may consider terminating the investigation. The agency may also consider resuming the investigation under the following three conditions: (1) the business operator fails to implement the promise; (2) significant changes occurred in the facts on which the suspension was made; (3) the information, based on which the suspension was made was incomplete or inaccurate.[55]

In addition, Article 53 specifies that parties may appeal the decisions pursuant to Articles 28 and 29 of the AML, the party may apply for an administrative reconsideration; and if the party is not satisfied with the reconsideration decision, it may lodge an administrative lawsuit. When parties are dissatisfied by other agency decisions, it may apply for administrative reconsideration or file an administrative lawsuit.[56]

2.4.2.2 Provisional Rules by SAIC and NDRC

SAIC issued the Provisions for the Procedures for the Administrative Departments for Industry and Commerce to Investigate and Handle Cases of Monopolization Agreements and Abuse of Dominant Market Position on May 26, 2009.[57] Article 5 of the provision clarifies the type of information that should be included when individuals or entities report suspected monopolistic behaviour, including (1) basic information of the informant (2) basic information about the reported business operator (3) relevant facts of suspected monopolization (4) relevant evidence, including documentary evidence, material evidence, testimony of witness, audio-visual materials, computer data, authentication conclusions, etc. (5) a statement of whether the same facts have been reported to other administrative agencies or have been brought

[54] Article 44, AML.

[55] Article 45, AML.

[56] Article 53, AML.

[57] Gongshang Xingzheng Guanli Jiguan Chachu Longduan Xieyi Lanyong Shichang Zhipei Diwei Anjian Chengxu Guiding (工商行政管理机关查处垄断协议、滥用市场支配地位案件程序规定) [Provisions on the Procedures for the Administrative Departments for Industry and Commerce to Investigate and Handle Cases of Monopolization Agreements and Abuse of Dominant Market Position] (issued by the State Administration for Industry and Commerce on May 26, 2009 and effective on July 1, 2009, now expired).

before court. Article 6 of the provision stipulates that AIC branches below the provincial level must submit the reporting materials to the provincial branch within five working days. Once receiving the materials (including those anonymous written reports), the authority should register and verify the contents of the report; and if the materials are incomplete, the informant should be notified to provide additional materials.[58] Article 10 restated Article 39 of the AML. Article 12 stipulates that the respondent should provide the following written materials: (1) basic information of the respondent, including the organization structure, name, contact person and contact information, operation licence, corporation code; if the operator is an individual, the ID card and contact information should be provided; (2) business operators should provide the last three years sales and operation status, annual sales revenue, tax payment, the business transaction with relevant dealers, information on foreign investment, and stock returns; (3) the industrial association should provide association structure, administrative guidance and policy in the relevant sector, the business operating plan and implementation of the sector, other relevant materials on meetings, activities and documents related to monopolistic conduct; (4) explanations on the relevant questions raised by the authority; (5) other written materials that the authority considers to be necessary.[59] Article 14 states that conduct including refusal to provide information, not responding within the required time limits, providing untrue information, concealing, destroying or transferring evidence, or refusing to cooperate or impeding the investigation, will be subject to penalties under Article 52 of the AML.[60]

On the same date, the SAIC also issued Provisions on the Procedure for the Industrial and Commercial Administrations to Stop Acts of Abusing Administrative Power for Excluding or Limiting Competition.[61] Article 4 of the provision empowered the AIC branches to give suggestions to higher authority on how to handle administrative monopoly case when local government or affiliated department at provincial level has abused its administrative power to exclude or restrict competition. Article 5 of the provision stipulates that monopolistic conduct designated or authorized by administrative agency or organizations are subject to the same procedural rules as monopoly or abuse of dominance cases.

NDRC issued the Provisions on the Administrative Procedures for Law Enforcement against Price Fixing on December 29, 2010.[62] Article 5 of the provision specifies that after the agency receives the report by individuals or entities about suspected

[58] Article 6, id.

[59] Article 12, id.

[60] Article 14, id.

[61] Gongshang Xingzheng Guanli Jiguan Zhizhi Lanyong Xingzheng Quanli Paichu Xianzhi Jingzheng Xingwei Chengxu Guiding (工商行政管理机关制止滥用行政权力排除、限制竞争行为程序规定) [Provisions on the Procedure for the Industrial and Commercial Administrations to Stop Acts of Abusing Administrative Power for Excluding or Limiting Competition] (issued by the State Administration for Industry and Commerce on May 26, 2009 and effective on July 1, 2009, now expired).

[62] Fan Jiage Longduan Xingzheng Zhifa Chengxu Guiding (反价格垄断行政执法程序规定) [Provisions on the Administrative Procedures for Law Enforcement against Price Fixing] (issued by the

price-fixing conduct, an investigation should be initiated and should cover[63]: (1) whether the individual or entity has reported to other administrative organs or whether he has brought a private action; (2) the basic information on the accused person; (3) the facts and evidence provided by the informant; (4) other relevant issues. Article 6 of the provision restated Article 39 of the AML. Article 7 states that the investigation may take the form of interview, telephone conversation, or in writing. Article 8 stipulates that the investigation should be taken by at least two law enforcement officers who should present their identifications during the investigation. Articles 9 and 10 requires the government officials to keep confidential the commercial secrets that they may have access to, and requires the persons under investigation to comply with the investigation and not to refuse or obstruct the investigation.

In 2013, NDRC issued Provisions on the Procedures for Price-related Administrative Penalties, and Provisions on Evidence for Administrative Penalty for Price-related Violations. In 2014, NDRC published the Rules on the Hearing and Review of Price-related Administrative Punishment cases and Several Provisions on Regulating the Price-related Administrative Penalty Power. In January 2014, the NDRC published the amended Provisions on Handling Reports about Price-related Regulations (2014 Revision), and this regulation specified the acceptance, handling and notice of complaints of price-related violations that are filed with the NDRC.[64] Article 2 states that the provision applies to citizens, legal persons or other organizations when filing a report about violations of prices and fees regulations. Article 3 of the regulation requires the authority to publish the relevant information including the 12,358 hotline, online reporting platform, mailing address, time and location for receiving visitors on public. Article 4 of the regulation states that an informant can file the report to the price authority by means of the 12,358 report hotline, or through letters, fax, the Internet, or visit the authority office. Article 8 requires the price authority to notify the informant whether the report has been accepted or transferred to other administrative agencies within seven working days. NDRC also published the Guiding Opinions on the Online Handling of Cases Involving Administrative Penalties for Price-related Violations, the Model Text for Documents Relating to Complaints of Price-related Violations, and amended Measures for the Rewards for Complaints of Price-related Violations.

On August 3, 2008, the State Council released the Provisions on Thresholds for Prior Notification of Concentrations of Undertakings. A prior notification must be filed when the participating undertaking' combined worldwide turnover exceeds RMB 10 billion, and the turnover of at least two participating undertakings within China are both worth more than RMB 400 million in the previous accounting year; or when the participating undertakings' combined turnover within China exceeds

State Development and Reform Commission on December 29, 2010 and effective on February 1, 2011, now expired).

[63] Article 5, id.

[64] Jiage Weifa Xingwei Jubao Chuli Guiding (价格违法行为举报处理规定,, 2014 修订) Provisions on Handling Reports about Price-related Violations (2014 Revision), Order No. 6 of the National Development and Reform Commission, issued by the State Development and Reform Commission on January 15, 2014, effective on May 1, 2014).

RMB 2 billion, and the turnover of at least two participating undertakings in China is worth more than RMB 400 million in the previous accounting year.[65] The notification procedure has to comply with the Guiding Opinions of the Anti-monopoly Bureau of the Ministry of Commerce on the Declaration Documents and Materials of the Concentration of Business Operators issued by MOFCOM in January 2009, and failure to notify will be sanctioned by administrative fines.

According to Articles 25 and 26 of the AML, after MOFCOM accepts the notification application, the Phase I review should be completed within 30 days. The investigation may be continued to Phase II review for 90 days, and this procedure can be further extended by no longer than 60 days. Article 27 of the AML has listed six factors that the authority should take into account when assessing the anti-competitive effects: (1) the participating undertakings' market share in the relevant market, and the controlling power in that market; (2) the level of concentration in the relevant market; (3) the concentration's technological impact; (4) the concentrations' effects on consumers and other business operators; (5) the concentration's effects on national economic development; (6) other elements considered by the authority. Details of the merger control notification provisions will be provided in Chap. 7 of this book.

2.4.2.3 Provisional Rules by SAMR

In 2018, SAMR published the Interim Provisions on the Procedures for Administrative Punishments for Market Supervision and Administration.[66] Article 17 of the provision stipulates that the market regulatory department should verify the clues for violation by complaint, report, transfer by other government agencies or an authority at a higher level within 15 working days and decide on whether to file the case. Under special circumstances it may extend for 15 working days. Article 20 listed the evidence that will be collected by case handling personnel, and the evidence includes documentary evidence, physical evidence, audio-visual materials, electronic data, witness testimony, statements of the parties, authentication opinions and on-site investigation transcripts. Articles 21–23 specified that in case of difficulties of obtaining the original documents and articles, duplications, photocopies, transcriptions and videos may be taken as evidence after verification by the evidence provider. In the same month, the SAMR issued the Interim Measures for the Hearings

[65] Guowuyuan Guanyu Jingyingzhe Jizhong Shenbao Biaozhun De Guiding (国务院关于经营者集中申报标准的规定) [Provisions of the State Council on Thresholds for Prior Notification of Concentrations of Undertakings] (adopted at the 20th Executive Meeting of the State Council on 1 August 2008, effective on 3 August 2008).

[66] Shichang Jiandu Guanli Xingzheng Chufa Chengxu Zanxing Guiding (市场监督管理行政处罚程序暂行规定) [Interim Provisions on the Procedures for Administrative Punishments for Market Supervision and Administration] (issued on December 21, 2018 and effective on April 1, 2019).

for Administrative Punishments for Market Supervision and Administration.[67] This chapter (Articles 5–7) explains the process of applying for hearings, and Chap. 3 (Articles 8–17) specifies the organisers, personnel and participants of the hearing, and Chap. 4 (Articles 18–22) listed the requirements for preparations of the hearing. Chapter 5 (Articles 23–30) provides the procedures and the general holding of hearings. Article 16 of the SAMR Interim Provisions on Prohibiting Monopoly Agreements[68] listed the information that is required when reporting monopolistic conduct related to price monopoly: (1) the basic information of the informant; (2) the basic information of the person reported; (3) relevant facts and evidence of the suspected monopoly agreement; (4) whether the informant has reported the same facts to another administrative authority or has brought a lawsuit before a people's court. In accordance to Article 24 of the SAMR Interim Provisions on Prohibiting Abuse of Dominant Market Positions[69] and Article 12 of the Interim Provisions on Prohibiting the Acts of Eliminating or Restricting Competition by Abuse of Administrative power,[70] the information required for reporting anti-competitive behaviour related to abuse of dominant position and abuse of administrative power is the same. Article 20 of the Interim Provisions on Prohibiting Monopoly Agreements stipulates that the anti-monopoly enforcement agency must issue a written decision when imposing administrative penalties and the decision should include: (1) the name, address, and other basic information of the business operator; (2) source and the investigatory process of the case; (3) facts and evidence of the illegal conduct; (4) the statement in defence of the business operator, and reasons for acceptance; (5) the contents and basis for the administrative penalties; (6) the method and time limit for performing the penalties; (7) the approach and time limits for applying for administrative reconsideration or bringing administrative litigation; (8) the name of the anti-monopoly enforcement agency and the date of the decision made.

---

[67] Shichang Jiandu Guanli Xingzheng Chufa Tingzheng Zanxing Banfa (市场监督管理行政处罚听证暂行办法) [Interim Measures for the Hearings for Administrative Punishments for Market Supervision and Administration] (issued on December 21, 2018 and effective on April 1, 2019).

[68] Jinzhi Longduan Xieyi Zanxing Guiding (禁止垄断协议暂行规定) [Interim Provisions on Prohibiting Monopoly Agreements] (issued on June 26, 2019 and effective on September 1, 2019).

[69] Jinzhi Lanyong Shichang Zhipei Diwei Xingwei Zanxing Guiding (禁止滥用市场支配地位行为暂行规定) [Interim Provisions on Prohibiting Abuse of Dominant Market Positions] (issued on June 26, 2019 and effective on September 1, 2019).

[70] Zhizhi Lanyong Xingzheng Quanli Paichu Xianzhi Jingzheng Xingwei Zanxing Guiding (制止滥用行政权力排除、限制竞争行为暂行规定) [Interim Provisions on Prohibiting the Acts of Eliminating or Restricting Competition by Abuse of Administrative Power] (issued on June 26, 2019 and effective on September 1, 2019).

2.5 Conclusions

The AML has experienced a 13 years long legislative debate. The earliest rule of protecting competition was adopted in October 1980. In September 1987, the State Council promulgated administrative regulation on price control, and the Price Law was effective in May 1998. In 1993, the Anti-unfair Competition law was promulgated and it was revised in November 2017. A comprehensive competition law only came into force in August 2008. The AML followed a clear bureaucratic enforcement, and since August 2018, the State Administration for Market Regulation (SAMR) has become the enforcement agency of the AML. In addition, provisions issued by the SAIC, NDRC, MOFCOM and SAMR are relevant to understand the procedural rules of the AML.

The structure and contents of the Anti-monopoly Law have been influenced by the EU competition law. The AML is composed of 57 articles in 8 chapters. Chapter 1 provides general provisions, and Chap. 2 (Articles 13–16) deals with monopoly agreements. Chapter 3 (Articles 17–19) covers the abuse of dominant position, and Chap. 4 (Articles 20–31) focuses on concentrations. Chapter 5 (Articles 32–37) deals with administrative monopolies. Chapter 6 is about investigative procedure (Articles 38–45), and Chap. 7 (Articles 46–54) is on legal liabilities and the last chapter is supplementary provisions. In addition, provisions issued by the SAIC, NDRC, MOFCOM and SAMR are relevant for an understanding of the procedural rules of the AML. Any entities or individuals may report suspicious monopolistic conduct to the enforcement agency. Once the investigation is initiated, the enforcement agency may enter the business offices, inquire into the business operators under investigation, review and copy relevant documents, seize and detain the evidence, and inquire about the bank accounts. The respondents must cooperate and assist the enforcement agency to conduct the inquiry. The parties may appeal the administrative decisions by applying for an administrative reconsideration or lodge an administrative lawsuit. According the 2018 SAMR Interim provisions on the Procedures for Administrative Punishments for Market Supervision and Administration, the enforcement agency should verify the clues for violation within 15 working days and decide on whether to file the case. Duplications, photocopies, transcriptions and videos may be taken as evidence. Furthermore, the Interim Measures for Hearings for Administrative Punishments for Market Supervision and Administration specify the process of hearings, including the application process, the organizers, personnel and participants of the hearing, the requirements for preparations, and the general procedures. The SAMR provisions of Interim Provisions on Prohibiting Monopoly Agreements, Interim Provisions on Prohibiting Abuse of Dominant Positions, and Interim Provisions on Prohibiting the Acts of Eliminating or Restricting Competition by Abuse of Administrative power clarified the additional information required for reporting anti-competitive behaviour related to price monopoly, abuse of dominant position, and abuse of administrative power.

References

Berry, J. A. (2005). Anti-monopoly law in China: A socialist market economy wrestles with its antitrust regime. *International Law and Management Review, 2,* 129–152.

Gerber, D. J. (2008). Economics, law and institutions: The shaping of Chinese competition law. *Journal of Law and Policy, 26,* 271–299.

Hittinger, C. W., & Huh, J. D. (2007). The People's Republic of China enacts its first comprehensive antitrust law: Trying to predict the unpredictable. *New York University Journal of Law and Business, 4,* 246–284.

Howell, T. R., Wolff, A. W., Howe, R., & Oh, D. (2009). China's new anti-monopoly law: A perspective from the United States. *Pacific Rim Law and Policy Journal, 18*(1), 53–96.

Huang, Y. (2008). Pursuing the second best: The history, momentum and remaining issues of China's Anti-monopoly Law. *Antitrust Law Journal, 75,* 117–132.

Huang, Y., & Li, Z. (2013). An overview of Chinese competition policy: Between fragmentation and consolidation. In A. Emch & D. Stallibrass (Eds.), *China's Anti-monopoly Law: The first five years*. Frederick: Kluwer International Law.

Jung, Y. J., & Hao, Q. (2003). The new economic constitution in China: A third way for competition regime? *Northwestern Journal of International Law and Business,* 24, 107–172.

Neumann, P. (2003, December 23). The slow boat to antitrust law in China. *Faegre Baker Daniels.* Retrieved from http://www.faegrebd.com/4709.

Owen, B. M., Sun, S., & Zheng, W. (2008). China's competition policy reforms: The anti-monopoly law and beyond. *Antitrust Law Journal, 75,* 231–266.

Samuels, J. R. (2007). "Tain't what you do" effect of China's proposed anti-monopoly law on state owned enterprises. *Pennsylvania State International Law Review, 26,* 169–202.

Van den Bergh, R., & Faure, M. (2011). Critical issues in the enforcement of the Anti-monopoly Law in China: A law and economics perspective. In M. Faure & X. Zhang (Eds.), *Competition policy and regulation, recent developments in China, the US and Europe* (pp. 54–72). Cheltenham: Edward Elgar.

Wei, D. (2011). China's anti-monopoly law and its merger enforcement: Convergence and flexibility. *Journal of International Economic Law, 14*(4), 807–844.

Wei, D. (2013). Antitrust in China: An overview of recent implementation of anti-monopoly law. *European Business Organization Law Review, 14*(1), 119–139.

Wu, Z. (2008). Perspectives on the Chinese anti-monopoly law. *Antitrust Law Journal, 75,* 73–116.

Zheng, W. (2010). Transplanting antitrust in China: Economic transition, market structure and state control. *University of Pennsylvania Journal of International Law, 32*(2), 643–721.

Chapter 3
Goals of the Competition Law

Abstract The AML incorporates five goals in Article 1: preventing and restraining monopolistic conduct, protecting fair competition in the market, enhancing economic efficiency, safeguarding the interests of consumers and social public interest, and promoting the healthy development of a socialist market economy. The revised AML adds one more goal: to promote innovation. The academic debate focuses on whether consumer welfare, efficiency or protecting fair competition should serve as a functional goal or the ultimate goal. It is believed that a more balanced approach should be adopted. The goal of promoting a socialist market economy is mentioned in Article 4. Industrial policy concerns on SOEs are reflected in Article 7 of the AML. The exemptions mentioned in Article 15 refer to the broad definition of public interest. A fair competition system has been implemented since 2017 to coordinate competition and industrial policy.

3.1 Introduction

Since Robert Bork wrote the book *The Antitrust Paradox* in 1978, the goals of antitrust law are a mysterious topic that arouses interesting debates between lawyers, economists, philosophers, and politicians. Goals of competition law have been evolving, shifting between non-economic concerns and economic ones, and economic considerations are consequently subject to interpretation on key terms of total welfare, consumer welfare, consumer choice, efficiency, and distribution issues.

As discussed in Chap. 2, the drafting process of the AML was to a large extent influenced by the specific competition goals in China. Although the AML followed the structure of the competition law and policy in the EU which deals with monopoly agreements, abuse of dominant position, and concentrations, a particular aspect that makes the AML distinct from the competition policy in both the US and the EU is that it incorporates various non-economic goals.[1] The AML contains several articles which indicate that the competition policy in China does not solely focus on

[1]Farmer (2013, p. 22).

J. Ma, *Competition Law in China*,
https://doi.org/10.1007/978-981-15-5105-5_3

economic goals. Article 1 of the AML states that this law is enacted for five objectives, including restraining monopolistic behaviour, protecting competition, promoting efficiency, protecting the interest of consumers and the public, and contributing to the development of the socialist market economy.

This chapter indicates that the AML pursues various economic and non-economic goals, including the consumer welfare standard, the total welfare standard, and public interest concerns.[2] Following Article 1, the AML contains several articles that address the goal of contributing to a socialist market economy, strengthening the development SOE, industrial policy concerns and the goal of promoting public interest. These concerns will be explained in detail in the following sections.

3.2 The Debate of Competition Goals in China

3.2.1 Economic and Non-economic Goals of the AML

Competition policy in many jurisdictions used to define their goals in a clear hierarchy. During the early years of European integration after the Second World War, market integration clearly ranked higher than other considerations, such as the goal of protecting consumer welfare. In Korea, after Jung Hee Park became president, it was declared that the number one priority of the government was economic growth, and to facilitate economic growth, all sectors should implement the "export-oriented industrial policy".[3] A series of *5 Year Economic Development Plans* were instituted by the Economic Planning Board, and a number of "national champions" received favourable treatment from the government in bank loans, export subsidies, and tax credits.[4] During the thirteen year-long legislative debate of the Anti-monopoly Law in China, the drafting process of the competition act follows the main goal of market reform, that is to develop a socialist market economy.

Most scholars in China agree that the goal of the AML should include economic goals, in particular the goal of promoting efficiency.[5] The reason is that although China has experienced a rapid economic development in recent years, it is still on its way to becoming a high-income country. Therefore, the goals of promoting economic growth, as well as enhancing efficiency, should be included in the AML. Meanwhile, although some scholars in China argue that efficiency should be the primary goal, most scholars argue that the efficiency goal needs to be balanced with the goal of promoting fairness.[6] Li argues that in addition to protecting consumers, competition law should also take into account the interests of small and medium enterprises,

[2]Shan et al. (2011, p. 7).

[3]Yi and Jung (2007, p. 156).

[4]Yi and Jung (2007, p. 156).

[5]Ding (2011, p. 128), Lyu and Tao (2008, p. 27).

[6]Gao and Dong (2008, p. 97).

and the goal of providing a fair competitive economic environment is important for small and medium enterprises.[7] With respect to the hierarchy between these different goals, Ding argued that the goal of protecting fair competition under Article 1, serves as a functional goal, which laid the basis for the competition policy in China. The other three goals—improving efficiency, protecting consumer welfare and social interests—are the results that the AML is expected to achieve. Because the AML was enacted to achieve these three results, the fundamental functions of the law are the production function and the distribution function, with the production function superior to the distribution function.[8] Lan argues that competition law should not limit itself on protecting consumer interests, as competition law is to protect competition mechanism and consumers are protected even when consumer welfare is not taken as the criteria in competition case analysis.[9] By contrast, Lyu and Tao argue that maximizing consumer welfare should be the ultimate goal of the competition law in China. The reason is that the economic growth should benefit the majority of the society. The goal of promoting competition and efficiency, are only of the two most useful instruments to serve the goal of maximizing consumer welfare.[10] Wu and Wei argued that when the goals of competition law conflict with each other, which goal should be taken as the superior goal should be decided according to the economic, social and political situation in the country as well as the international environment.[11] Sun argues that when other goals conflict with the goal of consumer welfare, the goal of protecting consumer welfare should be prioritized as the ultimate goal.[12] Yan shares the similar view that compared with the ultimate goal of protecting consumer welfare, the goal of protecting fair competition order plays only a functional role.[13]

Lin proposed a 'competition-neutral principle' to deal with the relationship between the industrial policy and the competition policy.[14] This principle is that industrial policy should only be considered in the situation where a transaction has neither anti-competitive nor pro-competitive effects. To be more precise, industrial policy should not be taken as the critical factor to determine competitive effects.[15] This principle proposed by Lin indicates that when the competition policy is in conflict with the industrial policy, the criteria to be used to decide the case should be the competitive effects of the merger. In any situation, an anticompetitive merger should not be allowed and a procompetitive merger should not be banned.[16] The ultimate goal of a competition law should be promoting competition.[17] According to Lin,

---

[7]Li (2008).

[8]Ding (2011, p. 128).

[9]Lan (2016, p. 80).

[10]Lyu and Tao (2008, p. 27).

[11]Wu and Wei (2005, p. 98).

[12]Sun (2008).

[13]Yan (2005).

[14]Lin (2009), Lin and Zhao (2012, p. 129).

[15]Lin and Zhao (2012, p. 129).

[16]Lin and Zhao (2012, p. 129).

[17]Lin and Zhao (2012, p. 129).

this principle can not only be applied to concentrations, but also to other domains of competition law, such as cases related to abuse of dominant position and monopolist agreements.

3.2.2 The Development of a Socialist Market Economy

Article 1 of the AML states that the law is to sustain a healthy development of a socialist market economy. Article 4 states that competition rules will be applied in a way which fits into the socialist market economy. The implementation of these rules must contribute to the establishment of a unified, open, competitive and well-ordered market system. This article signals that the role of the AML is to achieve the broader goals of establishing a well-functioning market system with a specific characteristic of 'socialist market economy'. Competition law itself was developed under the market reform after 1978. Professor Huang Yong argued that there are three stages in the reform of socialist market economy and the development of competition law[18]: (1) 1978–1993, the discussion of competition law in the Communique of the Third Plenary Session of the Eleventh Central Committee of the CPC[19] and Decision of the CPC Central Committee on Economic System Reform.[20] (2) 1993–2003, the early draft of competition law and the competition legal framework under the implementation of Decision of the Central Committee of the Communist Party of China on Several Issues Concerning the Establishment of a Socialist Market Economy.[21] (3) 2003–2013, the improvement of competition law under the Decision of the Central Committee of the Communist Party of China on Some Issues Concerning the Improvement of the Socialist Market Economy.[22] According to Prof. Gerber, the AML in China has been influenced by the incentive structures, due to the important role that the central government has played in the economic development in China.[23] The incentives to take actions are motivated by specific ideological goals,

---

[18] Huang (2018, p. 126).

[19] Zhongguo Gongchandang Di Shiyijie Zhongyang Weiyuanhui Disanci Quanti Huiyi Gongbao (中国共产党第十一届中央委员会第三次全体会议公报) [Communique of the Third Plenary Session of the Eleventh Central Committee of the Communist Party of China], December 22, 1978.

[20] Zhonggong Zhongyang Guanyu Jingji Tizhi Gaige De Jueding (中共中央关于经济体制改革的决定) [Decision of the CPC Central Committee on Economic System Reform], October 20, 1984.

[21] Zhonggong Zhongyang Guanyu Jianli Shehui Zhuyi Shichang Jingji Tizhi Ruogan Wenti De Jueding (中共中央关于建立社会主义市场经济体制若干问题的决定) [Decision of the Central Committee of the Communist Party of China on Several Issues Concerning the Establishment of a Socialist Market Economy], November 14, 1993.

[22] Zhonggong Zhongyang Guanyu Wanshan Shehui Zhuyi Shichang Jingji Tizhi Ruogan Wenti De Jueding (中共中央关于完善社会主义市场经济体制若干问题的决定) [Decision of the Central Committee of the Communist Party of China on Some Issues Concerning the Improvement of the Socialist Market Economy], adopted at the 3rd Plenary Session of the 16th CPC Central Committee on October 14, 2003.

[23] Gerber (2008, p. 277).

such as pursuing social equality, which are announced by the government or other institutions.[24]

Wu and Wei argued that the goal of the economic reform in China is to establish a socialist market economy, which promotes both economic efficiency and social fairness. Therefore, it is necessary to balance the efficiency goal and the fairness goal in antitrust enforcement, if the ultimate goal is to ensure a healthy development of the socialist market economy, and to establish a harmonious socialist society.[25] Hamp-Lyons argued that the goal of establishing a socialist market economy indicates China's strong interest in sustaining social stability. Therefore, the goals of competition policy in China will be different from those of the United States or the European Union.[26] Montinola et al. and Wang accepted that the term of socialist market economy reflects the ideology of socialism.[27] Shan et al. argued that the goal of promoting the healthy development of the socialist market economy mentioned in Article 1 of the AML may give preference to the gains to the SOEs, or it could be understood as protecting the interests of specific producers.[28] According to Hamp-Lyons, when a merger forces an inefficient competitor to close down, the Chinese government might prohibit this merger and choose to protect the inefficient local firms, because closing a firm will result in workers losing their jobs. In this way, when the goal of efficiency and the socialist goal conflict with each other, the social stability goal might have a higher weight.[29] Fox argued that it is reasonable for the Chinese government to take employment into account, as stability is a clear social goal. She proposed that Chinese antitrust authorities should prohibit the mergers which will create no clear harm or benefit for consumers, but which will lead to the bankruptcy of local firms.[30]

3.2.3 SOE

Article 7 of the AML pays attention to the State-owned economy. This article states that for State-controlled industries, which are crucial for the national economy and national security, as well as industries operating exclusive operations and sales, their lawful business will be protected by the State.[31] Moreover, their business operations, as well as the prices of their products and services, will be supervised and controlled

[24]Gerber (2008, p. 277).

[25]Wu and Wei (2005, p. 98).

[26]Hamp-Lyons (2009, p. 1580).

[27]Montinola et al. (1995, p. 52), Wang (2008, p. 133).

[28]Shan et al. (2011, p. 6).

[29]Hamp-Lyons (2009, p. 1580), see Footnote 15.

[30]Fox (2007, p. 211, 228, 229).

[31]Article 7 of the AML: With respect to the industries controlled by the State-owned economy and concerning the lifeline of national economy and national security or the industries lawfully enjoying exclusive production and sales, the State shall protect these lawful business operations conducted by the business operators therein, and shall supervise and control these business operations and

by the State, for the purpose of safeguarding consumer interests and promoting technical progress. Article 7 leaves room for future interpretation, and adds uncertainties in antitrust enforcement concerning the tradeoff between the interests of industries that are controlled by the State and the welfare gains of consumers. As Prof. Huang Yong, an advisory expert of the drafting of the AML, said that the most challenging task of enacting an antitrust law during this transition is to strike a balance between promoting competition and maintaining the dominant control of the SOEs in strategic industries.[32]

Liu and Qiao argued that this article puts particular weight on the protection of industries that are controlled by the state-owned economy and that are critical to the well-being of the national economy.[33] Similarly, in the context of abuse of dominant position, the AML has described several rules with the statement of 'without any justifiable causes', the question of how to interpret these rules has to be answered by the enforcement agency, and how these rules will be balanced with the industrial policy, is still uncertain.[34] Williams pointed out that it is doubtful whether SOEs will be granted special protection and whether domestic and foreign enterprises will be equally treated.[35] Fox argued that this article indicates that SOEs are regulated and controlled by the State. The State, not the enforcement agency of the AML, is empowered to make a decision on their anti-competitive conduct.[36] Fels saw this article as a compromise between the competition policy and the industry policy in China. According to Fels, this article can be interpreted in three ways: the SOEs are completely exempted, or not exempted at all, or an intermediate position where in most cases the AML is also applied to SOEs; however, in situations where SOEs are undertaking activities that are required by the State, they will be protected by the AML.[37] Li argues that this article indicates four types of SOEs will be exempted for monopolistic behaviour: (1) SOEs in special regulatory industries or strategic industries (2) SOEs which have sovereignty functions (3) SOEs which have public interest functions (4) SOEs which are regulated by special laws.[38] In the debate of revising the AML, Wang argues that Article 7 should be deleted because it has never been applied during the 12 years enforcement experience of the AML, and this Article is in conflict with fair competition review and is not applicable in practice.[39]

---

the prices of these commodities and services provided by these business operators, so as to protect consumer interests and facilitate technological advancements. The business operators mentioned in the previous paragraph shall operate according to law, be honest, faithful and strictly self-disciplined, and accept public supervision, and shall not harm consumer interests by taking advantage of their controlling or exclusive dealing position. Translation adopted from en.pkulaw.cn.

[32] Huang (2008, p. 119).

[33] Liu and Qiao (2012, p. 103).

[34] Liu and Qiao (2012, p. 104).

[35] Williams (2009, p. 137).

[36] Fox (2008, p. 178).

[37] Fels (2012, p. 15).

[38] Li (2017, p. 122).

[39] Wang (2020, p. 12).

In addition, Article 15 of the AML provides the circumstances for granting exemptions for business operators who are involved in monopoly agreements. There are seven circumstances where exemptions can be applied. The first situation is when the agreement is for the purpose of promoting research and development for new products. The second circumstance is when the agreement is for the purpose of improving product quality, increasing efficiency, unifying product standards, and upgrading product specialization. The third situation is when the agreement is for the purpose of increasing efficiency for small and medium-sized operators and improving their competitiveness. The fourth circumstance is when the agreement is for the purpose of protecting the environment, saving energy, helping victims after natural disasters, and other social public interests. The fifth circumstance is the agreement is signed during economic recessions and for the purpose of mitigating the loss because of sales decreasing or excessive production. The sixth circumstance is when the agreement is for justifiable interests in international trade and international economic cooperation. The seventh is other circumstances that are justified by laws and stipulated by the State Council. When a monopoly agreement falls under one of the first five circumstances, to receive an exemption from Articles 13 and 14, the business operator has to prove that this agreement ensures consumers will share the benefits generated, and the agreement will not severely restrict competition in the relevant market. The seven circumstances listed in this article indicate several different goals that the competition rules in China can take into account. For example, the goal of promoting technological improvement mentioned in the first circumstance, the concerns of protecting small and medium-sized operators under the third circumstance, and the emphasis on the social public interest in the fourth circumstance. The sixth circumstance particularly focuses on the lawful interest of domestic firms in international trade.

Furthermore, the concentration among SOEs has been supported by the State Council. In September 2010 the State Council issued the Opinions of the State Council on Promoting Enterprise Merger and Restructuring[40] and the Opinion supports the trans-regional merger and restructuring, in particular in industries include automobile, steel, cement, machinery manufacturing, electrolytic aluminum and rare earth, to improve industrial centralization and promote large enterprise groups with international competitiveness. On November 12, 2013, the Decision of the Central Committee of the Communist Party of China on Several Important Issues Concerning Comprehensively Deepening the Reform[41] states that the functions of different SOEs should be accurately defined. SOEs with public interest functions should make greater contributions in providing public services, while in the natural monopoly industry where state-owned capital continues to operate as a controlling entity, reforms focus

[40]Guowuyuan Guanyu Cujin Qiye Jianbing Chongzu De Yijian (国务院关于促进企业兼并重组的意见) [Opinions of the State Council on Promoting Enterprise Merger and Restructuring], issued by State Council on August 28, 2010, effective on August 28, 2010.

[41]Zhonggong Zhongyang Guanyu Quanmian Shenhua Gaige Ruogan Zhongda Wenti De Jueding (中共中央关于全面深化改革若干重大问题的决定) [Decision of the Central Committee of the Communist Party of China on Several Important Issues Concerning Comprehensively Deepening the Reform], issued on November 12, 2013.

on the separation of government and enterprises to improve the competitiveness of the enterprises and ensure public resources are allocated by marketization. In September 2015, the Guiding Opinions of the CPC Central Committee and the State Council on Deepening the Reform of State-owned Enterprises[42] made clear that SOEs should be divided into commercial SOEs and SOEs in public welfare nature. Commercial SOEs should engage in commercial operations in accordance with market requirements and independently carry out production and business activities. On March 6, 2015, the General Office of the SASAC issued the Notice of the General Office of the State-owned Assets Supervision and Administration Commission (SASAC) of the State Council on the Development of the 13th Five-Year Plan for Central Enterprises[43] and states that concentrations among SOEs at central level should be encouraged in order to develop strong super-SOEs that are able to compete in the international market. It is argued that those industrial policies raised concerns on the enforcement of merger control policy on SOEs.[44] The concentration among SOEs should be reviewed by AML by taking efficiency, consumer welfare, public interest and national interest criteria into account to prevent the concentration of market power and thus impede market competition between SOEs and other types of enterprises, as the concentration between SOEs is often not reviewed by the competition authority.

3.2.4 Industrial Policy

Since the beginning of the market reform, industrial policy has become an effective instrument in economic development. The most commonly adopted tools are administrative interventionist mechanisms including provisions, guidelines, decisions, notices and replies on market entry, application and review systems on project, land, capital and other types of mandatory requirements. Few industrial policies are adopted through legal procedures. In March 2015, the State Council published the Several Opinions of the CPC Central Committee and the State Council on Deepening the Reform of Systems and Mechanisms to Accelerate the Implementation of Innovation-driven Development Strategies, which states that competition policy and industrial policy share the same goal of improving market innovation.[45] In

[42]Zhonggong Zhongyang Guowuyuan Guanyu Shenhua Guoyou Qiye Gaige De Zhidao Yijian (中共中央, 国务院关于深化国有企业改革的指导意见) [Guiding Opinions of the CPC Central Committee and the State Council on Deepening the Reform of State-owned Enterprises], issued by the State Council on August 24, 2015.

[43]Guowuyuan Guoyou Zichan Jiandu Guanli Weiyuanhui Bangongting Guanyu Kaizhan Zhongyang Qiye "Shisanwu" Fazhan Zhanlue He Guihua Bianzhi Gongzuo De Tongzhi (国务院国有资产监督管理委员会办公厅关于开展中央企业 "十三五" 发展战略和规划编制工作的通知) [Notice of the General Office of the State-owned Assets Supervision and Administration Commission of the State Council on the Development of the 13th Five-Year Plan for Central Enterprises] effective on March 6, 2015.

[44]Dai (2016), Ye (2017).

[45]Zhonggong Zhongyang Guowuyuan Guanyu Shenhua Tizhi Jizhi Gaige Jiakuai Shishi Chuangxin Qudong Fazhan Zhanlue De Ruogan Yijian (中共中央、国务院关于深化体制机制改革加快实

May 2016, the State Council published The Notice on Approving and Forwarding the Opinions of the National Development and Reform Commission on the Pivotal Work of Deepening the Reform of the Economic System in 2015 and Article 5 of the Notice stipulated that regulations and practices that hinder the national market and fair competition should be reviewed and repealed. A market access negative list system should be developed and industrial policy and competition policy should be coordinated effectively, and to establish a review mechanism on a fair and competitive industrial policy.[46] In Article 17 of the State Council Notice on Circulating the Opinions of the National Development and Reform Commission on Deepening the Reform of the Economy System issued in March 2016, it is stressed the importance of coordinating competition and industrial policy and a fair competition review system, and the pilot program of the market access negative list system should be developed in Shanghai, Guangdong, Tianjin and Fujian.[47]

In 2016, the State Council published the Opinions of the State Council on Establishing A Fair Competition Examination System in the Building of the Market System, which states that the core of the market reform is to make the market play a *decisive* role in the allocation of resources. A fair competition examination system is to be established to prevent the government's excessive and inappropriate intervention in the market.[48] The Opinion states four exceptional provisions in which industrial policy can be implemented even when it has anti-competitive effects: (1) to protect state economic security and cultural security, or involve national defense construction (2) to achieve reducing poverty, disaster relief and other social security purposes (3) for the conservation of energy resources, the protection of the ecological environment, and the protection of other public interests (4) other circumstances prescribed by laws and administrative regulations. In October 2017, the NDRC, Ministry of Finance, Ministry of Commerce, SAIC and the Legislative Office of the State Council published the Detailed Rules For the Implementation of the Fair

---

施创新驱动发展战略的若干意见) [Several Opinions of the CPC Central Committee and the State Council on Deepening the Reform of Systems and Mechanisms to Accelerate the Implementation of Innovation-driven Development Strategies, effective on March 13, 2015 ("Market Competition has the fundamental role to stimulate innovation, create a fair, open, and transparent market environment, strengthen the guidance of innovation by competition policies and industrial polices, promote the survival of the fittest, and enhance the innovation momentum of market players").

[46]Guowuyuan Zhuanpi Fazhan Gaigewei Guanyu 2015 nian Shenhua Jingji Tizhi Gaige Zhongdian Gongzuo Yijian De Tongzhi (国务院转批发展改革委关于2015年深化经济体制改革重点工作意见的通知) [Notice of the State Council on Approving and Forwarding the Opinions of the National Development and Reform Commission on the Pivotal Work of Deepening the Reform of the Economic System in 2015] issued by the State Council on May 8, 2015.

[47]Guowuyuan Pizhuan Guojia Fazhan Gaigewei Guanyu 2016 nian Shenhua Jingji Tizhi Gaige Zhongdian Gongzuo Yijian De Tongzhi (国务院批转国家发展改革委关于2016年深化经济体制改革重点工作意见的通知) [Notice of the State Council on Circulating the Opinions of the National Development and Reform Commission on Deepening the Reform of the Economic System in 2016] effective on March 25, 2016.

[48]Guowuyuan Guanyu Zai Shichang Tixi Jianshe Zhong Jianli Gongping Jingzheng Shencha Zhidu De Yijian (国务院关于在市场体系建设中建立公平竞争审查制度的意见) [Opinions of the State Council on Establishing A Fair Competition Examination System in the Building of the Market System] issued by the State Council on June 1, 2016, effective on June 1, 2016.

Competition Review System.[49] Article 2 of the Notice stipulates that administrative agencies should conduct a fair competition review when developing rules, policies and regulatory documents for market entry, the development of industry, investment, bidding, government procurement, business operation codes, qualification standards and other types of policy measures for economic activities. In the Notice on Issuing the Plan for Market Regulation During the 13th Five-Year Plan Period published by State Council in January 2017, it made clear that strengthening and improving market supervision is an urgent need to improve the socialist market economic system. Competition policy has the function of regulating market order, protecting fair competition, encouraging market innovation, strengthening institutional reform, improve market efficiency and social benefits. Competition policy plays a fundamental role in the development of the socialist market economy and it is urgent to strengthen and improve market supervision to remove obstacles of inadequate market competition in order to improve the economic system.[50] In the 2020 draft revision of the AML, Article 9 was added and it explicitly states that the State establishes and implements a fair competition review system, regulates government administrative actions, and prevents the introduction of policies and measures that exclude or restrict competition.

3.2.5 Public Interests

Article 27 provides the six factors that are to be taken into account in merger review, and the third factor is the impact of concentration on market access and technological advancements, and the fifth factor is the impact of the concentration on national economic development.[51] Article 28 states two situations when a concentration can be exempted from a prohibition. The first situation is when the concentration can

[49]Guojia Fazhan Gaigewei, Caizhengbu, Shangwubu Deng Guanyu Yinfa Gongping Jingzheng Shencha Zhidu Shishi Xize Zanxing De Tongzhi (国家发展改革委, 财政部, 商务部等关于印发《公平竞争审查制度实施细则(暂行)》的通知) [Notice of the National Development and Reform Commission, the Ministry of Finance, the Ministry of Commerce and Other Departments on Issuing the Detailed Rules for the Implementation of the Fair Competition Review System (For Interim Implementation)], issued on October 23, 2017 and effective on October 23, 2017.

[50]Guowuyuan Guanyu Yinfa Shisanwu Shichang Jianguan Guihua De Tongzhi (国务院关于印发 "十三五" 市场监管规划的通知) [Notice of the State Council on Issuing the Plan for Market Regulation During the 13th Five-Year Plan Period] issued by the State Council on January 12, 2017, effective on January 12, 2017.

[51]Article 27 AML: In the case of the examination on the concentration of business operators, it shall consider the relevant elements as follows: (1) the market share of the business operators involved in the relevant market and the controlling power thereof over that market, (2) the degree of market concentration in the relevant market, (3) the influence of the concentration of business operators on the market access and technological progress, (4) the influence of the concentration of business operators on the consumers and other business operators, (5) the influence of the concentration of business operators on the national economic development, and (6) other elements that may have an effect on the market competition and shall be taken into account as regarded by the Anti-monopoly Authority under the State Council. Translation adopted from en.pkulaw.cn.

prove that the potential positive effects will be larger than the negative effects that it has on competition. The second situation is when the concentration pursues public interests.[52] On May 25, 2010, the SAIC issued Regulations on the Prohibition of the Abuse of Dominant Market Positions, and Article 8 of this regulation listed the factors which will be included to assess competitive effects. One important factor is the effects on social public interests and economic development.

Articles 15 and 28 of the AML grant exemptions for monopolistic behaviour that promotes public interest,[53] but to some commentators it is not clear that whether the interest of the universal good of the Chinese people also includes the interest of certain business operators.[54] To explain this, Wu and Jin argued that the choice of the competition policy goal is affected by national industrial policy, trade and economic policy.[55] Granting exemptions may leave room for future interpretations, and a decision will be made by the authority to strike a balance between the goals of competition law and the goals of other social and economic policies.[56] According to Wei, the compromise between competition policy and industrial policy is covered under the public interest defence in the AML. Wei argued that it is common for many emerging countries to include public interest concerns in their antitrust laws, as the goals of antitrust law are affected by the process of market liberalization and the process of economic development.[57] Berry argued that economic development is facilitated through the trade-offs between liberalizing the market and retaining the centralized system,[58] as any increase in economic freedom requires the reduction of the control from the central government.[59] Berry also pointed out that the extent to which the AML can achieve its goals is dependent on precisely how the policy makers define and interpret the key terms stated in the law and in the provisions, for example, the definition of the relevant market and the monopoly market share.[60] In addition, the enforcement agencies will have to work together to ensure the consistent application of the AML.[61]

---

[52] Article 28 of the AML: Where the concentration of business operators will or may eliminate or restrict competition, the Anti-monopoly Law Enforcement Agency under the State Council shall make a decision to prohibit the concentration. However, if the business operators can prove either that the favourable impact of the concentration on competition obviously exceeds the adverse impact, or that the concentration meets the public interests, the Anti-monopoly Law Enforcement Agency under the State Council may decide not to prohibit the concentration. Translation adopted from en.pkulaw.cn.

[53] Wang (2008, p. 143).

[54] Wang (2008, p. 142).

[55] Wu and Jin (2009, p. 44).

[56] Wu and Jin (2009, p. 44).

[57] Wei (2013, p. 126).

[58] Berry (2005, p. 143).

[59] Berry (2005, p. 143).

[60] Berry (2005, p. 148).

[61] Berry (2005, p. 149).

3.2.6 National Security Review

Article 31 of the AML states that when a foreign investor participates in the concentration, besides the examination of competition effects, an additional examination on national security might also be applied, which is conducted under other relevant State provisions. On August 25, 2011, the MOFCOM published the Regulation on the Implementation of the Security Review System for Mergers and Acquisitions of Domestic Enterprises by Foreign Investors[62] to implement a previous circular Notice on Establishing a Security Review System in Respect of Acquisitions of Domestic Enterprises by Foreign Investors,[63] issued by the State Council on February 3, 2011. This regulation draws attention to the issue of national security and imposes challenges on future antitrust decisions regarding the question of how to make a wise trade-off between other industry policies and competition policies.

Delury argued that the definition of national security used by Chinese regulators is broader than that is used in the context of Western laws.[64] It not only refers to the national defense security, but also covers three other areas, such as national economic stability, the basic societal order, and the research and development capacity for key technologies related to national security.[65] In the Notice issued by the State Council, the security review procedure will be applied in two situations. The first is when the acquisition targets industries or supports activities that are related to national defense security. The second situation is when the acquisition targets industries that are related to national economic security, such as important sectors in agricultural production, energy resources, infrastructure, transportation services, technology and major equipment manufacturing.[66]

[62]Shangwubu Shishi Waiguo Touzizhe Binggou Jingnei Qiye Anquan Shencha Zhidu Youguan Shixiang De Zanxing Guiding (商务部实施外国投资者并购境内企业安全审查制度有关事项的暂行规定) [The Interim Measures on Relevant Matters Concerning the Implementation of Security Review of Mergers and Acquisitions of Domestic Enterprises by Foreign Investors] (issued by the Ministry of Commerce on 4 March 2011, effective on 5 March 2011), available at http://wzs.mofcom.gov.cn/article/n/201103/20110307432685.shtml.

[63]Guowuyuan Bangongting Guanyu Jianli Waiguo Touzizhe Binggou Jingnei Qiye Anquan Shencha Zhidu De Tongzhi (国务院办公厅关于建立外国投资者并购境内企业安全审查制度的通知) [Notice of the General Office of the State Council on the Establishment of the Security Review System for Mergers and Acquisitions of Domestic Enterprises by Foreign Investors] (issued by the General Office of the State Council on 3 February 2011, effective on 3 March 2011).

[64]Delury (2008, p. 35).

[65]Goldstein (2011, p. 31).

[66]Lin and Zhao (2012, p. 117).

3.3 Trading off Different Competition Goals

3.3.1 Efficiency and Welfare Standards

When discussing the trade-offs of economic goals of the AML, academic scholars have not agreed on whether efficiency, consumer welfare or total welfare goal should be prioritized when deciding cases in monopoly agreement, abuse of dominant position and merger reviews. Lin and Zhao argued that although the MOFCOM did not officially announce how efficiencies were treated, there is no doubt that efficiencies are one of the countervailing factors in merger decisions.[67] Article 28 of the AML indicates that efficiencies might be taken into account after deciding whether a merger is anti-competitive or not.[68] In this way, efficiency considerations, such as the effects of cost savings and economies of scale, can only serve as offset factors in the anticompetitive mergers, not as factors to decide whether a merger is competitive or anticompetitive.[69] This article is also more in line with the total welfare standard than a consumer welfare standard.[70]

With respect to the welfare standard applied in China, Shan et al. argued that Article 1 of the AML includes both a consumer welfare standard and a total welfare standard. In addition, public interest concerns, environmental and national securities issues also have to be integrated in antitrust decisions.[71] In particular, the goal of promoting economic development seems to be more consistent with the total welfare standard.[72] Nevertheless, their examination of the published merger case lead to the conclusion that the MOFCOM tends to apply a consumer welfare standard.[73] However, to Berry, this argument could be troublesome, as he argued that consumer interests played a very limited role during the development of the AML and the merger policy.[74] According to Berry, consumers in China may benefit from the increased efficiency of the society, however, he is not convinced that policy makers in China are incentivized to consider the welfare of consumers at the first stage of their decisions.

From a normative view, Lan argued that the efficiency goal has its limitations and cannot deal with competition cases in China in particular administrative monopoly

---

[67]Lin and Zhao (2012, p. 12). Lin and Zhao mentioned that Articles 9 and 12 of the Interim Provisions on Assessing the Impact of Concentration of Business Operators on Competition, *See* Shangwubu Guanyu Pinggu Jingyingzhe Jizhong Jingzheng Yingxiang De Zanxing Guiding (商务部关于评估经营者集中竞争影响的暂行规定) [Interim Provisions on Assessing the Impact of Concentration of Business Operators on Competition] issued Announcement No. 55 (2011) of the MOFCOM issued on August 29, 2011 effective on September 5 2011. Lin and Zhao argued that in accordance with the provision, efficiency may be taken as a countervailing factor.

[68]Lin and Zhao (2012, p. 127).

[69]Lin and Zhao (2012, p. 127).

[70]Shan et al. (2011, p. 7).

[71]Shan et al. (2011, p. 7).

[72]Shan et al. (2011, p. 8).

[73]Shan et al. (2011, p. 26).

[74]Berry (2005, p. 150).

cases. Multiple goals set in AML Article 1 are applicable and efforts should be made to improve legal interpretations to make a balance between different considerations in the competition system.[75] Lin and Zhao argued that under the total welfare standard, efficiencies should be taken into account to decide the competitive nature of a merger. Moreover, from a normative view, the total welfare standard is more likely to be the welfare standard that the AML strives to follow. The reason is that the AML has put considerable emphasis on the industrial policy considerations, which indicates that the producer surplus should not be ignored.[76] Hence, for Lin and Zhao, it is more practical to follow the total welfare standard than a consumer welfare standard.[77] Ying argued that the definition of consumers should be broadened to all citizens in the society and there is no clear difference between consumer welfare and total welfare.[78]

According to Ding, the language of the AML tends to indicate a message of a total welfare standard.[79] For example, the seven circumstances in which the exemptions are granted in Article 15 have showed the process of negotiating between different interests. Granting exemptions for a monopolistic agreement for the reasons of improving technologies, upgrading product quality, enhancing operational efficiency, or mitigating decreases in sales, may show a clear preference towards the productive function of the AML, instead of the distributive function.[80] The primary concern of this law is more likely to maximize the economic cake and how to fairly distribute the welfare between consumers and producers is only a secondary concern.[81] Ding's argument was supported by Yu Donghua, who argued that only a total welfare standard can explain the third, the fifth and sixth factors listed under Article 27 of the AML. The second reason is that under Article 28 of the AML, the concentration will not be prohibited if it has positive effects on public interest. This also proved that an efficiency defence can only be used under a total welfare standard. The third reason listed by Yu is that an efficiency defence can be applied during the notification procedure. Only under the total welfare standard can efficiency defence be applied.[82] Jiao argued that non-economic goals can also be economically measured, and if they can be transferred to efficiency, it is possible to trade-off pro-and anti-competitive effects by applying an efficiency standard. If the monopolistic behaviour has larger benefits than costs, it is possible to exempt that conduct by applying efficiency defence.[83]

[75] Lan (2014).
[76] Lin and Zhao (2012, p. 127).
[77] Lin and Zhao (2012, p. 127).
[78] Ying (2010).
[79] Ding (2011, p. 128).
[80] Ding (2011, p. 128).
[81] Ding (2011, p. 128).
[82] Yu (2012, p. 103).
[83] Jiao (2017, p. 135).

3.3.2 The Legislative Debate

The legislative process of the AML took more than a decade. It has been widely argued that an antitrust law may not have been necessary for China at that time.[84] The legislators in China were concerned that the Chinese enterprises might not be capable of competing with multinational firms in global markets.[85] Concentrations in certain industries between Chinese enterprises should be tolerated, as they were not comparable with enterprises in developed economies.[86]

During the drafting process of the AML, representatives from various groups debated the goal of the AML.[87] For example, in June 2006, during the 22nd meeting of the 10th Standing Committee of the National People's Congress, representatives from Guangdong, Beijing and Shanghai proposed to delete the goal of promoting economic efficiency, and representatives from Guangdong, Guangxi and Anhui proposed to delete the goal of maintaining the legitimate rights and interests of producers. Representatives from Guangxi and the China University of Political Science and Law proposed to delete the goal of protecting consumers' interest. Representatives from Beijing and the National Lawyers Association proposed to add the goal of protecting the national interest. In June 2007, during the 28th meeting of the 10th Standing Committee of the National People's Congress, representative Nan Zhenzhong proposed to add the goal of protecting the legitimate interests of producers,[88] and representative Chen Shu proposed to delete the goal of promoting efficiency.[89] Shang Ming, the first director of the antitrust bureau of the MOFCOM, has acknowledged that the success of the economic development in China for the last 30 years shows that a free and fair market competition order is 'necessary' to ensure that the market economy is developed healthily, efficiently and in an orderly way.[90]

In July 2005, the Minister of the NDRC, Ma Kai, said in a forum in Beijing that by the end of 2004, China had basically completed' the procedure of transforming the highly centralized economy to a socialist market economy. The socialist market economic system is characterized as public ownership playing the major role, with the coexistence of other types of ownerships.[91] Shang Ming perceived the Anti-monopoly Law as a significant landmark in the development of the socialist market economy system within the socialist legal system with Chinese characteristics.[92]

---

[84]Huang (2008, p. 118); International scholars have also argued that competition policy may not be served as a pre-condition for the development of the Chinese economy. *See for example*, Ulen (2011, pp. 13–44).

[85]Huang (2008, p. 118).

[86]Huang (2008, p. 118).

[87]Ding (2011, p. 128).

[88]Ding (2011, p. 128).

[89]Ding (2011, p. 128).

[90]Shang (2009, p. 4).

[91]China has socialist market economy in place, *People's Daily Online*, 13 July 2005, available at http://en.people.cn/200507/13/eng20050713_195876.html (accessed 28 March 2020).

[92]Shang (2009, p. 4).

The special characteristics of China's economic and political structure mean that the AML does not follow the patterns of competition laws in other jurisdictions, and there are a few implications that could be drawn from the debate on competition goals of the AML. The first implication is that the AML targets various economic and non-economic goals, and does not restrict itself to the economic goal of promoting efficiency. After publishing the new Judicial Interpretation in June 2012, a spokesperson of the Intellectual Property Tribunal of the Supreme People's Court highlighted the multiple goals that China's Anti-monopoly Law is trying to achieve,[93] including the maintenance of the market order, the protection of consumers and undertakings, promotion of the public interest, enhancing competitiveness and economic security, and the promotion of a healthy development of the socialist market economy. Zhao Xiaoguang, the Director of the Department of Industry, Communications and Commerce at the Legal Affairs Office of the State Council, argued that the ultimate goal of the competition law is to maximize the total benefit to the society.[94] The focus of this law should be the entire society, not any individuals in any specific market. To implement the competition law in China, Zhao argued, it is important to consider the specific social and political characteristics in China in its transition from a planned economy to a socialist market economy.[95] Competition law can be enforced differently in different countries, and in different time periods. Zhao argued that this difference lies in the fact that countries are at different stages of economic development. As a result, the enforcement of the AML has to be in accordance with the specific social, political and economic characteristics of China.[96]

The second implication is that the treatment of foreign investors has to be aligned with the goal of protecting national security. On the one hand, the positive effects of the foreign investments have been widely acknowledged. The MOFCOM recognized that foreign investments have made an important contribution to the economic development in China. Given the positive influences of the foreign companies, the officials confirmed that the AML will be equally applied to both domestic and foreign enterprises.[97] During an interview in December 2004, Director Shang Ming confirmed that there is no clause in the draft of the Anti-monopoly Law targeting multinational companies. The AML will be applied to domestic and foreign enterprises with all types of ownerships.[98] Wu Zhenguo, the Deputy Director General of the Department of Law and Treaties and the Anti-monopoly Investigation Office of the MOFCOM, confirmed this standpoint and argued that the AML is enforced to

[93]Responses to Reporters' Requests to the Draft for Comments of the Judicial Interpretation of the Anti-monopoly Law from a Superintendent of Intellectual Property Tribunal of Supreme People's Court (25 April 2011), cited by Farmer (2013, p. 15).

[94]Zhao (2008).

[95]Zhao (2008).

[96]Zhao (2008).

[97]Howell et al. (2009).

[98]Wang (2004), Interview: Shang Ming: Anti-Monopoly Law is not only for Multinational Companies, *Xinhua Net*, 23 December 2004.

guarantee that all enterprises compete at the same stage.[99] Zhang Qiong, the associate director of the Legislative Affairs Office of the State Council, confirmed in an interview that AML will be equally applied to foreign and domestic enterprises. The AML does not specifically target mergers by multinationals. On the other hand, to mitigate the negative effects of foreign investments is a clear goal of the AML and its merger policies. Zhang emphasizes that mergers which will affect national economic security will be prohibited.[100]

The third implication is that given the special features of the AML and its role of contributing to a socialist market economy, the enforcement system of the AML in China might be different from other jurisdictions. An officer from the SAIC stated that the SAIC has been fully aware that the experiences of antitrust enforcement in western countries had shown the antitrust authority should be maintained as professional, independent and non-political.[101] In particular, the goal of protecting employment, or promoting economic growth, should not override the goal of competition. However, this officer mentioned that China faces challenges in establishing an independent competition authority, given that its political system requires the officials to follow the leadership from the authority at the higher level. The authority at higher level might prioritize other values than competition, and in this situation antitrust law in China might not be properly enforced.[102]

The fourth implication is that when the competition act has incorporated a multitude of different goals, the challenge of balancing both economic and social, even political goals has to be laid at the door of the competition agency itself. It substantially weakens the enforcement of competition law because on the one hand, the agency has to shoulder extra responsibility to define the meaning, the priorities, and the instruments of competition goals; meanwhile, when it becomes difficult to find the right direction, the performance of the agency can only be ill-assessed. Apparently, to develop a "brand" of the competition agency itself, it is the agency that needs to clarify the goals and the central aim of their daily work. The statement on the agency's goals needs to be clear both to the internal employees and the outsiders.[103] Therefore, there has been an argument to take non-competition goals out and to put them into separate laws. For example, Sang-Seung Yi and Youngjin Jung have argued that the goals of protect minority shareholders should be taken out of the Korean Competition Law MRFTA, and put into the Corporation Part of Korea's Commercial Code, or to enact another law titled "A Special Law on the Protection

[99]Wu (2008, p. 100).

[100]Legislative Affairs Office of the State Council: The AML does not Affect Legitimate Mergers and Acquisitions of Enterprises (国务院法制办:《反垄断法》不影响企业正当并购), *Xinhua Net*, September 10 2007, available at http://news.sina.com.cn/c/2007-09-10/193212542684s.shtml (accessed 26 March 2020).

[101]Wang (2004, p. 3).

[102]Wang (2004, p. 3).

[103]Kovacic et al. (2011, p. 31).

of Minority Shareholders of Large Business Groups".[104] The topic of developing an effective enforcement agency under multiple policy goals will be further discussed in Chap. 9 of this book.

3.4 Conclusions

Article 1 of the AML incorporates five different goals and the 2020 draft revision of the AML adds one more goal of encouraging innovation. Academic scholars in China have not reached consensus on which goal should be taken as the functional or ultimate goal. Some argued that the goal of protecting fair competition is the fundamental function of the law, whereas some others argued maximizing consumer welfare should be the ultimate goal. It is also debated on whether efficiency, consumer welfare or total welfare should be the prioritized economic goal.

Various non-economic concerns have also been reflected in Articles 4, 7, 15, 27, 28 of the AML. Article 4 of the AML states that competition rules are to be applied with the development of a socialist market economy. Industrial concerns on protecting SOEs are reflected in Article 7. Article 15 provides seven circumstances for granting exemptions for business operators who are involved in monopoly agreements. Article 27 lists six factors that the enforcement agency should consider in the assessment of concentrations. Broad industrial policy also covers the goal of promoting innovation. The State Council Notice in 2016 stresses the importance of adopting a fair competition system to coordinate competition policy and industrial policy. Since October 2017, the fair competition review system has been implemented. Furthermore, the definition of public interest also connects with national security concerns and Article 31 of the AML requires foreign investors to apply for national security examinations. The regulation published by MOFCOM in 2011 specifies the procedure for such a review. The debate on multiple policy goals also gives rise to the discussion on establishing an independent competition authority and the competition agency also has to take the responsibility to clarify the goals and apply appropriate instruments to make the trade-off at the same time implement the economic as well as non-economic policy goals.

References

Berry, J. A. (2005). Anti-monopoly law in China: A socialist market economy wrestles with its antitrust regime. *International Law and Management Review, 2,* 129–152.

Dai, L. (2016). The perspectives on merger of SOEs from the anti-monopoly law (国企合并的反垄断法视角评析). *Competition Policy Research* (竞争政策研究) (2), 78–86.

Delury, J. (2008). 'Harmonious' in China. *Policy Review, 148,* 35–44.

[104] Yi and Jung (2007, p. 155).

Ding, M. (2011). On the functions and its optimization of antitrust law (反垄断法的目标选择及其功能优化刍议). *Journal of Tianjin University of Finance and Economics* (天津财经大学学报) (8), 123–129.

Farmer, S. B. (2013). Recent developments in regulation and competition policy in China: Trends in private civil litigation. In M. Faure & X. Zhang (Eds.), *The Chinese anti-monopoly law, new developments and empirical evidence* (pp. 15–72). Cheltenham: Edward Elgar.

Fels, A. (2012). China's Antimonopoly Law 2008: An overview. *Review of Industrial Organization, 41,* 7–30.

Fox, E. M. (2007). Economic development, poverty, and antitrust: The other path. *Southwestern Journal of Law and Trade in the Americas, 13,* 211–236.

Fox, E. M. (2008). An anti-monopoly law for China—Saling the walls of government restraints. *Antitrust Law Journal, 75,* 173–194.

Gao, H., & Dong, X. (2008). The goal and the values of the AML (论我国反垄断法的价值目标及其实现). *Socialism Studies* (社会主义研究), serial no. 180(4), 95–100.

Gerber, D. J. (2008). Economics, law and institutions: The shaping of Chinese competition law. *Journal of Law and Policy, 26,* 271–299.

Goldstein, K. B. (2011). Reviewing cross-border mergers and acquisitions for competition and national security: A comparative look at how the United States, Europe, and China separate security concerns from competition concerns in reviewing acquisitions by foreign entities. *Tsinghua China Law Review, 3,* 215–256.

Hamp-Lyons, C. (2009). The dragon in the room: China's anti-monopoly law and international merger review. *Vanderbilt Law Review, 62*(5), 1577–1622.

Howell, T. R., Wolff, A. W., Howe, R., & Oh, D. (2009). China's new anti-monopoly law: A perspective from the United States. *Pacific Rim Law and Policy Journal, 18*(1), 53–96.

Huang, Y. (2008). Pursuing the second best: The history, momentum and remaining issues of China's antimonopoly law. *Antitrust Law Journal, 75,* 117–132.

Huang, Y. (2018). On the fundamental role of china's competition policy under the rule of law (论中国竞争政策基础性地位的法制保障). *Business and Economic Law Review* (经贸法律评论), 119–134.

Jiao, H. (2017). Antitrust law exemption standards for social policy objectives (社会政策目标的反垄断法豁免标准). *Law Review* (法学评论) (4), 124–138.

Kovacic, W. E., Hollman, H. M., & Grant, P. (2011). How does your competition agency measure up. *European Competition Journal, 7*(1), 25–45.

Lan, L. (2014). Questioning the efficiency standard of competition law (反垄断法唯效率论质疑). *Journal of the East China University of Political Science and Law* (华东政法大学学报) (4), 116–129.

Lan, L. (2016). Debunking myths on consumer interests in antitrust law (Part II) (反垄断法上消费者利益的误用批判(下)). *Competition Policy Research* (竞争政策研究) (6), 73–84.

Li, J. (2008). The value in the antitrust law (论反垄断法的价值取向). *Law and Social Development* (法制与社会发展) (1), 13–22.

Li. (2017). On the exemption of state-owned enterprises by antitrust law (论反垄断法对国有企业的豁免). *Law Review* (法学评论) (4), 115–123.

Lin, P. (2009). *Balancing competition policy and industrial policy under China's AML, presentation at the 5th summer workshop on industrial organization and management strategy*. Beijing: Tsinghua University.

Lin, P., & Zhao, J. (2012). Merger control policy under China's anti-monopoly law. *Review of Industrial Organization, 41,* 109–132.

Liu, Z., & Qiao, Y. (2012). Abuse of market dominance under China's 2007 anti-monopoly law: A preliminary assessment. *Review of Industrial Organization, 41,* 77–107.

Lyu, Z., &Tao, W. (2008). The ultimate goal of the AML (浅谈我国反垄断法的终极目标). *Study on China Administration for Industry & Commerce* (中国工商管理研究) (4), 25–28.

Montinola, G., Qian, Y., & Weingast, B. R. (1995). Federalism, Chinese style: The political basis for success in China. *World Politics, 48*(1), 50–81.

Shan, P., Tan, G., Wilkie, S. J., Williams, M. A. (2011). China's anti-monopoly law, what is the welfare standard. University of South California (USC), Center in Law, Economics and Organization, Research Paper Series No. C 11–18, and USC Legal Studies Research Paper No. 11–25.
Shang, M. (2009). Antitrust in China—A constantly evolving subject. *Competition Law International, 5,* 4–11.
Sun, Y. (2008). On protection of competition law for consumers (论竞争法对消费者的保护). *Journal of CUPL* (中国政法大学学报) (4), 88–98.
Ulen, T. S. (2011). The uneasy case for competition law and regulation as decisive factors in development: some lessons for China. In M. Faure & X. Zhang (Eds.). *Competition policy and regulation, recent developments in China, the US and Europe* (pp. 13–44). Cheltenham: Edward Elgar.
Wang, X. (2004, January 9). Challenges/obstacles faced by competition authorities in achieving greater economic development through the promotion of competition. Speech at the OECD Global Forum on Competition, Center for Co-operation with Non-members Directorate for Financial, Fiscal and Enterprise Affairs.
Wang, X. (2008). Highlights of China's new anti-monopoly law. *Antitrust Law Journal, 75,* 133–150.
Wang, X. (2020). Reflections on the revision of China's antimonopoly law (我国《反垄断法》修订的几点思考). *Law Review* (法学评论) (2), 11–21.
Wei, D. (2013). Antitrust in China: An overview of recent implementation of anti-monopoly law. *European Business Organization Law Review, 14*(1), 119–139.
Williams, M. (2009). Foreign investment in China: Will the anti-monopoly law be a barrier or a facilitator? *Texas International Law Journal, 45*(1), 127–156.
Wu, Z. (2008). Perspectives on the Chinese anti-monopoly law. *Antitrust Law Journal, 75,* 73–116.
Wu, H., & Jin, S. (2009). The social goals of the AML (论《反垄断法》的社会公共目标—以《反垄断法》的实施为契机). *Journal of Capital Normal University* (首都师范大学学报), *188*(3), 41–46.
Wu, H., & Wei, W. (2005). The value and goals of the AML (论反垄断法的价值目标). *The Jurist* (法学家) (3), 92–98.
Yan, Y. (2005). The ultimate aim of antitrust law and its judicial protection (反垄断法的终极目的及其司法保障). *Presentday Law Science* (时代法学) (6), 45–53.
Ye, W. (2017). Industrial restructuring and implementation of antitrust law (产业重组与反垄断法实施). *Law-Based Society* (法治社会) (6), 1–8.
Yi, S. S., & Jung, Y. (2007). A new kid on the block: Korean competition law, policy and economics. *Competition Policy International, 3*(2), 153–183.
Ying, P. (2010). The welfare standards of anti-monopoly control on concentration of business operators: A comparison study and the choice of China (经营者集中反垄断控制的福利标准—类型化之研究及我国的选择). *Journal of Lanzhou University of Finance and Economics* (兰州商学院学报) (4), 114–121.
Yu, D. (2012). A study on the Choose of welfare standards in merger antitrust control (横向并购反垄断控制的福利标准选择研究). *Fudan Journal* (复旦学报) (6), 94–104.
Zhao, X. (2008). The nature, status and features of the AML and its main institutional ideas (反垄断法的性质、地位、特征及其主要制度理念). *Price Supervision and Anti-Monopoly in China* (中国价格监管与反垄断), *2008*(9), 7–12.

Part II
Substantive Law of the AML

Chapter 4
Horizontal Restrictions

Abstract Monopolistic agreements in Chap. 2 of the AML are divided into horizontal and vertical agreements. Article 13 of Chap. 2 prohibits horizontal monopoly agreement and Article 14 prohibits vertical restrictions. By summarizing the openly published administrative decisions on horizontal agreements by SAIC, NDRC, SAMR and their local branches in China from 2010 till 2018, the average number of participating firms is 12.65. Among the total of 91 cartel cases, 31 of them were led by industrial associations. The most represented industries of cartels include auto dealing, insurance, concrete and bricks, pharmaceutical, food industry, tourism and transportation. Cartel fines in China range from 1 up to 10% of the sales revenue in the previous year. In accordance with the leniency guidelines, the first operator who actively reports evidence and fully cooperates with investigation may receive exemption from punishment, while others may receive a reduced penalty in appropriate circumstances.

4.1 Introduction

Cartel, as defined by the UK Office of Fair Trading, is "an agreement between business not to compete with each other", the three components for a cartel include: (1) an agreement (2) among competitors (3) to restrict competition. Cartels often take four categories of conduct: price fixing, restrictions on output, market allocation and bid rigging.[1] Cartel members have to exchange information to engage in agreements, in the form of oral, written, or other types of tacit agreements. In economic terms, collusion refers to the situation when prices are set higher than the benchmark of competitive prices. The outcome of reaching a monopoly price is more relevant than the formalities through which the outcome is reached[2] Communication between participating parties is the core factor when deciding on collusion as the agreement has to be self-enforcing. Communication is more evident in the first period during the process of fostering coordination and collusion, and in the later stages communication is 'necessary' to sustain the collusion when parties are facing uncertainties on costs

[1]ICN Report (2005, pp. 9–10).

[2]Motta (2004, p. 138).

J. Ma, *Competition Law in China*,
https://doi.org/10.1007/978-981-15-5105-5_4

and discount factors.[3] Cartels are formed with an exclusive objective to collude between competitors, in order to increase prices and to gain monopoly profits. With no countervailing benefits, there is no need to conduct a cost and benefit assessment for cartels,[4] and most jurisdictions prohibit cartels per se.

Monopolistic agreements in Chap. 2 of the AML are divided into horizontal and vertical monopoly agreements. Horizontal monopoly agreement refers to the monopoly agreement reached by business operators with competitive relations, and the competitors are at the same economic level, and operate in the same competitive market and have a competitive relationship. Vertical monopoly agreement refers to the monopoly agreement reached between business operators who do not have a competitive relationship and they often do not operate at the same business level and only have a transactional relationship. Articles 13–15 follow the "prohibition + exemptions" approach: Article 13 of the Chap 2 of the AML prohibits horizontal monopoly agreement and Article 14 prohibits vertical relationship. Article 15 provides exemptions and Article 16 regulates industrial associations.

In addition to the AML, monopoly agreements are subject to the NDRC Provisions against Price Fixing[5] issued on December 29, 2010, and the SAIC Provisions for the Industry and Commerce Administrations on the Prohibition of Monopolistic Agreements issued on December 31, 2010.[6] On June 26, 2019, the SAMR issued Interim Provisions on Prohibiting Monopoly Agreements,[7] and this provision was effective from September 1, 2019. The newly promulgated SAMR provision has consolidated the NDRC and SAIC provisions, and has specified the definitions and explanations of the concepts related to monopolistic agreement. In the SAMR provision, monopoly agreements are no longer separated as price or non-price related cases, and it made clear that when the market share of the entities is less than 15% for horizontal agreements and <25% for vertical agreements, the conduct may be considered as having limited prohibitive or restrictive effect (the 'Safe Harbour Policy').[8] Besides, prohibitions on collusive behavior are included in Article 14 of the Price Law and Article 32 of the Bidding Law.

---

[3] Aubert et al. (2006, p. 1245).

[4] Monti (2001, p. 15).

[5] Fan Jiage Longduan Guiding (反价格垄断规定) [Provisions against Price Fixing] (issued by the State Development and Reform Commission on December 29, 2010 and effective on February 1, 2011, now expired).

[6] Gongshang Xingzheng Guanli Jiguan Jinzhi Longduan Xieyi Xingwei de Guiding (工商行政管理机关禁止垄断协议行为的规定) [Provisions for the Industry and Commerce Administrations on the Prohibition of Monopolistic Agreements] (issued by the State Administration for Industry and Commerce on December 31, 2010 and effective on February 1, 2011, now expired).

[7] Jinzhi Longduan Xieyi Zanxing Guiding (禁止垄断协议暂行规定) [Interim Provisions on Prohibiting Monopoly Agreements] (issued by the State Administration for Market Regulation on June 26, 2019 and effective on September 1, 2019).

[8] Zhan et al. (2018).

4.2 Cartel Agreements in Economic Theory

4.2.1 Cartel Stability and Duration

Cartel agreements have to be enforceable and sustainable. Rational participants estimate the costs and benefits of maintaining cartel surcharges and may break the agreement when the potential costs exceed the benefits. Cartel participants face coordination costs to implement collusive agreements, to monitor costs of deterring defections and preventing entries, and firms take a wide range of strategies to prevent cheating.[9] Incentives and self-enforcing mechanisms between cartel members have been widely studied in economic literature. For example, Levenstein and Suslow studied the determinants of cartel duration for 81 international cartels found by the US, or the EC or both engaged in agreements on price fixing or market division since 1990, and the average duration of cartels is 8.1 years with a standard deviation of 5.8 years, and the median life span is 7 years. Only about 10% of the cartels in the sample lasted no more than 2 years.[10] In Combe and Monnier's study, the average duration of cartels was 7 years,[11] and Smuda estimated that the average cartel duration is 8.35 years.[12] In the sample studied by Posner in 1970,[13] the average duration of cartels prosecuted was 7.5 years, and the study by Gallo et al.[14] found in 2000 that the average cartel duration in the US was 5.4 years.[15] About 80% of the cartels ended because of the intervention by antitrust authorities.[16] The data from US DOJ Commerce Clearing House Trade Regulation Reporter showed that from 1992 to 2010, a period when cartel penalties have been increased dramatically, there were over 36 cartel convictions per year, with approximately 700 DOJ cartel convictions in total, and the average duration of cartel price fixing cases was about eight years.[17]

In Hay and Kelley's study of horizontal price-fixing cartels in the US between 1963 and 1972, it was concluded that 80% of the cartels were organized by 10 or less firms, and when more than 15 firms participated in the cartel, it was often the trade associations who were involved to facilitate coordination. The empirical evidence also proved that the cartel is more likely to survive when there is high concentration market share and the products are homogeneous.[18] Feinberg et al. studied the cartel decisions published by Korea Fair Trade Commission (KFTC) between 1989 and 2012, and found that when the number of participating firms increases, the cartel

[9]Levenstein and Suslow (2006, p. 44).

[10]Levenstein and Suslow (2011, pp. 462–463).

[11]Combe and Monnier (2011).

[12]Smuda (2014).

[13]Posner (1970).

[14]Gallo et al. (2000).

[15]Levenstein and Suslow (2011, p. 464).

[16]Levenstein and Suslow (2011, p. 466).

[17]Levenstein and Suslow (2012, p. 4).

[18]Hay and Kelley (1974).

stability is reduced, although the participation of foreign companies may lead to greater cartel duration.[19] Harrington and Chang proposed that cartel duration is likely to be affected by the strength of antitrust enforcement,[20] and Miller proved that a more active enforcement of the leniency program could increase cartel detections.[21]

Velijanovski[22] summarized the cartels prosecuted by the EU Commission from 1999 to 2006, it was reported that cartels detected and prosecuted had an average duration of 7.1 years, with a median duration of 5.5 years and the longest cartel case lasted for 29 years. On average, cartels had 5.2 members, ranging from 2 members (in 7 cartels) to 16 members. Cartels are concentrated in chemicals and it composed 47% of the total cartel cases. Based on the dataset of 249 hard-core cartels prosecuted in over 20 developing countries from 1995 to 2013, Ilvadi et al. analyzed the descriptive data in these cases including relevant market, the number of colluding firms, cartel duration, cartel's sales, penalties applied and estimated price overcharges. They found that the median number of colluding firms was 5, and the median cartel duration was 27 months. Compared with the median cartel durations in North America (50 months) and in the EU (70 months), cartel duration in developing countries was less sustainable.[23] Hüschelrath et al. studied 73 cartel cases with 471 cartel members in European Commission's decision between 2000 and 2011, and concluded that the average number of cartel firms was 6.45 and the average overall cartel duration was 8.81 years (106 months).[24]

Cartels are more likely to maintain their stability when the industry is concentrated, and products are often homogeneous, and companies share similar cost structures and mature technologies.[25] In the data sample of 64 cartels convicted by the European Commission from 1975 to 2009, Monnier and Combe concluded that 40% of the cartel operated with the chemical sector, and two thirds of the cartels operated in the manufacturing industry of intermediary products, while other well represented industries included the metal and mineral sector, machinery and equipment.[26] Hüschelrath et al.'s research showed that among all cartel cases decided by the European Commission between 2000 and 2011, 75% of the cartels are referred to the manufacturing industry, and 25% are in wholesale trade, transporting and storage.[27] Levenstein and Suslow summarized that frequent cartel industries include agriculture, stone, glass, machinery, chemical, agricultural food products, textiles, steel, highway construction, street construction, electrical contracting.[28] Cartels in unconcentrated markets or with large number of participants are often facilitated and coordinated by trade

[19] Feinberg et al. (2016).
[20] Harrington and Chang (2009).
[21] Miller (2009).
[22] Velijanovski (2007).
[23] Ivaldi et al. (2015, p. 20).
[24] Hüschelrath et al. (2012).
[25] Monti (2001, p. 15).
[26] Monnier and Combe (2011, p. 243).
[27] Hüschelrath et al. (2012).
[28] Levenstein and Suslow (2006, p. 57).

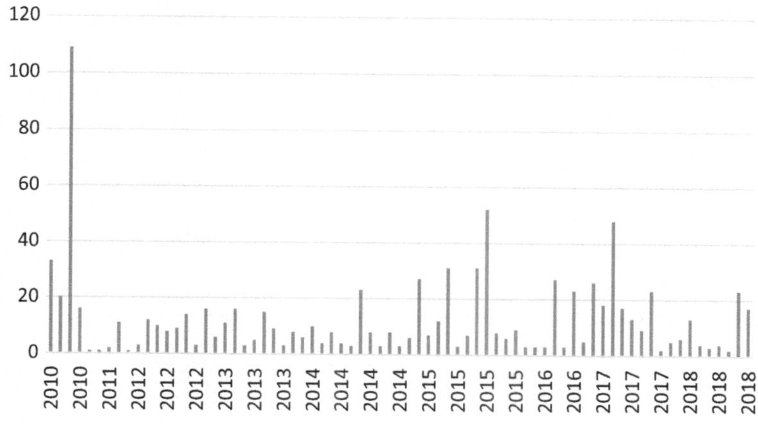

Chart 4.1 The number of participating firms in Cartel (2010–2018)

and industry associations.[29] Trade associations are often involved when the number of participating firms is larger than ten.[30]

When summarizing the openly published administrative decisions on horizontal agreements by NDRC, SAIC, SAMR and their local branches in China from 2010 till 2018, the average number of participating firms is 12.65, with the median number of 8, ranging from the minimum of 2 to maximum number 109 (Chart 4.1). Among the total 97 cartel cases, 31 of them were led by an industrial association. Among the 31 cartel cases led by industrial organization, 9 (29%) of them received fines only on the association, and 8 (26%) of them received fines only on the participating firms, and 14 (45%) of them received fines on both the association and the firms.

As shown in the Chart 4.2, the most represented industries of cartels include auto dealing (12 cases), insurance (12 cases), concrete and bricks (12 cases), pharmaceutical (7 cases), food industry (4 cases), tourism (4 cases), transportation (3 cases), paper making (2 cases), energy supply (2 cases), manufacturing (2 cases), liquor (2 cases), fireworks (2 cases), vision care (2 cases), accounting (2 cases).

4.2.2 *Cartel Surcharges and Detection*

The expected benefits for cartels have been proved to be substantial, however, the detection rate of cartels remain low. Based on the original dataset containing 1517 cartel overcharge estimates in 381 product markets between 1990 and 2009 in European market, Smuda calculated that the mean cartel overcharge is 20.7% of the selling

[29] Levenstein and Suslow (2006, p. 60).

[30] Monti (2001, p. 16).

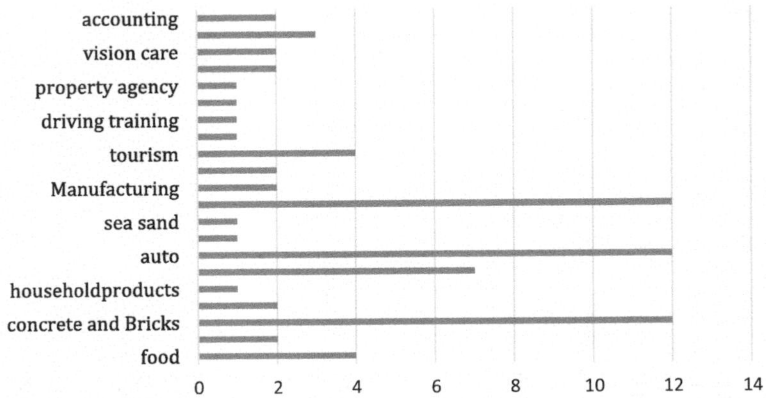

Chart 4.2 Cartel Industries (2008–2018)

price, and the median is 18.37 of the selling price, and overcharges imposed by international cartels are higher than domestic cartels.[31] The estimation of the probability of detection of cartels varies between 10 and 17% in the US[32] and in Europe. From 1996 till 2008, 75 cartels were detected in 12 years, on average 6.25 cartels were detected per year; in the 28 years before 1996, only 35 cartels were detected and this equals 1.4 cartels being detected on average per year.[33] Combe, Monnier and Legal's model published in 2008 shows that the probability of detecting cartels in the EU is between 12.9 and 13.3% annually.[34] A selected sample chosen by Ivaldi, Jenny and Khimich shows that the estimated maximum detection rate in developing countries is 24%.[35] To increase the detection rate, since the early 1990s both the US and EU have implemented leniency policies. Recent studies show that although leniency programs could substantially increase the detection rate, the deterrence effect on preventing future cartels is rather insignificant,[36] and even with a leniency program, the rate of recidivism remains very high and the specific deterrent effect is still rather weak.[37] The cartel penalties, including fines imposed, and imprisonment also remain below

[31] Smuda (2014).

[32] In 1986, according to the estimation by Douglas Ginsburg, the Assistant Attorney General for Antitrust, the probability of cartels being detected was only around 10%. See Sentencing Options Hearing before the United States Sentencing Commission, in United States Sentencing Commission: Unpublished Public Hearings, 15 July 1986. There are concerns about whether this estimation is valid. See Connor and Lande (2005, p. 519). Bryant and Eckard estimated that in the sample period from January 1961 to December 1987, this probability in the US in a given year was around 13–17%. Bryant and Eckhard (1991, p. 531).

[33] Monnier and Combe (2011, p. 239).

[34] Combe et al. (2008). In 2010, Connor concluded that "most scholars believe that it (the probability of being apprehended) averages <30%". Connor (2010, p. 3).

[35] Ivaldi et al. (2015, p. 20).

[36] Harrington and Chang (2009), Miller (2009), Brenner (2006, p. 639).

[37] Hinloopen and Soetevent (2008), Connor (2010); Note that Werden, Hammond and Barnett responded Connor's empirical research by using their data from 1999 to 2012: Werden et al. (2011).

the deterrent level.[38] By studying collusion in 75 cartel cases, Connor and Lande's research showed that although illegal cartel members face sanctions including corporate fines, individual fines and imprisonment, as well as house arrest, collusion is still a profitable business strategy, and the cartel sanctions in the US today counted only 7–17% of the amount that would have been optimal to protect victims of cartels.[39]

By using the sample data of international cartels sanctioned in major antitrust jurisdictions (including the US, EU, Canada and other countries) between 1990 and 2005, Bolotova and Connor found that the average gain from cartel price-fixing was 27.8% of affected commerce, while the average fine imposed by the administrative authority was 10.2% of affected sales. The result shows that government fines imposed were not sufficient to perform a compensatory function and have not achieved an optimal deterrent effect, because the government fines are not adjusted in accordance to the cartel duration.[40] Ilvadi et al.' study shows that on average, the penalties imposed on developing countries was 19% of the excess profits, and it was much below the level in the US (57%) and in the EU (26%); however, the under-enforcement of competition fines does not lead to the high overcharge rate in developing countries, and it was rather similar (20%) to what it is in the EU countries (19.5–22.48%) and in the US and Canada (16.7–19%). The maximum annual probability of cartel detection was 24%, and this result could partially be explained by the close cooperation between neighbouring countries, for example, between Argentina, Brazil, Chile, Colombia and Mexico in cartel investigation.[41]

4.2.3 Cartel Punishment

Most antitrust jurisdictions rely on monetary sanctions (high fines) to deter cartel conduct. This is based on the economic rationale that the optimal sanction should be calculated as external harm to the society divided by the probability of detection. According to Katsoulacos et al., monetary sanctions on cartels in economic literature could be categorized in four types: fines based on revenue,[42] fines based on illegal gains,[43] fines based on cartel overcharge, and fixed fines. Katsoulacos et al. argued that penalties on cartels should not be based on revenue or illegal gain, but the penalty

---

[38]In Europe: see Combe and Monnier (2011) ("Fines imposed against cartels by the European Commission are overall sub-optimal.") Allain et al.'s research shows that although recent EC-imposed cartel fines are close to meeting the deterrence goal, some fines seem to be too high, and some are too low (Allain et al. 2015).

[39]Connor and Lande (2012). For similar results in Europe, see Connor and Miller (2009). Their research is consistent with the commonly accepted view by empirical economists that the worldwide cartel sanctions today are sub-optimal.

[40]Bolotova and Connor (2008).

[41]Ivaldi et al. (2015).

[42]Bageri et al. (2013), Katsoulacos and Ulph (2013).

[43]Harrington (2004, 2005), Houba et al. (2010, 2012).

should be based on cartel overcharge.[44] On the one hand, it has been advocated that antitrust fines should be increased even more substantially in order to offset the cartel gains and the low probability rate, when the fine is not high enough, industries may find it is "worthwhile" to keep cartel illegal profits.[45] According to Connor, in the US, the maximum fine for corporations and individuals was set at USD 50,000 from 1955 until 1974, and it accounted for only 0.4% of the affected sales. This amount increased to 1.4% when the maximum fine rose to USD 1 million from 1974 till 1980, although most corporations paid about 86% discount (USD 140,000) maximum statutory fine from 1974 till 1980 because of plea bargaining. In the late 1980s, the US Sentencing Commission Guideline set 20% of affected sales as "base line" and it could be increased up to 80% of affected sales, resulting in an increase of an average fine to USD 160,000 per company in the mid-1980s.[46] Between 1990 and 2004, the maximum corporate fine was limited to USD 10 million.[47] In 2004, this statutory limit was increased to USD 100 million by the Antitrust Criminal Penalty Enhancement and Reform Act signed by President George W. Bush, and the maximum individual fine was increased from USD 350, 000 to USD 1 million.[48] Since then, the average fines imposed on corporate cartels have increased dramatically. The average annual cartel fines rose from USD 297 million between the fiscal year 1995 and 1999, to USD 558 million in fiscal years 2005–007. Since 1995, the major source of these cartel fines is from non-US firms.[49] The amount of cartel fines set by the Antitrust Division in the US, however, is not the highest worldwide. Between 2000 and 2004, the fines set by the EU were 200% higher than the cartel fines by the Antitrust Division.[50] The cartel fines by all EU authorities amounted to USD 11.6 billion in 2005, account for 77% of the cartel fines that are charged by all antitrust authorities around the globe. The amount of total fines imposed by the European Commission increased from 0.271 billion euro from the 1995–1999 period, to 3.2 billion euros in the 2000–2004 period, to 8.2 billion euros in the 2005–2009 period.[51] In 2008, EU Commission imposed 1.38 billion euros in total—the highest fine in the history of antitrust enforcement worldwide—on companies participating in a car glass cartel.[52] In particular, the fine for Saint Gobain which amounted to 896 million euros, was

---

[44] Katsoulacos et al. (2015).

[45] Normann and Tan (2013), Smuda (2014), Connor and Lande (2012); Comparing another survey conducted among representatives of the general population by Andreas Stephan in 2014: when the US citizens were asked "Is price fixing illegal in your country?", 43% replied "Don't know". See Stephan (2014, p. 13).

[46] Connor and Lande (2005), Connor (2006, p. 207, 208).

[47] Antitrust Amendments Act of 1990, Pub. L. No. 101-588, 104 Stat. 2879 (Codified at 15 U.S.C. section 1, 2000). See Ginsburg and Wright (2010, p. 4).

[48] Clarke (2012, p. 82), Hammond (2005, p. 1).

[49] Connor (2008, p. 104).

[50] Connor (2008, p. 106).

[51] Smuda et al. (2015, p. 1352).

[52] Anderson and Cuff (2011, p. 402), Commission Decision Summary No. COMP/39125 (*Car Glass*), 2009 O.J. C 173/13.

at the time the highest cartel fine ever imposed on a single company.[53] After the Regulation No 1/2003 came into force, the violation of Article 101 of the TFEU can be punished with fines up to 30% of the undertakings or association of undertakings' global turnover in the preceding business year.[54] Since 2006, for the recidivist of hardcore cartel cases this fine can be charged from 30% of relevant sales, up to 100%.[55]

A closer look at the amount of fines on global cartel cases, however, indicates that the amount of fines imposed by the EU and US are at a comparable level.[56] In the Lysine case, the fine imposed by the US antitrust authority was USD 92.5 million, whereas in Europe this amount was USD 97.9 million. In the Citric Acid case, the US authority charged USD 110.4 million and the European antitrust authority charged USD 120.4 million. Similarly, in the Vitamins case, the company was fined USD 906.5 million and in Europe it was fined USD 756.9 million.[57] Competition authorities in Europe usually calculate fines based on the affected commerce, rather than on the loss of consumer surplus or the unlawful profits, or they link the amount of fines to the annual turnover of the firms.[58] Starting from the end of 2008, the total fines imposed on cartels by the European Commission increased dramatically. From 2008 till 2011, the total amount of fines imposed on 110 cartels reached 12 billion euros, equal to 116 million euros per cartel, and the largest fine reached 1.3 billion euros.[59] Based on the guidelines published by the European Commission in 2006, the Commission will first determine a basic amount by considering the previous turnover of the undertaking, the gravity and duration of the cartel, then add about 15–25% (30% for cartels) of the sales value in order to achieve deterrence. The basic amount could be adjusted if the aggravating conditions are met, and the cap of the maximum fine is 10% of the worldwide annual turnover in the preceding year.[60] In the US, the Sentencing Guidelines 2006 set the base line level at 20% of the affected commerce, and this amount was made in accordance to the estimate that the average benefits of the cartel were 10% of the sale price.[61] Setting the base line as 20% of the affected commerce is theoretically flawed. The most famous argument is that the

---

[53] Anderson and Cuff (2011, p. 402).

[54] The sales are counted as the sales of products covered by the infringement during the previous year. The assessment of fines depends on the factors including the nature of the infringement, the geographic scope, and whether the infringement has been implemented. The fines on cartels are in the range of 15–20%. See European Commission Factsheet "Fines for breaking EU Competition Law", available at https://ec.europa.eu/competition/cartels/overview/factsheet_fines_en.pdf.

[55] Guidelines on the Method of Setting Fines, Official Journal C 210, 1 September 2006. See Ginsburg and Wright (2010, p. 4).

[56] Note that the fines imposed by the European Commission have increased dramatically during the last fifteen years, see European Commission, Cartels: Overview, available at: http://ec.europa.eu/competition/cartels/overview/index_en.html.

[57] Buccirossi and Spagnolo (2005, p. 10).

[58] Bageri et al. (2013, p. 545).

[59] Combe and Monnier (2011, p. 239).

[60] Bageri et al. (2013, p. 547).

[61] U.S. Sentencing Guidelines Manual section 2R1.1(d)(1) (2006).

level of fine is still too low. Connor and Lande's study on seventy-five recent US and international cartels shows that the sanctions imposed on cartels (a median sanction of 17% of the sales value) was almost the same as their overcharge (approximately 19% of the sales value). However, if the average rate of detection and conviction is only between 20 and 24%, the level of sanction should be increased by five times.[62]

On the other hand, it is also argued that antitrust fines may not achieve their deterrence goal, and thus should develop alternatives, such as confiscating illegal gains or develop antitrust rewards. It has been argued that a reward system rather than a deterrence-based punishment scheme could be more effective. When comparing the impact of a leniency program of reduced fines and providing positive rewards for corporations and individuals, Aubert et al. found that reward could deter collusion more effectively. In their model, positive rewards, in particular on individuals, achieve a more significant deterrence effect than reduced fines.[63] Collusion is not sustainable when facing large rewards and thus deterrence could be strong, and the deterrence effect is more significant when the cartel leader is accessible to rewards. The Korean Fair Trade Commission (KFTC) has provided the substantial award amount of 1 billion KRW to incentivize informants to report cartels, and in 2008 rewards have been granted in fifteen cases with the total amount of 333 million KRW.[64]

4.3 Chapter 2 of the AML

4.3.1 Definition of Monopoly Agreements

Chapter 2 of the AML deals with the legal definition of monopoly agreements and Article 13 defines the concept of horizontal agreements between competitors, and Article 14 defines vertical agreements between firms at upstream manufacturing and downstream dealing processes. Article 13 of the AML stipulates that monopoly agreements refer to "agreements, decisions, or other concerted behaviour that may eliminate or restrict competition".[65] Article 6 of the NDRC Provisions against Price Fixing explains the concept of "concerted behaviour", that the act must be determined on the basis of two factors: (1) the price-related acts are consistent; (2) business operators have communicated with each other. Article 3 of the Provisions for the Industry and Commerce Administrations on the Prohibition of Monopolistic Agreements adds a third factor: whether the business operators are able to justify their actions. Both provisions have mentioned that the market structure, competition status in the relevant market, changes in the market, and general conditions of the industry should also be considered. Article 6 of the Interim Provisions on Prohibiting Monopoly

---

[62]Connor and Lande (2012, p. 478).

[63]Aubert et al. (2006).

[64]Sokol (2011, p. 5).

[65]Article 13, AML.

Agreements issued by the SAMR[66] have combined both provisions and concluded that there are four factors to be considered when identifying "concerted practice": (1) whether the market behaviour of the business operators are consistent; (2) whether business operators had communicated with each other or had exchanged information; (3) whether the business operators can provide justifications for their concerted behaviour (4) the relevant conditions of the market structure, competition status and changes in the market. Article 5 of the SAMR provision defines that an agreement or a decision may be in the form of writing or oral, and concerted practice which means that although business operators have not entered into agreement or decision, they have "substantially conducted a concerted practice". Article 13 adds seven factors that should be taken into account when determining monopoly agreements: (1) the facts that business operators have reached a monopoly agreement and have enforced the agreement; (2) market competition status; (3) the market share and market power of the business operator; (4) the effects of the monopoly agreement on product prices, quantities and qualities; (5) the effects of the monopoly agreement on market entry, technology development and other aspects; (6) the effects of the monopoly agreements on consumers and other producers; (7) other relevant factors that are related to determining monopoly agreements.

4.3.2 Types of Horizontal Agreements Under the AML

Article 13 of the AML prohibits six types of horizontal agreements[67]: they are the agreements (1) Fixing or changing the price of commodities (price cartel); (2) Restricting the production quantity or sales volume of commodities (quantity cartel); (3) Dividing the sales market or the raw materials supply market (regional cartel); (4) restricting the purchase of new technology or new facilities or the development of new technology or new products; (5) joint boycotting transactions; (6) other monopoly agreements determined by the AML enforcement agency.

Article 7 of the Provisions against Price Fixing explains the eight types of price fixing cartel,[68] including (1) agreement fixes or changes to the price level of commodities and services; (2) agreement fixes or changes to the spread of changes in prices; (3) agreement fixes or changes to the handling charges, discounts or other fees that have effects on prices; (4) agreement that sets agreed prices on the transactions with a third party; (5) agreement that sets a standard formula for calculating price; (6) agreements that prohibit price changes without the consent of the participating business operators; (7) agreement that fixes or changes prices by other means; (8) other types of agreements determined by the price bureau. In Article 7 of the SAMR

[66] Jinzhi Longduan Xieyi Zanxing Guiding (禁止垄断协议暂行规定) [Interim Provisions on Prohibiting Monopoly Agreements], issued by the SAMR on June 26, 2019 and effective on September 1, 2019.

[67] Article 13, AML.

[68] Article 7, Provisions against Price Fixing.

Interim Provisions on Prohibiting Monopoly Agreements, the eight types of price fixing agreements have been reduced to four types[69]: (1) monopoly agreement that fixes or changes the level of the price, range of price changes, profit level or other fees including discount, commission fees and other expenses; (2) agreement that adopts a standard formula for calculating prices; (3) agreement restricts the participating business operator's right to determine prices; (4) agreement that fixes or changes prices by other means.

Article 4 of the Provisions for the Industry and Commerce Administrations on the Prohibition of Monopolistic Agreements[70] prohibits two types of quantity cartels: (1) agreement that restricts the production quantity through imposing restrictions on production, fixing production, stopping production, or restricts the production quantity of specific types or models; (2) agreement that restricts the quantity through refusing to supply, restricting the supply quantity or imposing restrictions on the sales quantity of specific types of models. In addition to these two types of agreements, Article 8 of the SAMR Interim Provisions on Prohibiting Monopoly Agreements adds a third one, that is agreement which restricts production quantity or sales quantity by other means.

Article 5 of the Provisions for the Industry and Commerce Administrations on the Prohibition of Monopolistic Agreements defines three types of monopolistic agreements as regional cartel[71]: (1) agreement that divides sales market, sales target or types and quantities of the products sold; (2) agreement that divides the territory, types and quantities of raw materials, semi-finished products, components and relevant equipment; (3) agreement that restricts suppliers for raw materials, semi-finished products, components and relevant equipment. Article 9 of the SAMR Interim Provisions on Prohibiting Monopoly Agreements has expanded the definition of regional cartel and has included the agreements with restrictions on time. Article 9 prohibits agreements that (1) divide sales territory, market share, sales target, sales revenue, sales profits or the type, volume and time on sold products; (2) divide the procurement area, category, volume, time or suppliers for raw materials, semi-finished products, components, and related equipment; (3) divide the sales market or raw materials procurement market by other means. Raw materials include technologies and services that are required for production and business operation.

Article 6 of the Provisions for the Industry and Commerce Administrations on the Prohibition of Monopolistic Agreements[72] prohibits agreements that (1) restrict the purchase or use of new technology and new techniques; (2) restrict the purchase, lease or use of new equipment; (3) restricts the investment in or research and development

[69] Article 7, SAMR Interim Provisions on Prohibiting Monopoly Agreements.

[70] Article 4, the Provisions for the Industry and Commerce Administrations on the Prohibition of Monopolistic Agreements.

[71] Article 5, Provisions for the Industry and Commerce Administrations on the Prohibition of Monopolistic Agreements.

[72] Article 6, Provisions for the Industry and Commerce Administrations on the Prohibition of Monopolistic Agreements.

of new technologies, new techniques or new products; (4) refuse to adopt new technology, new techniques or equipment; (5) refuse to adopt new technological standards. Article 10 of the SAMR Interim Provisions on Prohibiting Monopoly Agreements has kept the five types of monopoly agreements, and added "new products" to the second and the fourth and the fifth type of restrictive agreements.

Article 7 of the Provisions for the Industry and Commerce Administrations on the Prohibition of Monopolistic Agreements[73] prohibits agreements with concerted behaviour of boycotting, in particular (1) refusal to supply or sell to certain business operators; (2) refusal to purchase or to sell products to certain business operators; (3) imposing restrictions on trading with a competing business operator. Article 11 of the SAMR Interim Provisions on Prohibiting Monopoly Agreements adds the fourth type: concerted boycotting behaviour by other means.

4.3.3 Exemptions

As mentioned in Chap. 3 of this book, Article 15 of the AML stipulates that if business operators could prove that the monopolistic agreements falls within one of the seven circumstances,[74] the monopolistic agreement could be exempted from Articles 13 and 14. The seven circumstances include: the monopolistic agreement is for the purpose of (1) improving technologies, developing new products; (2) upgrading product quality, reducing costs, improving efficiency, harmonizing product standards, specifications or the implementation of professional division of labour; (3) improving the competitiveness and efficiency of small and medium sized business operators; (4) protecting social public interest such as energy conservation, environmental protection and providing disaster relief; (5) mitigating severe decreases of sales or excessive production during economic recessions; (6) protecting justifiable interests in foreign trade and economic cooperation; (7) other circumstances stipulated by law and the State Council.

On May 12, 2016, NDRC published the Guideline on the General Conditions and Procedures for Exemption of Monopolistic Agreements (draft version) for public consultation.[75] Article 7 of the Guideline explains the factors that should be considered when determining exemptions: (1) the extent to which the agreements has achieved the forms and effects of Article 15(1)–(6) of the AML; (2) the causal relationship between the agreement and the effects; (3) the importance of the agreement to achieving the effects; (4) other factors that could be adopted to prove exemptions. Article 8 of the Guideline listed the factors that the competition agency will take into

[73]Article 7, Provisions for the Industry and Commerce Administrations on the Prohibition of Monopolistic Agreements.

[74]Article 15, the AML.

[75]Guanyu Longduan Xieyi Huomian Yibanxing Tiaojian He Chengxu de Zhinan (Zhengqiu Yijian Gao) (关于垄断协议豁免一般性条件和程序的指南(征求意见稿)) [Guideline on the General Conditions and Procedures for Exemption of Monopolistic Agreements (draft version)] issued by the NDRC on May 12, 2016.

account when assessing whether the agreement significantly impede competition: (1) the definition of the relevant market; (2) the market share of the agreement participants and main competitors, as well as the competition status of the relevant market; (3) agreement participants' capacity of controlling market and raw material procurement market; (4) agreement participant's financial and technology capacities; (5) other business operators' transactional dependability to the agreement participants; (6) the difficulties of market entry; (7) the availability of potential competitors; (8) other factors that could prove the agreement will significant exclude or restrict competition. Article 9 of the Guideline explains the factors which should be taken into account when assessing the welfare effects on consumers, including (1) product or service innovation; (2) increase in categories and quantities; (3) improve qualities and safety; (4) reducing prices; (5) improving convenience in consumption; (6) other circumstances.

There has been no published document on whether the Guideline has been implemented; nonetheless, Article 7 of the Guideline has been adopted by Article 27 of the SAMR Interim Provisions on Prohibiting Monopoly Agreements. Article 27 also mentioned Article 9 of the Guideline, that the competition authority should consider whether the agreement has benefited consumers in products prices, qualities, categories and other aspects.

4.3.4 Cartel Fines

Compared with the corporate and individual fine that is charged by the antitrust authorities in the US and the EU, the sanction set by the Chinese antitrust authority is rather low. Article 46 of the AML states "Where business operators reach a monopoly agreement and perform it in violation of this law, the anti-monopoly authority shall order them to cease doing so, and shall confiscate the illegal gains and impose a fine of 1 up to 10% of the sales revenue in the previous year. In the instance where the monopoly agreement has yet to be implemented: a fine of less than RMB 500,000 shall be imposed. The Anti-monopoly law enforcement agency may impose a fine of less than RMB 500,000 on industrial associations that organizes business operators to implement a monopoly agreement." The 2020 draft revision of the AML has significantly increased the level of antitrust fines and in the revised Article 53,[76] the

[76]Article 53 of the 2020 draft revision of the AML: If a business operator violates the provisions of this law and implements a monopoly agreement, the anti-monopoly law enforcement agency shall order it to stop the illegal behaviour, confiscate the illegal income, and impose 1–10% of its sales in the previous year. For those who did not have sales in the previous year or have not implemented the monopoly agreement reached, they may be fined <50 million yuan. In the case of organizing and helping the operator to reach a monopoly agreement, the provisions of the preceding paragraph shall apply. Where an operator actively reports to the anti-monopoly law enforcement agency about the conclusion of a monopoly agreement and provides important evidence, the anti-monopoly law enforcement agency may reduce or exempt the operator's punishment as appropriate. If an industry association violates the provisions of this law and organizes an operator to reach a

fine on business enterprises (RMB 500,000) increased to RMB 50 million, and the fine on industrial associations (RMB 500,000) increased to RMB 5 million.

In 2010, Guangxi DRC reported a cartel case. The cartel was organized by manager Que Zhihe, from Nanning Xian Yi Ge Food Plant in November 2009 and 18 producers joined this cartel and jointly raised the price of rice noodles in Nanning. In January 2010, this cartel was extended to Liuzhou and another 15 rice noodle producers participated, resulting in an approximately 26% increase of wholesale rice noodle prices and an average 14% increase of retail prices.[77] The penalty that was imposed by the NDRC on the cartel participants was an administrative fine. The three major organizers received a RMB 100,000 fine, and 18 other participants received fines ranging from RMB 30,000 to RMB 80,000, and the remaining 12 producers who cooperated with the investigation only received administrative warnings.[78] It is not clear whether this sanction was imposed according to Article 46 of the AML, Article 15 of the Regulations on Administrative Sanctions for Price-related Illegal Conduct and the Law of Administrative Sanctions, or Article 39 of the Price Law.[79]

The Green Mung Bean Cartel was another case that was brought by the NDRC after the Rice Noodle Cartel case.[80] On October 17, 2009, over 100 distributors in Jilin Province attended a meeting to increase the price of green mung beans. This meeting led to a price increase of 220% of green mung beans in May 2010 across the country. The organizer of this cartel, Jilin Corn Center Exchange (JCCE), received a fine of RMB 1 million from the NDRC and this amount was the highest fine that the NDRC imposed after the promulgation of the AML.[81] Three other companies were charged a fine from RMB 300,000 to RMB 500,000. Other participants, however, only

monopoly agreement, the anti-monopoly enforcement agency will be ordered to stop the illegal act and a fine of <5 million yuan may be imposed; if the circumstances are serious, the registration organization of the social organization may cancel the registration according to law.

[77] First Price Cartel Cases under the Chinese AML, Cleary Gottlieb Steen & Hamilton LLP Alert Memo, May 21 2010, available at https://www.clearygottlieb.com/-/media/organize-archive/cgsh/files/publication-pdfs/first-price-cartel-cases-under-the-chinese-aml.pdf.

[78] According to Article 46 of the AML "where any business operator voluntarily reports the conditions on reading the monopoly agreement and provides important evidence to the anti-monopoly authority, it may impose a mitigated punishment or exemption from punishment as the case may be [...]". However, at that time, leniency policy had not been officially proposed by the NDRC. This decision may be issued according to the Article 15 of the Regulations on Administrative Sanctions for Price-related Illegal Conduct and the Law of Administrative Sanctions. See First Price Cartel Cases Under the Chinese AML, Cleary Gottlieb Steen & Hamilton LLP Alert Memo, May 21, 2010, available at https://www.clearygottlieb.com/-/media/organize-archive/cgsh/files/publication-pdfs/first-price-cartel-cases-under-the-chinese-aml.pdf (accessed 30 March 2020).

[79] According to Article 39 of the Price Law, if there are illegal gains, the violator might be fined up to 5 times the value of the illegal gains.

[80] See China Fines Agricultural Companies for Agreeing to Raise the Price of Their Products, Eversheds, LLP. July 16 2010.

[81] This NDRC decision was issued according to the Price Law, and the Provisions on Administrative Penalty against Unlawful Price-Related Practices. See China Fines Agricultural Companies for Agreeing to Raise the Price of Their Products, Eversheds, LLP.

received administrative warnings.[82] On January 26 2011, the SAIC, another antitrust authority in China, imposed a fine of RMB 200,000 on the Committee for Concrete for the anticompetitive conduct of dividing the concrete market.[83] This Committee belongs to the Lianyungang City Construction Material and Machinery Association. The investigation started by receiving information from the whistleblower and was conducted by a special team from the SAIC Jiangsu province branch. Compared with the fines imposed by antitrust authorities in the EU and the US, the fine that cartel members received at that time was still modest.[84] In June 2019, the SAMR imposed RMB 162.8 million on Chang'an Ford for setting RPM with finished vehicles in Chongqing, and it was reported as the highest fines imposed by SAMR.[85]

On June 17, 2016, the NDRC published the draft Guideline on the Determination of Illegal Gains from Monopolistic Conduct by Business Operators and the Setting of Fines for public consultation. It provides calculation details for the amount of fine to be imposed. They should be based on the revenue and the penalty rate is determined by the cartel overcharge rate. The draft guideline was not implemented. According to Article 4 of the Measures for the Administrative Authorities for Industry and Commerce to Determine Illegal Proceeds in Administrative Punishment Cases, the illegal gains from the sale of commodities should be calculated as sales income minus the purchase price of the illegally sold commodities.[86] Wang and Fang's empirical research shows that from August 1, 2008 until January 15, 2018, among the 30 cases investigated by the NDRC, the agency only confiscated illegal gains of 3 cases, and among the 36 cases investigated by the SAIC, in only 17 cases the agency confiscated illegal gains. For the 41 cases that the agency did not confiscate illegal gains, the enforcement agencies did not provide explanations, and in 5 cases the authority stated that it was difficult to calculate the illegal gains. Their research shows that imposing antitrust fines on antitrust infringers is a more practical and realistic instrument for the AML enforcement.[87]

---

[82]It is not clear whether the NDRC has applied the leniency policies in this case. In addition to the decision from the NDRC, there was another distributor that was fined RMB 20,000 by the Guangdong Provincial Price Bureau.

[83]See First Cartel Fines in China Following New Regulations, McDermott Will & Emery, 25 February, 2011.

[84]McDermott Will & Emery, 25 February 2011, id.

[85]Liu et al. (2020).

[86]Gongshang Xingzheng Guanli Jiguan Xingzheng Chufa Anjian Weifa Suode Rending Banfa (工商行政管理机关行政处罚案件违法所得认定办法) [Measures for the Administrative Authorities for Industry and Commerce to Determine Illegal Proceeds in Administrative Punishment Cases] Order No. 37 of the SAIC, issued on November 21, 2008 and effective on January 1, 2009.

[87]Wang and Fang (2018).

4.3.5 Leniency

A leniency program has been widely adopted in antitrust jurisdictions based on economic arguments that in Prisoner's Dilemma leniency would induce defection of cartel members thus reduce cartel stability and increase cartel detection.[88] Cartel participants and third parties will be incentivized to report crucial information, thus reducing the administrative costs, resources and time to collect evidence.[89] It has been proved by theoretical model that in the US the leniency program could improve cartel detection rate by about 60%.[90] According to Kyung Jong Han's research, the 2004 leniency program increased total cartel discoveries by about 10 per year and the influential cartels discoveries about 9 per year.[91] The effectiveness of the leniency program in Korea has also been proved by Sae Ran Koh and Jinook Jeong's research, which shows that from 2005 until 2010, 49% of the cartel cases imposing a surcharge were detected by leniency applications.[92] In Europe, the European Commission amended the Leniency Notice in 2006,[93] which grants immunity to the first cartel participant who submits information and evidence. Such immunity has been granted in 25 decisions out of 31 cartel decisions with fines in 2006–2010 period, and in 21 out of 23 cartel decisions in 2011–2015 periods.[94]

The AML does not specify the conditions of how leniency could be granted and the extent to which applicants could receive exemptions. On February 2, 2016, the NDRC issued the draft Guideline on the Application of Leniency in Cases Involving Horizontal Monopoly Agreements (draft leniency guideline), and the draft Guideline on Commitments in Anti-monopoly Cases (draft commitment guideline) for public comment. The guideline made it clear that companies may apply for leniency by contacting the competition agency either orally or in writing, and submitting an application, as well as important evidence before or after an investigation has been initiated. The evidence includes information on the participants, the communications relating to the reaching of the agreement, and products, services, prices, quantities, geographical scope and size of the market; and duration of the agreement. After the application is received, the competition agency may request the company to provide supplementary materials within 30 days, and in special circumstances it could extend to 60 days. Once the company has started its application for leniency, it should immediately cease illegal practice and cooperate with the competition agency and do not disclose the information that it has already made the leniency application.

---

[88] Aubert et al. (2006).

[89] Wils (2016, p. 12).

[90] Miller (2009).

[91] Cartel leniency program in Korea was adopted in 1997 and revised in 2004. The leniency program increased total cartel fines USD 215 million, and average cartel fines per discovery USD 8 million (Han 2015).

[92] Koh and Jeong (2013).

[93] Commission Notice on Immunity from Fines and Reduction of Fines in Cartel Cases, [2006] OJ C 298/17.

[94] Wils (2016, p. 9).

The organizer of the cartel, who has initiated and implemented the monopolistic agreement will not be exempted from the penalty, but it may receive reduction in the fine if the leniency application is accepted.

The Guideline stipulates that in a single case, a maximum of three applicants could be considered, and only when the case is complex and a substantial number of companies are involved and each leniency applicant could provide different types of evidence, more than three applicants could be considered. The first-in-line applicant could receive 80–100% reduction of fine, and the second-in-line applicant may receive a 30–50% reduction in fine, and the third-in-line applicant may receive maximum 30% reduction. If the first-in-line applicant submitted evidence before the investigation, the competition agency must grant it exemption from all fines. Reduction, even exemption of the confiscated illegal gains can also be considered.

The Guideline provides that the competition agency should ensure confidentiality and all materials submitted should be stored separately and no information should be disclosed to any third party. The materials should not be used as evidence in civil litigation and no authority, organization, or individual is allowed to access the materials. If the leniency application is refused, these materials should not be considered when making decisions on the monopolistic agreement after the agency's investigation. This means that cartel members report to law enforcement agencies and actively cooperate with the investigation, thereby obtaining mitigation or exemption from punishment, before the cartel is discovered, or if the law enforcement agencies have found it but have not formally commenced the investigation, or have not obtained sufficient evidence. Article 12 provides for exemption from punishment for the first active reporting of the relevant circumstances of the monopolistic agreement reached, the provision of important evidence and the full initiative to cooperate with the operator of the investigation. Other operators who actively report to the administrative authorities for industry and commerce on the relevant circumstances of the monopolistic agreement reached and provide important evidence shall, as appropriate, have a reduced penalty.[95]

According to Article 14 of the Provisions on the Administrative Procedures for Law Enforcement against Price Fixing,[96] the price authority *may* reduce or exempt the penalties when the business operator voluntarily reports the relevant information of price fixing agreements and provides important evidence. A business operator who is the first to voluntarily report the information and provide evidence *may* be exempted from punishment. The second to voluntarily report relevant information and provide evidence *may* receive a reduced punishment by *not less than* 50%. All

---

[95]Article 12 stipluates that the first operator who actively reports the relevant situation, provides important evidence of the monopoly agreement and fully cooperate with the investigation, shall be exempted from punishment. For other operators who proactively report to the industry and commerce administrative authorities on the relevant situation and provide important evidence of the monopoly agreement, receive a reduced penalty according to circumstances. Translation adopted from en.pkulaw.cn.

[96]Fan Jiage Longduan Xingzheng Zhifa Chengxu Guiding (反价格垄断行政执法程序规定) [Provisions on the Administrative Procedures for Law Enforcement Against Price Fixing] issued on December 29 2010, effective on February 1 2011.

other business operators who report the relevant information and important evidence of the price fixing agreement *may* receive a reduced punishment by *not more than* 50%. Article 14 also clarifies that important evidence refers to evidence that "plays a key role in the determination of a price fixing agreement by the competent price department of the government."

Article 11 of the Provisions for the Industry and Commerce Administration on the Prohibition of Monopolist Agreements[97] provides a similar statement that business operators who report a monopolistic agreement and provide key evidence *may* receive reduced or exempted from punishment. When deciding the circumstances of granting reduced penalties, the industry and commerce administration should consider the factors including the time sequence of the voluntary reporting, the importance of evidence provided, information on the conclusion and implementation of the monopolistic agreement, and the cooperative attitude of the business operators. Important evidence refers to the evidence that plays a key role in initiating and determining monopolistic agreements, including the participating business operators, the range and type of products, contents and form of the agreement, and the circumstances of the implementation of the monopolistic agreement.

4.4 Industrial Associations

Article 16 of the AML prohibits trade associations from organizing business operators to implement monopolistic conduct. Article 11 of the AML requires trade associations to strenghthen self-discipline, and lead the business operators in the industry to lawful competition, maintain the market competition order. Article 9 of the Provisions for the Industry and Commerce Administrations on the Prohibition of Monopolistic Agreements prohibits industry associations from organizing business operators to engage in monopolistic agreements through (1) issuing rules, decisions, notices, standards of the association with terms on preventing and restricting competition in the industry; (2) organizing or assiting business operators in the industry to reach agreements, decisions, summary or memorandum with terms preventing or restricting competition. On July 20, 2017, the NDRC issued Guidelines on Pricing Behaviour

[97]Gongshang Xingzheng Guanli Jiguan Jinzhi Longduan Xieyi Xingwei de Guiding (工商行政管理机关禁止垄断协议行为的规定) [Provisions for the Industry and Commerce Administrations on the Prohibition of Monopolistic Agreements] issued on December 31, 2010 and effective on February 1, 2011.

of Trade Associations, prohibiting distortive price-related behaviour by trade associations.[98] Article 46 of the AML imposed penalties on industrial associations when organizing monopolistic agreements.[99]

In case law, among the 97 horizontal agreements, about one third of the cartels was led by industrial associations, and in about a half of the cases both industrial associations and participating firms received administrative penalties. One third only of the associations received a penalty and another one third of participating firms received a penalty. Industrial associations may impose direct restrictions on prices. For example, in 2012, three driving school associations in Guangzhou, Shenzhen and Foshan organized meetings to set a minimum price or a range of prices that would be implemented by its members. The Guangdong Price Bureau imposed RMB 350,000 for each association for the breach of Article 16 of the AML.[100] In Shale brick cartel, Hunan AIC investigated a shale brick cartel in the Mayang Miao Autonomous County from December 2014 to January 2015. The cartel was established by 27 (later 29) local shale brick companies through the Mayang County Shale Brick Industry Association. The companies reached agreements between March 2011 and September 2013 with terms on fixing the ex-factory and delivered prices of bricks, dividing markets, limiting production output, and preventing the competition from non-Mayang County bricks. Companies will have to pay management fees to the association, and those who fail to comply with the terms will be sanctioned. The Hunan AIC found that the agreements had an evident harmful effect on monopolizing the shale brick market, and to eliminate competition from non-local shale brick producers, which violated Articles 13(2) and 13(3) of the AML. The Hunan AIC imposed a total fine of RMB 1,389,400 on nine individuals and one company.

In the Guangdong Panyu Animation and Entertainment Industry Association cartel case, Guangdong AIC issued a decision on December 8, 2015 that Guangdong Panyu Animation and Entertainment Industry Association was fined RMB 100,000 for conducting collective boycott. It violates Articles 13(5) and 16 of the AML, and Article 9(2) of the SAIC's Regulations on Prohibiting Monopoly Agreements. The Guangdong Panyu Animation and Entertainment Industry Association requested its 52 members and associated companies to participate in an expo alliance agreement on May 25, 2012, and forced its members to agree that, starting from 2013, association members should only attend exhibitions in Guangzhou that were led, organized or hosted by the association. If not, the member had to submit a written request at

[98] Guojia Fazhan He Gaige Weiyuanhui Gonggao 2017 Nian Di Liu Hao (国家发展和改革委员会公告2017年第6号—行业协会价格行为指南) [NDRC Announcement No. 6 of 2017—Guidance for Price Behavior of Industry Associations] issued by NDRC on July 20, 2017, available at http://www.ndrc.gov.cn/zcfb/zcfbgg/201707/W020170725555925290946.pdf.

[99] Article 46 of the AML: Where a trade association organizes the business operators in its own industry to reach a monopoly agreement in violation of this Law, the Anti-monopoly Law Enforcement Agency may impose a fine of <500,000 yuan; where the circumstances are serious, the authority in charge of social group registration may deregister the trade association. Translation adopted from en.pkulaw.cn.

[100] Fels et al. (2014a, p. 2).

least 30 days before the expo to request the association's written permission. Guangdong AIC started the antitrust investigation against Guangzhou Panyu Animation Association on July 21, 2014. Guangdong AIC held that the relevant market was the animation entertainment expo market, and when 52 members signed and implemented the agreement, according to Article 13 of the AML, it has the anti-competitive effect of restricting and eliminating competition. The cartel agreement does not meet the conditions of Article 15 of the AML for exemption.[101] Industrial associations may also impose broad restrictions on production and sales through joint agreements or decisions. Insurance industry is one evident example.

In 2015–2016, Hubei and Jiangxi AIC imposed fines on insurance companies who signed market sharing monopoly agreements. In Hubei, 12 insurance companies signed a coinsurance agreement which states that the principal insurer China Pacific holds 12% of the total insured amount and the other 11 companies hold 8%. On behalf of the coinsurers, China Pacific would be in charge of collecting insurance premiums and distributing the premiums among co-insurers every month. Coinsurers should pay China Pacific 5% of the total premiums as a management fee. In Jiangxi, 10 insurance companies signed two co-insurance agreements to divide markets. Taikang Life became the principal insurer in Nanchang and the rest of Jiangxi province would be in the charge of China Life. According to the agreement, 31.5% of the total premium in Nanchang should be transferred to Taikang Life and 40% of the premium in the rest of Jiangxi province should be given to China Life. The rest of the premiums will be distributed among coinsurers. The agreement requires that the coinsurers should not insure businesses independently. The participants of the agreement increased to 17 insurance companies in 2012, and the agreements adjusted the insurance premium rates and included a basic and a shared bound system. Both naked market sharing agreements were found illegal under Article 13 of the AML and Article 5 of SAIC Regulations on Prohibiting Monopoly Agreements. Hubei AIC imposed fines of 6% of the previous revenue on China Pacific, and 2% on the rest of 11 insurance companies. Jiangxi AIC imposed fines of 5% of their insurance revenue in 2013 on China Life and Taikang Life, and the rest of the 15 insurance companies were fined 3%. No insurer could be granted leniency in accordance to Article 46(2) of the AML.[102]

Similarly, Hubei AIC initiated its investigations on Hubei Insurance Association in March 2013 for organizing and implementing market sharing agreements on the car insurance market and made its decision on May 5, 2016. Hubei Association asked four insurance companies to divide the market of new car insurance in Wuhan by signing an agreement in May 2003. The agreement included terms on the control of market shares and personnel management. The proportionality of market share was adjusted in 2004, 2006 and 2008 after new members joined the agreement. By taking into account of the cooperative behaviour, fines imposed on the Hubei Association have been reduced to RMB 200,000 from RMB 500,000.[103]

[101] Fels et al. (2016a, p. 7).

[102] Fels et al. (2016a, p. 10).

[103] Fels et al. (2016c, p. 4).

On March 20, 2017, Guangxi AIC imposed fines of RMB 100,000 on Hechi Insurance Association, and 5% of previous revenue for participating companies for implementing a market sharing monopoly agreement. Hechi Insurance Association was the organizer, and starting from July 2008 until March 2013, it asked 9 insurance companies to join self-discipline agreements which have terms on driving the market for motorcycle insurance in Hechi. The Association organized insurance companies in the Yizhou District to sign agreements in December 2009 and in March 2013, it arranged for companies in Du'an County, Dahua County and Bama County to sign self-discipline agreements. Guangxi AIC concluded that these agreements violated Articles 13 and 16 of the AML. The association was fined RMB 100,000.[104]

In Shannxi province, the motor vehicle inspection fees were regulated by the government, and after it became liberalized, Shannxi Motor Vehicle Inspection Industry Association organized 31 motor vehicle inspection businesses to collectively increase prices on the social media platform of WeChat. The meetings were held three times during November and December 2015. After the meeting, motor vehicle inspection fees increased 100% in Xi'an, Shangluo and Yangling in December 2015. Shaanxi Price Bureau imposed a fine of RMB 250, 000 on the association and 6-8% of previous sales on 26 businesses, and 3% on 4 businesses for the breach of Article 13(1) of the AML. 4 businesses received reduced fines because their illegal conduct was "minor" and they had quickly rectified their conduct.[105]

On May 4, 2015, the NDRC, the National Health and Family Planning Commission, the Ministry of Human Resources and Social Security, the Ministry of Industry and Information Technology, the Ministry of Finance MOFCOM, and China Food and Drug Administration issued the Opinion on Pushing Forward Pharmaceutical Pricing Reform. This opinion made clear that from June 1, 2015, pharmaceutical prices will be determined by the market. On the same day, NDRC issued the Notice on Strengthening the Supervision of Pricing Conduct in the Pharmaceutical Market, and it included ten types of unlawful activities that will be investigated by NDRC. On March 24, 2017, the NDRC released the draft guideline on the price-related self-disciplined conduct of industry associations.

4.5 Case Law

In case law, it may be more apparent that the agreement is reached through oral or written agreements. For example, in the express delivery cartel, the agreement was reached when the executives met for having meal. In December 2016, Guangdong DRC imposed RMB 0.65 million fine on five express delivery companies, namely, Huitong STO Express, Huian ZTO Express, Fuxin Express, Jidaneng Logistics, Sanhui YTO Express for jointly raising prices after a meeting at a restaurant in Huidong

[104] Fels et al. (2017b, p. 4).

[105] Fels et al. (2016b, p. 3).

county on October 12, 2016, and increased prices of express delivery from November 1 to 5 in 2016. In another case investigated by NDRC and Chongqing AIC, the three active allopurinol tablets (commonly used for the treatment of gout, or known as hyperuricemia) manufacturers in China, the Chongqing Qingyang Pharmaceutical, Jiangsu Tianjie and Shanghai Sine Pharmaceutical frequently held meetings from April 2014 to September 2015 to increase prices of allopurinol tablets. They increased the prices for allopurinol tablets from RMB 10/bottle to minimum RMB 23.8/bottle in provinces where allopurinol is listed as an "essential medicine" and to RMB 50/bottle in provinces where it is listed as a "low-cost drug". The agreement required that manufactures should only submit tenders in the markets divided to them and should not negotiate prices across provinces.[106]

The cartel may also be reached through professional meetings such as seminars or conferences. For example, in August 2014, NDRC imposed fines on eight Japanese auto parts manufacturers (Hitachi, Denso, Aisan, Mitsubishi Electric, Mitsuba, Yazaki, Furukawa, and Sumitomo Electric) and four Japanese bearing manufacturers for engaging in bilateral or multilateral talks on coordinating auto parts prices. NDRC found that NSK, NTN, Jtekt, and Nachi-Fujikoshi held seminars and conferences in Shanghai, from 2000 to June 2011 to exchange price information and following the meetings, the prices for bearings increased in China and other Asian countries. Hitachi and Nachi-Fujikoshi were the first reported to the NDRC, so they were exempted from the penalty, and for the other seven companies, fines between 4 and 8% were imposed and Sumitomo Electric received the highest fine of AML until 2014, amounting to RMB 290.4 million.[107]

The cartel agreement may also be similar to a business proposal of setting joint operations. In December 2016, Henan AIC imposed fines on five fireworks and firecrackers wholesalers in Henan for implementing market allocation agreements. The five companies joined an operation agreement in March 2015 and agreed to set up an operational centre and to centralize the management of purchases, storage and sales. The price had been unified and penalties would be imposed for non-compliance of the pricing guidelines. Sales revenues would be divided proportionally annually and the operational centre would be carried out by Gushi Zhaoxiang Fireworks. The Henan AIC found that this joint operational agreement is a market sharing cartel agreement, which violates Article 13(1)(3) of the AML. The Henan AIC confiscated the illegal profits, and Gushi Zhaoxiang Fireworks was fined 2% of the previous year's revenue and the other four companies were fined 1% of the previous year's revenue.[108]

Similarly, in the Yongzhou Concrete Companies cartel, participants signed a partnership agreement. There were seven companies participating in the concrete company partnership agreement on September 30, 2011 and they agreed to form an 'operational joint venture' by sharing the responsibilities on management, marketing, scheduling and production. The participating firms signed the Partnership

[106]Fels et al. (2016a, p. 11).

[107]Fels et al. (2014b, p. 3).

[108]Fels et al. (2017a, p. 4).

Agreement of Concrete Firms on September 30, 2011. The agreement had terms on the contributed assets and the plan of dividing profits in accordance to market share. Although the joint venture was not sanctioned and abandoned in December 2011, the Hunan AIC held that the agreement itself breached Article 13(3) of the AML and Article 5(1) of the SAIC Regulations on Prohibiting Monopoly Agreements. Six companies were fined RMB 30, 000 each and one company was exempted because it was the first to report to the agency, and had provided important evidence. Hunan AIC imposed fines on concrete companies in Yongzhou on November 3, 2015 for their cartel behaviour of market sharing. The decisions were published on December 29, 2015.[109]

In the shipping companies' cartel, important information has been communicated through phone calls, meetings, meals, emails and visits.[110] The NDRC started investigation in August 2014 and it was reported that the shipping companies discussed prices, tenders, and the division of consumers and shipping routes from 2008 to September 2012.[111] NDRC found that the price agreements on shipping services for roll on/roll off cargo manufactures on shipping routes in China were made and maintained, which eliminated or restricted competition and both the interests of Chinese importers, exporters and end consumers were harmed when the roll on/roll off cargo international shipping fees were increased. Among the eight companies fined, NSK was the first leniency applicant and it received exemption. The second (K Line) and the third (Mitsui) received reductions in fine at the amount of 4 and 7% of the relevant revenue. For the remaining five companies, Eukor Car Carriers and Wallenius Wilhelmsen were fined 9 and 8% for the reason of having provided important evidence. CSAV, Eastern Car Liner and CCNI were fined of 6%, 5% and 4% for the reason that their anti-competitive impact was relatively minor. NDRC issued the decision on imposing fines of RMB 407 million on eight shipping companies for the anti-competitive behaviour of fixing prices and bid rigging related to shipping services for roll on/roll off cargo on five shipping routes, including North America-China, Europe-China, China-South America, and coastal China shipping routes.

4.6 Conclusions

Monopolistic agreements in Chap. 2 of the AML are divided into horizontal and vertical monopoly agreements. The cartel provisions in the AML follow the "prohibition + exemption" approach. Article 13 of the Chap. 2 of the AML prohibits horizontal monopoly agreement, and Article 14 prohibits vertical restrictions. Article 15 provides exemptions and Article 16 regulates industrial associations. Article 13 of the AML includes six types of horizontal agreements and Article 6 of the SAMR Interim Provisions on Prohibiting Monopoly Agreements lists the four factors that

[109] Fels et al. (2016a, p. 9).

[110] Fels et al. (2016a, p. 9).

[111] Fels et al. (2016a, p. 9).

to be considered when defining "concerted practice". Article 13 of the AML lists seven factors to be taken into account when determining monopoly agreements.

Economic research tends to prove that cartel stability is negatively affected by the number of participating firms and the average cartel duration is about 5–8 years. Cartels are more stable when the industry is concentrated and producing homogeneous products. By summarizing the openly published administrative decisions on horizontal agreements by SAIC, NDRC, SAMR and their local branches in China from 2010 till 2018, this chapter concludes that the average number of participating firms in cartel agreements was 12.65 in China, and the most represented industries include auto dealing, insurance, concrete and bricks, pharmaceutical, food industry, tourist and transportation.

Although Articles 11 and 16 of the AML prohibit industrial associations from organizing business operators to implement monopolistic conduct, when examining the published cases about one third of cartel agreements was organized by industrial associations, and legal sanctions imposed on industrial associations were not severe compared with illegal gains. According to Article 46 of the AML, cartel fines in China ranged from 1 up to 10% of the sales revenue in the previous year. The 2020 draft revision of the AML has increased the fines of RMB 500,000 to RMB 50 million on business entities and RMB 5 million on industrial associations, and such a change is supported by economic arguments of cartel fines, that monetary sanctions need to be increased significantly to impose a 'cost' on cartel infringers. Business enterprises may apply for leniency by contacting the competition agency either orally or in writing, and submit applications and important evidence before or after an investigation is initiated. Others may receive a reduced penalty in certain circumstances.

References

Allain, M.-L., Boyer, M., Kotchoni, R., & Ponssard, J.-P. (2015). Are cartel fines optimal? Theory and evidence from the European Union. *International Review of Law and Economics, 42*, 38–47.

Anderson, D., & Cuff, R. (2011). Cartels in the European Union: Procedural fairness for defendants and claimants. *Fordham International Law Journal, 34*, 385–430.

Aubert, C., Rey, P., & Kovacic, W. E. (2006). The impact of leniency and whistle-blowing programs on cartels. *International Journal of Industrial Organization, 24*, 1241–1266.

Bageri, V., Katsoulacos, Y., & Spagnolo, G. (2013). The distortive effects of antitrust fines based on revenue. *Economic Journal, 123*, 545–557.

Bolotova, Y., & Connor, J. M. (2008). *Cartel sanctions: An empirical analysis*. Retrieved from https://papers.ssrn.com/sol3/papers.cfm?abstract_id=1116421.

Brenner, S. (2006). An empirical study of the European corporate leniency program. *International Journal of Industrial Organization, 27*, 639–645.

Bryant, P. G., & Eckhard, E. W. (1991). Price fixing: The probability of getting caught. *Review of Economics and Statistics*, 531–536

Buccirossi, P., & Spagnolo, G. (2005). *Optimal fines in the era of whistleblowers, should price fixers still go to prison?* Lear Research Paper 05-01.

Clarke, J. (2012). The increasing criminalization of economic law—A competition law perspective. *Journal of Financial Crime, 19*(1), 76–98.

Combe, E., & Monnier, C. (2011). Fines against hard core cartels in Europe: The myth of over-enforcement. *Antitrust Bulletin, 56*(2), 235–276.

Combe, E., Monnier, C., & Legal, R. (2008). *Cartels: The probability of getting caught in the European Union*. Bruges European Economic Research Papers no. 12.

Connor, J. M. (2006). Effectiveness of antitrust sanctions on modern international cartels. *Journal of Industry, Competition and Trade, 6,* 195–223.

Connor, J. M. (2008). Anti-cartel enforcement by the DOJ: An appraisal. *The Competition Law Review, 5*(1), 89–121.

Connor, J. M. (2010). Recidivism revealed: Private International Cartels 1991–2009. *Competition Policy International, 6,* 101. Retrieved from http://papers.ssrn.com/sol3/papers.cfm?abstract_id=1688508.

Connor, J. M., & Lande, R. H. (2005). How high do cartels raise prices? Implications for reform of sentencing guidelines. *Tulane Law Review, 80,* 513–570.

Connor, J. M., & Lande, R. H. (2012). Cartels as rational business strategy: New data demonstrates that crime pays. *Cardozo Law Review, 34,* 427–490.

Connor, J. M., & Miller, D. (2009). *Determinants of EC antitrust fines for members of global cartels*. Retrieved from https://papers.ssrn.com/sol3/papers.cfm?abstract_id=2229358.

Feinberg, R. M., Hyunchul, K., & Park, M. (2016). The determinants of cartel duration in Korea. *Review of Industrial Organization, 48,* 433–448.

Fels, A., Wang, X., Ng, W., & Emch, A. (Eds.). (2014a, January/February). *China competition bulletin* (30th ed.). A Publication of the Competition Law & Economics Network at Melbourne Law School, University of Melbourne.

Fels, A., Wang, X., Ng, W., & Emch, A. (Eds.). (2014b, July/August). *China competition bulletin* (33rd ed.). A Publication of the Competition Law & Economics Network at Melbourne Law School, University of Melbourne.

Fels, A., Wang, X., Ng, W., & Emch, A. (Eds.). (2016a, January/February). *China competition bulletin* (40th ed.). A Publication of the Competition Law & Economics Network at Melbourne Law School.

Fels, A., Wang, X., Ng, W., & Emch, A. (Eds.). (2016b, March/April). *China competition bulletin* (41th ed.). A Publication of the Competition Law & Economics Network at Melbourne Law School, University of Melbourne.

Fels, A., Wang, X., Ng, W., & Emch, A. (Eds.). (2016c, July/August). *China competition bulletin* (43rd ed.). A Publication of the Competition Law & Economics Network at Melbourne Law School, University of Melbourne.

Fels, A., Wang, X., Ng, W., & Emch, A. (Eds.). (2017a, March). *China competition bulletin* (46th ed.). A Publication of the Competition Law & Economics Network at Melbourne Law School, University of Melbourne.

Fels, A., Wang, X., Ng, W., & Emch, A. (Eds.). (2017b, June). *China competition bulletin* (47th ed.). A Publication of the Competition Law & Economics Network at Melbourne Law School, University of Melbourne.

Gallo, J. C., Dau-Schmidt, K., Craycraft, J. L., & Parker, C. J. (2000). Department of justice antitrust enforcement, 1955–1997: An empirical study. *Review of Industrial Organization, 17,* 75–133.

Ginsburg, D. H., & Wright, J. D. (2010). Antitrust sanctions. *Competition Policy International, 6*(2), 3–39.

Hammond, S. D. (2005, January 10). *An overview of recent developments in the antitrust division's criminal enforcement program*. Speech to the American Bar Association, Kona, HI.

Han, K. J. (2015, April 16). *Cartel leniency program and cartel enforcement in South Korea*. Capstone Paper for the 2015 MPA Class, University of Kentucky.

Harrington, J. (2004). Cartel pricing dynamics in the presence of an antitrust authority. *Rand Journal of Economics, 35,* 651–673.

Harrington, J. (2005). Optimal cartel pricing in the presence of an antitrust authority. *International Economic Review, 46,* 145–170.

Harrington, J. E., & Chang, M.-H. (2009). Modeling the birth and death of cartels with an application to evaluating competition policy. *Journal of the European Economic Association, 7*(6), 1400–1435.

Hay, G. A., & Kelley, D. (1974). An empirical survey of price fixing conspiracies. *Journal of Law and Economics, 17*(1), 13–38.

Hinloopen, J., & Soetevent, A. R. (2008). Laboratory evidence on the effectiveness of corporate leniency programs. *RAND Journal of Economics, 39,* 607–616.

Houba, H., Motchenkova, E., & Wen, Q. (2010). Antitrust enforcement with price-dependent fines and detection probabilities. *Economic Bulletin, 30*(3), 2017–2027.

Houba, H., Motchenkova, E., & Wen, Q. (2012). Competitive prices as optimal cartel prices. *Economic Letters, 114,* 39–42.

Hüschelrath, K., Laitenberger, U., & Smuda, F. (2012). *Cartel enforcement in the European Union: Determinants of the duration of investigations*. Center for European Economic Research Discussion Paper No. 12-071. Retrieved from http://ssrn.com/abstract=2179037.

ICN Report. (2005). Defining hard core cartel conduct effective institutions effective penalties. Report prepared by the ICN Working Group on Cartels, ICN 4th Annual Conference Bonn, Germany, 6–8 June 2005.

Ivaldi, M., Jenny, F., & Khimich, A. (2015). Cartel damages to the economy: An assessment for developing countries. In F. Jenny & Y. Katsoulacos (Eds.), *Competition law enforcement in the BRICS and in developing countries—Legal and economic aspects* (pp. 103–133). Springer.

Katsoulacos, Y., & Ulph, D. (2013). Antitrust penalties and the implications of empirical evidence on cartel overcharges. *Economic Journal, 123*(572), 558–581.

Katsoulacos, Y., Motchenkova, E., & Ulph, D. (2015). Penalizing cartels: The base for basing penalties on price overcharge. *International Journal of Industrial Organization, 42,* 70–80.

Koh, R., & Jeong, J. (2013). The leniency program in Korea and its effectiveness. *Journal of Competition Law and Economics, 10*(1), 161–183.

Levenstein, M. C., & Suslow, V. Y. (2006). What determines cartel success? *Journal of Economic Literature, XLIV,* 43–95.

Levenstein, M. C., & Suslow, V. Y. (2011). Breaking up is hard to do: Determinants of cartel duration. *The Journal of Law & Economics, 54*(2), 455–492.

Levenstein, M., & Suslow, V. (2012). *Cartels and collusion—Empirical evidence*. Ross School of Business Working Paper No. 1182. Retrieved November 2012, from http://ssrn.com/abstract=2182565.

Liu, C., Li, A., Bi, Y., Liu, S., Hong, L., & Liu, J. (2020, February 20). *China's anti-monopoly law enters its second decade.* King & Wood Mallesons. Retrieved from https://www.chinalawinsight.com/2020/02/articles/antitrust/chinas-anti-monopoly-law-enters-its-second-decade/.

Miller, N. H. (2009). Strategic leniency and cartel enforcement. *American Economic Review, 99*(3), 750–768.

Monnier, C., & Combe, E. (2011). Fines against hard core cartels in Europe: The myth of over enforcement. *The Antitrust Bulletin, 56*(2), 235–275.

Monti, M. (2001). Why should we be concerned with cartels and collusive behavior? In *Fighting cartels—Why and how?* Swedish Competition Authority 2001, printed in Sweden by Elanders Graphic Systems in Goeteborg, Sweden.

Motta, M. (2004). *Competition policy—Theory and practice* (1st ed.). Cambridge: Cambridge University Press.

Normann, H.-T., & Tan, E. S. (2013). Effects of different cartel policies: Evidence from the German power-cable industry. *Industrial and Corporate Change, 23*(4), 1035–1057.

Posner, R. A. (1970). A statistical study of antitrust enforcement. *Journal of Law and Economics, 13,* 365–419.

Smuda, F. (2014). Cartel overcharges and the deterrent effect of EU competition law. *Journal of Competition Law and Economics, 10*(1), 63–86.

Smuda, F., Bougette, P., & Hüschelrath, K. (2015). Determinants of the duration of European appellate court proceedings in cartel cases. *Journal of Common Market Studies, 53*(6), 1352–1369.

Sokol, D. (2011, September). Detection and compliance in cartel policy. In *Competition policy international CPI antitrust chronicle* (vol. 2).

Stephan, A. (2014). *Survey of public attitudes to price fixing in the UK, Germany, Italy and the USA*. University of East Anglia Law School, CCP Working Paper 15-8.

Velijanovski, C. (2007, forthcoming). The economic of cartels. In *Finnish competition law year book 2006*.

Wang, J., & Fang, X. (2018). The realistic dilemma and solutions for application of antimonopoly confiscation of illegal gains (反垄断没收违法所得适用的现实困境与解决思路). *Competition Policy Research (竞争政策研究), 1,* 20–37.

Werden, G. J., Hammond, S. D., & Barnett, B. A. (2011, September 22). Recidivism eliminated: Cartel enforcement in the United States since 1999. Georgetown Global Antitrust Enforcement Symposium, Washington, DC. Retrieved from www.justice.gov/atr/public/speeches/275388.pdf.

Wils, W. P. J. (2016). The use of leniency in EU cartel enforcement: An assessment after twenty years. *World Competition, 39*(3), 327–388.

Zhan, H., Song, Y., & Yang, Z. (2018). A new era comes–highlights of the anti-monopoly law of China in 2018. *Anjie Law Firm.* Retrieved from http://www.anjielaw.com/en/uploads/soft/190201/1-1Z2011P205.pdf.

Chapter 5
Vertical Restrictions

Abstract Manufacturers and retailers are observed as a principal agent relationship. When a product is produced and to be sold at a downstream distribution level, the manufacturer may choose either vertically integrate with the dealer (vertical integration), or choose an independent distributor from the market (market transaction). Vertical restrictive contracts are largely used to reduce the coordination problem in the principal-agent relationship, to prevent free-riding and locked-in, and thus to maximize the joint benefits. While restrictive provisions such as resale price maintenance (RPM), and restrictions on sales quantity and territory (exclusive dealing), restrictions on the type of purchased goods (tying) could reduce coordination problems and promote efficiency, they may have anti-competitive effects that harm inter-brand and intra-brand competition. Since the late 1960s, the per se illegal rules for vertical restraints have been challenged by Chicago school scholars and modern industrial organization economists, who provided economic arguments to prove the pro-competitive efficiency gains of vertical agreements. In 1977, efficiency considerations were taken into account by the Supreme Court in *Continental T.V., Inc. versus GTE Sylvania*, Inc. In June 2007, the *Leegin* case reversed the per se rule by rule of reason. Article 14 of the AML in China deals with vertical restrains and the first two provisions refer to RPM and the third provision refers to other types of non-price restrictions. In case decisions, both administrative agencies and courts tend to put emphasis on the anti-competitive effects of RPM and the pro-competitive effects were considered to be 'irrelevant' and cannot be taken to exempt the party from monetary penalties. The *Ruibang/Johnson & Johnson* case ruled by the Shanghai Higher People's Court provided the most detailed analysis on the economic effects of RPM.

5.1 Introduction

Vertical agreements refer to the binding agreements between business operators at different transaction levels, often between the manufacturer (supplier) and the distributor (dealer). Manufacturers and retailers are observed as a principal agent relationship. When a product is produced and to be sold at a downstream distribution

J. Ma, *Competition Law in China*,
https://doi.org/10.1007/978-981-15-5105-5_5

chain, the manufacturer may choose to either vertically integrate with the dealer, or to choose an independent distributor from the market (market transaction). In a complete market transaction, there is no condition imposed on sales and prices, but in such a situation each party has the tendency to make decisions to maximize the profit of its own without considering the externalities on other firms, rather than the joint profits of the vertical structure. Thus vertical contracts are developed to impose restrains on pricing and distribution to ensure a sustainable vertical relationship. Vertical restrictive contracts are largely used to reduce the coordination problem in the principal-agent relationship, to prevent free-riding and locked-in, and thus to maximize the joint benefits. Vertical restrains may take the form of resale price maximization and minimization (Resale Price Maintenance, RPM), exclusive dealing, exclusive distribution and territorial restrictions, conditional rebates, tying/bundling, price discrimination, royalty contracts, and refusal to supply. Until the late 1960s, price and non-price vertical restraints were accepted as harmful to competition. Lester Telser's article in 1960[1] provided economic justifications for efficiency arguments, that vertical restraints were to reduce the free-riding problem. In 1977, efficiency considerations were taken into account by the Supreme Court in *Continental T.V., Inc. versus GTE Sylvania*, Inc. In June 2007, the *Leegin* case[2] overturned the per se *illegal* rule in *Dr. Miles*[3] by *rule of reason* on all types of vertical restrains. Influenced by the Chicago school, after 1980, economists turned to research into the efficiency gains of vertical agreements. According to the Chicago School, vertical restrictions on competition agreements, because they are not agreements between competitors, are not intended to jointly limit the quantity of production or inflate the price of goods. On the contrary, the common interest of the parties to the agreement lies in the enhancement of output, which generally plays a role in increasing the wealth of society. It is now a generally accepted view that vertical agreements have both positive and negative effects. In the EU, economic analysis of vertical agreements has been incorporated since Regulation 2790/1999. Efficiency arguments are defined in the 2010 Block Exemption Regulation on Vertical Restraints[4] and the Guidelines on Vertical Restraints.[5] A rule of reason analysis requires a trade-off balance between the efficiency enhancing effects and the anti-competitive considerations. From the perspective of positive effects, the vertical agreements will mitigate the agency principal-agent problem and speculation; from the negative perspective, vertical agreements establish barriers to entry and increase the risk of complicity and lead to the danger of collusion.

---

[1]Telser (1960).

[2]Leegin Creative Leather products versus PSKS Inc, 551 US (2007).

[3]Dr. Miles Medical Co. versus John D. Park & Sons Co. 220 U.S. 373 (1911).

[4]Commission Regulation (EU) No 330/2010 of 20 April 2010 on the application of Article 101(3) of the Treaty on the Functioning of the European Union to categories of vertical agreements and concerted practices, OJ L 102, 23 April 2010.

[5]Guidelines on Vertical Restraints.

5.2 Economic Analysis of Vertical Agreements

The economic analysis of vertical agreements includes pro-competitive efficiency analysis and anti-competitive effects. Manufacturers and distributors sign vertical agreements to reduce the agency problem, prevent free-riding, build brands, extend distribution networks and to encourage distributors to invest in pre-sale promotions and services. The anti-competitive effects refer to the undesirable restraints on inter-brand and intra-brand competition. The rule of reason analysis has to evaluate the pro-competitive and anti-competitive effects.

5.2.1 Agency Problem

Manufacturers and distributors in vertical chain are perceived as principal and agent. Coordination problems may arise along the vertical structure because the agent makes decisions on behalf of the principal, and because there is substantial information asymmetry between the two parties; the agent often acts in accordance with his own interests rather than the interests of the principal. As information asymmetry occurs in decisions such as distribution prices, sales volume and quantities, marketing and promotion strategies, geographical locations, personnel control on the sales person, etc., decentralized decision-making is often observed when the distributors have information advantages and the principals are in need of control. By signing vertical agreements, producers and distributors can maintain each other's interests while maximize the total benefits along the vertical chain, and to reduce the risks, uncertainties and difficulties to mitigate the coordination problem in vertical structures.

In addition to information asymmetry, when manufacturers and distributors set prices and quantities without considering the externalities on other firms' profits, a double marginalization problem may occur.[6] When the upstream manufacturer has market power, they may add a "mark-up" on the price when selling the product to the distributor, without taking into account the externalities imposed on the profits of the retailers; and when the distributor in the vertical chain also has monopolistic market power, the price could be raised the second time, ending up a "double mark-up" for consumers. Thus, setting a minimum or maximum retail price as a type of effective vertical restraints can solve the externality problem in this way to prevent the distributor from raising monopoly prices, and to ensure the manufacturer and distributor both have a fair share of the profits.

[6]Spengler (1950).

5.2.2 Free-Riding

Lester Telser developed free rider theory in 1960 which argues that vertical restraints could be justified for efficiency benefits as they prevent the free-rider problem, enhance interbrand competition and increase distribution efficiency. Manufacturers often have to enter new markets through advertising and a series of promotional activities, and if manufacturers fix resale prices to distributors, they are encouraged to compete in the market through pre-sales services and promotional activities, such as advertising, display of products, product information, customer services. Consumers can "free-ride" the pre-sales services such as visiting the store to get free samples, ask questions, compare different product models, in order to get a full range of services without paying the cost. At the same time dealers without investing in pre-sales services can "free-ride" the efforts made by other dealers.

Setting maximum or minimum price restraints could prevent the free-riding problem at horizontal level among distributors, and the incentive to shirk the efforts is perceived as horizontal externality. The free-riding problem along the vertical chain is called a "hold-up" problem and it could be solved through exclusive dealing clauses in the vertical contract. A hold-up problem occurs when a sales agreement requires a party to make a specific investment. The upstream manufacturer may invest in the design of the retail outlets, promoting and marketing of the product, and training store managers, and that investment may be a "free-ride" for other brand manufacturers if the distributor also sells other products. Similarly, the downstream distributor may also invest in marketing a specific brand and improving the quality of service. When a vertical relationship is ended, the specific investment made by the distributors will be sunk. Vertical agreements with exclusive clauses could prevent opportunistic behaviour, and secure the vertical relationship, thus preventing the risk of underinvestment. Those clauses include granting the distributor rights of exclusive supply, division of the geographical territories of sales, and other types of exclusive dealing provisions.

5.2.3 Brand Impact

In order to ensure their brand reputation, manufacturers set a minimum resale price to prevent distributors from discounting their products, so consumers could feel the high status and quality of the product. For product value after-sales services, such as mobile phones, electronic products, manufacturers are willing to exert control on the quality of the services provided by the dealers, so setting a minimum price could encourage dealers to compete on services and to improve the long-term reputational benefits for the product. However, the economic benefits of building brand reputation do not apply to industries that do not value after-sales services, such as beer, ice cream sales, and general necessities.

5.2.4 Supply and Marketing Network

If the price competition between dealers is too fierce, from the manufacturer's point of view, it is not conducive to the construction of a continuous sales network. If the lowest price is fixed, control over the number of distributors can be relatively relaxed, or they can be given the freedom to choose the location of the store. In an economic sense, vertical agreement clauses, such as exclusive distribution (where producers choose only one distributor in a region), have the following benefits: preventing other dealers from free-riding; opening new markets; dealers are encouraged to maintain high-quality services and make dedicated investments; and to achieve economies of scale.

5.2.5 The Anti-competitive Effects of Vertical Agreements

While the impact of efficiency gains can be seen, vertical agreements also have an anti-competitive impact. Resale price fixing or setting minimum or maximum resale prices will dampen price competition between dealers. When prices among distributors become transparent, collusion among horizontal competitors will be much easier to facilitate and the market concentration is likely to be intensified. Price synergy between manufacturers, or divisions on sales territories and consumer groups are easier to implement, and dealers are also more likely to collude with manufacturers to reduce price competition. In addition, prohibiting vertical price maintenance could protect intra-brand competition and allow distributors to price differently and there could be a possibility of arbitrage. The more efficient distributor could get the highest sales volume by offering the lowest price, and consumers can choose the best distributor by comparing prices. Efficient dealers can reduce sales prices and inefficient dealers might be driven out of the market; eventually price competition could promote efficiency and innovation between distributors.

The most evident argument for the anti-competitive effects of vertical restraints is that it may strengthen the monopoly power of distributors and prevent competition at the downstream level and increase entry barriers. Exclusive territories will make the entry of potential competitors more difficult and the collusion between dealers will be more sustainable. When exclusive territorial clauses are applied to prevent free-riding problems, at the same time they strengthened the monopoly market power of distributors by reducing inter-brand competition. Thus, the anti-competitive effects of vertical restraints are often created by the same provision that is seen to have welfare-enhancing efficiency benefits. A balance of pro- and anti-competitive effects of vertical restraints requires a careful analysis of the effects of the restrictive provisions on competition as a whole.

5.3 Vertical Restrictions in the AML

5.3.1 Vertical Agreements

Vertical agreements refer to the agreements between business entities at different economic stages in the market. Manufacturers may impose various restrictions on the product transactions by retailers, such as restrictions on wholesale and retail prices, restrictions on distribution areas, limiting the scope of consumers. Vertical restrictions on competition agreements could be divided into price and non-price restraints. Manufacturers could set the maximum or minimum wholesale price (or mention a "recommended price" or "advertising price"), or fix a specific price. The supplier may also give discriminatory price discounts to retailers according to certain conditions, such as the purchase quantity, the consumer groups, or tie-in conditions. Non-price restrictions include exclusive dealing, which takes the form of exclusive territorial distribution, exclusive transactions, exclusive purchases, in which situation distributors are prohibited from purchasing or selling products by competitors. Manufacturers may also restrict specific sales methods such as pre-sales and after-sales services. Franchising is a typical type of vertical agreement and various vertical restrictions could be imposed to ensure the distributors operate in a chain manner.

5.3.2 Article 14 of the AML

Article 14 of China's Antimonopoly law prohibits the operator from entering into the following monopoly agreements with the counterparty to the transaction: (i) fixing the price of the goods for resale to a third party; (ii) Limiting the minimum price for the resale of goods to a third party; (iii) Other monopoly agreements as determined by the antimonopoly enforcement agencies of the State Council.

5.3.3 RPM Cases

The first and second type of agreement mentioned in Article 14 refer to Resale Price Maintenance (RPM), including fixing resale prices, setting the maximum or minimum retail prices. The economic reason for RPM is that it prevents free riding and when the prices at the distribution level are fixed, retailers cannot free ride on others' investment in pre-sale promotion and services, and consumers may choose retailers based on the quality of the service that they could provide. RPM can encourage retailers to put efforts into improving the quality of services, and to improve the distribution network. However, the anti-competitive effect of RPM is that it fixes the price of product distribution and therefore reduces competition between dealers, and consumers can no longer choose the best retailer based on price competition, and retailers are more likely to collude at the horizontal level.

Vertical restraints cases in China are mainly investigated by administrative agencies. In most RPM cases published by the price bureau and NDRC, it is observed that a strong per se illegal rule has been implemented. As Chap. 2 of the AML follows the EU approach on monopoly agreements, by defining provisions of "general prohibition and exemptions". The agency tends to apply the analysis of horizontal agreements on vertical restrains, where agreements on price fixing are perceived as anti-competitive, and efficiency arguments are not taken into account as exemptions listed on Article 15 of the AML, so there are limited economic arguments for efficiency gains being mentioned in the cases.

The two liquor cases *Maotai* and *Wuliangye* are the well-known RPM cases in China. In 2012, because of weak sales and the tension on the capital chain of the dealer of the high-end liquor, Maotai and Wuliangye, retailers began to sell at a low price. Seeing this, a dealer conference was held publicly at the end of 2012, which specified the minimum resale price of 53° Maotai should not be less than 1519 RMB/bottle, and the group retail price should not be lower than 1400 RMB/bottle. Distributors who sell at prices below the minimum resale prices with be punished by a deduction of supply or non-refunding of a cash deposit. At the same time, starting from 2009, 3200 dealers of Wuliangye nationwide signed a vertical agreement to set the minimum resale price. Non-cooperative dealers in 11 provinces were punished by deductions of supply, non-refunding of cash deposit, other types of restrictions or fines. In 2013, the NDRC initiated the investigation and on February 22, 2013, the Guizhou Provincial price bureau issued the administrative penalty decision. Retailers of Maotai were fined 247 million RMB for making and implementing vertical monopoly agreements on sale prices. Retailers of Wuliangye received administrative fines of 202 million RMB from Sichuan Provincial DRC for reaching RPM. The economic analysis on Wuliangye published by Sichuan DRC concluded that the vertical agreement eliminated intra-brand competition between distributors, and thus reduced economic efficiency; the agreement eliminated inter-brand competition because other brand suppliers may adopt similar agreements with dealers. In addition, the RPM will limit consumer choice and harm consumer welfare. The economic elements mentioned in the case showed that the agency acknowledged the existence of economic arguments, but mainly for anti-competitive effects, the pro-competitive effects are not mentioned and are not considered as a strong defence or exemption that could grant the firm a reduction of fines.

A widely-published case on milk powder enterprises in the early years of AML enforcement was also on RPM. On August 7, 2013, formula manufacturers including Mead Johnson, Dumex, Abbotts, Fonterra, and Biostime were fined RMB 668.73 million for implementing RPM. Wyeth, Beyoncé and Meiji received leniency for providing evidence and being cooperative with the enforcement agency. Downstream operators carried out various forms of strategies to implement RPM, including contract agreements, direct fines, deduction of rebates, restrictions on supply, refusal to supply, etc. The NDRC decision listed the economic reasons for the anti-competitive effects, eliminating and restricting intra-brand competition between the distributors selling the same brand and inter-brand competition among different producers, damaging fair market competition and harming consumer interests. The NDRC clarified that the economic justifications for reaching RPM do not meet the exemptions listed in Article 15.

RPM cases published with a per se illegal rule are also widely observed in the automobile industry. Shanghai Price Bureau imposed RMB 1.98 million on Speech Fresh Logistics on December 27, 2016 for illegally implementing resale price agreements with Guangming pasteurized milk products distributors. Shanghai Price Bureau accepted that the company had cooperated with the agency during the investigation and had revised the agreement prior to the investigation to partially cease the activity, and issued a reduced fine of 1% of the turnover of products in 2015.

Another similar case on *SAIC-GM*. On December 23, 2016, Shanghai Price Bureau imposed administrative fines of RMB 201 million, accounting for 4% of its turnover of relevant products on automobile manufacturer SAIC-GM in 2015, for violating AML Article 14 on resale price maintenance. SAIC-GM is the joint venture between Shanghai Automobile Industry Corporation (SAIC, a SOE) and US General Motors. Starting from 2014, SAIC-GM issued price notices to fix the resale price and limit the maximum discount with dealers for Cadillac models, and to fix the guidance price, gross margin and suggested promotional cash discount for Chevrolet models, and issued recommended resale price and discounts for Buick models. SAIC-GM could secretly collect information on the resale prices that dealers used to sell to third parties, and it would suspend supplying the popular models if the dealers fail to comply with the price notice. The Shanghai Price Bureau concluded that the joint venture has violated Article 14(2) of the AML, and it had eliminated competition, and had harmful effects on consumer interests and public interests.[7]

Medtronic Shanghai is also a RPM case. NDRC imposed administrative fines of RMB 118.5 million (4% of its turnover of relevant products in the previous year) on Medtronic (Shanghai) Management Corporation on December 9, 2016 for violating Article 14 of the AML by implementing vertical price agreements on fixed resale prices and resale price floors with primary distributors and e-commerce firms when supplying medical equipment for cardiovascular diseases, restorative therapies, and diabetes. The agreement specified the resale prices for distributors at different tiers, and fixed the minimum resale prices to hospitals. Distributors were only allowed to resell products to secondary distributors on the agreement terms and through which end-users could purchase the products. Medtronic refused to supply and terminated the distributorship with those who failed to comply with the agreement. NDRC found that Medtronic violated Articles 14 (1) and (2) of the AML and because of its cooperative behaviour on revising distribution agreements and the management policies, a fine of 4% of the sales revenue was imposed.[8]

In December 2016, the Shanghai Price Bureau imposed a fine of RMB 2 million on Shanghai Speed Fresh Logistics for its RPM restrictions on pasteurised milk products. Speed Fresh requested dealers and its distributors to comply with their pricing

[7] Fels et al. (2016, p. 3).

[8] Fels et al. (2016, p. 3).

and promotion policy. Those who did not implement the minimum prices policy would be sanctioned by deductions from security deposits, or cessation of supply, even terminating the distributorship. Speed Fresh issued price adjustment letters and monitored the market prices; retail stores who sold pasteurised milk products below the minimum prices would be reported. The Shanghai Price Bureau found that Speed Fresh had violated Article 14(2) of the AML and dealers were prohibited from setting prices independently. The fine of RMB 2 million was equal to 1% of the sales revenue of the company in 2015.[9]

Smith & Nephew was the RPM case investigated by the price bureau. The Shanghai Price Bureau initiated an investigation on Smith & Nephew for setting sale prices at each level of the distribution channel from exclusive distributor to secondary distributor and pharmacies. The Shanghai Price Bureau found that because the price policy had prevented distributors from determining their prices independently, competition had been eliminated and restricted. Smith & Nephew were fined over RMB 720,000 (6% of the sales revenue in 2014). The fine was calculated based on the nature, degree, duration and whether the parties had cooperated with the investigation.[10]

3 Haier-affiliated companies was the vertical agreement case with price and non-price restrictions. Shanghai Price Bureau imposed fines of over RMB 12 million (3% of the relevant revenue in the previous year) on three Haier-affiliated companies in August 2016. Haier is the manufacturer of consumer electronics in China, and since 2012, Haier had implemented distribution agreements with three companies in Shanghai, which specified the minimum resale prices on refrigerators, air conditioning units, range hoods and other products to supermarkets and other third parties. The three companies announced sale policies, a retail price guidebook, and required distributors to comply with the distribution agreements with restrictions on prices. Non-compliant distributors would be punished by the refusal of supply. Shanghai Price Bureau concluded that the agreement violated Article 14(2) of the AML and Article 8(2) of the NDRC's Anti-Price Monopoly Regulation.

Ruibang (Rainbow)/Johnson & Johnson was the first RPM case sued at court and in this case the court clearly used a rule of reason analysis. Ruibang Yonghe Technology and Trade Co., Ltd (Ruibang/Rainbow) sued Johnson & Johnson. In January 2018, Johnson forced Ruibang to maintain a specific price floor when reselling its products and after being informed that Ruibang lowered the price at the bidding held in Peking University Renmin Hospital, Johnson ceased to supply to Ruibang, deducted a deposit of RMB 20,000 and prohibited Ruibang from reselling Johnson's product at two hospitals. On August 11, 2010, Ruibang brought the case to court and asked Johnson to compensate its economic loss of more than RMB 14 million. The Shanghai No. 1 Intermediate People's Court ruled that to prove monopolistic agreement, the fact of whether the parties have signed an RPM contract is not sufficient, and it is necessary to prove that the agreement has prevented and restricted competition. But the evidence provided by Ruibang was insufficient and could not prove that the RPM had the negative effect of preventing and restricting competition. The court

---

[9]Fels et al. (2016, p. 4).

[10]Fels et al. (2016, p. 4).

concluded that the plaintiff failed to provide facts on how losses are caused by the monopolistic conduct in the RPM contract. Ruibang appealed on May 28, 2012. In August 2013, the Shanghai Higher People's Court used a 'rule of reason' analysis, and found that Johnson & Johnson held strong market power in the relevant market, and in particular it had a leading market share in the global and Chinese markets; it held strong pricing power and brand reputation, and thus could control the distribution system effectively.[11] Moreover it had the "intent" to restrict competition. The court analysed the anti-competitive effects including restrictions on intra-brand and inter-brand competition, the tendency to facilitate price cartels and eliminating price competition, increasing entry barriers for efficient dealers and harming consumer interests. The court held that arguments on pro-competitive effects could not stand because the pre-sale marketing efforts, improving the sales network and product reputation were not relevant as consumers are familiar with the products. The court concluded that the price floor set by Johnson had the anti-competitive effect of excluding competition, and ordered Johnson to compensate Ruibang by RMB 530,000. The Ruibang/Johnson case has the "most systematic and most elaborate discussion of economics"[12] in a RPM decision made by courts in China, and both defendant and plaintiff invited economists to give expert opinions. The first instance and second instance judges avoided using a clear definition of "per se illegal" or "rule of reason" approach; instead, they tended to list a few factors that are to be considered. The first instance judge focused on the causation between the economic loss suffered and the monopolistic conduct made by Johnson, and ruled that parties failed to provide sufficient evidence to support the claim. The second instance judges elaborated the factors on pro and anticompetitive effects, and applied an analytical framework of "four steps"—defining the competition status in the relevant market, the market position of the defendants, the motives and intentions of the defendant to impose vertical restrains and the competition effects of the vertical restraints.[13] but the court ruled the case with a strong focus on proving the anti-competitive effects of the RPM.

5.3.4 Other Types of Vertical Restrictions

The third type of agreement mentioned in Article 14 is too broad to be clearly defined. Usually other types of vertical agreements may refer to exclusive dealing, tying (tie-in purchasing), refusal to supply. Exclusive dealing is the situation when the agreement restricts a geographical area or a particular target consumer group that distributors could operate in, and prohibits the dealer from purchasing purchase or selling the products by other manufacturers, in order to control the distribution chain to ensure the quality and reputation of the product. When the manufacturer

[11] Liu and Qiao (2017, p. 29).

[12] Jiang and Sokol (2015, p. 15).

[13] Liu and Qiao (2017, p. 31).

holds a market dominant position, exclusive dealing agreements may have an anti-competitive foreclosure effect. Tying agreements refer to the restrictions on buyers to purchase one type of product instead of purchasing another one. Refusal to supply is the situation when a manufacturer refuses to supply products to distributors who have not signed the agreement.

5.4 Evaluating Pro- and Anti-competitive Effects

Article 13(2) of the AML stipulates that monopolistic agreements are the agreements, decisions or concerted practices that prevent and restrict competition. Article 13 is not clear on whether defining a monopolistic agreement has to prove that the agreement prevents and restricts competition, and it is also argued that since Article 13(2) is written under the section of horizontal agreements, it may not apply to vertical restrictions.[14] The 2020 draft revision of the AML moved Article 13(2) to Article 14 directly under the heading of Chap. 2, and such a change tended to unify the definition of monopolistic agreement for horizontal and vertical restrictions. Thus, to prove the effects of preventing and restricting competition would be necessary when defining a monopolistic agreement. The Shanghai High People's Court provided analysis of 4 factors to prove whether the defendant's behaviour had anti-competitive effects: (1) the competitiveness in the relevant market (2) the market power of defendant (3) the intent to implement RPM (4) the competition effects of RPM. The enforcement agencies do not mention any information in most case decisions on how to analyse the effects of preventing and restricting competition, and it is not clear whether it is necessary to prove that both the *purpose* and *effects* of the monopolistic conduct was to "prevent and restrict competition".[15] Also, while both the administrative agencies and courts briefly introduced economic arguments in the case decisions, the use of economic analysis tends to be 'selective' as the anti-competitive effects were strongly elaborated while the pro-competitive effects were either ignored or considered to be 'irrelevant'. The enforcement agencies applied a similar methodology of horizontal agreements and treated efficiency arguments as a type of exemptions. It is claimed that the AML followed the EU "general prohibition plus exemptions" model, so there is no need to clarify whether the agency has applied a per se illegal rule or rule of reason analysis. However, the EU model has developed "prohibition-block exemption-case by case exemption" approach[16] and the detailed case-by-case analysis on pro and anti-competitive effects was not implemented by the agency. Although the court tends to apply a more balanced "rule of reason" approach as it discussed both the pro and counter arguments in the *Ruibang/Johnson* case, the court simplified the economic analysis into a four factor based analytical framework, and while it showed efforts in finding evidence on market power (market shares), and the definition of relevant

---

[14] Liu (2012).

[15] Wang (2014, p. 39).

[16] Jiang and Sokol (2015, p. 17).

market, the court did not provide sufficient economic evidence on anti-competitive effects when it concluded that the vertical restraints violated the AML.

On March 23, 2016, NDRC published the Auto Sector Draft Antitrust Guidelines for public consultation. It specifies how anti-competitive effects could be analyzed when a vertical agreement is reached between automakers, auto parts manufacturers, distributors and after-sales service providers.

5.5 Conclusions

Unlike horizontal agreements, economic arguments for vertical restraints are straightforward: RPM can prevent free riding and ensure product reputation by encouraging distributors to improve service qualities and achieve efficiency at the distribution network. RPM can further eliminate double marginalization problem and serves as a mechanism to solve coordination problem between manufacturers and distributors in the contractual structure. Exclusive dealing could prevent lock-in problems and ensure that specific investment is made at the horizontal as well as vertical levels. Nonetheless, the economic arguments for pro-competitive effects of vertical agreements are challenged by the economic reasons for anti-competitive effects, such as strengthening the monopoly power of distributors, and it makes the collusion between manufacturers more likely and stable. Exclusive dealing and retail cartels also increase the entry barriers and reduce inter-brand and intra-brand competition.

Article 14 of the AML in China deals with vertical restraints. The first two provisions deal with RPM and the third one refers to other types of vertical restraints. The legal provision is broad and ambiguous on the pro-and anti-competitive balance, and how economic arguments could be taken into consideration remains uncertain. While courts ruled that it is not sufficient to prove that the agreement has been implemented, but also that the agreement has effects on preventing and restricting competition, the price bureau and NDRC tend to rely on the same methodology of horizontal agreements, which prohibits agreements with price-fixing terms. The court ruled that it is important to prove whether the agreement has effects on preventing and restricting competition, and the factors to be taken into account include whether the relevant market is competitive, whether the market power of the defendant is strong, the intent of the defendant to enforce RPM, and the competition effects of RPM. Administrative agencies and courts tend to avoid clarifying either a "per se illegal" or a "rule of reason" approach, while agencies claimed the AML has followed the EU approach of "general prohibition plus exemptions". The parties bear the burden of proof to provide evidence on the pro-competitive effects and the enforcement agencies decide on whether those arguments could be taken as an exemption. While economic arguments are mentioned in the case, they are mainly on the aspect of anti-competitive effects. In the administrative decisions issued by the competition agencies, the pro-competitive arguments are not mentioned and the balance of pro and anti-competitive justification is missing. The *Ruibang/Johnson & Johnson* case decision made by Shanghai Higher People's Court provides the most detailed analysis on competition effects of the RPM, and it showed that the court tended to adopt a sort of "rule of reason" approach by listing the pro and counter arguments, although in the final ruling the pro-competitive effects were considered to be irrelevant and not sufficient to support the case that the RPM was applied in a fair and efficient manner.

References

Fels, A., Wang, X., Ng, W., & Emch, A. (Eds.). (2016, November/December). *China competition bulletin* (45th ed.). A Publication of the Competition Law & Economics Network at Melbourne Law School, University of Melbourne.

Jiang, S., & Sokol, D. (2015). Resale price maintenance in China: An economic perspective. *Journal of Antitrust Enforcement,* i132–i154.

Liu. (2012). On the formal logic problems of the concept of monopoly agreement in the anti-monopoly law of China (试析我国<反垄断法>垄断协议概念的形式逻辑问题). *Journal of Beijing University of Chemical Technology (Social Sciences Edition)* (北京化工大学学报 (社会科学版)) (4), 11–15.

Liu, Z., Qiao, Y. (2017). Vertical restraints, the Sylvania case, and China's antitrust enforcement. *Review of Industrial Organization,* 193–215.

Spengler, J. (1950). Vertical integration and antitrust policy. *Journal of Political Economy, 58,* 347–352.

Telser, L. (1960). Why should manufacturers want fair trade. *Journal of Law and Economics, 3,* 86–105.

Wang. (2014). A study on the relationship between monopoly agreement identification, exclusion and restriction of competition (垄断协议认定与排除、限制竞争的关系研究). *Law Science* (法学) (3), 35–49.

Chapter 6
Abuse of Dominant Position

Abstract Article 17 of the AML gives the definition of market dominance, that is when the business operator has the ability to prevent or restrict other business operators from entering the relevant market. The method to define relevant market is stated by the Guide of the Anti-monopoly Committee of the State Council for the Definition of the Relevant Market, and supply and demand substitutability is the main method. However, *Qihoo 360 versus Tencent* case shows that the SSNIP test has its limitations in market dominance cases when the parties operate in the online market. In the 2020 draft revision of the AML, Article 21 adds that to determine whether the Internet operators have a dominant market position, factors such as network effects, economies of scale, lock-in effects and the ability to master and process related data should be considered. Another challenge is that the refusal to do business and imposing restrictive conditions on trading is often conducted by public enterprises, and the abusive behaviour could be understood as a type of administrative monopoly.

6.1 Introduction

Article 17 of the AML states that a business operator holds a dominant position when it has the ability to control the price, quantity, or other trading conditions of the product, or has the ability to prevent or restrict other business operators from entering the relevant market. According to the Guide of the Anti-monopoly Committee of the State Council for the Definition of the Relevant Market,[1] demand and supply substitutability is the main method to define the relevant market. The Small but Significant and Non-transitory Increase in Price (SSNIP) test has its limitation in market dominance cases when the parties operate in the online market. Instead of paying prices, consumers provide information and attention when consuming online services and in the two-sided market the demand of user at one side of the platform has network externalities and influences the profitability of the other side user.

[1] Guowuyuan Fanlongduan Weiyuanhui Guanyu Xiangguan Shichang Jieding De Zhinan (国务院反垄断委员会关于相关市场界定的指南) [Guide of the Anti-monopoly Committee of the State Council for the Definition of the Relevant Market], issued on July 6, 2009 and effective on July 6, 2009.

J. Ma, *Competition Law in China*,
https://doi.org/10.1007/978-981-15-5105-5_6

Thus, defining the relevant market may become a challenge in market dominance cases. In defining the market dominance conduct, Article 17 of the AML lists seven types of behaviour (1) selling products at unfairly high prices or buying products at unfairly low prices; (2) selling products at prices below cost without justifiable reasons; (3) refusing to trade with the trading party without justifiable reasons; (4) without justifiable reasons, imposing restrictions on the trading parties on choosing other trading partners; (5) without justifiable reasons, tying and bundling, or imposing other unreasonable trading conditions; (6) without justifiable reasons, applying discriminatory treatment on the prices and trading conditions of trading partners with same conditions; (7) other acts that are deemed as abuse of dominant position by the anti-monopoly enforcement agency under the State Council. In refusal to trade and imposing restrictions on the trading party cases, it is common to observe the business operator is a public enterprise. The abusive conduct could be understood as a type of administrative monopoly.

6.2 Defining Dominant Position

Article 17 of the AML defines the concept of 'dominant position' as a market position in which the business operator has the ability to control the price, quantity, or other trading conditions of the product, or has the ability to prevent or restrict other business operators from entering the relevant market. Article 5 of the SAMR Interim Provisions on Prohibiting Abuse of Dominant Market Positions[2] defines 'other trading conditions' as factors other than prices, quantities that can have a substantial impact on the transaction, including varieties and qualities of the products, terms of payment, mode of delivery, after–sales services, transaction selection, technical constraints and so on. Article 5 also defines the term 'preventing or restricting other business operators from entering the market' as excluding or delaying other business operators from entering the market within a reasonable period of time, or substantially increases the costs of entering the market, and prevents potential competitors from competing with the incumbents.

Article 19 of the AML refers to the criteria of market share in determining dominant position: (1) one business operators' market share accounts for 1/2 in the relevant market; (2) two business operators' market shares account for 2/3 in the relevant market; (3) three business operators' market shares account for 3/4 of the relevant market. For the latter two situations, when one business operators' market share is below 1/10, that business operator should not be considered to have a dominant position.

The AML focuses on market share when defining market dominance and the definition of relevant market is also important for determining market power. A clear

[2]Jinzhi Lanyong Shichang Zhipei Diwei Xingwei Zanxing Guiding (禁止滥用市场支配地位行为暂行规定) [Interim Provisions on Prohibiting Abuse of Dominant Market Positions], Order No. 11 of the SAMR, issued on June 26, 2019 and effective on September 1, 2019.

example is the *Qihoo 360 versus Tencent* case. Qihoo 360 Technology Co., Ltd. (Qihoo) filed a lawsuit in November 2011 to sue Tencent Technology (Shenzhen) Co., Ltd., the operator of QQ software at Guangdong Higher People's Court, for RMB 150 million damage compensation. Qihoo said Tencent Technology Co., Ltd., in the instant messaging software and services related markets had a dominant market position. In March 2013, the Guangdong provincial Higher People's Court ruled that the plaintiff Qihoo company failed to appropriately define the relevant product market, and the evidence provided was not sufficient to prove that Tencent had a monopoly position, and rejected Qihoo technology litigation request. Qihoo filed an appeal with the Supreme People's Court.

The dispute centered on how to define whether the parties have a dominant position. The question was will QQ software Manager and instant messaging software bundled to upgrade QQ software Manager in the name of the installation of QQ Doctor, constitute bundled sales. The supreme court took up the case in June 2013 and heard the case in public in November 27, 2013, which revolved around 22 questions about whether Tencent, the defendant, had a dominant market position and whether it constituted abuse. The case revolved around whether the relevant product market is a comprehensive instant messaging service or a single instant messaging service, and whether the relevant regional market is mainland China or the global market.

Qihoo 360 versus Tencent case raised the concern of defining relevant market in online markets. According to Articles 12 of the AML and Articles 2 and 3 of the Guideline,[3] relevant market is the product and geographic scope within which business operators compete. In *Qihoo versus Tencent* case, Qihoo argued that the relevant market is instant communication services, while Tencent argued the relevant market is instant messaging including email, social networks and business communications. Both software operators are in a two-sided market, and the case raised concerns on the issue of defining relevant market in online markets in cases of abuse of dominant position. Online markets challenge traditional antitrust analysis because online services are often available to users for free, and the "price" that the consumer pays is calculated as attention and information that is often used for direct relevant advertising. Economic and business participants interact through the platform and such a system is often called two-sided or multi-sided market. The inter-dependencies across those actors may make the traditional SSNIP test unsuitable for market definition and market power analysis for non-price competition in a multi-sided market. In *Qihoo 360 versus Tencent*, the Supreme People's Court rejected the SSNIP test and refused to analyse Tencent market power through calculating price elasticity, on the basis that the increase in price to the platform, which does not require users to pay has a different business model than traditional business services. The crucial issue

[3] Article 3 of the Guide of the Anti-monopoly Committee of the State Council for the Definition of the Relevant Market: Relevant commodity market refers to a market comprised of a group or a category of commodities that are considered by consumers to have a relatively strong substitution relationship based on the characteristics, uses and prices of the commodities. These commodities have a relatively intense competitive relationship, and it may be considered as the commodity scope within which business operators compete with each other in the anti-monopoly law enforcement. Translation adopted from en.pkulaw.cn.

is, in a multi-sided market, all sides of the market need to be analyzed because the benefits of indirect network externality effects can only be achieved when multiple agents are coordinated,[4] because consumers with different preferences are treated as independent groups while in a one-sided market consumers and producers are often considered as a whole.[5] The participation of one particular consumer group will create an externality to other consumer groups through the use of the platform, although the preferences and lock-in effects of consumers are difficult to measure. In *Qihoo 360 versus Tencent* case, a definition of the market power of Tencent has to consider the multiple effects of restricting competition and limiting consumer choices, and therefore harming consumer welfare, as Article 7 of the Guideline stressed, the definition of relevant market has to fit the basic functions of consumer preferences.[6] In the 2020 draft revision of the AML, Article 21 (Article 19 of the AML) adds that to determine whether Internet operators have a dominant market position, factors such as network effects, economies of scale, lock-in effects, and the ability to master and process related data should be considered. Article 11 of the SAMR Interim Provisions on Prohibiting Abuse of Dominant Market Positions[7] also mentioned that in determining market dominance for business operators in the industry of Internet or other new economic formats, factors such as competition characteristics, business models, number of users, network effects, locking effects, technical features, market innovation, capacity of mastering and handling relevant data, the business operator's market force in the relevant market could be taken into account.

6.3 Defining Abusive Conduct

Article 6 of the AML prohibits business operators from eliminating or restricting competition through abusing market dominant position. Chapter 3 (Articles 17–19) of the AML prohibits abuse of dominant position. Article 17 reads that a business operator with a dominant market position is prohibited from conducting the following acts: (1) selling products at unfairly high prices or buying products at unfairly low prices; (2) selling products at prices below cost without justifiable reasons; (3) refusing to trade with the trading party without justifiable reasons; (4) without justifiable reasons, imposing restrictions on the trading parties on choosing trading partners; (5) without justifiable reasons, tying and bundling, or imposing other unreasonable trading conditions; (6) without justifiable reasons, applying discriminatory treatment

---

[4] Evans and Schmalensee (2014).

[5] Sokol and Ma (2017, p. 51).

[6] Article 7 of the Guide of the Anti-monopoly Committee of the State Council for the Definition of the Relevant market: No matter which method is adopted to define the relevant market, it must consider commodities' basic attribute of meeting the demands of consumers, and this attribute should also be taken as the basis for correcting any obvious deviation in defining the relevant market. Translation adopted from en.pkulaw.cn.

[7] Jinzhi Lanyong Shichang Zhipei Diwei Xingwei Zanxing Guiding (禁止滥用市场支配地位行为暂行规定) [Interim Provisions on Prohibiting Abuse of Dominant Market Positions], Order No. 11 of the SAMR, issued on June 26, 2019 and effective on September 1, 2019.

on the prices and trading conditions of trading partners with the same conditions; (7) other acts that are determined as abuse of dominant position by the anti-monopoly enforcement agency under the State Council.

Chongqing AIC's investigation in Chongqing Qingyang Pharmaceutical and Chongqing Southwest No. 2 Pharmaceutical Factory are the first two cases in refusal to deal.[8] When the party holding a dominant position refuses to provide products or services, it may become difficult to search for substitutes and thus strengthen the dominant position of the party. On December 22, 2015, Chongqing AIC announced its decision on Chongqing Qingyang Pharmaceutical Co. Ltd., for a refusal to deal under abuse of dominance. Qingyang Pharmaceutical was fined 3% of the previous year's revenue, amounting to RMB 439,308.53. Qingyang Pharmaceutical reached a selling agreement with Hunan Xiangbaihe Pharmaceutical in September 2013 on allopurinol active pharmaceutical ingredients. Chongqing AIC initiated the investigation in December 2014 and concluded that Qingyang Pharmaceutical violated Article 17 of the AML on refusal to deal.[9] On June 7, 2016 Chongqing AIC investigated Chongqing Southwest No. 2 Pharmaceutical Factory Co. Ltd., and issued its decision on November 14, 2016. The company abused its dominant position and refused to supply products in the phenol active pharmaceutical ingredients market from February to April 2014. It only supplied to six companies from May 2014 to December 2015. The company received an administrative fine of 1% of previous annual turnover, amounting to RMB 17, 240 and confiscating illegal gains of RMB 482,883.9 for its practice of refusal to supply for 23 months.

Similarly, In January 2017, Hubei AIC imposed a fine of RMB 2.2 million on Wuhan Xinxing Jingying Pharmaceutical for abusing its dominant position and imposing unreasonable conditions. Xinxing Jingying had 100% market share in methyl salicylate API in China and it is the exclusive distributor for two producers of methyl salicylate API, so it can decide on the condition to supply and the prices. After signing exclusive distribution agreements with two methyl salicylate API producers, Xinxing Jingying increased the prices from RMB 20,000/tonne to RMB 60,000–150,000/t. The Hubei AIC confiscated illegal gains of RMB 1.8369 million and imposed a fine of over RMB 372, 000 (3% of the sales revenue in 2015). The fine was reduced because of Xinxing Jingying's cooperative behavior with the investigation.[10]

Suqian Yinkong Water Supply Company case is an example of imposing restrictions on trading parties by public enterprises. According to Article 2 of the Regulation, public enterprises refer to enterprises that provide public services, including electricity and gas supply, post and communication.[11] The market monopolistic conduct by public enterprises could be understood as a type of administrative monopoly,

---

[8] Anti-monopoly Enforcement Trends in Healthcare Industry, AnJie Law Firm, September 14, 2017.

[9] Cao et al. (2016).

[10] China Competition Bulletin, Edition 46, March 2017, at p. 5.

[11] Guojia Gongshang Xingzheng Guanli Ju Guanyu Jinzhi Gongyong Qiye Xianzhi Jingzheng Xingwei De Ruogan Guiding (国家工商行政管理局关于禁止公用企业限制竞争行为的若干规定) [Certain Regulations on Prohibiting Anti-competitive Practices of Public Enterprises], issued on December 24, 1993. Article 2 stated that public enterprises mentioned in these Regulations refer to the operators of public utilities, including those engaged in postal service, telecommunication,

and the case analysis is similar to a case mentioned in Chap. 8 administrative monopolies. In the reform of industrial policy and the development of a fair competition review system, competition enforcement agencies have strengthened their enforcement power to investigate market dominance cases by public enterprises. The Opinion[12] published by the State Council in 2015 stresses the importance of preventing market divisions and monopolies set by industrial policies. The challenge of dealing with market dominance cases by public enterprises is to coordinate the enforcement power between competition agencies and industry regulators.[13] In the development of a fair competition review system, particular attention has been paid to the coordination between industrial policy and competition law, and it will be equally important to coordinate the enforcement power when investigating market dominance cases. On April 1, 2016 the SAIC published the Announcement on Prominent Issues Concerning the Acts of Public Utility Enterprises to Restrain Competition and Practice Monopoly.[14] The Announcement states that public utility enterprises in water supply, electricity and gas supply, public transport, funeral services and other sectors restrain competition in the manner of forced transactions, arbitrary charges, selling tie-in products and imposing unreasonable trading conditions.

On June 8, 2015, Jiangsu AIC investigated Suqian Yinkong Water Supply Company and issued its decision on November 28, 2016, imposing an administrative fine of 3% of the company's previous annual turnover, amounting to RMB 1.84 million and confiscating illegal gains of RMB 3.67 million for the practice of restricting real estate companies to deal exclusively with one water facility installation company in the relevant market. *Urumqi Water Industry Group* is a similar case. On December 18, 2014, Xinjiang AIC investigated against Urumqi Water Industry Group and issued its decision on October 12, 2016. The Group abused its monopolistic position in the public water supply market in the Urumqi inner city area by restricting consumer's choices and competition in the relevant market, to require consumers to exclusively deal with only one supplier. An administrative fine of 1% of the annual turnover in the previous year, amounting to RMB 1.49 million was imposed for the restrictive behaviour.

In 2015, the Jilin Price Bureau ruled that Jihua Group Information Network Technology violated Article 17 (1)(5) of the AML. As the only supplier for broadband services in the district, it required costumers who did not use its fixed-line services

---

transportation, as well as the supplying of water, electricity, heat and gas, etc. Translation adopted from en.pkulaw.cn.

[12]Zhonggong Zhongyang Guowuyuan Guanyu Shenhua Tizhi Jizhi Gaige Jiakuai Shishi Chuangxin Qudong Fazhan Zhanlve De Ruogan Yijian (中共中央、国务院关于深化体制机制改革加快实施创新驱动发展战略的若干意见) [Several Opinions of the CPC Central Committee and the State Council on Deepening the Reform of Systems and Mechanisms to Accelerate the Implementation of Innovation-driven Development Strategies] issued on March 13, 2015.

[13]Wang (2014), Shi and Xiao (2005).

[14]Guojia Gongshang Zongju Guanyu Gongyong Qiye Xianzhi Jingzheng He Longduan Xingwei Tuchu Wenti De Gonggao (国家工商总局关于公用企业限制竞争和垄断行为突出问题的公告) [Announcement of the SAIC on Prominent Issues Concerning the Acts of Public Utility Enterprises to Restrain Competition and Practice Monopoly], issued on April 1, 2016.

to pay a RMB 5/month security fee. The Jilin Price Bureau ruled that Jihua Group abused its dominant position and imposed unreasonable conditions on its broadband supply service. The Bureau confiscated illegal gains of RMB 528,000 and fined RMB 300,000 (5% of the previous year revenue). Similarly, the Liaoning Price Bureau ruled that China Unicom's branch in Dandong had abused its dominant position. The Dandong branch tied the sale of cable broadband services to landline telephone services, and signed a cooperative agreement with Dandong Cable TV, so it could determine the types and prices of cable broadband services that Dandong Cable TV resold to residents. The Liaoning Price Bureau found that China Unicom's Dandong branch has violated Article 17(1)(5) and Article 14(1) of the AML, and imposed a fine of RMB 670,000 (1% of the previous year's revenue).[15]

In a similar case, the Inner Mongolia AIC announced on April 22, 2016 that the Alxa Zuoqi Water Supply and Drainage Company had abused its dominant position. Alxa Zuoqi had been the only supplier of urban public water services in the Alxa Zuoqi Bayanhaote area, and the entry barriers for competitors are high due to the strict legal requirements and limited water sources. Starting from May 2013, Alxa Zuoqi required users of the urban public water supply network to also use the water meter and the construction services provided by Alxa Zuoqi, whose prices were much higher than similar products in the market, and Alxa Zuoqi would not supply water for those who do not use its water meter or constructions services. The Inner Mongolia AIC found that Alxa Zuoqi has breached Article 17(1)(5) of the AML and confiscated its illegal gains of RMB 300,000 and imposed a fine of RMB 450,000.[16]

In June 2016, the Inner Mongolia AIC announced that the Xilin Gol branch of the Inner Mongolia Radio and Television Network Group violated Article 17(5) of the AML, and confiscated its illegal gains of RMB 91,600 and imposed a fine of RMB 98,000. Xilin Gol Radio and Television is one of the only two service providers in the market of cable and Internet Protocol television (IPTV) services and it had a market share of 98.6%. The market control power is a significant entry barrier for potential competitors because of the requirements for licenses and administrative approvals. Starting from March 2015, without informing its users, Xilin Gol Radio and Television forced consumers to purchase an additional optional viewing package, besides their standard viewing package. After consumers raised objections, the company refused or used excuses to delay dealing with the issue. The inner Mongolia AIC concluded that Xilin Gol Radio and Television had practised tying and had abused its dominant position.[17]

In November 2016, the Jiangsu AIC found that Suqian Yinkong Water Supply Company, the exclusive urban public water supplier in Sucheng, Yanghe, Susu and City Economic Development Zone districts of Suqian City had abused its dominant position. Yinkong Water required real estate developers to use its subsidiary's water supply infrastructure construction services. The Jiangsu AIC concluded that Yinkong

[15]China Competition Bulletin, Edition 46, March 2017, at p. 3.

[16]China Competition Bulletin, Edition 42, May/June 2016, at p. 8.

[17]China Competition Bulletin, Edition 42, May/June 2016, at p. 8.

Water had violated Article 17(1)(4) of the AML and Article 5(2) of the SAIC Regulation on the Prohibition of Conduct Abusing a Dominant Market Position. The Jiangsu AIC confiscated illegal gains of RMB 3.6 million and imposed a fine of RMB 1.8 million.

Hunan Salt Industry Group case is the example for tie-in and bundling. On July 15, 2015, Hunan AIC conducted an investigation against Hunan Salt Industry Group, and a decision was issued on October 26, 2016. Hunan AIC imposed administrative fines of RMB 0.27 million (1% of the previous annual turnover of relevant products in Jianghua, Xintian, Qiyang and Jiangyong) and confiscating illegal gains of RMB 0.69 million, for their practice of abusing their dominant position in the salt wholesale market and tied-in the high-price salt production with ordinary salt production. The tie-in practice could not be supported by any justifiable reasons. *Tobacco wholesaler bundling case in Fushun* is another case of bundling. Liaoning AIC initiated the investigation in June 2014 and imposed fines of over RMB 4 million (1% of the bundled sales in 2013) on Fushun Tobacco on August 12, 2015, and concluded that Fushun Tobacco abused its dominant position in the cigarette wholesale market in Fushun, Liaoning province. Fushun Tobacco was the only approved cigarette wholesaler and could bundle the sales of cigarettes that were in short supply with the sale of other brands of cigarettes. Retailers could only purchase the brands and volumes of cigarettes based on the proportion set by Fushun Tobacco, and those who did not cooperate with such strategy were forced to reduce order volumes or to replenish stock.[18]

In November 2014, Jiangsu AIC fined Xuzhou Tobacco Company Pizhou branch for abusing its dominant position and engaging in discriminatory treatment. As the only supplier with a cigarette wholesale licence, Pizhou Tobacco obtained the dominant position in cigarette wholesale market in Pizhou. In 2009, to comply with the State Tobacco Monopoly Administration and China Cigarette Sales Company's notice, Pizhou Tobacco categorized cigarette retailers into 42 groups. Since 2010, Pizhou Tobacco had implemented a "KA customers management policy" and Jiangsu AIC found that the policy had given different treatment among customers Golden Eagle, Jiangsu Happy Buy, and Xuzhou Happy Buy. Pizhou Tobacco breached Article 17(6) of the AML because providing customers with different quantities of supply cannot be justified. Jiangsu AIC imposed a fine of RMB 1,723,745 (1% of the sales of bestselling cigarettes in 2012) on Pizhou Tobacco.[19]

[18]Fels et al. (2015b, p. 2).

[19]Fels et al. (2015a, p. 4).

6.4 Determining Abusive Conduct

Article 18 of the AML listed the factors that should be taken into account when determining abusive conduct: (1) business operator's market share in the relevant market and the competition status in the relevant market; (2) the business operators' capacity to control the sales market or the raw material procurement market; (3) the business operator's financial and technological capacity; (4) the extent to which other business operators rely on the entity's transactions; (5) the level of difficulty for other business operators to enter the market; (6) other relevant factors in deciding the business operator's dominant position.

Articles 6 and 7 of the SAMR Interim Provisions on Prohibiting Abuse of Dominant Market Position further explained the criteria of the six factors mentioned by Article 18 of the AML. Article 6 mentioned that when deciding on the market share of the business operator, the proportion of the sales amount, sales volume or other indicator of the product in the relevant market within a certain period of time should be taken into account. When analyzing the competition situation in the relevant market, the development status of the relevant market, number and market share of existing competitors, degree of diversity of products, innovation and technical changes, sales and procurement models, situation of potential competitors, and other factors should be considered.[20] Article 7 of the Provision specified that when determining the business operator's capacity to control the sales market or the raw material procurement market, factors to be considered include the business operator's capacity in control the upstream and downstream markets of the industrial chain, the ability to control the sales or procurement channels, the ability to affect or decide price, volume, contract term or other transaction conditions, and the ability to obtain raw materials, semi-finished products, spare parts, relevant equipment and other sources that are required for production and operation.[21]

6.5 Conclusions

The challenge of enforcing market dominance provisions of the AML includes two important issues. One is the defining of relevant market and market power, as the State Council Guidelines stress the use of SSNIP test and in the online market the test may have its limitations. In a non-price market, consumers may or may not switch to another platform provider when the price increases, as the indicator of price has been changed by consumer choices, consumer behaviour and the indirect network externality effect. The *Qihoo 360 versus Tencent* case shows the different attitude between the Shanghai Intermediate and the High People's Court when defining the

[20] Article 6 of the Interim Provisions on Prohibiting Abuse of Dominant Market Positions, translation adopted from en.pkulaw.cn.

[21] Article 7 of the Interim Provisions on Prohibiting Abuse of Dominant Market Positions, translation adopted from en.pkulaw.cn.

relevant market. Article 19 of the AML also lists the requirements of market shares when defining market power, and such provisions may become outdated when market dominance cases are conducted through platforms and online markets. Another challenge is that the refusal to deal and imposing restrictive conditions on trading cases are often conducted by public enterprises and enforcing market dominance provisions requires a smooth coordination between competition agency and industry regulators. The recent case has shown a more active enforcement and it is expected that the fair competition review system could further strengthen the enforcement of competition policy on abusive conduct by administrative monopolies.

References

Cao, M., Qin, Y., Chen, Z., Gu, T., Hou, H., Hong, L., Jin, M., & Xu, J. (2016, January). *Competition Law Bulletin*. Zhong Lun Law Firm Antitrust Practice Group, (12).

Evans, D. S., & Schmalensee, R. (2014). The antitrust analysis of multi-sided platform businesses. In R. D. Blair & D. D. Sokol (Eds.), *Oxford handbook of international antitrust economics* (vol. 1).

Fels, A., Wang, X., Ng, W., & Emch, A. (Eds.). (2015a, January/February). *China competition bulletin* (35th ed.). A Publication of the Competition Law & Economics Network at Melbourne Law School, University of Melbourne.

Fels, A., Wang, X., Ng, W., & Emch, A. (Eds.). (2015b, July/August). *China competition bulletin* (38th ed.). A Publication of the Competition Law & Economics Network at Melbourne Law School, University of Melbourne.

Fels, A., Wang, X., Ng, W., & Emch, A. (Eds.). (2015c, May/June). *China competition bulletin* (42th ed.). A Publication of the Competition Law & Economics Network at Melbourne Law School, University of Melbourne.

Fels, A., Wang, X., Ng, W., & Emch, A. (Eds.). (2015d, March). *China competition bulletin* (46th ed.). A Publication of the Competition Law & Economics Network at Melbourne Law School, University of Melbourne.

Shi, J., & Xiao, Z. (2005). Comparative study of anti-monopoly law and industry legislation, anti-monopoly institutions and industry regulators (<反垄断法>与行业立法、反垄断机构与行业监管机构的关系之比较研究及立法建议). *Journal of Political Science and Law* (政法论丛) (4), 48–54.

Sokol, D., & Ma, J. (2017). Understanding online markets and antitrust analysis. *Northwestern Journal of Technology and Intellectual Property, 15*(1), 43–52.

Wang, X. (2014). Coordination of monopoly industry supervision and enforcement of antitrust law (垄断行业监管与反垄断法执法之协调). *Law Science* (法学) (2), 111–117.

Chapter 7
Merger Control

Abstract Before the establishment of the SAMR, MOFCOM was the enforcement agency of merger control policy. Merger control policy adopted a mandatory pre-merger notification system. The State Council Provisions on Thresholds for Prior Notification of Concentrations of Undertakings specify the thresholds for notifications and Article 27 of the AML lists the factors that are to be taken into account when assessing the anti-competitive effects of the concentration. Merger policy has been frequently enforced after the AML came into force, and since 2014, MOFCOM has adopted the simplified procedure. Compared with the practice in the US and EU, MOFCOM is particularly in favour of behaviour remedies. The number of filings and reviews increased fivefold from 2008 to 2018 and most conditionally approved mergers were imposed with behavioural remedies. The anti-competitive effects of the mergers are reviewed by taking various factors into account and business enterprises are often required to submit remedies when the merger raises anti-competitive concerns.

7.1 Introduction

Chinese Anti-monopoly Law and its merger policy entered into force in August 2008. The enforcement agency—the Ministry of Commerce Anti-monopoly Bureau (MOFCOM) was established in 2003, being responsible for the implementation of the Interim Provisions for Foreign Investors to Merge Domestic Enterprises, an administrative regulation on mergers and acquisitions. In June 2011, an Anti-monopoly Commission office under the supervision of the State Council was established within MOFCOM. This office undertakes responsibilities including receiving concentration notifications, reviewing, investigating and assessing concentrations, as well as guiding domestic enterprises overseas in antitrust litigations, and facilitating international cooperation on multilateral and bilateral competition policy.

Chinese merger control policy has adopted a mandatory pre-merger notification system. The State Council released the Provisions on Thresholds for Prior Notification of Concentrations of Undertakings in August 2008, and the notification procedure has to comply with the Guiding Opinions of the Anti-monopoly Bureau of

J. Ma, *Competition Law in China*,
https://doi.org/10.1007/978-981-15-5105-5_7

the Ministry of Commerce on the Declaration Documents and Materials of the Concentration of Business Operators issued by MOFCOM in January 2009. Since 2014, MOFCOM has adopted the simplified procedure[1] that transactions which meet the criteria would not have to go through the normal filing, and will be able to be cleared within 30 days upon acceptance. The criteria include transactions with combined post-merger market shares lower than 15% (for horizontal) and 25% (for vertical and mergers without vertical relationships), or joint ventures outside China where no economic activities are involved within China. A list of unconditionally approved transactions can be found on MOFCOM website every month. Until December 31, 2016, among the total filed 395 merger cases, 76% of them were simple cases, and 98.6% of the simple cases were cleared within 30 days after the official acceptance.[2] According to MOFCOM Interim Measures on the Investigation and Handling of Concentrations of Undertakings that failed to notify in accordance with laws in 2011, when companies fail to comply with the ex-ante filing obligation, MOFCOM may impose an administrative fine lower than RMB 500,000 and may make a public announcement of the penalty. The 2020 draft revision of the AML increased the fines for enterprises that failed to notify to up to 10% of the annual sales revenue in the previous year.

According to Articles 25 and 26 of the Anti-monopoly Law, after MOFCOM accepts the notification application, the Phase I review should be completed within 30 days. The investigation may be continued to Phase II review for 90 days, and this procedure can be further extended to no longer than 60 days. Article 27 of the Anti-monopoly Law has listed six factors that the authority should take into account when assessing the anti-competitive effects: (1) the participating undertakings' market share in the relevant market, and the controlling power in that market; (2) the level of concentration in the relevant market; (3) the concentration's technological impact; (4) the concentrations' effects on consumers and other business operators; (5) the concentration's effects on national economic development; (6) other elements considered by the authority.

After going through the assessment procedure, MOFCOM is required to issue orders on the merger, including three options—prohibition, approval, and approval with conditions. The restrictive conditions include structural remedies, behavioural remedies and combined remedies. A written determination will only be issued when the merger is prohibited or approved with conditions. An official document on the assessment and reasoning of the economic effects published for approved cases is rare. Based on Article 53 of the Anti-monopoly Law, dissatisfaction with the MOFCOM decisions may cause administrative reconsideration or the option of filing an administrative lawsuit according to law.

Merger policy has been frequently enforced in China after the Anti-monopoly Law came into force. From 2008 until August 31, 2017, MOFCOM has cleared

---

[1]Guanyu Jingyingzhe Jizhong Jianyi Anjian Shiyong Biaozhun De Zanxing Guiding (关于经营者集中简易案件适用标准的暂行规定) [MOFCOM Interim Regulation on the Applicable Standards for Simple Cases of Concentrations between Business Operators].

[2]Hui (2017).

1936 transactions, and 70% of them were reviewed after 2013. Among the cleared transactions, only 30 were cleared with remedies, with 28 related to foreign-to-foreign transactions, and two were blocked.[3] From August 2008 to June 2010, 140 mergers were notified and 95% of them were approved unconditionally.[4] In 2011, 160 merger reviews were completed and 151 cases were cleared without condition. In the four cases approved under certain conditions, a behavioural remedy was imposed in three cases, and a structural remedy was imposed in one case. In 2012, 154 merger reviews were completed and 142 merger cases were cleared without condition. In the six merger cases approved under certain conditions, four of them received a behavioural remedy; in one case a structural remedy was imposed. As of June 2013, the MOFCOM—the merger enforcement authority in China, has received 754 notifications, and 690 cases have been reviewed. In the 643 cases in which a decision was issued, 624 were approved without conditions, 18 were approved with restrictions and one was prohibited. From August 2008 to June 2013, only the *Coca Cola/Huiyuan* merger was blocked by the MOFCOM. Among all the 18 cases that were granted remedies, nine received combined structural and behavioural remedies. Compared with the conditionally approved merger cases in the EU, it seems that the MOFCOM is particularly in favour of behavioural remedies. According to Mario Mariniello, from 2008 to August 2013, 60% of MOFCOM's conditionally cleared mergers were imposed with behavioural remedies, with 20% for structural remedies, and the rest was for combined remedies. For the same period, the EU Commission imposed structural remedies for 77% of the mergers cleared with restrictions, and 7% for behavioural remedies. The remaining 16% was for combined remedies.[5] In 2018, the newly established competition agency SAMR imposed tailored behavioural remedies on Essilor/Luxottica, and combined structural and behavioural remedies on Bayer/Monsanto, Linde/Praxair, and UTC/Rockwell Collins.

7.2 Economic Analysis of Concentrations

Horizontal mergers may lead to both unilateral restrictions on competition and inter-firm coordination problem. After the merger between competitors, the number of competing firms in the relevant market decreases, and the remaining operators are more likely to enter into cartel agreements thus the risk for inter-firm cartelistic behaviour increases. Meanwhile, after the merger the competitive pressure for the enterprise decreases and when the business operator gain a considerable market share, it is possible to impose unilateral restrictions on products and the risk of increasing product prices and impeding a competition may increase.

Vertical merger refers to merger between enterprises at different stages of production for the same product, from raw materials to semi-finished products to sales

[3]Antitrust in Asia (2017, p. 23).

[4]Healey (2010, p. 58).

[5]Mariniello (2013, pp. 6–8).

channels integration, vertical consolidation can improve production efficiency and save transaction costs, but it will also have an anti-competitive impact. The merger may block the market and limit opportunities for potential competitors to enter the market, thus impeding existing competition at the same time as increasing entry barriers.

Mixed merger means that the enterprises participating in the merger come from a completely different market, and there is neither a competitor nor a buying or selling relationship between them. Such mergers are usually aimed at improving the flow of funds between enterprises or at reducing market risk through diversified production. Mixed merger may increase the market power or even obtain a dominant influence on another enterprise by means of acquiring entity, assets or through contractual terms.

Article 20 of the AML made clear that 'concentration' in the AML include three circumstances: (1) merger between business operators (2) a business operator obtains control of another operator through acquiring equities or assets (3) a business operator obtains control or exerts a decisive influence over another operator by contract or any other means.[6] The 2020 draft revision of the AML adds one paragraph after the three circumstances and explains that the term 'control right' refers to the right or actual status of the business operators directly or indirectly, individually or collectively, that has or may have a decisive influence on the production and operation activities or other major decisions of other operators.

7.3 Chapter 4 of the AML on Merger Control

7.3.1 Notification

The notification provision is issued by the State Council, and several guidelines have been issued to follow this provision. It is the same for the market definition provision. These guidelines, although they were drafted by the MOFCOM, have to be approved and issued by the Anti-monopoly Commission. This is to confirm that the standards stated in the guidelines, such as the market definition, are to be applied in all fields of the antitrust investigations by all enforcement authorities. The thresholds for filing merger control applications is that in the previous fiscal year, the total global turnovers of all undertakings concerned exceeds RMB 10 billion, and if at least two parties are concerned each has a turnover of more than RMB 400 million in China, or in the previous fiscal year, the total Chinese turnovers of all undertakings concerned exceeded RMB 2 billion, and if at least two parties are concerned each has a turnover of more than RMB 400 million in China.

[6] Article 20 of the AML, translation adopted from en.pkulaw.cn.

(1) **Prior-Merger Notification**

Article 21 of the AML stipulates that business operators should declare in advance the concentration when it reaches the threshold proscribed by the State Council Anti-monopoly Law Enforcement agency, and those who fail to notify must not implement the concentration. It is clear that the AML applies a prior-merger notification system. The 2020 draft revision of the AML adds two paragraphs to Article 21, and states that the anti-monopoly law enforcement agency of the State Council can formulate and modify reporting standards based on the level of economic development and industry scale, and make them publicly available. Where the concentration of undertakings meet the reporting standards, but the concentration does not comply with the notification requirement, or the concentration does not meet pre-merger notification requirements but has or may have the effects of excluding or restricting competition, the enforcement agency shall investigate in accordance with the law.

On August 3, 2008, the State Council released the Provisions on Thresholds for Prior Notification of Concentrations of Undertakings.[7] The Provisions have five articles and especially specify the thresholds for the declaration of concentrations, and state that even if the enterprises do not reach this standard, they may also have to be examined if anticompetitive effects are expected to occur. Article 3 of the Provisions list two thresholds and when a concentration reaches these thresholds, a prior notification should be filed. The first circumstance is when the participating undertaking's combined worldwide turnover is more than RMB 10 billion in the previous accounting year, and at least two participating undertaking's turnover within China are both more than RMB 400 million in the previous accounting year. The second circumstance is when the participating undertakings' combined turnover within China is more than 2 billion yuan in the previous accounting year, and at least two participating undertakings' turnover in China is more than RMB 400 million in the previous accounting year.[8] According to Article 4, concentrations below this threshold may also be subject to an anti-monopoly investigation, when this concentration may have anti-competitive effects.

If the combined market share of the participating undertakings is below 15%, and each undertaking's market share does not exceed 25% for the upstream, or the downstream market, and the market share of each market related to the merger or acquisition is below 25%, or the offshore joint venture outside of China or the overseas acquired enterprise does not engage in any economic activity within China, or one or more undertakings which control the joint venture acquires sole control through the concentration, the proposed merger control filing will be accepted through the simplified procedure. The Guiding Opinions of the Anti-monopoly Bureau of the SAMR on Declaration for Simple Cases of Concentration of Business Operators

---

[7] Guowuyuan Guanyu Jingyingzhe Jizhong Shenbao Biaozhun De Guiding (国务院关于经营者集中申报标准的规定) [Provisions of the State Council on the Standard for Declaration of Concentration of Business Operators] issued on August 3, 2008. The Provision was amended on September 18, 2018.

[8] Article 3 of the Provisions of the State Council on the Standard for Declaration of Concentration of Business Operators.

(Revised in 2018)[9] lists the four documents that to be submitted in the simplified procedure: the declaration form, explanations of the influence of the concentration on the competition status of the relevant market, concentration agreements and the financial accounting report of the previous fiscal year of each business operator participated in the concentration.

(2) **Contents of the Notification**

Declaration documents and information according to Article 23 of the AML, when the operator declares to the Ministry of Commerce, the material should be submitted including (1) the notification application; (2) the focus on the relevant market competition in the impact of the description; (3) the centralized agreement and related documents; (4) the financial accounting report of the last fiscal year audited by the accounting firm of the operators participating in the concentration; (5) other documents and materials requested by the Ministry of Commerce (Anti-monopoly Service). The filer should submit at the same time two sets of the declaration documents, the public version of the information and the confidential version, and submit two sets of electronic discs of the same content.

Following this provision issued by the State Council, several guidelines were implemented which further clarify the information to be submitted and the procedure to be followed. On January 5, 2009, the MOFCOM issued the Guiding Opinions of the Anti-monopoly Bureau of the Ministry of Commerce on the Declaration Documents and Materials of the Concentration of Business Operators.[10] On July 15, 2009, the Measures for Calculating the Turnover for the Declaration of Business Concentration in the Financial Industry[11] was issued by the China Banking Regulatory Commission, the China Insurance Regulatory Commission, the China Securities Regulatory Commission, and the Ministry of Commerce and People's Bank of China. This provision provides guidance on the calculation of turnover for financial institutions. On November 21, 2009, the MOFCOM issued the Measures for the Undertaking Concentration Declaration.[12] On December 30, 2011 the MOFCOM issued the Interim

---

[9] Guojia Shichang Jiandu Guanli Zongju Fanlongduan Ju Guanyu Jingyingzhe Jizhong Jianyi Anjian Shenbao De Zhidao Yijian (2018 xiuding) 国家市场监督管理总局反垄断局关于经营者集中简易案件申报的指导意见 (2018修订) [Guiding Opinions of the Anti-monopoly Bureau of the State Administration for Market Regulation on Declaration for Simple Cases of Concentration of Business Operators (Revised in 2018)] issued on September 29, 2018 and effective on September 29, 2018.

[10] Shangwubu Fanlongduanju Guanyu Jingyingzhe Jizhong Shenbao Wenjian Ziliao De Zhidao Yijian (商务部反垄断局关于经营者集中申报文件资料的指导意见) [Guiding Opinions of the Anti-Monopoly Bureau of the Ministry of Commerce on the Declaration Documents and Materials of the Concentration of Business Operators] (issued by the Ministry of Commerce, 5 January 2009, effective on 5 January 2009).

[11] Jinrongye Jingyingzhe Jizhong Shenbao Yingye'e Jisuan Banfa (金融业经营者集中申报营业额计算办法) [Measures for Calculating the Turnover for the Declaration of Business Concentration in the Financial Industry] (issued by the China Banking Regulatory Commission, the China Insurance Regulatory Commission, the China Securities Regulatory Commission, the Ministry of Commerce, and People's Bank of China, on 15 July 2009, effective on 15 August 2009).

[12] Jingyingzhe Jizhong Shenbao Banfa (经营者集中申报办法) [Measure for the Undertaking Concentration Declaration] (promulgated by the Ministry of Commerce on 21 November 2009, effective on 1 January 2010).

Measures for Investigating and Handling Failure to Legally Declare the Concentration of Business Operators.[13] On September 8, 2017, MOFCOM issued the Notice on Soliciting Public Comments on the Measures on the Review of Concentrations of Business Operators (Revised Draft for Comments).[14]

7.3.2 *Review Process*

According to Article 25 of the AML, the anti-monopoly enforcement agency must, within 30 days from the date of receipt of the documents and information submitted by the enterprise in conformity with the provisions provided by Article 23 of the Anti-monopoly Law, after consulting relevant government authorities, and industrial associations, conduct a preliminary review of the declaration and a decision on whether to further continue the review, and notify the enterprises in written documents. For the simplified procedure, within the 30 calendar days in Phase I, a ten-day public consultation should be included. Phase II for further review will take a maximum of 90 calendar days, and it can be extended by 60 days. Most filings should be cleared within 90 days, and it is only possible to extend the review days when the parties request the agency to do so, or there is an inaccuracy in the filing documents, or there are significant changes in the circumstances of the transaction.[15] The 2020 draft revision of the AML adds Article 30 following Articles 25 and 26 and explains that in the following situations the time required is not included in the time limit for the investigation (1) the examination period is suspended with the consent of the applicant; (2) the applicant submits additional documents and materials in accordance with the requirements of the enforcement agency; (3) The enforcement agency consults on the proposal of remedies in accordance with Article 33 of this law. The specific provisions on the suspension of the investigation period shall be formulated separately by the anti-monopoly enforcement agency of the State Council.

According to Article 28 of the AML, if the concentration has or may have the effect of excluding or restricting competition, the anti-monopoly enforcement agency of the State Council will make provisions prohibiting the concentration. The transaction should not be processed until the anti-monopoly enforcement agency of the State Council makes a decision. In 2017, the average official launch time upon accepting

---

[13] Wei Yifa Shenbao Jingyingzhe Jizhong Diaocha Chuli Zanxing Banfa (未依法申报经营者集中调查处理暂行办法) [Interim Measures for Investigating and Handling Failure to Legally Declare the Concentration of Business Operators] (issued by the Ministry of Commerce, 30 December 2011, effective on 1 February 2012).

[14] Shangwubu Guanyu Jingyingzhe Jizhong Shencha Banfa Xiuding Caoan Zhengqiu Yijiangao Gongkai Zhengqiu Yijian De Tongzhi (商务部关于《经营者集中审查办法(修订草案征求意见稿)》公开征求意见的通知) [Notice of the Ministry of Commerce on Public Solicitation of Measures for the Concentration Review of Operators (Revised Draft for Soliciting Opinions) published on August 8, 2017.

[15] Hui (2017).

merger reviews was 28 days, and the length of merger reviews was 39 days.[16] In the ASE/SPIL case closed in November 2017, MOFCOM took 111 days to accept the filing and 345 days to review and complete Phase III. The merging parties were requested to refile by the end of Phase III and went through the review for the second time, resulting in a total review time of 456 days.[17] Based on the data of cleared mergers in 2019, it was reported that the average time of merger reviews under the simplified procedure by SAMR was 16.4 days.[18]

7.3.3 Assessment

According to Articles 25 and 26 of the AML, after the notification is accepted, the authority (specifically MOFCOM) has to conduct a preliminary review of the proposed concentration and issue a written decision within 30 days. If the MOFCOM decides to conduct an in-depth review, this process takes 90 days, and can be extended to no more than 150 days. After the review, a written decision should be issued and notified to the business operators.

There are three categories of guidelines that have been issued and implemented to assess merger effects after the AML came into force. The first category is guidelines that are applied to define the relevant market. In 2009, the Guidelines for Defining the Relevant Market, was issued by the Anti-monopoly Commission. However, this guideline does not have binding force. On May 24, 2009, the State Council issued the Guide of the Anti-monopoly Committee of the State Council for the Definition of the Relevant Market.[19]

The second category of guidelines refers to the guidelines that are applied to assess competitive effects. Article 27 of the AML lists six elements that the authority will consider during the investigation of anti-competitive effects: (1) the participating undertakings' market share in the relevant market, and the controlling power in that market; (2) the level of concentration in the relevant market; (3) the concentration's technological impact; (4) the concentration's effects on consumers and other business operators; (5) the concentration's effects on national economic development; (6) other elements considered by the authority. On August 29, 2009, the MOFCOM issued the Interim Provisions on the Assessment of Competitive Effects of Concentrations of Undertakings.[20] On November 24, 2009, the MOFCOM issued the Measures for

[16]MLex, "China's MOFCOM lifts remedies in 11 transactions, 23 still under supervision, official says" (released December 15, 2017).

[17]Deng and Huang (2018).

[18]Liu et al. (2020).

[19]Guowuyuan Fanlongduan Weiyuanhui Guanyu Xiangguan Shichang Jieding De Zhinan (国务院反垄断委员会关于相关市场界定的指南) [Guide of the Anti-Monopoly Committee of the State Council for the Definition of the Relevant Market] (issued by the Ministry of Commerce on 24 May 2009).

[20]Shangwubu Guanyu Pinggu Jingyingzhe Jizhong Jingzheng Yingxiang De Zanxing Guiding (商务部关于评估经营者集中竞争影响的暂行规定) [Interim Provisions on Assessing the Impact of

the Undertaking Concentration Examination.[21] On March 11, 2010, the MOFCOM issued the Working Guidelines of the Anti-monopoly Bureau of the Ministry of Commerce on Concentrations of Undertakings[22] and in 2011 the MOFCOM issued the Interim Rules on the Assessment of Competitive Impacts of Concentrations of Undertakings.

The third category of guidelines in merger analysis is the application of remedies. Article 29 of the AML formulates the basic rules for merger remedies. On July 5, 2010, the MOFCOM issued the Interim Provisions on the Divestiture of Assets or Business in the Concentration of Business Operators.[23] In August 2010, the MOFCOM issued the Provisional Rules on the Implementation of Business Divestiture in Concentrations between Undertakings.

7.3.4 Merger Remedies

On July 8, 2010 MOFCOM issued the Interim Measures on Implementing Assets or Business Divestitures by Concentrations of Undertakings, and MOFCOM issued the provision on Imposing Restrictive Conditions on Concentrations of Undertakings (trial implementation) on December 4, 2014. The provision became effective on January 5, 2015. It specified the types of restrictive conditions, the determination of restrictive conditions and the standard for choosing buyers, the procedure of divestment, the supervision of implementing restrictive conditions. This regulation replaced the Interim Regulation on the Implementation of Asset or Business Divestiture in Concentrations between Business Operators in July 2010.

7.3.5 National Security Review

Article 31 of the AML provides that transactions involving a domestic firm will have to be subject to a national security review. The State Council established the national security review on February 3, 2011, by issuing the Notice on Launching

---

Concentration of Business Operators on Competition] (issued by the Ministry of Commerce on 29 August 2011, effective on 5 September 2011).

[21] Jingyingzhe Jizhong Shencha Banfa (经营者集中审查办法) [Measure for the Undertaking Concentration Examination] (issued by the Ministry of Commerce 24 November 2009, effective on 1 January 2010).

[22] Jingyingzhe Jizhong Fanlongduan Shencha Banshi Zhinan (经营者集中反垄断审查办事指南) [Working Guidelines of the Anti-Monopoly Bureau of the Ministry of Commerce on Concentrations of Undertakings] (issued by the Ministry of Commerce on 11 March 2010).

[23] Shangwubu Guanyu Shishi Jingyingzhe Jizhong Zichan Huo Yewu Boli De Zanxing Guiding (商务部关于实施经营者集中资产或业务剥离的暂行规定) [Interim Provisions on the Divestiture of Assets or Business in the Concentration of Business Operators] (issued by the Ministry of Commerce on 5 July 2010, effective on 5 July 2010).

the Security Review System for Mergers and Acquisition of Domestic Enterprises by Foreign investors. This notice came into force on March 5, 2011. The Notice specifically targets mergers and acquistions in which foreign investors aquire actual control rights in the industries of agricultural products, energy and resources, infrastructure, transport and important technology and assembly manufactoring. According to Articles 2 and 3 of the Notice, the review will be administered by MOFCOM's Foreign Investment Administration Department, and will be conducted by a ministerial panel consisting of representatives from governmental departments in the relavant industry, based on the transaction' impact on national security, national economic stability, societal order, and the key technology's R&D capacity.[24] On August 25, 2011, MOFCOM published Regulations of the Implementation of a Security Review System for Mergers and Acquisitions of Domestic Enterprises by Foreign Investors, and this Regulation came into force on September 1, 2011.

7.4 Overview of the Cases

During 2007, the MOFCOM has conducted over 220 reviews on merger cases.[25] The number of filings and reviews increased five fold from 2008 to 2018 (see Chart 7.1). These practices made the MOFCOM more experienced in investigating antitrust cases and implementing other merger control guidelines after the enactment of the AML.

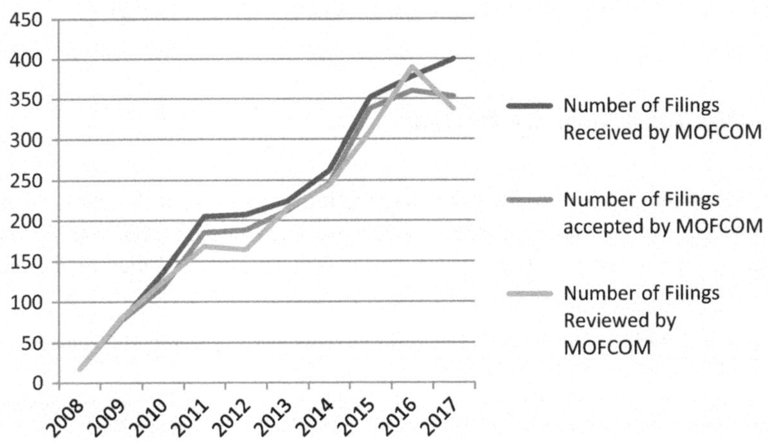

Chart 7.1 The number of filings received, accepted and reviewed by MOFCOM (The data is provided by Deng and Huang 2018)

[24] Article 2 of the National Security Review Notice.

[25] Wu (2008, p. 115).

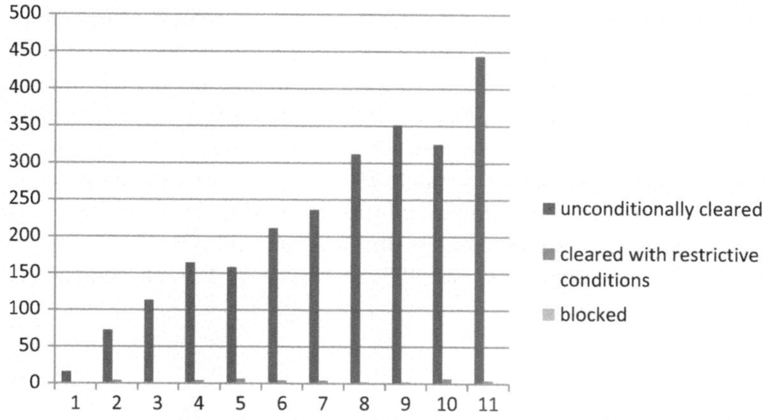

Chart 7.2 Number of filings and the percentage of cases with restrictive conditions (Zhan et al. 2018, p. 5; Li and Xu 2017; Deng 2014)

Up to the first quarter of 2018, MOFCOM completed the review of 2151 filings and among them, 36 were cleared with conditions, 2 filings were blocked and 2052 were cleared unconditionally, and 750 cases were filed through the simplified procedure.[26] The percentage of cases cleared with restrictive conditions is particularly low (see Chart 7.2).[27] The published merger cases cover a large range of industries, from consumer goods to pharmaceutical products, and most involved foreign companies which are global players and which produce and sell products both in China and in the global market. Electronics, services, automotive, chemicals and consumer goods are the top five industries filed for merger review from 2008 to 2018. The percentage of the service industry increased from 6% during the first five years to 12% when counting the filings for the first ten years.[28]

From 2008 until 2013, most conditionally approved mergers were between foreign companies,[29] and only four published cases were between a foreign and a domestic company: Coca Cola/Huiyuan, GE/Shenhua Group JV, Henkel Hongkong/Tiande Chemical, and Walmart/Niuhai. The merger GE/Shenhua Group JV involves both a foreign company and a SOE. Until August 2013, no merger between two domestic companies was cleared with restrictions by the MOFCOM. According to a press release published by the MOFCOM in November 2012,[30] 90% of the unconditionally approved cases were between foreign companies. To explain the low percentage of merger cases involving domestic firms, it might be possible that some domestic mergers failed to notify the MOFCOM, for example the merger between China

[26]Deng and Huang (2018).

[27]Deng and Huang (2018).

[28]Deng and Huang (2018).

[29]For a comprehensive study on the MOFCOM's decisions on foreign companies from a perspective of extraterritorial effects of the AML, see Faure and Zhang (2013).

[30]MOFCOM (2012).

Telecom and China Unicom was not filed.[31] According to Mario Mariniello, from October 2012 to September 2013, only 15% of the notified mergers in China were between domestic enterprises.[32] However, when counting the merger filings for the last ten years, the observation is different: 46% the filings were between foreign and foreign companies, and 29% were between Chinese firms, and 15% were when a foreign firm acquired a Chinese firm, and 11% were when a Chinese firm acquired a foreign firm. The percentage of domestic firms involved in the acquisition increased significantly. In non-acquisition mergers (mostly joint ventures), 50% were between foreign and Chinese companies, and 40% involve only foreign companies, 10% between only Chinese firms.[33]

7.4.1 The Extensive Use of Behavioural Remedies

Most conditionally approved mergers were imposed behavioural remedies. Compared with the conditional approved merger cases in the EU, it seems that the MOFCOM is particularly in favour of behavioural remedies.[34] According to Mario Mariniello, from 2008 to August 2013, 60% of MOFCOM's conditionally cleared mergers were given behavioural remedies, with 20% for structural remedies, and the rest was for combined remedies. For the same period, the EU Commission has imposed structural remedies for 77% of the mergers cleared with restrictions, and 7% for behavioural remedies.[35] The remaining 16% was for combined remedies. The reason why MOFCOM has relied on behavioural remedies might be two-sided: on the one hand, behavioural remedies have an advantage of being flexible, so they are easier to negotiate and to impose on the merging parties[36]; on the other hand, the flexible use of behavioural remedies may give the MOFCOM the opportunity to achieve a broader goal of competition policy,[37] in particular to pay more attention to the role of competitors instead of consumers. In addition, as some commentators observed, both for the proposal and for the implementation of remedies, the MOFCOM tends to rely on the negotiations as well as the voluntary cooperation from the merging parties.[38]

In several cases, the merging parties were either required to maintain the price and quantity level for a given product in the market, such as in Uralkali/Silvinit, Henkel Hong Kong/Tiande, or were prohibited from increasing the market power of this product by acquiring other producers or by building new plants,

---

[31] Wang and Emch (2013, p. 267), Wang (2009).

[32] Mariniello (2013, p. 8).

[33] Deng and Huang (2018).

[34] Mariniello (2013, p. 6).

[35] Mariniello (2013, p. 6, 7).

[36] Mariniello (2013, p. 7).

[37] Mariniello (2013, p. 7).

[38] Hao (2010, p. 19).

such as in InBev/Anheuser-Bush, Walmart/Newheight, Novartis/Alcon and Mitsubishi Rayon/Lucite.[39] The MOFCOM gave remedies to InBev/Anheuser-Busch, Mitsubishi Rayon/Lucite, GM/Delphi, Seagate/Samsung, and Google/Motorola, whereas these mergers were unconditionally cleared by the antitrust authorities in the US and in the EU.[40] In Thermo Fisher/Life Tech, Dow/DuPont and Agrium/PotashCorp, MOFCOM imposed behavioural and structural remedies, while US and EU only required divestitures.[41] Merger cases Uralkali/Silvinit, Penelope (AlphaV)/Savio, Henkel Hongkong/Tiande Chemical, Microsoft/Nokia, Merck/AZ Electronic, Nokia/Alcatel, HP/Samsung, ASE/SPIL, on which MOFCOM imposed behavioral remedies, did not meet the notification requirement in the US and in the EU.[42] In particular, using behavioural remedies to maintain price and quantity for one product may not be well explained by competition theory. The issue of preventing a merged firm from entering an area of business or from expanding the operation line seems to be more relevant to industrial policy, which should be the concern of a regulator, but not a competition authority.[43] The remedies MOFCOM requested in cases Microsoft/Nokia, Merck/AZ Electronics, Nokia/Alcatel, Broadcom/Brocade, HP/Samsung, Agrium/PotashCorp, Maersk/Hamburg Süd, ASE/SPIL are stricter than the remedies imposed by the US and EU competition authority. Remedies in NXP/Freescale, AB InBev/SAB Miller, Abbott/St. Jude Medical and Bayer/Monsanto are less strict or the same.[44]

In several decisions, for example, in Mitsubishi Rayon/Lucite and GM/Delphi, the MOFCOM has mentioned that the increased competitiveness of the merging party would restrict the access to a product market for other competitors. In Coca Cola/Huiyuan, the MOFCOM claimed that the merged firm would squeeze the market space for domestic small and medium-sized fruit juice producers.[45] However, economic theory of competition generally shows that the enhanced competitiveness of the merging party would benefit consumers by promoting efficiency.[46] It would only become an anticompetitive concern when the antitrust authority pays particular attention to the competitors.[47] In this view, it was more likely that the merger policy in China was implemented to fulfill industrial policy goals, and in particular to support the development of domestic firms.[48] In some other cases, when there was no major domestic competitor involved in that industry, it seems that the MOFCOM

[39] Mariniello (2013, p. 7).

[40] Wang and Emch (2013, p. 254), Chin (2012, p. 7, 12).

[41] Deng and Huang (2018, p. 10).

[42] Chin (2012, p. 7).

[43] Healey (2010, p. 44).

[44] Deng and Huang (2018, p. 10).

[45] MOFCOM's decision on the Coca Cola/Huiyuan case http://fldj.mofcom.gov.cn/aarticle/ztxx/200903/20090306108494.html.

[46] Mariniello (2013, p. 7).

[47] Mariniello (2013, p. 7).

[48] Sokol (2013, p. 12).

imposed behavioural remedies to mitigate the negative effects on the domestic market. For example, in Seagate/Samsung and Western Digital/Hitachi, the MOFCOM investigated in detail how the hard disk drive (HDD) market functions, such as the issue of how large computer manufacturers bid for the order in HDD procurement, as well as how market entry, capacity usage and innovation affect the development of the HDD industry. In both cases, the MOFCOM has explicitly mentioned the transaction's impact on consumers because China is one of the major consuming countries of personal computers.

In some cases, the consideration of the domestic market has also been extended to markets relying on international trade. In Glencore/Xstrata and Marubeni/Gavilon two global mergers, the MOFCOM specifically focused on the effects of the transaction on the import market. In Glencore/Xstrata, the MOFCOM mentioned that China is the major copper importing country and constitutes 50% of the global copper demand. In 2011, the imported copper formed 68.5% of the total supply of copper in China. In both cases, the MOFCOM focused on the analysis of the transaction on the import supply of major natural resources. In Glencore/Xstrata, as a remedy to mitigate the anticompetitive effects, the MOFCOM imposed a detailed trade requirement on the long-term contract (from 2013 to 31 December 2020) between Glencore and the Chinese buyers. In Marubeni/Gavilon, the MOFCOM put emphasis on the merger's effects on the import market of soya beans. MOFCOM's investigation shows that 99% of the soya beans operated by Marubeni are exported to China. In 2012, 80% of the supply of soya beans in China relied on imports. As the bargaining power from domestic firms is low, MOFCOM imposed behavioural remedies to require Marubeni and Gavilon to keep their business in soya beans independent. The MOFCOM expressed similar concerns in Uralkali/Silvinit, and in that case the MOFCOM even mentioned that this merger may negatively affect agricultural development in China. On the one hand, MOFCOM's concern of the importing market could be explained from the goal of promoting domestic economy, as well as the welfare impact on domestic consumers and producers. On the other hand, this concern can be explained by the role of the MOFCOM itself, as it is a bureau that operates under the leadership of the Ministry of Commerce, of which the major responsibility is to deal with commercial affairs involved in the international trade. It is also possible that the MOFCOM staff members have applied their expertise in dealing with other commercial issues to the implementation of a newborn antitrust law.

To benefit domestic consumers, MOFCOM may request the merging parties to commit to specific supply terms. In GM/Delphi, MOFCOM imposed behavioural remedies to ensure that the merged entity will maintain non-discriminatory, timely and reliable supply to consumers in the Chinese market. The terms on supplies have also been imposed on Uralkali/Silvinit, Glencore/Xstrata, MediaTek/MStar, Dow/DuPont, HP/Samsung, Broadcom/Brocade, ASE/SPIL, and Agrium/PotashCorp. The terms imposed on MediaTek/MStar have been specified in maintaining the pre-transaction cycle and the scope of price cuts. Terms with pricing commitments could also be observed from the remedies on Thermo Fisher/Life Tech, which required the merging parties to lower catalog prices in China by one percent per year for two products. Similarly, in Dow/DuPont, the prices for Chinese customers on certain active ingredients should be lower than the 12-month average level before approval.[49] In addition, the merging party should supply Chinese producers with ingredients and preparations for rice herbicides at a reasonable price for 5 years on a non-exclusive basis.[50] Behavioural remedies with terms on price commitments would reflect concerns beyond a pure economic analysis of the anti-competitive effects.

Another aspect of the extensive use of behavioural remedies is that in some cases, such as in Novartis/Alcon, Seagate/Samsung, Uralkali/Silvinit, Walmart/Newheight, and Google/Motorola, the MOFCOM required a monitor to facilitate the implementation of the behavioural remedies. To some scholars, the goal of appointing a monitor is to ensure compliance.[51] However, to some lawyers who have followed the Seagate/Samsung case closely, this requirement was clearly based an industrial policy concerns.[52] The reason was that although China is the largest personal computer market, it does not have a competitive Chinese firm in this industry. In their views, it was highly likely that the government wished to learn from the operation of Western competitors through the process of monitoring.[53]

It may become evident when behavioural remedies are extensively applied to provide tailored benefits for domestic producers. In Bayer/Monsanto, MOFCOM specifically required Bayer and Monsanto to provide access for agricultural application developers in China to their digital agricultural platform, and such a remedy can only be explained from the perspective of benefiting domestic competitors.[54] In Google/Motorola Mobility, Nokia/Alcatel, Merck/AZ Electronics, and Microsoft/Nokia, MOFCOM imposed FRAND-related conditions. In Bayer/Monsanto, MOFCOM requested the merging parties to guarantee Chinese agricultural application developers to access the merging parties' digital agricultural platform through connecting their software, based on FRAND terms for five years after entering the Chinese market. Local producers should also be allowed to register and employ their digital agricultural products.[55] In Essilor/Luxottica, SAMR designed behavioural remedies to benefit domestic retail firms, for example, the merging party should not provide exclusivity conditions to Chinese spectacles retailers, but should supply all frame and sunglasses products and offer necessary trademark licensing to retailers in China on FRAND terms.[56] In Linde/Praxair, SAMR held that the transaction would eliminate and/or restrict competition in the industrial gas product markets and strengthen the combined company's controlling market power. In addition to imposing structural remedies of divestiture, SAMR requested the merging

[49] Deng and Huang (2018, p. 14).

[50] Fels et al. (2017, p. 2).

[51] Zhang and Zhang (2013, p. 34).

[52] Sokol (2013, p. 13).

[53] Sokol (2013, p. 13).

[54] China Competition Review 2018, Davis Polk & Wardwell LLP.

[55] Deng and Huang (2018, p. 13).

[56] China Competition Review 2018, Davis Polk & Wardwell LLP, at p. 3.

parties to assist the buyers of the assets in transporting the gas to China, and supply gas mixtures at a reasonable price in China.[57] In Rockwell Collins/UTC, SAMR held that the acquisition would raise anti-competitive concerns in the markets of trimmable horizontal stabilizer actuators, and go beyond the structural remedies on dividing assets, so the SAMR imposed behavioural remedies on prohibiting merging parties to conduct tie-in sales or bundling.[58]

The Table 7.1 lists the merger cases cleared with conditions that are published by MOFCOM.

7.4.2 The Investigation Process

MOFCOM starts the investigation by describing the market shares of each party. As most decisions are rather brief, it was unclear how economic analysis of market share, and market concentration was calculated.[59] Nevertheless, all of the decisions have mentioned from which sources the MOFCOM collected the information, such as whether it is from government, trade associations, or from downstream firms, and all the cases decisions have mentioned that the information was collected from government and trade associations.[60] Besides, most cases have mentioned downstream firms and experts, and a few cases have mentioned the competitors in the same industry. As far as consumers are concerned, only downstream customers and dealers were mentioned in some cases, but the role of the end-users and consumer associations was ambiguous. A possible explanation might be that the MOFCOM seems to rely more on the information received from producers, governmental agencies and trade associations. The investigation source might imply that industrial policy considerations and other political goals may play an important role in merger analysis.

MOFCOM tends to focus on the market share of the merging firms. It is highly likely for a merged firm to obtain a dominant position when its post-merger market share is high,[61] and a merger would be considered highly likely to restrain competition if it creates a dominant position. For example, in Mitsubishi Rayon/Lucite, the MOFCOM claimed that the post-merger company held 64% of the market share in the MMA product, and that this would lead to a dominant position, which could restrict the market access for other competitors.[62] Similar logic was also applied to

[57] China Competition Review 2018, Davis Polk & Wardwell LLP, at p. 3.

[58] China Competition Review 2018, Davis Polk & Wardwell LLP, at p. 4.

[59] It was argued that the accuracy and transparency of MOFCOM decisions have been improved in later cases. See Wang and Emch (2013, p. 255).

[60] Trade associations in China are usually established as government agencies which play a role of monitoring a specific industry (Healey 2010, p. 25). In practice, trade associations would coordinate with ministries or SOE members, and impose political pressure on merger cases (Sokol 2013, p. 11).

[61] Hao (2010, p. 17).

[62] Healey (2010, p. 46).

Table 7.1 MOFCOM published merger cases (2008–2020)

Date	Merger case	Industry/Product	Buyer country	Target country	Type of transaction	Decision	Type of remedy
November 18, 2008	InBev/Anheuser-Busch	Beverage manufacturing	Belgium	US	Foreign/Foreign	Conditional approval	Behavioral
March 18, 2009	Coca Cola/Huiyuan	Fruit juice beverage	US	China	Foreign/Domestic	Prohibited	No remedy
April 24, 2009	Mitsubishi Rayon/Lucite	Methylmethacrylate ('MMA'), a material for making plastics	Japan	UK	Foreign/Foreign	Conditional approval	Behavioural and structural
September 28, 2009	GM/Delphi	Auto Manufacturing	US	US	Foreign/Foreign	Conditional approval	Behavioural
September 29, 2009	Pfizer/Wyeth	Pharmaceutical products	US	US	Foreign/Foreign	Conditional approval	Behavioural and structural
October 30, 2009	Panasonic/Sanyo	Battery Manufacturing	Japan	Japan	Foreign/Foreign	Conditional approval	Behavioural and structural
August 13, 2010	Novartis/Alcon	Healthcare (Ophthalmic anti-inflammatory Compound and contact lens care products)	Switzerland	Switzerland	Foreign/Foreign	Conditional approval	Behavioural
June 2, 2011	Uralkali/Silvinit	Fertilizer (Potash or potassium chloride)	Russia	Russia	Foreign/Foreign	Conditional approval	Behavioural
October 31, 2011	Penelope (AlphaV)/Savio	Electronic yarn cleaner	France	Italy	Foreign/Foreign	Conditional approval	Structural

(continued)

Table 7.1 (continued)

Date	Merger case	Industry/Product	Buyer country	Target country	Type of transaction	Decision	Type of remedy
November 10, 2011	GE/Shenhua Group JV	Coal-water slurry gasification technology	US	China	Foreign/Domestic	Conditional approval	Behavioural
December 12, 2011	Seagate/Samsung	Hard disk drive	US	Korea	Foreign/Foreign	Conditional approval	Behavioural
February 9, 2012	Henkel Hongkong/Tiande Chemical	Chemicals	Germany	China	Foreign/Domestic	Conditional approval	Behavioural
March 2, 2012	Western Digital/Hitachi	Hard Disk Drives (HDD)	US	Japan	Foreign/Foreign	Conditional approval	Behavioural and structural
May 19, 2012	Google/Motorola	Smart mobile terminals and operating systems	US	US	Foreign/Foreign	Conditional approval	Behavioural
June 15, 2012	Goodrich/UTC	Aviation Electronic Systems	US	US	Foreign/Foreign	Conditional approval	Structural
August 13, 2012	Walmart/Yihaodian	B2C online retail business	US	China	Foreign/Domestic	Conditional approval	Behavioural
December 6, 2012	Advanced RISC Machines/G&D/Gemalto Joint venture	Trusted Execution Environment	UK, Germany, Netherlands		Foreign/Foreign	Conditional approval	Behavioural
April 16, 2013	Glencore/Xstrata	Natural resource	Switzerland	UK	Foreign/Foreign	Conditional approval	Behavioural and structural

(continued)

Table 7.1 (continued)

Date	Merger case	Industry/Product	Buyer country	Target country	Type of transaction	Decision	Type of remedy
April 22, 2013	Marubeni/Gavilon	Agricultural products (Export market of beans)	Japan	US	Foreign/Foreign	Conditional approval	Behavioural
13.082013.8.8	Baxter Int./Gambro	Medical device (CRRT)	US	Sweden	Foreign/Foreign	Conditional approval	Behavioural and structural
August 27,2013	MediaTek/Mstar Semiconductor	Electronic (LCD)	Taiwan region	Taiwan region	Taiwan region/Taiwan region	Conditional approval	Behavioural
January 14, 2014	Thermo Fisher Scientific/Life Technologies	biotechnology	US	US	Foreign/Foreign	Conditional approval	Structural and behavioural
April 8, 2014	Microsoft/Nokia	IT/Software/Mobile equipment	US	Finland	Foreign/Foreign	Conditional approval	behavioural
April 30, 2014	Merck/AZ	Mobile device manufacturing	Germany	Luxemburg	Foreign/Foreign	Conditional approval	Behavioural
June 17, 2014	Maersk/Mediterranean Shipping/CMA CGM	Shipping	Denmark	Switzerland, France	Foreign/Foreign	rejection	no remedy
July 2, 2014	Corun/Toyota/PEVE/ZhongYuan/Toyota Tsusho	Automotive	Japan	China	Foreign/Domestic	Conditional approval	Behavioural
2015	Nokia/Alcatel	Consumer technology	Finland	France	Foreign/Foreign	Conditional approval	Behavioural
November 27, 2015	NXP/Freescale	Semiconductor	Global	Global	Foreign/Foreign	conditional approval	structural

(continued)

Table 7.1 (continued)

Date	Merger case	Industry/Product	Buyer country	Target country	Type of transaction	Decision	Type of remedy
2016.7	AB InBev/SABMiller	Brewing	Belgium	UK	Foreign/Foreign	conditional approval	Structural
2016.8	Dell/EMC	technology	US	US	Foreign/Foreign	approval	no remedy
2016.9	Marriott/ Starwood	hotel operation	US	US	Foreign/Foreign	approval	no remedy
October 27, 2016	Qualcomm/NXP Semiconductors	Semi-conductor	US	Netherlands	Foreign/Foreign	The review took over 20 months long and in July 2018 Qualcomm withdrew the deal	no remedy
December 30, 2016	Abbott Laboratories/St. Jude Medical	Healthcare	US	US	Foreign/Foreign	conditional approval	structural
2017	Dow/DuPont	Agriculture and Chemicals	US	US	Foreign/Foreign	Conditional approval	Structural and behavioural
2017	Broadcom/Brocade	Semi-conductor	Singapore	US	Foreign/Foreign	Conditional approval	Behavioural
2017	HP/Samsung	printer	US	Korea	Foreign/Foreign	Conditional approval	Behavioural
2017	Agrium/Potash Corp	Fertilizer	Canada	Canada	Foreign/Foreign	Conditional approval	Structural and behavioural

(continued)

Table 7.1 (continued)

Date	Merger case	Industry/Product	Buyer country	Target country	Type of transaction	Decision	Type of remedy
2017	Maersk/Hamburg süd	shipping	Denmark	Germany	Foreign/Foreign	Conditional approval	Behavioural
2017	ASE/SPIL	Semi-conductor	Taiwan Region	Taiwan Region	Foreign/Foreign	Conditional approval	Behavioural
2017	Becton Dickinson/C.R. Bard	Healthcare	US	US	Foreign/Foreign	Conditional approval	Structural
2018.3	Bayer/Monsanto	Agricultural	Germany	US	Foreign/Foreign	Conditional approval	Structural and behavioural
2018.7	Essilor/Luxottica	Optical industry	France	Italy	Foreign/Foreign	Conditional approval	Behavioural
2018.9	Linde AG/Praxair	Industrial gas product	Germany	US	Foreign/Foreign	Conditional approval	Structural and behavioural
2019.2	KLA-Tencor/Orbotech	Semiconductor	US	Israel	Foreign/Foreign	conditional approval	Behavioural
2019.7	Cargotec/TTS Gruppen	Marine engineering industries	Finland	Norway	Foreign/Foreign	Conditional approval	Behavioural
2019.9	II–VI/Finisar	Engineering materials and optoelectronic components	US	US	Foreign/Foreign	Conditional approval	Behavioural

(continued)

Table 7.1 (continued)

Date	Merger case	Industry/Product	Buyer country	Target country	Type of transaction	Decision	Type of remedy
2019.10	Zhejiang Garden Biochemical/Royal DSM	Life science and materials science, nutrition	China	The Netherlands	Domestic/Foreign	Conditional approval	Behavioural
2019.12	Novelis/Aleris	Manufacturing and sales of rolled aluminum products	Canada	US	Foreign/Foreign	Conditional approval	Structural and behavioural
2020.2	Danaher/GM	Biopharmaceutical	US	US	Foreign/Foreign	Conditional approval	Structural and behavioural

Sources MOFCOM official website http://fldj.mofcom.gov.cn/article/ztxx/ SAMR official website http://www.samr.gov.cn/fldj/tzgg/ftjpz/; Healey (2012, pp. 13–15); Davis and Wardwell (2016, 2018)

the merger analysis of Pfizer/Wyeth, where the MOFCOM claimed that the post-merger firm held a market share of 49.4%, with the second producer in the market holding 18.35% market share.[63] Most behavioural remedies were imposed by the MOFCOM for the purpose of mitigating the potential anticompetitive effects; however, these decisions did not provide a detailed analysis regarding to what extent the remedies would indeed reduce the anticompetitive effects.[64] It also remains unclear how to enhance monitoring efforts and how to deal with the situation if the merging party fails to comply.[65]

MOFCOM also requests the business operators to submit proposals on remedies when the merger raises anti-competitive concerns. Take *NXP acquisition of Freescale*[66] as an example. On November 27, 2015, MOFCOM approved NXP Semiconductors N.V. (NXP)'s acquisition of Freescale Semiconductor Ltd. (Freescale) with conditions. MOFCOM assessed the affected markets included micro-controllers, analogue integrated circuits for power supply for automobile applications, and radio frequency power transistors. In the radio frequency power transistors market, the concentration level is high, and the top eight market players held over 90% of the market. Products used LDMOS and gallium nitride process technologies that were manufactured by Freescale and NXP and accounted for 84% in 2012 and were expected to reach a market share of 92% in 2018. Therefore, the merger between these two leading companies, which share similar client networks and process technologies, would eliminate competition in the radio frequency power transistor market. The acquisition would limit the supply choices for consumers, and reduce the motivation for companies to invest in research and innovation in new technology, which leads to an increase in barriers to entry. NXP proposed that to mitigate the negative anti-competitive effects, it should completely divest its business in radio frequency power transistors, and divesting the business to JAC Capital should be completed before the acquisition was closed by complying with the Samba Agreement and Final Commitments submitted by NXP to MOFCOM. The divestiture remedy was similar to those submitted to the US FTC, the European Commission, and the Korea FTC. This proposal was accepted by MOFCOM, and for the first time, MOFCOM required the parties to complete the divestiture before closing the proposed acquisition.

7.5 Conclusions

Before the establishment of SAMR, MOFCOM was responsible for the enforcement of merger policy. Merger policy has been frequently enforced in China after the AML came into force. Article 21 of the AML specifies the thresholds of prior

[63] Healey (2010, p. 47).

[64] Hao (2010, p. 17).

[65] Hao (2010, p. 16, 17).

[66] http://fldj.mofcom.gov.cn/article/ztxx/201511/20151101196182.shtml.

merger notification and Article 23 of the AML lists the materials to be submitted for merger notification. Article 25 of the AML requires the agency to review the case and issue a written decision within 30 days from the date of receipt of the documents. Furthermore, Article 31 of the AML provides that transactions which involve a domestic firm will have to be subject to a national security review. From 2008 until 2018, the number of filings and reviews increased fivefold and most conditionally approved mergers were imposed behavioural remedies. Various types of behavioural remedies are applied for the purpose of mitigating anti-competitive effects. During the investigation process, MOFCOM relies on the information collected from government, trade associations, or downstream firms. Market share is a clear indicator for assessing market dominance.

The summary of merger cases gives a general impression that the MOFCOM has paid particular attention to domestic producers who operate in the same industry as the merged firm. By reviewing the cases approved with conditions, it seems that non-economic goals may have played a role in MOFCOM's analysis of merger effects. This finding could be explained by the competition goals of protecting the interest of social public, and contributing to the development of the socialist market economy listed in Article 1 of the AML. In addition, the consideration of domestic competitors also indicates that merger policy in China might have been influenced by industrial policy. As no published case was between two domestic companies, it is difficult to compare whether merger policy has been equally applied to domestic and foreign competitors. However, when a merger between two foreign companies is cleared, it seems that it is always a major concern for the MOFCOM to investigate whether this merger will restrain competition for other domestic competitors in the same industry. Therefore, the boundary between competition policy and industrial policy might not be completely clear-cut in China.

References

Antitrust in Asia, The Business Impact of Fast-evolving Competition Laws, Freshfields Bruckhaus Deringer, October 2017, p. 23.

Chin, Y. W. (2012). *The high-wire balancing act of merger control under China's anti-monopoly law*. Retrieved from http://ssrn.com/abstract=2120280.

Davis, P., & Wardwell, L. L. P. (2016). *China antitrust review*. Retrieved from https://www.davispolk.com/files/2017-01-25_china_antitrust_review_2016.pdf.

Davis, P., & Wardwell, L. L. P. (2018). *China competition review*. Retrieved from https://www.davispolk.com/files/2019–01-31_china_antitrust_review_2018.pdf.

Deng, F. (2014, June 2). *Merger review and private litigation under China's anti-monopoly law*. US–China Business Council Annual Meeting.

Deng, F., & Huang, C. (2018, August). A ten-year review of merger enforcement in China. *The Antitrust Source*. Available at https://www.antitrustsource.com.

Faure, M., & Zhang, X. (2013). Towards an extraterritorial application of the Chinese anti-monopoly law that avoids trade conflicts. *George Washington International Law Review, 45*(3), 501–538.

Fels, A., Wang, X., Ng, W., & Emch, A. (Eds.). (2017, June). *China competition bulletin* (47th ed.). A Publication of the Competition Law & Economics Network at Melbourne Law School, University of Melbourne.

Hao, Q. (2010). Merger remedies in China: Developments and issues. *Competition Law International,* 13–21.

Healey, D. (2010). Anti-monopoly law and mergers in China: An early report card on procedural and substantive issues. *Tsinghua China Law Review, 3,* 17–58.

Healey, D. J. (2012). Strange bedfellows or soulmates: A comparison of merger regulation in China and Australia. *Asian Journal of Comparative Law, 7*(1), 1–40.

Hui, J. (2017, February/March). *Fundamentals and latest developments of China merger control filing.* JunHe LLP.

Li, F., & Xu, H. (2017, September 29). *Brief introduction to china antitrust regime.* UC Berkeley Law School.

Liu, C., Li, A., Bi, Y., Liu, S., Hong, L., & Liu, J. (2020). *China's anti-monopoly law enters its second decade.* King & Wood Mallesons. Retrieved February 20, 2020, from https://www.chinalawinsight.com/2020/02/articles/antitrust/chinas-anti-monopoly-law-enters-its-second-decade/#_ftn18.

Mariniello, M. (2013). The dragon awakes: Is Chinese competition policy a cause for concern? *Bruegel Policy Contribution* (2013/14).

MOFCOM. (2012, November 16). *Statistics of unconditionally approved concentration cases* (经营者集中反垄断审查无条件批准案件信息统计情况). Retrieved from http://fldj.mofcom.gov.cn/article/zcfb/201211/20121108437868.shtml.

Sokol, D. D. (2013). *Merger control under China's anti-monopoly law.* Minnesota Legal Studies Research Paper No. 13-05. Retrieved from http://papers.ssrn.com/sol3/papers.cfm?abstract_id=2207690.

Wang, B. (2009, April 30). Official with MOFCOM confirms that merger of China Unicom and China Netcom is allegedly illegal. *The Economic Observer.*

Wang, X., & Emch, A. (2013). Five years of implementation of China's anti-monopoly law—Achievements and challenges. *Journal of Antitrust Enforcement, 1*(2), 247–271.

Wu, Z. (2008). Perspectives on the Chinese anti-monopoly law. *Antitrust Law Journal, 75,* 73–116.

Zhan, H., Song, Y., &Yang, Z. (2018). A new era comes—Highlights of the anti-monopoly law of China.

Zhang, X., & Zhang. V. Y. (2013). Revisiting China's merger control, where are we going after the three-Year milestone? *Dovenschmidt Quarterly* (1), 26–35.

Chapter 8
Administrative Monopolies

Abstract "Administrative monopolies" refers to monopolistic behaviour that is supported by government or regulatory agencies at both central and regional levels. The central government protects specific sectors or departments through exercising administrative authority. Local government exerts administrative power over enterprises within the region and protect the profits of these enterprises by creating market barriers and restricting the flow of products. Administrative monopolies in China developed due to historical reasons and administrative monopolies are defined as sectorial, regional monopolies and public utilities. It has been argued that the enforcement of Chap. 5 of the AML on administrative monopolies is ineffective. After the establishment of the fair competition review system in 2016, more active measures have been taken to investigate administrative cases and to prohibit monopolistic behaviour conducted by public utility enterprises.

8.1 Introduction

Chinese economists and lawyers have long acknowledged that administrative monopolies generate considerable efficiency losses and consumer welfare losses[1]; provisions on prohibiting administrative monopolies entered into force even decades before the promulgation of the AML. However, the enforcement of these provisions was rather ineffective.[2] During the thirteen-year legislative history of the AML, it remained a debated issue whether prohibiting administrative monopolies should be included as one of its main objectives. Some commentators argued that administrative monopolies were *the* monopoly problem in China that the competition law should tackle,[3] whereas others proposed that given the specific economic and political characteristics of China during its transition from a centrally planned system to a market economy, the AML could only play a limited role in preventing governmental agencies from imposing anti-competitive restrictions.[4] Being influenced by this

[1]Chan (2009, p. 267), Guo and Hu (2004, p. 277), Yu and Yu (2011).

[2]Owen et al. (2008, p. 235), Liu and Qiao (2012, p. 79).

[3]Wang (2004, p. 286).

[4]Owen et al. (2008, p. 256, 257).

J. Ma, *Competition Law in China*,
https://doi.org/10.1007/978-981-15-5105-5_8

debate, provisions on prohibiting administrative monopolies were first included in several drafts of the AML that were released for comments after 2002; however, in the drafts of December 2005 and June 2006, the entire chapter on "prohibiting administrative monopolies" was completely deleted by the State Council. This chapter was reinserted in 2006 when the draft was submitted to the Standing Committee of the National People's Congress (NPC) for its first reading, and was kept until this law was promulgated in August 2007.[5]

The enforcement of Chap. 5 of the AML has been criticized as ineffective. Starting from 2013, the CPC Central Committee and the State Council have issued opinions on advocating the establishment of a fair competition review system to coordinate industrial policy and competition policy, thus solving the difficulties in investigating administrative cases. In June 2016, the State Council issued the Opinions on Establishing Fair Competition Review in the Development of a Market System, and stipulates that administrative regulations made by governmental agencies on economic activities should be reviewed before implementation. Since then effective measures have been taken to investigate administrative cases. It is expected that the fair competition system will be effectively applied to enhance the enforcement power of Chap. 5 of the AML.

8.2 Administrative Monopolies in China

As a general definition, administrative monopolies usually refer to monopolistic behaviour that is supported by government or regulatory agencies at both central and regional levels. The governmental agencies and departments tend to protect certain sectors or industries through exercising their administrative power and thus impede competition in these sectors.

Administrative monopolies have developed due to historical reasons. Prior to the Market Reform in 1978, the Chinese economy was organized through a system of national planning.[6] State-owned Enterprises (SOEs), which played a dominant role in almost all industries, were under the direct control of the central authority.[7] Learning from the former Soviet Union, before the reform, in every major industry in China, there was a corresponding ministry to ensure government control and management.[8] The State directly regulated production, price, supply of raw materials, entry and exit into the market, even the salary of enterprises' managers and employees.[9] SOEs had to produce according to central plans, and to deliver all outputs and revenues to the

[5]Chan (2009, p. 264), Owen et al. (2008, p. 254, 255).

[6]Shang (2009, p. 4).

[7]Lin et al. (1998, p. 423).

[8]Owen et al. (2008, p. 240), Berry (2005, p. 133), Yang (2002, p. 170).

[9]Lin et al. (1998, p. 423).

State.[10] The tight control over industries was gradually relaxed after the 1978 Market Reform. SOEs were allowed to retain part of their profits. Nevertheless, because the Market Reform followed a top-down, planned approach,[11] one of the most challenging tasks during the transition was the separation of the administration from the enterprise.[12] By implementing certain economic regulatory policies, governments in all regions are often involved in activities that have anti-competitive effects.[13]

Yang defines three types of administrative monopolies in China: sectorial monopolies, regional monopolies and public utilities.[14] Sectorial monopolies refer to large enterprise groups affiliated with government ministries that may receive favourable treatment, because government departments often play a regulatory role in industries such as nonferrous metal, electronics, shipbuilding, tobacco, and freight transport. Regional monopolies refer to local governments and administrative agencies which may establish trade barriers in order to prevent the flow of goods and services from a particular local region to other regions. Such behaviour is also called local protectionism. Public utility monopolies refer to sectors that are considered as natural monopolies, such as water, power, heat, gas, postal services, telecommunications, civil aviation, and railways. Their monopolistic position is often protected.[15] Although, in general, administrative monopolies include monopolistic conduct by both central and local governments, it is more likely that the central government tends to conduct sectorial monopolies, and local governments are involved in regional monopolies. According to Chan, in the analysis of administrative monopolies, restrictive behaviour by the central government is often excluded, because many scholars perceive such behaviour as implementing a type of national industrial policy.[16] In most cases, administrative monopolies refer to the abusive conduct by local governments which impose territorial restrictions on the free flow of economic resources or tend to protect local enterprises. Administrative monopolies can also refer to the abusive conduct by ministries and departments subordinated to the central government which protects certain industries or sectors by restricting market entry.[17]

To understand the administrative monopoly at regional level, it is important to discuss China's territorially based economic hierarchy. Before the 1978 market reform, the economic structure was decentralized twice. The first decentralization wave was in 1958, after the Third Plenary Session of the Eighth Congress of the Communist Party of China decided to delegate almost all SOEs to the local governments. The SOEs under the control of the central government only accounted for 14% of national total industrial output. Given the coordination failures during the 1958 Great Leap Forward, there was a recentralization trend during the period 1958–1963. The

[10] Lin et al. (1998, p. 423).

[11] Yang (2002, p. 175).

[12] Guo and Hu (2004, p. 272).

[13] Guo and Hu (2004, p. 272).

[14] Yang (2002, p. 172).

[15] Yang (2002, p. 172).

[16] Chan (2009, p. 264).

[17] Guo and Hu (2004, p. 273).

control over SOEs was allocated to the local governments again during the second wave of decentralization in the 1970s; the industrial output of the SOEs controlled by the central government went down to 8% of national production. The reform of the fiscal revenue system decentralized the banking system, and gave great authority to the local governments in setting price levels, establishing firms, making investments, having direct control over land, energy, raw material and other resources, being responsible for local economic development, as well as providing education, improving local infrastructure and other public goods. This decentralization wave aimed at giving local governments incentives to promote economic development. As a consequence, local governments were incentivized to promote economic growth in their own region,[18] and some of them were willing to set up trade barriers to block the inflow of products and services from other regions in order to support the development of SOEs in their own region. Moreover, governments retain their influence in two additional ways; this may also lead to an administrative monopoly. One is industrial associations, also named trade associations, that were created by government ministries after the 1990s. These associations play a very important role in facilitating price stabilization in specific industries[19] and are responsible for market supervision and have to maintain a market environment for fair competition. The second way is establishing affiliate companies under governmental agencies and giving them preferential treatment.[20]

8.3 Anti-competitive Effects of Administrative Monopolies

Both lawyers and economists in China have acknowledged that administrative monopolies create anti-competitive effects, and a few empirical studies have been conducted to measure the efficiency losses that are caused by administrative monopolies. Many have agreed that the most significant effect of administrative monopolies is market fragmentation.[21] The empirical study by Poncet shows that the trade flow between provinces in China decreased significantly from 1987 to 1997. In 1987, consumers purchased products that were produced in the local region 12 times more than those were produced in other provinces. This number increased to 16 in 1992 and 27 in 1997.[22] By applying the Institution-Structure-Conduct-Performance (ISCP) framework, Yu and Yu claimed that market segmentation could be significantly reduced by implementing a successful regional development policy and a cross-region competition policy.[23] For example, between 1985 and 2006, the degree of regional administrative monopoly in eastern provinces decreased more significantly

[18]Saich (2011), Ip and Law (2011, p. 358).

[19]Howell et al. (2009, p. 87).

[20]Owen et al. (2005).

[21]Chan (2009, p. 267), Guo and Hu (2004, p. 277).

[22]Poncet (2003).

[23]Yu and Yu (2011).

than in western provinces.[24] One reason to explain such observations, according to their study, was that the regional development policy implemented during the market reform reduced the level of administrative monopolies in eastern provinces.[25]

In addition to the market fragmentation problem, it was argued that administrative monopolies may impose harm on consumer welfare, because administrative monopolies may incentivize inefficient firms to provide expensive products and services for local consumers, since the efficient ones in other regions are often prohibited from entering the local market.[26] Imposing restrictions on the free movement of economic resources may also lead to allocative inefficiency.[27] The empirical study conducted by Yu and Zhang shows that in the industries of electricity, telecommunications, oil and railway, administrative monopolies cause substantial efficiency losses both at the micro and macro level.[28] Lastly, some commentators have raised the issue that administrative monopolies not only cause economic losses but also generate other social costs, since they may incentivize business operators to engage in rent-seeking activities.[29]

8.4 Chapter 5 of the Anti-monopoly Law

In the earliest competition rules, the Provisional Rules on the Development and Protection of Socialist Competition, Article 6 made it clear that competition must break regional blockades and division. No region or department is allowed to block the market and prevent the inflow of products from other provisions or departments. Relevant departments in industry, transportation, finance and trade, must revise their current rules and regulations on impeding competition, and it is illegal to apply administrative measures to block the circulation of products. Starting from the early 1990s, several administrative rules have been promulgated to break down the trade barriers established by local governments. The earliest rule on administrative monopoly was promulgated by the State Council in November 1990,[30] named as the Notice Concerning the Breaking of Local Market Blockades and Further Encouraging Commodity Circulation. It targets breaking down trade barriers established by the local governments. In December 1993, the SAIC promulgated the Certain Regulations on Prohibiting Anti-competitive Practices of Public Enterprises.[31] This regulation focuses on the

[24] Yu and Yu (2011, p. 94).

[25] Yu and Yu (2011, p. 94).

[26] Chan (2009, p. 267), Yang (2002, p. 172).

[27] Yu and Yu (2011, p. 79), Chen and Zhu (2012, 2014, p. 203).

[28] Yu and Zhang (2013, p. 216).

[29] Chan (2009, p. 267), Ding (2011, p. 119), Wang (2014, p. 6).

[30] Mehra and Meng (2009).

[31] Guanyu Jinzhi Gonggong Qiye Xianzhi Jingzheng Xingwei De Ruogan Guiding (关于禁止公共企业限制竞争行为的若干规定) [Certain Regulations on Prohibiting Anti-competitive Practices

abuse of market position of public utility companies. In addition, this administrative provision emphasizes the problem of administrative monopoly. In April 2001, after the SAIC was upgraded to a ministerial level,[32] the State Council enacted the Provisions of the State Council on Prohibiting Regional Blockades in Market Economic Activities.[33] This provision specifically focuses on the problem of regional protectionism, although it was critically argued that the implementation of these rules has been rather ineffective.[34] In the same month, the State Council enacted another decision on rectifying and standardizing the order in the market economy.[35] Administrative monopoly and local protectionism are both prohibited in the Article 11 of this decision. It is worth mentioning that in addition to the anti-monopoly regulations, administrative monopoly is also addressed by the Administrative Reconsideration Law[36] and by the Administrative Procedure Law.[37]

During the legislative process of the AML, the question of whether prohibiting administrative monopolies should be taken as one of the objectives of the AML has been intensively debated.[38] Proponents have argued that given the substantial social harm that administrative monopolies create, a chapter on prohibiting administrative monopolies is an "indispensable part" of the AML.[39] Moreover, by including provisions on prohibiting abuse of administrative power, the AML could contribute to the political regulatory reform by drawing attention from government officials on anti-monopoly issues.[40] Opponents claimed that administrative monopolies would be better dealt with by administrative law or constitutional law, rather than a competition law.[41] For example, Huang Yong, an advisory expert on the AML, argued that the ultimate solution for administrative monopolies is economic and political reform. Given the difficulty and the long process of such reform, adopting provisions

---

of Public Enterprises] (promulgated by the State Administration for Industry and Commerce, 24 December 1993, effective on 24 December 1993).

[32]Mehra and Meng (2009).

[33]Guowuyuan Guanyu Jinzhi Zai Shichang Jingji Huodong Zhong Shixing Diqu Fengsuo De Guiding (国务院关于禁止在市场经济活动中实行地区封锁的规定) [Provisions of the State Council on Prohibiting Regional Blockade in Market Economic Activities] (promulgated by the State Council on 21 April 2001, effective on 21 April 2001).

[34]Owen et al. (2008, p. 235).

[35]Guowuyuan Guanyu Zhengdun He Guifan Shichang Jingji Zhixu De Jueding (国务院关于整顿和规范市场经济秩序的决定) [Decisions of the State Council on Rectifying and Standardizing the Order in the Market Economy] (promulgated by the State Council on 27 April 2001, effective on 27 April 2001).

[36]Zhonghua Renmin Gongheguo Xingzheng Fuyi Fa (中华人民共和国行政复议法) [Administrative Reconsideration Law of the People's Republic of China] (promulgated by the National People's Congress, 29 April 1999, effective on 1 October 1999, revised on 27 August 2009).

[37]Zhonghua Renmin Gongheguo Xingzheng Susong Fa (中华人民共和国行政诉讼法) [Administrative Procedure Law of the People's Republic of China] (promulgated by the National People's Congress, 4 April 1989, effective on 1 October 1990).

[38]Chan (2009, p. 271).

[39]Wang (2008, p. 12).

[40]Wang (2004, p. 294).

[41]Chan (2009, p. 275), Li and Wu (2006, pp. 73–75).

restraining administrative power in the AML may be only a "second-best option".[42] Jung and Hao argued that the goal of tackling monopolistic behaviour by administrative power is "far-reaching" and "ambitious".[43] Some foreign scholars expressed similar views. For example, Fox argued that the abusive administrative restraints on economy should be dealt with by other legal instruments rather than an antitrust law.[44] Haley expressed his worries of applying an antitrust model that originated in the US and Europe to developing countries, because none of these models were designed to deal with the state power or need for state actions to create "conditions for effective market competition".[45]

In 2002, the drafting team of the AML, consisting of staff members from the State Economic and Trade Commission (SETC),[46] submitted a draft version to the Legislative Affairs Office of the State Council.[47] The 2002 Draft Anti-Monopoly Law included provisions prohibiting administrative monopolies in the Chap. 5, and the enforcement competence of these provisions is shared by "administrative authority at the higher level", and the Anti-Monopoly Management Body of the State Council.[48] The 2002 draft clearly reveals the concern of establishing a legislative framework to tackle the administrative obstacles for a competitive market.[49] However, the argument opposing the inclusion of administrative monopolies in the draft gained wide support during the legislative process[50] and the chapter on prohibiting administrative monopolies was completely deleted in the draft of the AML that was published in November 2005.[51] Harris argued there were two major reasons for excluding provisions against administrative monopolies: one is that, as it was argued by many commentators at that time, administrative monopolies might be better dealt with by a separate legal instrument or through regulatory reforms in the future, rather than by an anti-monopoly law. Another major issue is that administrative monopolies are often conducted to support the development of SOEs, and including provisions combating administrative monopolies would receive significant political pressure.[52]

[42] Huang (2008, p. 122).

[43] Jung and Hao (2003, p. 134).

[44] Fox (2008, p. 173).

[45] Haley (2004, p. 277).

[46] In the reform of government structure in 2003, the SETC was abolished. Meanwhile, the MOFCOM was established and was responsible for many of the duties of the former Ministry of Foreign Trade and Economic Cooperation (MOFTEC) and the SETC. Since then, the Ministry of Commerce (MOFCOM) participated in the drafting of the AML. See Owen et al. (2008, p. 260).

[47] Harris (2006, p. 178), Wang (2004, p. 285).

[48] Harris (2006, p. 178), Wang (2004, p. 290).

[49] Jung and Hao (2003, p. 108).

[50] Huang (2008, p. 131).

[51] New Changes on the Draft of the AML—Provisions on Prohibiting Administrative Monopolies were deleted (反垄断法面临新变数,禁止行政性垄断条款被删除), *China News*, 4 April 2006, available at http://www.chinanews.com/news/2006/2006-04-04/8/712394.shtml (accessed 30 March 2020).

[52] Harris (2006, p. 214).

However, after receiving criticisms, in the draft published in June 2006 this chapter was reinserted[53] and kept until the final version of the AML.

In the Chap. 1(General Provisions) of the AML, Article 8 states that it was prohibited for any administrative organ to abuse its administrative power to eliminate or restrict competition.[54] Chapter 5 (Article 32–37) of the AML prohibits abuse of administrative power to eliminate or restrict competition.[55] Administrative organs or organizations are not allowed to abuse administrative power to prevent entities and individuals from operating, purchasing, or using certain commodities provided by business operators selected by these organs (Article 32). Administrative agencies or organizations are not allowed to create trade barriers between regions through imposing discriminative terms, technical requirements, exerting administrative licensing, or setting barriers on the free distribution of commodities between regions (Article 33). Administrative organs or organizations are not allowed to abuse administrative power by imposing restrictions on business operators from outside regions participating in the tendering and bidding activities in the local region (Article 34). Governmental agencies should not impose restrictions on business operators from other regions on the investment in or set up of branches in the local region through granting unequal treatment for outside business operators compared with local operators (Article 35). Administrative agencies are not allowed to abuse administrative power to urge business operators to conduct monopolistic activities (Article 36), or to issue provisions to eliminate or restrict competition between regions (Article 37).

The issue of how Chap. 5 of the AML is enforced is dealt with by Article 51 of the AML. Article 51 states that when the abuse of administrative power occurs, "the higher authority shall order it to make correction, and impose punishments on the directly liable person(s)-in-charge and other directly liable persons." According to Article 51, the enforcement competence of the anti-monopoly authority with respect to administrative monopoly is that it may provide suggestions for the relevant superior authority regarding how to handle the case. From Article 51 of the AML, it seems that the enforcement competence of administrative monopoly remains the same as the previous legal rules and administrative regulations, that is, the "higher authority".[56] From this article, it also remains unclear how individuals or firms can file administrative lawsuits if they suffer a loss due to the anti-competitive conduct of administrative organs.[57] Given the weak enforcement of the competition rules before the AML prohibited administrative monopolies, commentators have expressed the worry that administrative monopolies may not be effectively restrained even if it is included in an anti-monopoly law.[58] For example, Fox argued that the enforcement powers against administrative abuses are "so weak as to nearly undermine

[53]Owen et al. (2008, p. 255).

[54]Article 8 of the AML.

[55]Chapter 5 of the AML.

[56]Chan (2009, p. 270), Wang (2014, p. 7).

[57]Sun (2010), Ip and Law (2011, p. 365).

[58]Howell et al. (2009, p. 84), Huang (2008, p. 131), Wang (2007).

the effort".[59] Huang stated that the provisions on administrative monopolies are "so mild that no meaningful enforcement can be foreseen".[60] In the 2020 draft revision of the AML, the "higher authority" still holds the enforcement competence of administrative monopoly.[61]

8.5 The Fair Competition Review System

Back to 2013, the Decision of the Central Committee of the CPC on Several Important Issues Concerning Comprehensively Deepening the Reform[62] states that a unified, competitive economic market system has to be established and the market plays a decisive role in resource allocation. In 2015, the State Council issued Several Opinions of the CPC Central Committee and the State Council on Deepening the Reform of Systems and Mechanisms to Accelerate the Implementation of Innovation-driven Development Strategies[63] and to facilitate the development of fair competition review. This Notice was followed by the Notice of the State Council on Approving and Forwarding the Opinions of NDRC on the Pivotal Work of Deepening the Reform of the Economic System in 2015[64] which stresses the importance of a fair competition review system to coordinate competition policy and industrial policy. In June 2015, the State Council issued the Opinions of the State Council on Several Policies and Measures for Vigorously Advancing the Popular Entrepreneurship and

[59] Fox (2008, p. 173).

[60] Huang (2008, p. 131).

[61] Article 51 of the AML is changed to Article 58 of the 2020 draft revision of the AML: Where an administrative organ and organizations authorized by laws and regulations with the function of managing public affairs abuse administrative power and impose exclusions or restrictions on competition, the anti-monopoly law enforcement agency may order corrections and make recommendations to relevant higher authorities. Directly responsible persons shall be punished by higher authorities in accordance with law. Administrative agencies and organizations shall complete the corrective actions within the time prescribed by the competition enforcement agency, and report the relevant corrections in writing.

[62] Zhonggong Zhongyang Guanyu Quanmian Shenhua Gaige Ruogan Zhongda Wenti De Jueding (中共中央关于全面深化改革若干重大问题的决定) [Decision of the Central Committee of the Communist Party of China on Several Important Issues Concerning Comprehensively Deepening the Reform].

[63] Zhonggong Zhongyang Guowuyuan Guanyu Shenhua Tizhi Gaige Jiakuai Shishi Chuangxin Qudong Fazhan Zhanlve De Ruogan Yijian (中共中央, 国务院关于深化体制改革加快实施创新驱动发展战略的若干意见) [Several Opinions of the CPC Central Committee and the State Council on Deepening the Reform of Systems and Mechanisms to Accelerate the Implementation of Innovation-driven Development Strategies].

[64] Guowuyuan Pizhuan Fazhan Gaigewei Guanyu 2015 nian Shenhua Jingji Tizhi Gaige Zhongdian Gongzuo Yijian de Tongzhi (国务院批转发展改革委关于2015年深化经济体制改革重点工作意见) [Notice of the State Council on Approving and Forwarding the Opinions of the National Development and Reform Commission on the Pivotal Work of Deepening the Reform of the Economic System in 2015].

Innovation,[65] which proposed that the fair competition review system has to be developed within a short period. In October 2015, the CPC Central Committee and the State Council issued Several Opinions of the CPC Central Committee and the State Council on Advancing the Pricing Mechanism Reform,[66] to implement the fair competition review system and to coordinate competition policy and other industrial policy. The State Council issued the Opinions on Establishing Fair Competition Review in the Development of a Market System on June 14, 2016.[67] The Opinion marks the establishment of the fair competition review system. It distinguishes two types of policies that should be reviewed.[68] To comply with this provision, local governments, including Hubei, Jiangsu,[69] Hunan, Hebei,[70] Liaoning,[71] Beijing,[72]

---

[65]Guowuyuan Guanyu Dali Tuijin Dazhong Chuangye Wanzhong Chuangxin Ruogan Zhengce Cuoshi De Yijian (国务院关于大力推进大众创业万众创新若干政策措施的意见) [Opinions of the State Council on Several Policies and Measures for Vigorously Advancing the Popular Entrepreneurship and Innovation] issued by the State Council on June 11, 2015.

[66]Zhonggong Zhongyang Guowuyuan Guanyu Tuijin Jiage Jizhi Gaige De Ruogan Yijian (中共中央、国务院关于推进价格机制改革的若干意见) [Several Opinions of the CPC Central Committee and the State Council on Advancing the Pricing Mechanism Reform], issued on October 12, 2015.

[67]Guowuyuan Guanyu Zai Shichang tixi Jianshe Zhong Jianli Gongping Jingzheng Shencha Zhidu de Yijian (国务院关于在市场体系建设中建立公平竞争审查制度的意见) [Opinions of the State Council on Establishing A Fair Competition Examination System in the Building of the Market System] issued by the State Council on June 1, 2016.

[68]The Opinions divides the review objects into two categories: the first category is the administrative regulations and other policy measures made by administrative agencies on market access, industrial development, investment, bidding and tendering, government procurement, qualification standards and other policy measures related to the economic activities of market entities; the other category is administrative regulations, policy measures and local regulations formulated by the State Council.

[69]Jiangsusheng Gongping Jingzheng Shencha Zhidu Shishi Yijian (江苏省公平竞争审查制度实施意见) [Opinions on the Implementation of the Fair Competition Review System in Jiangsu Province], issued on August 22, 2016.

[70]Hebeisheng Guanyu Zai Shichang Tixi Jianshe Zhong Jianli Gongping Jingzheng Shencha Zhidu De Shishi Yijian (河北省关于在市场体系建设中建立公平竞争审查制度的实施意见) [Implementation Opinions of Hebei Province on Establishing a Fair Competition Review System in the Construction of the Market System] issued on September 22, 2016. Details *see* Notice on Implementing Fair Competition System in the Market Development has been issued by Hubei Province on December 1, 2016 (省人民政府关于在市场体系建设中建立公平竞争审查制度的通知) available at http://gkml.hubei.gov.cn/auto5472/auto5473/201612/t20161215_928465.html.

[71]Liaoningsheng Renmin Zhengfu Guanyu Zai Shichang Tixi Jianshe Zhong Jianli Gongping Jingzheng Shencha Zhidu De Shishi Yijian (辽宁省人民政府关于在市场体系建设中建立公平竞争审查制度的实施意见) [Implementation Opinions of the People's Government of Liaoning on Establishing a Fair Competition Review System in the Construction of the Market System], issued on October 9, 2016.

[72]Beijingshi Renminzhengfu Guanyu Zai Shichang Tixi Jianshe Zhong Jianli Gongping Jingzheng Shengcha Zhidu De Shishiyijian (北京市人民政府关于在市场体系建设中建立公平竞争审查

Ningxia, Guangdong,[73] Guizhou and Shaanxi have issued their respective provisions to facilitate implementation. On April 8, 2016, SAIC published The Announcement on Prominent Issues Concerning the Acts of Public Utility Enterprises to Restrain Competition and Practice Monopoly, and announced that from June to October 2016, SAIC will take a special enforcement action nationwide to solve restrictive behaviour by public utility enterprises.[74] In April and May 2016, SAIC and local branches conducted a national campaign targeting the anti-competitive activities by public utilities, and 289 antitrust investigations have been launched and 59 of them have been concluded.[75] In Sichuan province, between April and June of 2016, the Sichuan AIC required public entities to self-correct monopolistic behaviour in industries including supply of water, electricity, gas, and public transportation. In the enforcement action, 59 cases were reported and 24 of them were closed.[76]

In July 2016, the NDRC published the Notice on the Working Procedure of Implementing the 'Opinions on Establishing A Fair Competition Review System in the Construction of the Market System'.[77] The Notice states that the agency that is responsible for drafting industrial policies will be responsible for fair competition review and is required to issue written review conclusions. Seeing the limitations of self-review and self-correct the industrial policies, in December 2016, the State Council issued the Letter on Approval of the Establishment of the Inter-Ministerial Joint Meeting System for Fair Competition Review,[78] and agreed to establish a co-chair

制度的实施意见) [Implementation Opinions of the Beijing Municipal People's Government on Establishing a Fair Competition Review System in the Construction of the Market System], issued on October 21, 2016.

[73]Guangdongsheng Renmin Zhengfu Zhuanfa Guowuyuan Guanyu Zai Shichang Tixi Jianshe Zhong Jianli Gongping Jingzheng Shencha Zhidu Yijian de Tongzhi (广东省人民政府转发国务院关于在市场体系建设中建立公平竞争审查制度意见的通知) [Guangdong Provincial People's Government Forwarded the State Council's Notice on Establishing a Fair Competition Review System in the Construction of the Market System], issued on July 25, 2016.

[74]Guojia Gongshang Zongju Guanyu Gongyong Qiye Xianzhi Jingzheng He Longduan Xingwei Tuchu Wenti De Gonggao (国家工商总局关于公用企业限制竞争和垄断行为突出问题的公告) [Announcement of the SAIC on Prominent Issues Concerning the Acts of Public Utility Enterprises to Restrain Competition and Practice Monopoly], issued on April 1, 2016.

[75]China Competition Bulletin, Edition 42, May/June 2016, p. 10.

[76]Sichuan Gongshang Jizhong Zhengzhi Gongyong Qiye Xianzhi Jingzheng He Longduan Xingwei (四川工商集中整治公用企业限制竞争和垄断行为) [Sichuan AIC Concentrates on Regulating Restricting Competition and Monopoly by Public Utility Enterprises] available at http://www.xinhuanet.com//politics/2016-04/14/c_128895051.htm.

[77]Guanyu Guanche Luoshi Guanyu Zai Shichang Tixi Jianshe Zhong Jianli Gongping Jingzheng Shencha Zhidu De Yijian Weinei Gongzuo Chengxu de Tongzhi (关于贯彻落实<关于在市场体系建设中建立公平竞争审查制度的意见>委内工作程序的通知) [The Working Procedure of Implementing the 'Opinions on Establishing A Fair Competition Review System in the Construction of the Market System'], issued on July 27, 2016.

[78]Guowuyuan Bangongting Guanyu Tongyi Jianli Gongping Jingzheng Shencha Gongzuo Buji Lianxi Huiyi Zhidu De Han (国务院办公厅关于同意建立公平竞争审查工作部际联席会议制度的函) [Letter of the General Office of the State Council on Approval of the Establishment of the Inter-ministerial Joint Meeting System for Fair Competition Review] issued on December 22, 2016.

meeting system with the participation of 28 ministries including NDRC, the Ministry of Education, the Ministry of Science and Technology, the Ministry of Industry and Information Technology, the Ministry of Civil Affairs, the Ministry of Finance, the Ministry of Land and Resources, the Ministry of Environmental Protection, the Ministry of Housing and Urban-Rural Development, the Ministry of Transport, the Ministry of Water Resources, the Ministry of Agriculture, the Ministry of Commerce, the Ministry of Culture, the National Health and Family Planning Commission, the People's Bank of China, the State-Owned Assets Supervision and Administration Commission, the State Administration of Taxation, the State Administration for Industry and Commerce, the General Administration of Quality Supervision, Inspection and Quarantine, the State Administration of Press, Publication, Radio, Film and Television, the China Food and Drug Administration, the State Intellectual Property Office, the Legislative Affairs Office of the State Council, the China Banking Regulatory Commission, the China Securities Regulatory Commission, the China Insurance Regulatory Commission, and the National Energy Administration. The co-chair meeting system is to provide additional reviews by other agencies under the guidance of State Council. In October 2017, the NDRC, Ministry of Finance, Ministry of Commerce, SAIC, the Legislative Office of the State Council published the Detailed Rules for the Implementation of the Fair Competition System.[79]

In January 2019, the new competition agency SAMR published the Regulations on Prohibiting of Abuse of Administrative Power Eliminating or Restricting Competition (draft version).[80] The regulation has 31 articles and elaborated the jurisdiction, the definition, investigation and results of investigation due to abuse of administrative power restricting competition. In the 2020 draft revision of the AML, Article 37 of the AML was revised to Article 42, and it made clear that administrative agencies and organizations authorized by laws and regulations with the function of managing public affairs shall not abuse administrative power and formulate provisions containing contents that excludes or restricts competition. Administrative agencies and organizations should conduct fair competition review in accordance with relevant state regulations when formulating regulations that involve market-driven economic activities.

8.6 Cases

The case analysis mentioned in Chap. 6 has briefly introduced the monopolistic conduct by public enterprises in China. Article 6 of the Anti-unfair Competition Law in 1993 prohibits public enterprises with a market dominant position from preventing

[79]Guojia Fagaiwei Caizhengbu Shangwubu Deng Guanyu Yinfa Gongping Jingzheng Shencha Zhidu Shishi Xize (zanxing) De Tongzhi (国家发改委、财政部、商务部等关于印发《公平竞争审查制度实施细则(暂行)》的通知) [Notice of the NDRC, the Ministry of Finance, the Ministry of Commerce and Other Departments on Issuing the Detailed Rules for the Implementation of the Fair Competition System (for Interim Implementation) issued on October 23, 2017.

[80]Zhan et al. (2018).

consumers from purchasing its own products to prevent competition between the public enterprises and other business operators.[81] Articles 11 and 12 of the Anti-unfair Competition Law prohibits monopolistic behaviour in particular predatory pricing and imposing unfair trading conditions. In Article 18 of the Price Law published in 1998, it stipulates that for the prices set by public enterprises, the government may impose government guiding prices or government-set prices. Article 18 of the Price law prohibits predatory pricing and price discrimination. Articles 39–41 of the Price Law sets legal liabilities for violations on setting prices. Article 26 of the Electricity Law[82] prohibits the refusal to trade in electricity supply enterprises. Telecommunication Regulation[83] prohibits refusal to trade, trading with restrictive conditions, charging extra prices, discriminatory trading and predatory pricing.

Shaanxi Price Bureau investigated against Yulin Municipal Bureau of Environmental Protection on administrative monopoly in October 2016. The Yulin Municipal Bureau of Environmental Protection violated the Article 37 of the AML on administrative monopolies when requiring lower-level environmental protection agencies, insurance agencies and companies to recognize Changcheng Insurance Brokers as the only supplier for environmental pollution liability insurance services for enterprises. Shaanxi Price Bureau concluded that the monopolistic practice restricted the market for environmental pollution insurance within Yulin region and the unlawful documents should be abolished. The investigation enhanced the understanding of the fair competition mechanisms for the municipal government officials.

In July 2016, Hubei Price Bureau imposed fines of 2% (on two suppliers) and 4% (on three suppliers) of their previous revenue on five piped natural gas suppliers for violating Article 17 of the AML on charging unfairly high prices and abused dominant position. The Price Bureau found that the five suppliers charged high fees

---

[81]Zhonghua Renmin Gongheguo Fan Buzhengdang Jingzheng Fa (中华人民共和国反不正当竞争法) [Anti-unfair Competition Law of the People's Republic of China], issued on September 2, 1993 and effective on December 1, 1993. Article 6: Public Utilities or other businesses legally in a monopolistic position shall not require others to purchase commodities from businesses designated by them in order to elbow out the fair competition of others. Translation adopted from en.pkulaw.cn. Note that this article has been removed in the 2019 amendment.

[82]Zhonghua Renmin Gonghe Guo Dianli Fa (2018 Xiuzheng) 中华人民共和国电力法 (2018修正) [Electric Power Law of the People's Republic of China (2018 Amendment), Article 26: The power-supply enterprise in any electricity service area shall be obligated to supply electricity to the consumers within its service area in accordance with the regulations of the State. It may not, in violation of State regulations, refuse to supply electricity to any unit or individual within their service area that has applied for power supply.

[83]Zhonghua Renmin Gongheguo Dianxin Tiaoli (中华人民共和国电信条例 (2016修订)) [Telecommunication Regulation of the People's Republic of China (2016 Revision)], issued by the State Council on February 6, 2016. Article 40: The telecommunications service providers shall not do any of the following acts when providing services: (1) Limit, in any form, the users to any service appointed by themselves, (2) Request the users to buy and use certain telecommunications terminal equipment appointed by themselves or do not allow the users to use their own access-licensed telecommunications terminal equipment; (3) Reject to provide, delay or terminate services without reasons; (4) Fail to honour their public promises or make false or misunderstanding PR efforts for their services; (5) Create difficulties to or retaliate on purpose against the users who complaint their services. Translation adopted from en.pkulaw.cn.

because they obtained dominant positions after signing piped natural gas infrastructure installation contracts with non-residential users. The contract limited the choices of those users on design, construction and management of the infrastructure and the purchase of construction materials.[84]

In April 2014, Chongqing AIC imposed fines on Chongqing Gas for breach of the AML on abuse of dominant position in the gas the supply market of seven districts in Chongqing. Chongqing Gas unilaterally decided upon the terms on calculating the amount charged for non-residential customers and required them to pay by a "correction factor" (based on the reading of gas meter, gas pipeline pressure and temperature) but not actual gas consumption. Chongqing AIC required it to stop the illegal conduct and imposed a fine of RMB 1,794,000.[85]

On November 2, 2015, NDRC issued its decision on the abuse of administrative power on centralized medicine procurement by Sichuan and Zhejiang Province Health and Family Planning Commission (HFPC). By issuing official notices, Sichuan HFPC restricted the percentage of medicine that are procured by local medical institutions, and non-local medicines were prevented from entering the local market. Those who failed to comply with the quota would be sanctioned. In a similar manner, HFPC in Zhejiang province also created entry barriers for non-local medicine firms and protected the local market through administrative powers. NDRC held that the behaviour of HFPC in Zhejiang and Sichuan provinces has violated articles 32–34 of the AML and requested them to rectify their monopolistic conduct.[86] This decision followed NDRC's decision three months earlier on Bengbu Municipal Health and Family Planning Commission. NDRC held that Bengbu Health Commission abused its administrative power in drug procecurement. In one of the three tender notices that were issued by the Bengbu Health Commission for 30 types of drugs for hospitals and public healthcare institutions in Bengbu, the Commission specified one producer and refused to let other producers to participate in the tender. In the other two notices, the Commission set financial requirements for non-local businesses, which established entry barriers for non-local bidders. The NDRC held that the Commission has violated Articles 32, 34 and 37 of the AML. On August 17, 2015 NDRC issued a letter to Anhui Provincial Government to request Bengbu Health Commission to rectify its conduct and to eliminate the barriers for non-local businesses. Anhui Provincial Government was requested to respond within two weeks.[87]

In 2017, Shenzhen Municipal Health and Family Planning Commission appointed a Group Purchasing Organization (GPO) in charge of drug procurement services for public hostpitals. All public hospitals had to purchase essential drugs from the GPO. Drug producers could not sell drugs through any other platforms, such as other qualified GPOs, province-level centralized drug procurement platforms, and all distributors should be selected by the GPO. Guangdong DRC found that such conduct breached Articles 8 and 32 of the AML, and required Shenzhen Municipal Health

[84]Fels et al. (2016b, p. 3).

[85]Fels et al. (2015a, p. 5).

[86]Cao et al. (2016).

[87]Fels et al. (2015c, p. 2).

and Family Planning Commission to rectify its conduct in accordance with the fair competition review system and allow public hosptials to purchase drugs through other procurement platforms.[88] Similarly, Shandong AIC found that Guanxian Health and Family Planning Bureau selected two drug distributors for public hospitals in specific distribution areas in the county. Shandong AIC issued a letter to the Liaocheng Guanxian People's Government in April 2017, and the Government replied in a rectification report that it had ordered Guanxian Health and Family Bureau to rectify its behaviour.[89]

Car Maintenance in Wuwei was a case of price-fixing agreements organized by government agencies. Gansu DRC imposed fines on 22 car maintenance businesses in Wuwei for fixing car maintenance service fees by signing a 'self-discipline convention' through Wuwei Maintenance Industry Association. The agreement fixed secondary car maintenance service fees and the convention was carried out from May 2010 to December 2014. Gansu DRC imposed a total fine of 2% of the secondary car maintenance service revenue in 2013, amounting to RMB 90,000 on 22 car maintenance businesses.[90] In particular, the convention was supported by government agencies. On November 5, 2015, the Gansu DRC issued a recommendation letter to the Wuwei Transport Bureau with regard to the practice of Wuwei Road Transport Management Bureau and related road transport industry associations. Gansu DRC recommendation clarified that the administrative actions on allowing the transport industry association to reach self-discipline convention has breached Article 36 of the AML and should be rectified. Gansu DRC requested Wuwei Transport Bureau to report back on the rectification measures by November 30, 2015.[91] On November 5, 2015, Gansu DRC also published the decision of an anti-administrative monopoly advisory, and requested Wuwei Municipal Transport Bureau (WTB) to rectify their behaviour on excluding or restricting competition by abuse of administrative power. Gansu DRC clarified that the joint convention with participation by 24 vehicle repair and maintenance service providers was signed from April 21 to May 3, 2010 and the agreement fixed the vehicle repair and maintenance fees in the Class-II vehicle repair market, and established the unified service delivery system. Such an agreement had been supported by the WTB, and on November 8, 2010, WTB forced the implementation of the agreement by issuing a series of administrative notes to prevent competition on Class-II vehicle repair market. Gansu DRC announced that WTB's behaviour violated the AML and the Class-II vehicle repairs and maintenance fee charges should be refunded.[92]

Gansu DRC investigated administrative monopoly with GPS platforms was a similar case. Gansu DRC issued letter on December 1, 2015 to Gansu Transport Department on the administrative monopolies when adopting the GPS platform. After the Satellite Navigation and Communications Co. Ltd (SatNav) signed agreement with

---

[88] Fels et al. (2017b, p. 5).

[89] Fels et al. (2017a, p. 5).

[90] http://www.gsdrc.gov.cn/content/2015-11/33425.html.

[91] Fels et al. (2016a, p. 8).

[92] Cao et al. (2016).

the Gansu Transport Management Bureau on the GPS service platform, the Bureau issued a Notice to lower level authorities, requesting the implementation of a GPS platform across the province, and it should be installed on 70,000 heavy-duty trucks and could access data from the GPS device, in particular, the Notice required local authorities to select SatNav as the provider for funding, operating and maintaining the GPS system, and price for installation should not exceed RMB 2,600/unit. Although the Notice was abolished and replaced by another notice issued on May 28, 2015 with an announcement of 14 GPS suppliers, local authorities implemented the requirement and installed GPS platforms from SatNav. Gansu DRC defined the case as an administrative monopoly enforced by Gansu Transport Management Bureau and its local authorities, which had violated Articles 8, 32 and 37 of the AML. In the letter, Gansu DRC asked the Gansu Transport Department to allow full competition in the choices of accessing monitoring platforms and eliminating the restrictions, as well as the fixed prices on GPS devices. Local transport management departments should rectify their conduct and report the process of actions in 30 days.[93]

PetroChina Kunlun Gas was a case of public enterprises abused dominant position. Jiangsu AIC found that Suqian Petro China Kunlun Gas forced property developers to install its own gas pipeline in new residential areas in Suqian. Jiangsu AIC concluded that PetroChina Kunlun Gas held a dominant position in the relevant market of piped natural gas supply in urban areas in Suqian. The former Suqian Construction Bureau granted Petro China Kunlun Gas the exclusive franchise rights for supplying piped natural gas in urban areas of Suqian. To obtain the pipeline maintenance service, property developers also had to install natural gas pipelines and other construction materials from Petro China Kunlun Gas, and the standard price charged per household was RMB 2500. Jiangsu AIC found that Petro China KunlunGas violated Article 17 of the AML, and it was fined RMB 25 million (5% of the previous year revenue).[94]

In December 2016, Jiangsu AIC found that Wujiang Huayan Water held a dominant position in water supply and related construction and material services for residential building. The Jiangsu AIC concluded that Huayan Water was the only water supplier in Wujiang, so it held a dominant position. The trading conditions with real estate developers were unreasonable and requesting real estate developers to contract with Huayan Water's subsidiary on water construction services had eliminated fair competition in the market of water supply construction and equipment. Because Huayan Water did not show an intention of rectifying its behaviour, Jiangsu AIC imposed a total fine of 21.4 million (7% of the sales revenues in 2014) on Huayan Water.[95] In a similar case, in December 2013, the Guangdong AIC found that Huizhou Daya Bay Yiyuan Water Company held a dominant position for water supply, and since December 2009, it required property developers to contract with Yiyuan on both temporary water supply services and residential water meter projects. Yiyuan would stop providing water if the property developers refused to implement the contract. The Guangdong AIC concluded that those terms affected competition,

[93]Fels et al. (2016a, p. 15).

[94]Fels et al. (2017b, p. 5).

[95]Fels et al. (2017b, p. 4).

and confiscated illegal gains of RMB 860, 239.09, and imposed a fine of RMB 2,363,597.45.

On June 2, 2015, NDRC published the decision made by Yunnan DRC on the abuse of administrative power by Yunnan Province Communications Authority for organizing meetings between local branches of China Mobile, China Telecom, China Unicom and China Tietong. An agreement was signed at the end of 2009 which included terms on the content, amount, and frequency of discounts offered to consumers, and specified the value and types of offers and rewards programs. Those companies failing to comply with the agreement would be reported to the Yunnan Province Communications Authority and would be asked to rectify the conduct. Yunnan DRC held that the four telecommunications compete with each other through offering discounts and reward programs to consumers. The agreement significantly restricted and eliminated competition, and it violated Articles 8 and 36 of the AML. Yunnan DRC imposed a total fine of RMB 13.18 million on four telecommunication companies, and required the Yunnan Province Communications Authority to rectify its activity and has reported the case to NDRC, who communicated with the Ministry of Industry and Information Technology (MIIT). MIIT has replied that it will require provincial level authorities to strengthen the efforts to comply with the AML.[96]

In August 2016, the Inner Mongolia AIC found that the Inner Mongolia Chifeng Salt Company (Chifeng Salt, a SOE) held a dominant position in the wholesale supply of edible salt in Chifeng. Because of regulatory restrictions, edible salt retailers could not purchase or sell salt from across territorial boundaries. Chifeng Salt held exclusive control of procurement and sale of salt in Chifeng. In September 2014, Chifeng Salt supplied with retailers different types of salt based on their territorial location, and in some areas, Chifeng salt stopped supplying solar salt and pickling salt. The Inner Mongolia AIC found that Chifeng Salt had engaged in discriminatory treatment and had abused its dominant position. Chifeng Salt argued that the changes in salt supply was because of the government edible salt reserve requirement, and salt producers stopped producing a type of salt, and it was out of stock. It supplied solar salt because those areas had suffered natural disasters. Those arguments were not accepted by the Inner Mongolia AIC and it concluded that the behaviour has violated Article 17(1)(6) of the AML. The Inner Mongolia AIC confiscated illegal gains of RMB 2 million and imposed a fine of RMB 1 million.

8.7 Conclusions

Administrative monopolies in China refer to monopolistic behavior supported by government or regulatory agencies at both central and regional levels. The central government protects specific sectors and local governments exert administrative power over enterprises within the region and protect profits of these enterprises by creating market barriers and the problem of local protectionism could be explained

[96]Fels et al. (2015b, p. 2).

by the economically decentralized structure after the reform of fiscal revenue system. Lawyers and economists have acknowledged the anti-competitive effects of administrative monopolies, and how to investigate and prohibit monopolistic behaviour by administrative agencies was intensively debated during the legislative history of the AML. After the AML came into force, commentators have criticized the weak enforcement of Chap. 5 of the AML. Starting from 2013, the CPC Central Committee and the State Council have issued opinions on establishing a fair competition review system to effectively coordinate competition policy and industrial policy. The cases mentioned in this chapter show a more effective enforcement of prohibiting monopolistic conduct by public enterprises after the fair competition review system was established, and indicates a positive prospect on dealing with administrative monopolies.

References

Berry, J. A. (2005). Anti-monopoly law in China: A socialist market economy wrestles with its antitrust regime. *International Law and Management Review, 2,* 129–152.

Cao, M., Qin, Y., Chen, Z., Gu, T., Hou, H., Hong, L., Jin, M. & Xu, J. (2016, January). *Competition Law Bulletin*. Zhong Lun Law Firm Antitrust Practice Group, (12).

Chan, G. Y. M. (2009). Administrative monopoly and the anti-monopoly law: An examination of the debate in China. *Journal of Contemporary China, 18*(59), 263–283.

Chen, L., & Zhu, W. (2012). The economic performance of regional administrative monopoly: An empirical research based on the instrumental variable method (中国地区性行政垄断与区域经济绩效—基于工具变量法的实证研究). *Comparative Economic and Social Systems (经济社会体制比较), 4,* 195–204.

Chen, L., & Zhu, W. (2014). Causes and governance of regional administrative monopoly (中国地区性行政垄断的成因与治理). *Journal of Systems and Management (系统管理学报), 23*(2), 229–237.

Ding, Q. (2011). Research on the formation and reformation of administrative monopoly (行政垄断的形成机制及改革思路研究). *Industrial Economic Review (产经评论), 2011*(3), 119–132.

Fels, A., Wang, X., Ng, W., & Emch, A. (Eds.). (2015a, January/February). *China competition bulletin* (35th ed.). A Publication of the Competition Law & Economics Network at Melbourne Law School, University of Melbourne.

Fels, A., Wang, X., Ng, W., & Emch, A. (Eds.). (2015b, May/June). *China competition bulletin* (37th ed.). A Publication of the Competition Law & Economics Network at Melbourne Law School, University of Melbourne.

Fels, A., Wang, X., Ng, W., & Emch, A. (Eds.). (2015c, July/August). *China competition bulletin* (38th ed.). A Publication of the Competition Law & Economics Network at Melbourne Law School, University of Melbourne.

Fels, A., Wang, X., Ng, W., & Emch, A. (Eds.). (2016a, January/February). *China competition bulletin* (40th ed.). A Publication of the Competition Law & Economics Network at Melbourne Law School, University of Melbourne.

Fels, A., Wang, X., Ng, W., & Emch, A. (Eds.). (2016b, July/August). *China competition bulletin* (43th ed.). A Publication of the Competition Law & Economics Network at Melbourne Law School, University of Melbourne.

Fels, A., Wang, X., Ng, W., & Emch, A. (Eds.). (2017a, March). *China competition bulletin* (46th ed.). A Publication of the Competition Law & Economics Network at Melbourne Law School, University of Melbourne.

Fels, A., Wang, X., Ng, W., & Emch, A. (Eds.). (2017b, June). *China competition bulletin* (47th ed.). A Publication of the Competition Law & Economics Network at Melbourne Law School, University of Melbourne.

Fox, E. M. (2008). An anti-monopoly law for China—Scaling the walls of government restraints. *Antitrust Law Journal, 75*(1), 173–194.

Guo, Y., & Hu, A. (2004). The administrative monopoly in China's economic transition. *Communist Post-communist Studies, 37*(2), 265–280.

Haley, J. O. (2004). Competition policy for East Asia. *Washington University Global Studies Law Review, 3,* 277–284.

Harris, H. S., Jr. (2006). The making of an antitrust law: The pending anti-monopoly law of the People's Republic of China. *Chicago Journal of International Law, 7*(1), 169–230.

Howell, T. R., Wolff, A. W., Howe, R., & Oh, D. (2009). China's new anti-monopoly law: A perspective from the United States. *Pacific Rim Law and Policy Journal, 18*(1), 53–95.

Huang, Y. (2008). Pursuing the second best: The history, momentum and remaining issues of China's anti-monopoly law. *Antitrust Law Journal, 75*(1), 117–132.

Ip, E. C., & Law, M. K. H. (2011). Decentralization, agency costs, and the new economic constitution of China. *Constitutional Political Economy, 22,* 355–372.

Jung, Y. J., & Hao, Q. (2003). The new economic constitution in China: A third way for competition regime? *Northwestern Journal of International Law and Business,* 24,107–172.

Li, B., & Wu, Y. (2006). Administrative monopolies—A perspective from the anti-monopoly law (行政垄断的反垄断法反思). *Guangxi Social Sciences (广西社会科学), 2,* 73–75.

Lin, Y. F., Cai, F., & Li, Z. (1998). Policy burdens, and state-owned enterprise reform. *American Economic Review, 88*(2), 422–427.

Liu, Z., & Qiao, Y. (2012). Abuse of market dominance under China's 2007 anti-monopoly law: A preliminary assessment. *Review of Industrial Organization, 41,* 77–107.

Mehra, S. K., & Meng, Y. (2009). Against antitrust functionalism: Reconsidering china's anti-monopoly law. *Virginia Journal of International Law, 49*(2), 379–430.

Owen, B. M., Sun, S., & Zheng, W. (2005). Antitrust in China: The problem of incentive compatibility antitrust in China. *Journal of Competition Law and Economics, 1*(1), 23–148.

Owen, B. M., Sun, S., & Zheng, W. (2008). China's competition policy reforms: The anti-monopoly law and beyond. *Antitrust Law Journal, 75*(1), 231–266.

Poncet, S. (2003). Measuring Chinese domestic and international integration. *China Economic Review, 14,* 1–21.

Saich, T. (2011). *Governance and politics of China* (3rd ed.). New York: Palgrave Macmillan.

Shang, M. (2009). Antitrust in China—A constantly evolving subject. *Competition Law International, 5,* 4–11.

Sun, J. (2010). On the defects of administrative monopoly in China's "Anti-Monopoly Law" and its improvement. *Canadian Social Science, 6*(2), 1–19.

Wang, X. (2004). Issues surrounding the drafting of China's anti-monopoly law. *Washington University Global Studies Law Review, 3,* 285–296.

Wang, X. (2007). Four main obstacles of anti-monopoly law enforcement (反垄断法实施面临四大瓶颈). *Cai Jing Magazine.* Retrieved December 5, 2007, from http://china.caixin.com/2007-12-05/100058461.html.

Wang, X. (2008). Highlights of China's new anti-monopoly law. *Antitrust Law Journal, 75,* 133–150.

Wang, X. (2014). Difficulties and implications of regulating administrative monopoly (行政垄断规制的困境与展望). *China Price (中国物价), 3,* 6–8.

Yang, J. (2002). Market power in China: Manifestations, effects and legislation. *Review of Industrial Organization, 21*(2), 167–183.

Yu, L., & Yu, D. (2011). The measure of regional administrative monopoly in China. In M. Faure & X. Zhang (Eds.), *Competition policy and regulation: Recent developments in China, the US and Europe* (pp. 79–97). Cheltenham: Edward Elgar.

Yu, L., & Zhang, W. (2013). Research on the intensity and effect of industrial administrative monopoly in China. In M. Faure & X. Zhang (Eds.), *The Chinese anti-monopoly law: New developments and empirical evidence* (pp. 194–217). Cheltenham: Edward Elgar.

Zhan, H., Song, Y., & Yang, Z. (2018). A new era comes–highlights of the anti-monopoly law of China in 2018. *Anjie Law Firm*. Retrieved from http://www.anjielaw.com/en/uploads/soft/190201/1-1Z2011P205.pdf.

Part III
The Enforcement of the AML

Chapter 9
Enforcement of Competition Law: Public Enforcement and Competition Agencies

> The prime key to the improvement of the administrative process is the selection of qualified personnel. Good men can make poor laws workable; poor men will wreak havoc with good laws
> —James M. Landis, Report on Regulatory Agencies to the President-Elect (Washington: December, 1960)

Abstract The increased focus on an effective enforcement of competition law in both developed and transitional economies has highlighted the debate on enforcement tools and institutions. Designing antitrust institutions became crucial, not only because a desirable substantive outcome of competition issues relies on an appropriate definition of competition policy enforcement organs, but also for the reason that a meaningful reform on the substances of law would be mediated through the reform of how competition institutions investigate and implement the substantive and procedural rules. It is argued that administrative agency policy making is superior to judicial or private systems because agencies are more specialized, while at the same time regulatory agencies may also suffer from insufficient human or financial resources, and being exposed to regulatory pressure and public choice concerns. To design an ideal enforcement agency, the general criteria of structural independence, independence in resourcing, the utility of the agencies should be fulfilled. To build agency capacity, training professional stuff, improving the organization of the agency and improving the leadership of the agency will be the key. Competition agencies in China include SAIC, NDRC, MOFCOM and SAMR. Before the establishment of the SAMR, the division of enforcement power between SAIC, NDRC and MOFCOM had been criticized for inefficiencies and creating overlaps and inconsistencies. It is expected that the institutional reform of establishing SAMR could improve the organizational design, and the agency capacity could be built through training professional staff, preventing regulatory capture and building connections between departments to solve coordination problems.

J. Ma, *Competition Law in China*,
https://doi.org/10.1007/978-981-15-5105-5_9

9.1 Introduction

The increased focus on an effective enforcement of competition law in both developed and transitional economies has highlighted the debate on enforcement tools and institutions. Designing antitrust institutions became crucial, not only because a desirable substantive outcome of competition issues relies on an appropriate definition of competition policy enforcement organs, but also for the reason that a meaningful reform on the substances of law would be mediated through the reform of how competition institutions investigate and implement the substantive and procedural rules.[1] Developing a "mix" of administrative, criminal and private enforcement, although desirable in theory, would be challenging in practice because of the institutional and cultural barriers, and most antitrust jurisdictions strongly rely on competition agencies to investigate and make judgements on competition issues.[2] It is therefore not a surprise to observe the discussion of competition agencies is as popular as the debate on competition laws itself.[3] For more experienced antitrust jurisdictions, reflecting on the life cycle of the agency could be valuable to understand the process of how an antitrust system was formed;[4] for countries where competition law was adopted under a strong foreign influence, pressures are imposed on a reform of competition authority, hoping for a more effective antitrust enforcement.[5] The central focus of the study of competition agency is measuring its effectiveness.[6]

The debate about competition agencies is in parallel with two sources of literature in academic research. The first area of study is concerned with the increasingly important role that a regulatory agency could play in domestic and international governance. Since the 1970s, the trend of granting discretionary power and increasing responsibilities to agencies have been named as a "new paradigm of European governance" in the EU,[7] and regulatory agencies have shifted countries across the Atlantic towards a regulatory state. The second area of research falls within the debate among law and economics scholars with regard to how public and private enforcement instruments could be combined to achieve regulatory goals. Notably, in recent decades research on the extent to which the advantages of public and private enforcement instruments have to be balanced with their deficiencies, have evolved

---

[1] As Kovacic, Hollman and Grant put it, "Brilliant theory without skillful implementation is a bad match. Great ideas from economics, law or other disciplines require equally great implementing institutions to move a system of competition policy forward." Kovacic et al. (2011, p. 25); *see also* Trebilcock and Iacobucci (2010, p. 455).

[2] See First and Shiraishi (2005).

[3] As Kovacic and Eversley once claimed, "Both older and newer competition systems have come to realize that a body of competition laws is only as good as the institutions entrusted with their implementation." Kovacic and Eversley (2007).

[4] Winerman and Kovacic (2010, pp. 145–203).

[5] In many countries, when blaming the weak enforcement of the competition law, it is the competition agency that receives the most criticism. For example, in Japan, in 2001, the competition authority JFTC was criticized for being a "watch dog that does not bite." Itoda (2001).

[6] Kovacic et al. (2011).

[7] Geradin et al. (2005).

into a more complex interaction between multiple enforcers themselves. The institutional dynamics with interdependent enforcement actors including agencies, state attorneys general, judiciary, and litigants has shown a more challenging regulatory framework.[8] In the light of this new era of enforcement debate, it worth the efforts to re-examine the specific characteristics of administrative enforcement in antitrust law by exploring the role that a competition policy should and could play.

Nevertheless, it was not until recent years that antitrust lawyers and economists have devoted efforts to the discussions of how to design antitrust institutions, and to provide operational guidelines and normative criteria for antitrust enforcement agencies.[9] Although there has been a growing consensus about the main factors that constitute good performance of the agency itself,[10] research projects on policy implementation have been conducted worldwide to study the performance details of competition agency,[11] a deeper analysis on the application of law and economics theories of regulatory agencies to antitrust enforcement is still underdeveloped. Particularly, when the institutional problems of the competition agency are discussed within the antitrust system, it is often suggested that external factors should be introduced, such as a specialized court, to combat the shortcomings of the agency design. These suggestions often cannot fully solve the institutional problem, because when an additional enforcement actor is introduced, it will complicate the existing interrelationship between the external actor and the current one;[12] let along to mention the side effects of legal transplantation when the introduced institutional reform is not embedded within the local culture. Moreover, although lawyers and economists have long advocated improving mechanisms for private damage litigation and for an active participation of public prosecutors in cartel criminal enforcement, in many civil law countries, the administrative agency alone is still the most important enforcer of the competition law. Seeing this, focusing on the organization structure and capacity building of the agency would be more pressing and realistic in practice.

This chapter focuses on the institutional design of the competition agency itself. It will take a more comprehensive view on what role the competition agency would

---

[8]Engstrom (2013, pp. 616–712).

[9]For example, in 2008, it was claimed that "relatively little emphasis has been placed on the institutions and operational considerations through which competition law and policy are implemented." Competition Policy Implementation Working Group: Subgroup 1, International Competition Network, Agency Effectiveness Report 3 (2008). For similar criticisms on implementation issues in the field of public policy, *see for example* Robichau and Lynn Jr (2009, p. 21).

[10]For example Fox (2010, p. 473); Kovacic (1997, pp. 403–453); Kovacic et al. (2011, pp. 25–45); Kovacic (2009, pp. 903–923).

[11]The most prominent research project on institutional design of competition agencies is Global Administrative Law Project of the New York University School of law, chaired by Professors Eleanor Fox and Michael Trebilcock.

[12]Daniel Sokol used the example that when snakes threatened Guam's bird population, the government introduced a mongoose; however, the mongoose also had a taste for birds and bird eggs. It is similar to introducing a specialized court to combat the antitrust institutional problems; but the specialized court may also run sub-optimally and create new problems. *See* Sokol (2010, pp. 1055–1056); Likewise, there were arguments against introducing private litigation, or doubting the benefits of class action in Europe. Wils (2003, pp. 473–488); Van den Bergh (2013).

play in antitrust enforcement, and how competition agencies could be designed to perform such a role. It holds the central claim that the normative criteria, the internal function and mechanism, and coherent logic of the competition agency must be clarified before new laws, administrative acts, and government agency reforms are undertaken. It studies the often inter-dependent relationship between competition policy and other ongoing economic reforms in the areas of macroeconomic policy, deregulation, and price control. It shows the theoretical foundations for understanding the complex policy issue that an agency is dealing with, and suggests the directions for institutional reform to improve the agency design.

An inter-disciplinary method will be employed to examine the literature related to the above-mentioned two sources of study. As a theoretical foundation, law and economics theories on regulatory agency, the administrative enforcement of law, and the optimal design of competition institutions will be explored. Following the theoretical discussion, a comparative legal study will be undertaken to evaluate the performance of competition agencies in the US, Europe, and Asia. The comparative study on the organization design of competition agencies is not aiming to answer the question of which agency is superior to another one based on the normative benchmarks; rather, is to understand the dynamics and evolution of agencies and to point out the institutional problems that the agency has overcome, as well as those inconsistent implementations of the competition policy due to the multiplicity of competition goals and the multitasking of their administrative duties.

The contribution of this study is to stress the important factors for designing a well-functioning competition agency, as well as to evaluate the extent to which the theoretical guidance on regulatory agency will be helpful to the practice of competition authority. Particularly, this chapter discusses when institutional and cultural infrastructures for enforcing competition law are not well-established, how competition agency could be modernized and reformed, in order to take a leading role in antitrust enforcement,[13] and what are the resulting implications for establishing the networks between a competition agency, political pressure, academic experts, business circles, and the general public. Based on developing a broad interdisciplinary theoretical framework, it discusses the normative criteria on how to improve the competition enforcement; moreover, it analyzes the pressing issues and institutional challenges that the competition agencies are facing, and discusses the practical strategies to dissolve those issues within the current administrative enforcement framework of competition law.

[13]The author shares the counter-arguments made by Mehra and Meng on antitrust functionalism, which argues that antitrust law can only be promulgated and enforced when institutional infrastructure, such as judicial review, is well-established. See Mehra and Meng (2009, pp. 379–429).

9.2 Economic Analysis of Public Enforcement of Law

Competition laws are enforced through different patterns. Some countries treat it as a type of economic policy and it is implemented through its centralized competition agency, which is an administrative organ and pursues regulatory goals. Anti-competitive conduct is prohibited by receiving administrative orders or fines. In some other countries, in particular in the US, antitrust law is enforced through private sanctioning powers and the court plays the dominant role in creating doctrines and making judgements in cases.

The different pattern of administrative versus judicial enforcement of competition law is reflected in several aspects. Firstly, when competition law is enforced through public regulators, the prioritized goals, substances, and procedures will follow the similar treatment of other public regulations.[14]In sharp contrast to US administrators, European state bureaucrats who enjoy high social status often enforce competition laws by following their own administrative values, customs, and traditions.[15] As a result of the specific differences in legal culture, history and economic environments, it was argued that is "unviable" to transplant the US enforcement system to Europe.[16]

Commentators argue that administrative agency policy-making is superior to judicial or private enforcement system because agencies are more specialized.[17] If agencies are structured based on a specialized function, regulatory expertise could be developed, knowledge of a particular industry will be accumulated and information will be collected at a lower cost. Bureaucratic expertise is the key factor to justify allocating more enforcement power to agencies. Whereas very often agency staff are no different from general judges who do not have sophisticated, technical training either when they started their career,[18] their expertise is often developed from practice.[19] Agency professionalization indicates that they could not only develop a deep knowledge on the subjects they are dealing with, but also a personal and professional network which may enhance their connection within the industry.[20] The fact that administrative agencies would have a high degree of expertise would then also be an argument in favour of regulatory discretion. A remarkable finding is that although the Anti-monopoly Bureau has been structurally separate from other departments of the Ministry of Commerce, for the reason that the bureau itself was established through an institutional reform and many of the staff working for the Ministry of Commerce are specialized in foreign trade, investment and economic policy, many of the merger decisions issued by the Anti-monopoly Bureau have reflected an integration of competition goals and industrial policy considerations. The overuse of behavioural remedies and the interventionist approach to international transactions

---

[14]Gerber (2002, p. 275).

[15]Gerber (2002, p. 276).

[16]Buxbaum (2005, p. 117).

[17]Landis (1938).

[18]Wright and Diveley (2012, p. 5).

[19]Eisner, at p. 130.

[20]Macey (1992, p. 103).

has been criticized for being a "protectionist" regulator, rather than an independent competition agency.

In addition, public enforcement may suffer from limitations that governmental agencies do not have sufficient human or financial resources to enforce the law, and they may generate substantial administrative costs because of the organization of the government institutions. Meanwhile, private enforcement could monitor regulatory agencies to prevent agency slack or shirking. Private parties are often more incentivized and informed than agencies to detect violations, to bring an enforcement action, and to monitor compliance.[21] Private actions could facilitate the allocation of social resources in law enforcement, and thus increase the efficiency and effectiveness of the enforcement of law,[22] and could develop litigation strategies and settlement techniques.[23] The advantages of public enforcement may also be impeded once regulators are exposed to regulatory pressure and public choice concerns. Building agency capacities will be critical for antitrust regimes that rely on public enforcement.

Moreover, a problem with the assumed higher expertise of administrative agencies and the related need for a high level of discretion is that these arguments may lack sufficient empirical support. By investigating 718 antitrust cases from 1976 until 2010 decided by the federal district court judges and FTC commissioners, Wright and Diveley found that case decisions by the FTC Commissioners are more likely to be appealed and reversed than cases decided by generalist judges.[24] Their research challenges the conventional view that agencies outperform general judges in deciding complex economic cases. In addition, when competition agencies have to combine multiple administrative duties,[25] competition authorities face the challenge of setting priorities and responsibilities, or sharing the resources with other regulatory agencies to deal with multiple duties.[26] Interviews with FTC staff by Susanne Weaver[27] and Robert Katzmann[28] showed that agencies may suffer from a bias when selecting cases, and that their choice was often influenced by private interests, such as career objectives and their personnel budgets. Although this explanation fits into the above-mentioned public choice argument that bureaucrats would often pursue personal rather than the public interest, the behavioural literature adds that the suboptimal decisions made by agencies may come from heuristic biases, in particular selection bias and myopia, overconfidence, coherence and anchoring. Chapter 12 of this

[21] Stephenson (2005, p. 108).

[22] Stephenson (2005, p. 107).

[23] Stephenson (2005, p. 107).

[24] Wright and Diveley (2012, p. 13).

[25] Most competition agencies have to combine the task of competition enforcement with consumer protection and other administrative duties. For example, in Peru, the competition authority INDECOPI is in charge of competition law, consumer protection, trade and intellectual property issues, as well as bankruptcy. see Kovacic and Hyman (2013, p. 2).

[26] Kovacic and Hyman (2013, p. 2).

[27] Weaver (1977).

[28] Katzmann (1980).

book will analyse to what extent these biases could play a role when administrative authorities decide competition cases.

9.3 Economic Analysis of Agency Design

In the US, the "success" of governmental agencies that have attracted attention from the press and congress is often measured by a few numbers: the number of new initiatives, the large cases, and the size of the companies involved in the case.[29] Hyman and Kovacic proposed seven criteria on evaluating the design, location and performance of agency: policy coherence, branding and credibility, capacity and capability, resilience, cohesion, and political implications.[30] The strength of the agency could be built up when agency's goals, priorities, duties are clarified and thus a "brand" could be promoted, and agencies with a good brand will receive credibility and respect before the courts, the public and regulated firms.[31] The allocation of functions, responsibilities and policy duties has to fit the capacity of the agency, including human talent, skills, and administrative resources.[32]

In addition, to implementing the administrative responsibilities, the agency should also be equipped with statutory powers, organizational structures and quality control mechanisms.[33] A match between policy commitments and agency capacity is crucial, as striving to achieve broad policy objectives with limited human talents and resources would lead to regulatory failure.[34] Trebilcock and Iacobucci defined the normative criteria for evaluating competition agencies, including independence and accountability, expertise, transparency and credibility, administrative efficiency, predictability and consistency.[35] Ideally, a competition agency is required to be institutionally separated from other governmental agencies and maintain independence in structural, resourcing, staffing and reporting. The mission and goals of the agency should be clearly defined. The level of difficulty that the agency encounters would increase once the policy goals are diverse and unrelated. The mix of policy goals will be meaningful if they are complementary, for example a mix of competition and consumer protection.[36] The core mission of the agency is derived from the institution itself and is fully understood and respected among the agency staff over a long time period; moreover, it has been supported by private entities, courts, government, and the academic community.[37] After defining the core mission, a positive agenda need

[29]Muris (2005, pp. 165–166).

[30]Hyman and Kovacic (2013a, pp. 1446–1516).

[31]Hyman and Kovacic (2013a, p. 1472).

[32]Hyman and Kovacic (2013a, p. 1474).

[33]Hyman and Kovacic (2013b, p. 1475).

[34]Hyman and Kovacic (2013b, p.1484).

[35]Trebilcock and Iacobucci (2010).

[36]Kovacic (2015, p. 242).

[37]Muris (2005, p. 167).

to be publicized to build a coherent strategy for an agency to exercise its authority.[38] To accomplish the mission, a long term investment in agency capacity building must be sustained and agency staff members should improve their knowledge and expertise in competition law and economics, through which agencies could respond to changing economic consequences, and to resist political pressure and politically motivated policy interventions.[39]

9.3.1 Structural Independence

The first criterion frequently used for designing a well-functioning agency is "regulatory independence", although the meaning of "independence" is far from clear—as it was claimed, it is a "magic concept".[40] The term "independence" often refers to the structural separation from other public organizations and the government,[41] and become a separate legal entity, no longer belonging to a government ministry, and it is identical to the term of "formal institutional separation"[42]; in the words of van Ooik, "(t)he agency concerned will be completely independent from the makers of law and politics. The agency's output may and should not be influenced by political consideration."[43] Thus, the prime meaning for 'independence' for a regulatory agency would mean structural independence, since structurally separated from the political institutions would guarantee a separation of power and interest from the political authority.[44] To a certain extent, the concept of "independence" has been used identical to the meaning of having an "organizational divorce" from their "parent bodies"—the overseer political organs, or called as a process of "formal institutional separation".[45] In the US, the most cited definition of "independence" in the case law is in *Humphrey's Executor v. United States*, where the court defines an independent agency is "a multi-member body whose members serve fixed terms and are protected from removal except for cause."[46] In theory, there is a trade-off between the level of independence and accountability. To reach maximum independence, the political interference will become zero; on the other hand, to become accountable, the competition agency would not be completely independent as it must be accountable with respect to appointments, budget and financial expenditures and performance review.[47]

---

[38] Muris (2005, p. 168).

[39] Hyman and Kovacic (2013b).

[40] Pollitt and Hupe (2011, pp. 641–658).

[41] Christensen and Laegreid (2006).

[42] Busuioc (2009, p. 602).

[43] Van Ooik (2005, p. 145).

[44] Jordana and Levi-Faur (2005).

[45] Busuioc (2009, p. 602).

[46] 295 U.S. 602 (1935), cited by Selin (2015, p. 972).

[47] Trebilcock and Iacobucci (2010, p. 457).

9.3.2 Independence in Resourcing, Staffing and Reporting

If a structural separation is the first step to be taken for establishing an independent agency, "complete independence" could only be achieved when the agency could achieve autonomy by having access to public funding, and the agency becomes accountable once the executive or legislative branch could oversee the agency's budget and courts could give deference to its judgements, and disclose information upon request from the public.[48] Socio-psychological and legal theories on autonomy would show that a structural separation would not be sufficient to secure autonomy of the regulatory agency until the key resources are under the control of the agency itself, such as manipulating resources, making decisions on financial budget, recruitment, and legal autonomy.[49]

Like other independent agencies, a competition agency is usually led by a group of commissioners, and the competition authority itself is named as a Commission. In the US, the commissioners are appointed by the President, and the Congress has to confirm the nomination.[50] Thus, an independent agency, in theory, would mean that it is an independent administrative agency being separated from the cabinet, or ministerial departments, and under the direct leadership of a group of commissioner that are appointed, but cannot be easily removed, by the President.[51]

9.3.3 Unity of Competition Agencies

For competition agencies, it is often claimed that the unity of competition-related regulatory agencies is crucial to guarantee the structural and resource independence of the competition agency. In recent years, many jurisdictions have taken measures to combine their regulatory agencies and to create a single united competition agency to implement the antitrust law. For example, in the UK, the Department for Business, Innovation and Skills (BIS) initiated a reorganization of the competition system in November 2010, and through which a new agency called Competition and Markets Authority (CMA) was granted the enforcement power that was previously assigned to the Office of Fair Trading (OFT) and Competition Commission (CC).[52] Regulatory reforms on combining several existing competition agencies into one have also been implemented in France, Portugal, Spain and Brazil.[53] In The Netherlands, the Competition Authority (NMa), the Post and Telecommunications Authority (OPTA) and the Consumer Authority (CA) merged into the Authority for Consumers and

---

[48] Kovacic and Hyman (2012, p. 530).

[49] Dworkin (1988); Jackson (2014, p. 259).

[50] Custos (2006, p. 616).

[51] Custos (2006, p. 616).

[52] Kovacic and Hyman (2012, p. 527).

[53] Kovacic and Hyman (2012, p. 528).

Markets (ACM) in April 2013.[54] Belgium Competition Bureau and the Competition Commission merged into the Belgium Competition Authority in 2013. In Spain, the regulators from six industries formed the Spanish National Competition Commission, and created the new agency on October 1, 2013 with the name of National Commission for Markets and Competition (CNMC).[55] In Finland, the consumer protection agency and the competition authority merged into KKV on January 1, 2013. The competition authority and consumer protection agency merged into Danish Competition and Consumer Authority (KFST) in Denmark in August 2010.[56] Similar measures on establishing a single, unified competition authority have also been taken in Ireland in 2014.[57]

Whereas it is not necessary to say that jurisdictions with competition laws should all conduct a regulatory reform to combine multiple enforcement agencies into one, it becomes clear that establishing a single enforcement agency could help with securing independence and autonomy for the competition authority, generating a reputation effect—a good "brand" for the agency. Kovacic et al. provided the criteria of assessing the effectiveness of a competition agency: the criterion of substantive results, that is, to use a mix of policy instruments to improve economic outcome, such as reducing costs and prices, increasing productivity, and the criterion of processes, that is to adopt administrative techniques to improve a continuous process.[58] The factors that contribute to the good agency process include: a clearly defined agency's aim, an internal planning mechanism, the employment of a problem-solving approach, recruiting administrative staff, lawyers and economists with skills and knowledge, and a long-term investment in knowledge building through domestic and international collaborations, and disclosing information and data to outside reviewers.[59]

Although multiplicity has the benefit of providing competition between different regulatory bodies and thus reduces the risk of capture, it has significant costs of creating tensions and conflicts between institutions and a decrease in social welfare would occur when agencies are engaged in a fight of political resources and interests.[60] Important decisions on litigation matters would be delayed because of the lack of responsibility, and a determinant agency, and international cooperation on competition issues would be impeded because of the complexity of internal collaboration between agencies.[61]

---

[54] Ottow (2014).

[55] Ottow (2014, p. 4).

[56] Ottow (2014, p. 4).

[57] Wan (2018, p. 7).

[58] Kovacic et al. (2011, pp. 30–31).

[59] Kovacic et al. (2011, pp. 30–36).

[60] Kovacic and Hyman (2012, p. 532).

[61] Kovacic and Hyman (2012, p. 532).

9.4 Agency Capacity Building

There is no doubt that investigating competition cases requires substantial knowledge and expertise in both law and economics. Building agency capacity, thus to build the "brand" of the agency is a long-term investment, including in human resources, institutional experience and knowledge and the infrastructure of the organization.[62] The performance of a competition agency is largely dependent upon how agency leaders and personnel can conduct professional and accurate analysis. There are various perspectives to discuss capacity building of the competition agency. First, for jurisdictions that have limited experience of competition law and competition culture, the first step to keep the agency running would be training the staff working at the agency to become professional. Universities and academic institutions may offer courses and training programs on competition law. Teaching materials, textbooks in both Chinese and English could be provided for students, practitioners and agency staff members. When the agency is capable of maintaining a basic operation, it may become a pressing issue to establish specific expert teams to deal with more technical issues of the case. Thus, a team with professional lawyers and another team with economist PhDs may work at different divisions and their analysis can be combined by the investigation staff.

In October 2002, EU Competition Commissioner Mario Monti announced the increased needs for economic knowledge and the importance of building a team of chief economists: "we are increasingly confronted with the need to investigate complex cases, which require in-depth fact-finding and rigorous economic and/or econometric analysis (…) we are, in particular, envisaging the creation of a new position of Chief Competition Economist within the DG… (…) I believe it needs to be closely associated with the day-to-day work of our case teams, giving guidance on analytical methodology, advice on the direction of investigations and direct assistance in the most complex cases."[63] After this speech, a Chief Competition Economist was appointed by the European Commission in July 2003, and 10 specialized economists with a PhD in industrial organization assisted the office of the Chief Competition Economist, and half of them are permanent officials of the EU and others are temporarily hired agents.[64] Once a member of the Chief Economist Team is assigned to the investigation of the case, she/he has complete access to the information and is able to request specific information or data for quantitative calculations.[65] In addition to the Chief Economist Team, an "Economic Advisory Group on Competition Policy (EAGCP)" was established in 2004, and leading academics are involved to provide professional knowledge and independent opinions. DG COMP discusses economic analysis with the EAGCP on an annual basis and

---

[62] Kovacic et al. (2011, p. 28).

[63] Speech by Commissioner Mario Monti "EU Competition Policy" at the Fordham Annual Conference on International Antitrust Law and Policy, New York, 31 October 2002, available at https://ec.europa.eu/competition/speeches/index_2002.html.

[64] Röller and Buigues (2005, p. 5).

[65] Röller and Buigues (2005, p. 7).

it is usually a one-day event held internally.[66] In 2010, the Bureau of Economics at the US Federal Trade Commission hired 75 PhD level economist and a group of accountants and research analysts. Professional staff and economic experts support the FTC to achieve competition-oriented policies and consumer protection goals.[67]

Agencies would need to cooperate with other governmental institutions to upgrade their investigation techniques. For example, already in the 1990s, the US DOJ has employed new investigatory techniques, such as videotaping, body wires, FBI photography, fingerprint identification, handwriting analysis, identification of typewriters after informants reported the meetings of cartel conspiracy.[68] Thirty to forty percent of antitrust criminal investigations by federal agencies received assistance from the FBI, Department of Defense, Department of Transportation, Environmental Protection Agency, and the US Postal Service.[69] Since the early 2000s, antitrust agencies including the Bureau of Economics at the US Federal Trade Commission and the competition authority in the Netherlands have widely adopted the screening techniques to use market data (prices or market shares) to detect collusion.[70] Developing investigatory tools, methods and techniques are crucial for competition agencies to improve their capacity in cartel detection.

9.4.1 Training Professional Agency Staff

When a competition agency is new and has obtained limited experience in antitrust analysis, the most practical solution to develop the human capital is to hire a number of professional staff working for the agency. Three mechanisms could be developed to provide law and economics expertise to agency officials.[71] First, academic infrastructure could be developed first, and once universities have started teaching competition law, micro-economics, industrial organization, and law and economics courses, graduate students could be recruited from those schools. Second, Teaching materials, journals, books in competition law should be accessible, and the recent publications including reports on the developments in a competition agency could improve the communication and transparency of the agency operation.[72] Third, professional associations and information networks could help facilitating the agency process and offer assistance in competition compliance. The reports on network guidance, annual seminars and meetings could also improve agency transparency.[73] Experiences in transitional economies such as Peru, Poland, Venezuela, Georgia,

---

[66] Röller and Stehmann (2006, p. 285).

[67] Farrell et al (2010, p. 263).

[68] Robinson (1991, p. 652).

[69] Robinson (1991, p. 653).

[70] Ghosal et al. (2007, pp. 5–6).

[71] The three mechanisms are based on Kovacic (1997, p. 409).

[72] Kovacic (1997, p. 410).

[73] Kovacic (1997, p. 411).

and Ukraine showed that hiring a small number of capable personnel to establish a "core team" would be much more efficient for the new agency than beginning by recruiting a large group of employees working for different divisions.[74] The key skills for the employees at the new agency include two types of techniques. The first area of knowledge and expertise is the understanding of basic microeconomic and legal concepts in competition law, and the second type of skill is solving practical competition cases. Both types of professional skills can be trained by organizing lectures, conferences, role-playing workshops, and exercises.[75]

With 20 staff members at the MOFCOM reviewing merger filings and 46 people at NDRC anti-monopoly division, the competition agency in China has a shortage of staff and experience.[76] The US DOJ Antitrust Division and FTC Competition Bureau have together 900 employees and the European Commission has around 100 staff members reviewing mergers.[77] The professionals are recruited through civil servant examinations, and they may shift from different bureaus in their career, so only in charge of competition enforcement responsibilities temporarily. Professional knowledge and expertise can only be obtained through organizing seminars and meetings with academics. Recruiting antitrust professionals and developing their expertise in economic knowledge is necessary.

9.4.2 Improve the Organization of the Agency

For a new agency, after the professional staff are hired and trained with basic knowledge and expertise, another important issue is to allocate control and responsibilities to each individual by designing a clear internal organization. It is often recommended to set up a central administrative office such as a secretariat, in order to coordinate the training of new employees, collect reports submitted from subdivisions and keep the records of the agency.[78] In addition, procedural rules for internal and external functions will have to be clarified, including the major responsibilities and tasks for each sub unit, as well as how complaints and requests can be filed externally by citizens or economic agents.[79]

---

[74] Kovacic (1997, p. 431).

[75] Kovacic (1997, p. 432–433).

[76] According to Deng and Huang (2018).

[77] US Chamber of Commerce (2014, p. 11).

[78] Kovacic (1997, p. 435).

[79] Kovacic (1997, p. 435).

9.4.3 *Leadership of the Agency*

Most competition agencies have a governing board; the advantage of having a board with members having diversified expertise and political preference is to resist capture, and being less influenced by the political power shifts. On the other hand, a diversified board may also have the disadvantage of failing to create a coherent and consistent agency agenda. The efficiency of decision making and implementation would be higher for a unitary hierarchical executive.[80] During the first decade after the FTC was established in the US, a customary rule was adopted that the chairmanship was rotated among the five Commissioners every year. There was criticism that such a rule imposed high operational costs, and impeded the effectiveness of the agency because the chair was not incentivized to make long-term plans and to make investment to improve the quality of their decisions. The opinions were a mere description of facts and a simple statement for the rationale.[81]

The Anti-monopoly Law in Japan granted the enforcement power to the competition agency Japanese Federal Trade Commission (JFTC). Articles 28, 29, 34 and 35 specify the structure, organization, and the authoritarian power of the agency. According to the law, the Commission is an independent agency with one Chairman, four Commissioners appointed by the Prime Minister, and the day-to-day competition investigation is made by antitrust professionals led by the Secretary General.[82] In practice, from 2001 until 2003, the JFTC was organized under the management control of the Ministry of Public Management, Home Affairs, Posts and Telecommunications (MPHPT). The structure of the agency is now placed under the supervision of the Cabinet Office.[83]

The competition agency in Korea—Korean Fair Trade Commission (KFTC)—was established in 1981 to enforce the Monopoly Regulation and Fair Trade Act (MRFTA) which was enacted in 1980. The agency was a division of the Economic Planning board, which was the coordination agency in charge of economic development. After the Economic Planning board was abolished under the bureaucratic reform in 1994,[84] it became a vice-ministerial agency under the directorship of the Prime Minister, and two years later it was promoted to be a ministerial level agency.[85] Today, the KFTC is the prime enforcement power for competition law in Korea. Private and criminal enforcement of anti-competitive conduct remains limited, and public prosecutors are not allowed to impose criminal liabilities on hard-core cartels until the KFTC refers to it. Decisions of the KFTC can be challenged before the Seoul High Court, and the Court is also responsible for private damage suits that can be filed without the investigation of the KFTC.[86]

---

[80] Kovacic and Hyman (2012, p. 531).

[81] Winerman and Kovacic (2010, p. 146).

[82] http://jftc.go.jp/e-page/about/role/organization.pdf.

[83] First and Shiraishi (2005, p. 5).

[84] For details, see Jung (2011, pp. 551-581).

[85] Yi and Jung (2007, p. 158).

[86] Yi and Jung (2007, p. 159).

The competition agency in Thailand, Trade Competition Commission (TCC), was established under the Price Determination Act and the Trade Competition Act in 1999. To become a Commissioner, the qualified person should not be politician, nor hold a position related to the administration of the political parties. The Chairman of the Trade Competition Commission is the Minister of Commerce, and the other members include the Vice Chairman, who is the Permanent Secretary for Commerce, the Secretary General of the TCC, who is the Permanent Secretary for Finance, and eight to twelves members. Among the members of the Commission, at least half of them have to be selected from the private sector.[87] The TCC is the single enforcement body of the competition law in Thailand, being granted the executive and the judicial power to consider merger notifications, market dominance cases, to react to complaints of allegedly illegal practices, as well as to take criminal proceedings.[88]

In practice, as Commissioners and other members at the Appellate Committee of the TCC are not full-time members, the Office of the Trade Commission (OTC) was established within the Department of Internal Trade at the Ministry of Commerce, and the Secretary General was the same person as the Director General of the Department of Internal Trade. The OTC is required to perform duties such as implementing the notifications, regulations and resolutions that are issued by the TCC, being responsible for most of the daily administrative work and to consider complaints filed by private parties. In addition, the appellate committee, or so-called sub-committees of the OTC are all appointed by the TCC.[89] Therefore, the TCC's decisions on abuse of market dominance, anti-competitive effects, and merger analysis are largely based on the investigation reports prepared by the OTC. Moreover, the OTC has limited human resources with regard to antitrust specialists. The officials were recruited from price regulators and other units of the Department of Internal Trade, together with inexperienced university graduates.[90] Given the heavy caseload, the administrative work borne by the OTC, and the shortage of professional staff, the investigations, for example on merger effects, are largely limited to the key factors, such as the size of the business, and the market shares. A more extensive use of economic techniques and a cost-benefit analysis is largely lacking.[91]

Clearly, since the director of the TCC and the OTC are the government officials at the Ministry of Commerce, and the administrative decisions are largely under the pressure from politicians and business sectors, neither the TCC nor the OTC could be considered independent.[92] Officials working at the OTC are under the leadership of the Department of Internal Trade, and the Director General is their direct monitor; they have a load of multiple administrative tasks in regulating price, maintaining market development and trade policies.[93] As mentioned above, the Director

[87] Poapongsakorn(2002, p. 190).

[88] Poapongsakorn(2002, p. 191).

[89] Poapongsakorn(2002, p. 191).

[90] Poapongsakorn (2002, p. 202).

[91] Poapongsakorn (2002, p. 201).

[92] Poapongsakorn (2002, p. 202).

[93] Poapongsakorn (2002, p. 202).

of the competition authority in Thailand, TCC and OTC, are the government officials working at the Ministry of Commerce, and the director himself has multiple administrative responsibilities, including regulating price, maintaining market development, and is in charge of trade policies. The director's own attitude towards competition law becomes important because he will have to balance the multiple administrative roles on his own.[94]

9.5 Competition Agencies in China

9.5.1 SAIC

The Law of the People's Republic of China for Countering Unfair Competition[95] was promulgated in 1993. The enforcement agency for the Law of Countering Unfair Competition is the Fair Trade Bureau of the SAIC and its local branches (AIC).[96] In 1994, both the SAIC and the AIC set up their offices, being especially responsible for fair trade affairs.[97] The enforcement agency for the Law of Countering Unfair Competition is the State Administration for Industry and Commerce (SAIC) with its local branches (AIC).[98] After the enactment of the AML, the function of dealing with anti-monopoly practices was formally regulated by the State Council and the SAIC became one of the enforcement agencies.[99] After the enactment of the AML, the function of dealing with anti-monopoly practices was formally regulated by the State Council and the SAIC became one of the enforcement agencies. In 2008, the Fair Trade Bureau was restructured and replaced by the Anti-monopoly and Anti-Unfair Competition Enforcement Bureau, and the bureau has two divisions, with 8–15 officials dealing with competition issues. SAIC has devoted substantial efforts to drafting regulations and guidelines, providing assistances for local enforcement by AICs.[100] By May 2015, SAIC had 15–20 staff members and 1–2 PhD economists working on non price-related violation cases.[101]

[94]Poapongsakorn (2002, p. 202).

[95]Zhonghua Renmin Gongheguo Fanbuzhengdangjingzheng Fa (中华人民共和国反不正当竞争法) [Anti-Unfair Competition Law of the People's Republic of China] (promulgated by the Standing Committee of the National People's Congress, 2 September 1993, effective on 2 September 1993).

[96]Jung and Hao (2003, p. 129).

[97]Mehra and Meng (2009, p. 403).

[98]Jung and Hao (2003).

[99]Guowuyuan Bangongting Guanyu Yinfa Guojia Gongshang Xingzheng Guanli Zongju Zhuyao Zhize Neishe Jigou He Renyuan Bianzhi Guiding De Tongzhi (国务院办公厅关于印发国家工商行政管理总局主要职责内设机构和人员编制规定的通知) [The State Council Notice on Major Duties, Internal Organization and Administration of the SAIC], July 11 2008.

[100]Hao (2013, p. 30).

[101]Wang (2015).

9.5.2 NDRC

NDRC was formed from the State Planning Commission, which serves the authority accommodating China's transition from a planned economy towards a market economy, and could oversee the ministerial work in industries including foreign investment, agriculture, employment, trade, social and environment development.[102] As the core responsibility, the administrative power of price control was solely allocated to the State Planning Commission, and it became the enforcing agency when the Price Law was drafted and promulgated in 1997.[103] In June 2003, NDRC issued the Interim Provisions on Preventing the Acts of Price Monopoly.[104] This regulation is in accordance with the 1997 Price Law. Article 3 of this regulation states that market predominance should be determined by three elements: the market share in the relevant market, the supply and demand substitutability, and the difficulty of market entry. This regulation also mentions the prohibition of abuse of market dominance, price coordination and the government agencies' illegal price intervention.[105] It indicates that the NDRC starts to share the responsibility of the enforcement of combating monopolistic practices, with a focus on the conduct of pricing.[106] In the first five years of the AML's enforcement, the enforcement power was allocated for one unit of the NDRC named "Department of Price Supervision", and only 3 officials in charge of day-to-day competition work, and in mid-2011 the number decreased to two, and most enforcement work has been conducted by local price authorities.[107] In July 2011, an additional 20 personnel were recruited and the antitrust team expanded to three units, and the name of the department was renamed as "Price Supervision and Anti-monopoly Bureau".[108] In 2014, the number of the staff members increased to 40, but not all of them work on competition issues.[109] By May 2015, NDRC had 40 staff members, and 5–6 PhD economists dealing with price-related violations.[110]

Both SAIC, NDRC and MOFCOM are ministerial agencies. SAIC and NDRC enforce competition law in collaboration with local branches. Local offices played a crucial role in detecting and investigating anticompetitive conduct. According to the report by NDRC, between 2011 and 2015, among the 97 price-related monopolistic agreement cases, NDRC investigated 29 cases, and local branches at province level

---

[102] Hao (2013, p. 27).

[103] Hao (2013, p. 28).

[104] Zhizhi Jiage Longduan Xingwei Zanxing Guiding (制止价格垄断行为暂行规定) [Interim Provisions on Preventing the Acts of Price Monopoly] (promulgated by the State Development and Reform Commission, June 18, 2003, effective on November 1, 2003).

[105] Interim Provisions on Preventing the Acts of Price Monopoly, id.

[106] Mehra and Meng (2009, p. 404).

[107] Hao (2013, p. 28).

[108] Hao (2013, p. 29).

[109] Emch (2014, p. 220).

[110] Wang (2015).

was in charge of 68 of them.[111] In June 2016, the Deputy Director of the SAIC reported that local bureaus initiated 1267 cases, and concluded 585 cases.[112]

9.5.3 MOFCOM

MOFCOM was established in 2003 by combining the State Economic and Trade Commission and the Ministry of Foreign Trade and Economic Cooperation.[113] The Ministry of Commerce established their antitrust office within the Department of Treaty and Law in 2004, showing their interest in investigating antitrust cases and in drafting legislation, especially in the field of merger and acquisitions. The office was named as the Ministry of Commerce Anti-Monopoly Bureau (MOFCOM). This office is responsible for the implementation of the Interim Provisions for Foreign Investors to Merge Domestic Enterprises, an administrative regulation on merger and acquisitions issued by six administrations in March 2003.[114] This provision has explicitly mentioned the pre-merger notification requirements in its Chap. 5, and the notification should be submitted both to the MOFCOM and the SAIC.

After the Anti-Monopoly Law in China came into effect in August 2008, the Anti-monopoly Investigation Office was promoted from a sub-unit of a department to an autonomous division of the Ministry of Commerce, and the Anti-monopoly Bureau became the enforcement organ for merger policy.[115]This office undertakes responsibilities including receiving concentration notifications, reviewing, investigating and assessing concentrations, as well as guiding domestic enterprises overseas in antitrust litigations, and facilitating international cooperation on multilateral and bilateral competition policy.

On June 17, 2011, MOFCOM announced the formal establishment of an AMC office, which will operate within MOFCOM.[116] This office undertakes nine major responsibilities:[117] (1) drafting regulations, provisions and documents of concentrations of undertakings; (2) reviewing, investigating and assessing concentrations; receiving concentration applications and notifications; taking related hearings and investigations; (3) investigating other concentration cases reported by antitrust enforcement agencies; (4) investigating monopolistic conduct in foreign trade, and taking action to mitigate negative effects; (5) guiding domestic enterprises overseas

---

111 国家发改委:"十二五"期间反价格垄断取得重大进展(NDRC: Significant Progress in the 12th Five-Year-Plan Period on the Enforcement of Price-related Monopolistic Agreements). http://www.sdpc.gov.cn/gzdt/201603/t20160304_791948.html

112 http://www.saic.gov.cn/fldyfbzdjz/gzdt/201706/t20170619_266335.html

113 Emch et al. (2016, p. 102).

114 Interim Provisions for Foreign Investors to Merge Domestic Enterprises (外国投资者并购境内企业暂行规定).

115 Emch, Han, and Ingen-Housz (2016, p. 103).

116 Ning and Yin (2011).

117 MOFCOM, The Responsibilities of the MOFCOM, June 13, 2011, *MOFCOM website,* available at http://fldj.mofcom.gov.cn/article/gywm/200809/20080905756026.shtml.

in antitrust litigations; (6) organizing negotiations on competition clauses in multilateral and bilateral agreements; (7) facilitating international cooperation on multilateral and bilateral competition policy; (8) other work assigned by the Anti-Monopoly Committee of the State Council; (9) other work assigned by the leaders.

Articles 20–31 of the AML formulate the competition rules for mergers and acquisitions. Following these rules, the MOFCOM implemented several guidelines which provided a few details in the enforcement of the merger control policy.[118] The Anti-monopoly Bureau has hired about 20–30 officials across seven divisions: the General Affairs Office, the Division of Competition Policy, the Consultation Division, the Supervision and Enforcement Division, the Legal Division, the Economic Division, and the Anti-monopoly Commission Coordination Division. Among them, the case investigators on mergers are about 15–20 officials.[119] By May 2015, the number of officials increased to around 30–40, and 3 PhD economists were recruited.[120]

9.5.4 SAMR

In May 2018, after a decade of enforcement of the AML, the SAIC, NDRC and MOFCOM were unified as one independent competition authority named the Sate Administration for Market Regulation (SAMR). With 27 bureaus and 805 staff members, the SAMR is in charge of various administrative duties related to market regulation, besides competition issues, it is responsible for product and safety regulation, food safety, standard-setting, issuing certifications and maintaining market order. On the official website, it makes clear that the Anti-monopoly Bureau of the SAMR has six responsibilities: (1) prepare anti-monopoly measures and guidelines (2) organize and implement anti-monopoly enforcement work (3) to undertake the work of guiding enterprises to respond to anti-monopoly lawsuits abroad (4) organize and guide the fair competition review (5) undertake international cooperation and exchanges (6) undertake the daily work of the Anti-monopoly Committee of the State Council. The Anti-monopoly Bureau has 10 divisions with 50 officials. Three of the departments in charge of merger control, another one dealing with those transactions that fail to notify and the issues related to remedy implementation specifically, and two divisions are assigned to monopoly agreements and abuse of dominant position, one for administrative monopoly, one for general matters, one for legislative works and one for international cooperation and the daily work of the antimonopoly commission.[121]

---

[118]Two guidelines were published by the MOFCOM right after the enactment of the AML: on 03 August 2008, the MOFCOM issued the Thresholds for Prior Notification of Concentrations of Undertakings, and the Guide of the Anti-Monopoly Committee of the State Council for the Definition of the Relevant Market, which was published on MOFCOM website on 24 May 2009.

[119]Emch, Han, and Ingen-Housz (2016, p. 104).

[120]Wang (2015).

[121]Zhan et al. (2018, p. 2).

The former minister of the SAIC, Mr Zhang Mao, became the minister of SAMR, and the former vice minister of the SAIC, Ms. Gan Lin, became the vice minister of the Anti-monopoly Bureau of the SAMR. The director is Mr. Wu Zhenguo, who is the former director of the Antimonopoly Bureau of MOFCOM.[122] On January 3, 2019, the SAMR published the Notice on Antitrust Enforcement Authorization, which provided the authorization to provincial branches of SAMR on antitrust enforcement. This authorization has replaced the authorization granted to local branches from the former antitrust bureau of the SAIC and NDRC.[123] Until now, no information has been disclosed with regard to the internal organization and detailed rules on agency process, in particular how governmental officials in charge of different antitrust issues are coordinated.

Overall, according to the AML, the enforcement agency of Chinese competition law and policy is called the Anti-monopoly Commission, which is a supra-ministerial commission that will coordinate multiple agencies. According to Notice on the Guidelines on the Definition of the Relevant Market, issued by the Anti-monopoly Commission on May 24, 2009, there are thirteen member agencies of the Anti-monopoly Commission: MOFCOM, NDRC, SAIC, Ministry of Industry and Information Technology (MIIT), Ministry of Supervision, Ministry of Finance, Ministry of Transport, SASAC, SIPO, Legislative Affairs Office of the State Council, PBC, National Bureau of Statistics, CBRC, CSRC, CIRC and the State Electricity Regulation Commission. After the consolidation of SAIC, NDRC and MOFCOM, it is clear that competition enforcement responsibilities have been shifted to SAMR, and personnel from three antitrust institutions have moved their position from MOFCOM, SAIC, NDRC, and their local branches to SAMR and its local branches, but SAMR may still be influenced by industrial policies issued by other regulatory agencies.

Since its establishment, the SAMR has taken effective actions to investigate anti-competitive conduct. In 2019, the SAMR has investigated 38 cases of monopolistic conduct in total and 17 of them were published on the official website. Among them, 6 cases were about horizontal agreements, 4 were about vertical agreements, 5 on abuse of dominance and 2 were monopolistic conduct organized by trade associations. The SAMR has also closed merger review of 432 cases and imposed remedies on 5 cases.[124]

9.6 Assessing the Competition Agencies in China

Shortly after the AML came into force in 2008, the enforcement power was divided between SAIC, NDRC and MOFCOM. The administrative enforcement by three agencies is subject to limited external judicial review. In practice, the enforcement

[122]Zhan et al. (2018, p. 2).

[123]Zhan et al. (2018, p. 4).

[124]Liu et al. (2020).

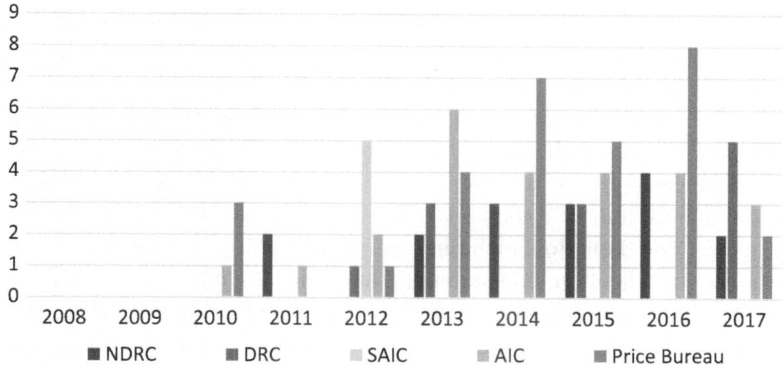

Chart 9.1 Number of Cartel Cases Initiated by Competition Agencies (2008–2017)

competence may not be equally divided between competition agencies. When calculating the number of cases initiated by SAIC, NDRC, the Price Bureau and their local branches from 2008 till 2017, it showed clearly that Price Bureau is the most active enforcement agency in horizontal agreement cases and has initiated 30 investigations in total. NDRC has initiated 16 cases, and DRC initiated 12 investigations. SAIC only published 5 case decisions in 2012, and AIC initiated 25 cases (Chart 9.1).

The division of enforcement power between SAIC, NDRC and MOFCOM has been criticized for inefficiencies, and separating price and non-price competition conduct may create overlaps and inconsistencies. Separating price-related behaviour from non-price related activities may not be clear, and agency powers are not effectively coordinated.[125] Multiplicity may also increase legal uncertainties and raise the cost of business transactions, and affect the overall authority of the enforcement agency. Such division of the competition enforcement power is rooted in political process, as SAIC used to be the enforcer of the Anti-Unfair Competition Law (AUCL) from 1993, and NDRC was formed within the State Planning Commission and was the enforcer of Price Law, and MOFCOM has been responsible for merger reviews and industrial policies related to international trade. Financial resources are provided through ministerial budges and professionals are recruited among the public servants.

After three agencies were united into one, the SAMR, the inefficiencies caused by the overlapping of decision making in three institutions may be mitigated; however, new challenges may arise because the single agent may fail to perform its responsibilities because of lack of an external monitor, capture, political influence or corruption,[126] after all, the new agency still operates under the direct control of the central government and ministries. The organization costs involved in coordinating different departments may have been reduced, but the extent to which the single agency has enhanced its independence and accountability is unclear, and its financial capacity may still be restrained by ministry budgets. As a theoretical basis for

[125]Hao (2013, p. 19).

[126]Kovacic and Hyman (2012, p. 532).

evaluating the overall function of a competition agency, the five institutional characteristics suggested by Kovacic and Hyman are to be examined: (1) the relationship to the political process, that is to make a trade-off between agency autonomy and receive political support to gain accountability; (2) the institution design of the governing board (3) positing the agency as a stand-alone institution or a sub-unit of a larger government body (4) whether the agency has exclusive or shared duties (5) the single or a multitude of policy goals, as well as the available policy instruments that the agency could employ, including enforcement tools, information disclosure, administrative adjudication, education and authority in civil and criminal enforcement.[127] Merging three agencies into one is only a change of organizations, as SAMR have not disclosed information on its internal institutional policy making rules, its relationship with other ministerial departments, and the investigatory process and coordination between staff members in dealing with monopoly agreements, abuse of dominant position and merger cases. It remains difficult to assess the performance of the SAMR based on the abovementioned five aspects. The policy goals for SAMR has been multiplied three times when goals for three agencies are combined, and SAMR has not clarified the hierarchy of all those multiple functions and purposes of the goals, although it has divided different responsibilities to 10 divisions and each has a particular administrative duty. In the past, competition agencies have been criticized for lack of structural independence, and policy decisions were made after going through negotiations with other government agencies.[128]The new agency may still have limited structural and operational independence and be influenced by political pressure from other departments within the SAMR.

When the three authorities in charge of competition, consumer protection and the post and communication merged into one authority for consumer and markets in the Netherlands, the main challenge for the institutional design was how different responsibilities could be allocated among each operating unit.[129] If the coordination problem could not be resolved, it would not matter whether the overlapping and conflicts on decision making are caused by different agencies or by separated units within the same agency. It was believed that the consolidation of the institutions could consolidate knowledge and expertise, thus anticipate market developments. The increased flexibility and the integrated organization will enhance the efficiency and effectiveness of competition regulation.[130] After the consolidation of the agencies, consumer interests and consumer welfare became the central focus of the new agency, and competition law will be assessed through the benefits and choices that are provided for consumers.[131] Based on the unified understanding on consumer interests and consumer behaviour, the new institution implemented procedural mechanisms to encourage cooperation between units. For example, detection officers who are in charge of collecting and analyzing information are connected through an internal

[127]Kovacic and Hyman (2013, p. 4).

[128]Ng (2015, p. 6).

[129]Ottow (2014, p. 3).

[130]Ottow (2014, p. 9).

[131]Ottow (2014, p. 14).

network, and this information is used for the entire institution.[132] Another major reform during the agency consolidation was the reshuffling of agency staff, and all staff members from three agencies had to reapply for positions at the new agency, and to participate in problem-oriented and cross-department teams with members having different expertise. This reform was to effectively prevent the risk of regulatory capture.[133] Ottow concluded that there are three factors that contribute to the success of the institutional design after the merging process. The first is to formulate the regulatory philosophy, culture, and organization structure as the new identity of the agency. The second factor is to select the right leaders to ensure the common culture is identified based on the value and vision of the new institution. The third factor is to introduce cross-departmental teams and to reallocate the positions to prevent the risk of regulatory capture.[134]

The factors could be applied during the process of agency consolidation in China. Building the common policy priorities and the organization culture among all competition staff members will be crucial, as the AML itself has incorporated multiple policy goals. Whether the new agency could resolve coordination problems, corruption and capture, will be dependent upon how procedural rules could be implemented and problem-solving investigatory teams could be formed, to create connections between departments, and to motivate sectoral regulators to participate in the investigatory activities in the new agency.

9.7 Conclusions

When most antitrust jurisdictions rely on administrative agencies to enforce competition law, particular attention has to be paid to the institutional design of the competition agency. Establishing an independent, autonomous enforcement agency is perhaps the most important step to begin the implementation of the antitrust law. The crucial issue in the institutional design is to reduce the risk of regulatory capture, and ensuring structural independence, and accountability in resource allocation, financial capacity and personal recruitment would be the key elements.

In terms of the agency design itself, multiplicity may have the advantages of creating internal checks and balances, thus reducing the risk of regulatory capture and being exposed to external monitoring; at the same time it suffers the cost of inefficiencies generated by overlapping and tensions in investigations as well as the interpretations of the law. There seems to be a global trend to unify competition-related institutions into one authority, while some nations have made such an institution in charge of competition law only, many others have formed a single multi-purpose

[132]Ottow (2014, p. 17).

[133]Ottow (2014, p. 17).

[134]Ottow (2014, p. 19).

authority, and combined administrative responsibilities of consumer protection, competition, and public procurement laws.[135] China has experienced a change from dividing competition enforcement powers among three ministerial agencies to unifying those responsibilities into a multi-purpose organ SAMR. Managers and staff members with knowledge and expertise from different agencies could thus be recruited, which could substantially improve the capacities of the new agency. Human talents and resources should be successfully applied and the problem of regulatory capture could be prevented, if a problem-solving approach is employed, and staff members with law or economics, or other backgrounds could form the project teams, as the experience in The Netherlands indicates. Obviously, the structural reform should be followed by a series of institutional designs in substantive and process tools, to build a transparent, accountable, and efficient competition agency.

References

Busuioc, M. (2009). Accountability, control and independence: the case of European agencies. *European Law Journal, 15*(5), 599–615.

Buxbaum, H. L. (2005). German legal culture and the globalization of competition law: a historical perspective on the expansion of private antitrust enforcement. *Berkeley Journal of International Law, 23*(2), 474–495.

Competition Policy Implementation Working Group Subgroup 1 (2008) International competition network, Agency effectiveness report 3.

Christensen T, & Laegreid P (Eds.) (2006) *Autonomy and Regulation: Coping with Agencies in the Modern State*. Cheltenham: Edward Elgar.

Custos, D. (2006). The rulemaking power of independent regulatory agencies. *The American Journal of Comparative Law, 54*, 615–639.

Dworkin, G. (1988). *The Theory and Practice of Autonomy*. Cambridge: Cambridge University Press.

Deng F, & Huang C (2018, August) A ten-year review of merger enforcement in China. *The Antitrust Source*.

Engstrom, D. F. (2013). Agencies as litigation gatekeepers. *The Yale Law Journal, 123*(3), 616–712.

Emch, A., Han, W., & Ingen-Housz, C. (2016). Merger control in China: procedural rights. In C. Cauffman & Q. Hao (Eds.), *Procedural Rights in Competition Law in the EU and China* (pp. 101–128). Berlin Heidelberg: Springer-Verlag.

Emch, A. (2014). Chinese antitrust institutions–many cooks in the kitchen. *Competition Policy International, 10*(1), 217–246.

Farrell, J., Pappalardo, J. K., & Shelanski, H. (2010). Economics at the FTC: Mergers, dominant-firm conduct, and consumer behavior. *Review of Industrial Organization, 37*, 263–277.

Fox, E. M. (2010). Antitrust and institutions: design and change. *Loyola University Chicago Law Journal, 41*(3), 473–488.

First, H., & Shiraishi, T. (2005). Concentrated power: The paradox of antitrust in Japan. In D. Geradin, & R. Muñoz, Petit N (Eds.). *Regulation Through Agencies in the EU, A New Paradigm of European Governance*. Edward Elgar.

[135] Kovacic and Hyman (2012, p. 533).

Gerber, D. J. (2002) Competition Law. *The American Journal of Comparative Law*, 50. (Supplement: American Law in a time of Global Interdependence: U.S. National Reports to the 16th International Congress of Comparative Law (Autumn, 2002)).

Geradin, D., Muñoz, R., & Petit, N., (Eds.) (2005). *Regulation through Agencies in the EU, A New Paradigm of European Governance*. Edward Elgar.

Ghosal, V., Harrington Jr, J. E., & Stennek, J. (2007). Issues in Antitrust Enforcement, in G. Vivek, & S. Johan (Eds.). *The Political Economy of Antitrust*. Elsevier.

Hao, Q. (2013) The multiple hands: institutional dynamics of China's competition regime. In A. Emch. & D. Stallibrass (Eds.). *China's Anti-Monopoly Law–The First Five Years,* Wolters Kluwer. Available at SSRN https://ssrn.com/abstract=2503274.

Hyman, D. A., & Kovacic, W. E. (2013a). Why who does what matters: governmental design and agency performance. *George Washington Law Review*, 1446–1516.

Hyman, D. A., & Kovacic, W. E. (2013b). Institutional design, agency life cycle, and the goals of competition law. *Fordham Law Review, 81,* 2163–2174.

Itoda, S. (2001, October 11) Competition in Japan's telecommunications sector: Challenges for the Japan fair commission.http://www.jftc.go.jp/e-page/speech/011011speech.pdf.

Jackson, C. (2014). Structural and behavioural independence: mapping the meaning of agency independence at the field level. *International Review of Administrative Sciences, 80*(2), 257–275.

Jung, Y. J., & Hao, Q. (2003). The new economic constitution in China: a third way for competition regime? *Northwestern Journal of International Law and Business, 24,* 107–172.

Jung, J. Y. (2011). How a powerful bureaucracy fell: the abolition of the economic planning board in South Korea. *Korea Observer, 42*(4), 551–581.

Jordana, J., & Levi-Faur, D (2005). The politics of regulation in the age of governance. In J. Jordana & D. Levi-Faur (Eds.). *The Politics of Regulation: Institutions and Regulatory Reforms for the Age of Governance*. Cheltenham: Edward Elgar

Katzmann, R. (1980). *Regulatory Bureaucracy: The Federal Trade Commission and Antitrust Policy*. Cambridge: MIT Press.

Kovacic, W. E. (1997). Getting started: Creating new competition policy institutions in transition economies. *Brooklyn Journal of International Law, 23*(2), 403–453.

Kovacic, W.E., & Eversley, D. (2007, May 23). An Assessment of institutional machinery: methods used in competition agencies and what worked for them. In *International Competition Network Competition Policy Implementation Working Group Subgroup 2 on Experiences of Younger Agencies*. Available at https://www.internationalcompetitionnetwork.org/wp-content/uploads/2018/09/AEWG_CPIInstitutionalMachinery2007.pdf.

Kovacic, W. E. (2009). Rating the competition agencies: what constitutes good performance. *George Mason Law Review, 16,* 903–926.

Kovacic, W. E., Hollman, H. M., & Grant, P. (2011). How does your competition agency measure up? *European Competition Journal, 7*(1), 25–45.

Kovacic, W. E., & Hyman, D. A. (2012). Competition agency design: what's on the menu? *European Competition Journal, 8*(3), 527–538.

Kovacic, W.E., & Hyman, D.A. (2013). Competition agencies with complex policy portfolios: divide or conquer. In *GW Law Faculty Publications & Other Works*.

Kovacic, W. E. (2015). Creating a respected brand: how regulatory agencies signal quality. *George Mason Law Review, 22,* 237–258.

Landis, J. M. (1938) *The Administrative Process*, Yale University Press.

Liu, C., Li, A., Bi, Y., Liu, S., Hong, L., & Liu, J. (2020, February 20). China's anti-monopoly law enters its second decade. *King & Wood Mallesons*. Available at https://www.chinalawinsight.com/2020/02/articles/antitrust/chinas-anti-monopoly-law-enters-its-second-decade/#_ftn18.

Mehra, S. K., & Meng, Y. (2009). Against antitrust functionalism: reconsidering China's Anti-monopoly Law. *Virginia Journal International Law, 49,* 379–430.

Muris, T. J. (2005). Principles for a successful competition agency. *The University of Chicago Law Review, 72*(1), 165–187.

Macey, J. R. (1992). Organizational design and political control of administrative agencies. *Journal of Law Economics and Organization, 8*(1), 93–110.

Ning, S., & Yin. R. (2011, June, 17) Formal establishment of anti-monopoly commission office within MOFCOM approved, *King & Wood Mallesons, China Law Insight.* Available at http://www.chinalawinsight.com/2011/06/articles/corporate/antitrust-competition/formal-establishment-of-antimonopoly-commission-office-within-mofcom-approved/.

Ng, W. (2015). The independence of Chinese competition agencies and the impact on competition enforcement in China. *Journal of Antitrust Enforcement, 2015,* 1–22.

Ottow, A. T. (2014). Erosion or innovation? The institutional design of competition agencies–a Dutch case study. *Journal of Antitrust Enforcement, 2014,* 1–19.

Poapongsakorn, N. (2002). The new competition law in Thailand: Lessons for institution building. *Review of Industrial Organization, 21*(2), 185–204.

Pollitt, C., & Hupe, P. (2011). Talking about government. *Public Management Review, 13,* 641–658.

Röller, L-H., & Buigues, P.A. (2005, May). The office of the chief competition economist at the European Commission. *European Commission Paper.* Available at https://ec.europa.eu/dgs/competition/economist/officechiefecon_ec.pdf.

Röller, L.-H., & Stehmann, O. (2006). The year 2005 at DG Competition: the trend towards a more effects-based approach. *Review of Industrial Organization, 29,* 281–304.

Robinson, C. K. (1991). Developments in criminal antitrust enforcement. *Antitrust Law Journal, 60*(2), 649–656.

Robichau, R. W., & Lynn, L. E., Jr. (2009). The implementation of public policy: Still the missing link. *Policy Studies Journal, 37*(1), 21–36.

Selin, J. L. (2015). What makes an agency independent? *American Journal of Political Science, 59*(4), 971–987.

Sokol, D. D. (2010). Antitrust, institutions, and merger control. *George Mason Law Review, 17*(4), 1055–1148.

Stephenson, M. C. (2005). Public regulation of private enforcement: the case for expanding the role of administrative agencies. *Virginia Law Review, 91*(1), 93–173.

Trebilcock, M. J., & Iacobucci, E. M. (2010). Designing competition law institutions: values, structure, and mandate. *Loyola University Chicago Law Journal, 41,* 455–471.

US Chamber of Commerce. (2014). *Competing Interests in China's Competition Law Enforcement: China's Anti-monopoly Law Application and the Role of Industrial Policy.* Available at https://www.uschamber.com/sites/default/files/aml_final_090814_final_locked.pdf.

Van den Bergh, R. (2013). Behavioral antitrust: not ready for the main stage. *Journal of Competition Law and Economics, 9*(1), 203–229.

Van Ooik, R. (2005). The Growing Importance of Agencies in the EU: Shifting Governance and the Institutional Balance. In D. Curtin, et al (Eds.). *Good Governance and the European Union, Reflections on Concepts, Institutions and Substance*. Intersentia.

Wan, J. (2018) 2008–2018: A retrospect of China's Anti-monopoly law enforcement system and prospect and commentary on the new system. CPI Asia Column. Available at https://www.competitionpolicyinternational.com/2008-2018-a-retrospect-of-chinas-anti-monopoly-law-enforcement-system-and-prospect-and-commentary-on-the-new-system/.

Weaver, S. (1977). *The Decision to Prosecute: Organization and Public Policy in the Antitrust Division*. Cambridge: MIT Press.

Winerman, M., & Kovacic, W. E. (2010). Outpost years for a start-up agency: The FTC from 1921–1925. *Antitrust Law Journal, 77*(1), 145–203.

Wright, J. D., & Diveley, A. M. (2012). Do expert agencies outperform generalist judges? Some preliminary evidence from the Federal Trade Commission. Available at SSRN https://www.ssrn.com/abstract=1990034.

Wils, W. P. J. (2003). Should private antitrust enforcement be encouraged in Europe? *World Competition, 26*(3), 473–488.

Yi, S. S., & Jung, Y. (2007). A new kid on the block: Korean competition law, policy, and economics. In *Competition Policy International* 3(2).

Zhan, H., Song, Y., & Yang, Z. (2018). A new era comes-highlights of the anti-monopoly law of China in 2018. Anjie Law Firm.

Chapter 10
Enforcement of Competition Law—Economic Analysis of Antitrust Sanctions

Abstract Socially desirable acts generate benefits whereas socially undesirable acts create substantial costs. Substantial amounts of public resources have been spent on law enforcement to detect, control, and deter socially undesirable acts. Law and economics literature studies how an optimal allocation of enforcement resources could be made by measuring the "social welfare versus costs" of law enforcement. The Becker Model defines the quantitative framework on how rational criminals calculate the expected benefits and costs of the crime. Only when expected private benefits exceeds private costs, which equals the perceived probability of detection (p) multiplies the magnitude of sanctions (S), would the infringer commit the crime. Economists have argued that the cost of committing monopolistic behaviour should be increased as the probability of detection remains low. Thus cartel criminalization has become a global trend. Cartel criminal and individual liabilities have not been introduced in China, and all of the three enforcement agencies strongly rely on administrative fines to deter anticompetitive violations. The level of fines rose dramatically in the second five years during the past decade, after the NDRC took positive actions on competition law in addition to the duty of enforcing Price Law. Studying the 97 monopoly agreement cases which received administrative fines, it seems to be evident that the enforcement competence between SAMR, SAIC, NDRC, Price Bureau and their local branches are not equally divided. NDRC and the Price Bureau imposed the fines most frequently and SAIC seems to be more lenient. The division of labour would be meaningful when the duties had been incorporated into SAMR after the three agencies merged into one in May 2018.

10.1 Introduction

Socially desirable acts generate benefits whereas socially undesirable acts create substantial costs. Substantial amounts of public resources have been spent on law enforcement to detect, control, and deter socially undesirable acts. Law and economics literature studies how an optimal allocation of enforcement resources could be made by measuring the social welfare (thus, the aggregate expected utilities of individuals) versus costs of law enforcement (including the costs of detection and

J. Ma, *Competition Law in China*,
https://doi.org/10.1007/978-981-15-5105-5_10

conviction, costs of law application and costs of imposing sanctions.[1]) In the landmark publication *The optimal Structure of Law Enforcement*, Steven Shavell distinguishes between the socially desirable and undesirable acts, and a potential law infringement would be socially undesirable when the expected harm exceeds the expected social benefits.[2] Methods of law enforcement can be compared to the timing of legal intervention (prevention, act-based or harm based), forms of sanction (monetary or non-monetary sanctions), and role of private actors and public agencies (private versus public enforcement).[3]

Economic analysis of antitrust sanctions is based on the theory of deterrence. The seminal work developed by Nobel Prize Winner Gary Becker defines the quantitative framework on how rational criminals calculate the expected benefits and costs of the crime. Only when expected private benefits exceeds private costs, which equals the perceived probability of detection (p) multiplied by the magnitude of sanctions (S), would the infringer commit the crime. The objective of antitrust sanctions is to deter future infringement by inducing criminals to internalize the social costs of the crime. In the optimal deterrence model, the sanction should be set to the same amount of social harm as the crime produced, while in the maximum deterrence model, the sanction should be set to the maximum level to deter future infringement.

As discussed in Chap. 4, the detection rate for cartels remains low and the potential illegal profits are substantial, but the magnitude of antitrust sanctions has been dramatically increased during the past decades. Three categories of solutions including increasing (maximum) cartel fines, introducing criminal liabilities and inducing individual liabilities on executives and managers have been widely adopted worldwide, although empirical studies show that cartel laws are still under-enforced. When promoting the three strategies, economic theory has provided criteria for choosing between monetary and non-monetary sanctions. The economic model on non-monetary sanctions, mainly imprisonment, concerns the question of how resources should be allocated to the criminal justice system as a whole, and how resources could be divided among branches of the systems. A balance between the private costs for law infringers, and the social cost, that is the harm caused by the offence plus the cost of the criminal justice system has to be made.[4]

Cartel criminal and individual liabilities have not been introduced in China, and all of the three enforcement agencies strongly rely on administrative fines to deter anti-competitive violations. The level of fines rose dramatically in the second five years during the past decade, after the NDRC took positive action on competition law in addition to the duty of enforcing Price Law. Studying the 97 monopoly agreement cases which received administrative fines, it seems to be evident that the enforcement competence between SAMR, SAIC, NDRC, Price Bureau and their local branches is not equally divided. NDRC and the Price Bureau imposed the fines most frequently and SAIC seems to be more lenient. The division of labour would be meaningful

---

[1]Shavell (1993, p. 261).

[2]Shavell (1993, p. 257).

[3]Shavell (1993, pp. 255–287).

[4]Avio (1998).

when the duties were incorporated into SAMR after the three agencies merged into one in May 2018.

10.2 Economic Analysis on Antitrust Sanctions

10.2.1 The Deterrence Goal

From an economic point of view, the reason why criminal sanctions are needed is to reach the goal of deterrence.[5] The deterrence theory developed by economists provides a scientific explanation and a rational prediction for the relationship between crime rate and the threat of punishment.[6] According to Cook, the theory of criminal deterrence deals with two issues, one is that assuming potential criminals are rational, deterrence theory explains how criminal sanctions influence the choices made by individuals on whether to participate in criminal activities; and the second issue is to analyze the effectiveness of different types of criminal justice systems in threatening infringers.[7] Criminal justice may function differently on deterring potential criminal acts because individuals may have different risk preferences when the probability of detection and conviction is uncertain, and different expectations of the outcome of the criminal act, when their evaluation of benefits is not monetary value, as well as individual's personal circumstances including skills, income, reputation. Thus, individuals may evaluate private costs and benefits of criminal opportunities to different extents.[8]

Public resources could be allocated to increase the probability of detection or the magnitude of sanctions to improve deterrence, while economists argued that increasing the severity of punishment could be less costly, although increasing the probability of detection could be more effective and have greater deterrence effect.[9] The legal sanction is set at the optimal level when potential infringers could internalize the external harm of the violation, thus those "inefficient violations"—when social harm exceeds the benefits could be deterred. To effectively deter future violations, the level of sanctions must be higher than the damage caused. The compensation that victims receive under civil law is often not sufficient to deter offences. By imposing criminal sanctions, offenders are not allowed to do certain things that are prohibited by the criminal law, even if they are willing to compensate the victims.[10] In particular, the sanction of imprisonment should be imposed when monetary sanctions, such as fines, are not sufficient to reach the deterrence goal. This refers to the situation where

[5]Shavell (1985) and Coffee (1980).

[6]Cook (1980, p. 212).

[7]Cook (1980, p. 216).

[8]Cook (1980, pp. 217–218).

[9]Cook (1980, pp. 230).

[10]Faure (2000) and Bowles et al. (2008, pp. 402–403).

the probability of detection is low and the risk of defendants being judgment-proof is high.[11] However, criminal sanctions also suffer some drawbacks in achieving the deterrence goal.[12] In most cases, the possibility of apprehending law infringers is not high enough. Given the large benefits of the infringement, in order to reach the deterrence goal, the sanction level should be set very high[13] to offset the low probability of detection. However, this will make the crime more risky, which imposes additional costs on those who are risk averse.[14]

10.2.2 Becker Model and Criminal Law

In economic theory, public and private resources have to be devoted to apprehend and convict offenders. Gary Becker has identified a cost minimization model of law enforcement.[15] To determine the optimal amount of resources to be spent on punishment, three factors, including the cost of detecting and convicting offenders, the choice of sanctions (fine or imprisonment) and the responses of offenders to the penalty have to be taken into account.[16] A potential infringer will only commit a crime when the expected utility exceeds the costs, and the cost is calculated as the probability of conviction multiplied by the severity of sanctions. Potential criminal activities are altered when the costs of the consequences are increased by law enforcement.

The Becker Model shows that the decision on sanction mechanisms depends on the information on the gain to the offender as well as the probability of detection.[17] The expected punishment cost, which is equal to the expected social cost of the crime, is calculated as the probability that the sanction will be imposed on the criminal multiplied with the magnitude of the punishment.[18] Becker identified the trade-offs involved in minimizing the costs in law enforcement and one of the most important trade-offs is the probability of being punished (p), as contrasted with the severity of the sanctioning (S). The potential offender makes a calculation ex ante, considering the probability of being apprehended and the level of punishment and compares this to the utility that could be derived from committing the crime.[19] Consequently, the magnitude of the sanctions multiplied by the probability that the sanction will be

[11] Bowles et al. (2008, p. 405).
[12] Shavell (1993, p. 275).
[13] Shavell (1993, p. 275).
[14] Easterbrook (1983, p. 293).
[15] Becker (1968).
[16] Becker (1968, p. 170).
[17] Van den Bergh and Faure (2011, p. 64).
[18] The theory of economic analysis to punishment was firstly developed by Jeremy Bentham in the eighteenth century. *See* Bentham (1789).
[19] Schwartz (1979, p. 1076).

applied equals the 'price' of engaging in activities that violate the law.[20] This price must be set at an efficient level. If the price is too low, there will be an excessive amount of harmful activities. Conversely, if the price is set too high, the process and punishment costs involved in law enforcement would be too high and the social cost of punishing offenders will exceed the social benefit. Shavell argues that to achieve the goal of deterring socially undesirable acts, the criminal sanction should increase when the probability of conviction falls.[21]

From an economic perspective, the goal of the criminal law is not to eliminate all crime, but to reduce the level of crime to a level where the social loss is minimized.[22] In that respect an optimal balance has to be found between the probability of detection (p) and the sanction (S). Hence, when the probability of being apprehended is low, the severity of sanctions should be set high, to offset the decreased expected price, in order to reach the expected optimal level of deterrence. Therefore, the enforcement structure will be desirable when the price is efficiently established, in which situation the process and punishment costs must be justified by the benefits that are generated from deterring harmful conduct.[23] Easterbrook argues that the optimal price is to be set equal to the externalities caused by the harm, divided by the probability of prosecution.[24]When the cost of allocating resources to reach this level of the optimal price is too high, this price might be reduced until the marginal benefit of the crime is equal to the marginal cost in crime control.[25] This is an application of Stigler's idea that society should not strive for a reduction of all crime at all costs, but rather for an optimum enforcement of laws, taking into account the costs of crime control.[26]

Economic theory perceives deterrence as the main goal of criminal law. This to some extent contrasts with the legal theory where criminal law is viewed as aimed at punishing morally unacceptable acts, and the goals of criminal law include retribution, rehabilitation, incapacitation and education.[27]However, from an economic perspective the question arises of whether the economic goal of deterrence can only be reached via the criminal law. The answer to that question largely depends on which type of sanction is needed. The economic justification for the use of sanctions and punishment is to make law infringers internalize the social costs. The level of penalty should be set equal to the social cost of the crime.[28] There are basically two types of penalties, monetary and nonmonetary (usually referred to imprisonment). From a legal perspective, monetary sanctions can either be administrative fines or take the form of criminal fines.

---

[20]Schwartz (1979, p. 1079).

[21]Shavell (2004, p. 551).

[22]King (2010, p. 15).

[23]Schwartz (1979, pp. 1079–1080).

[24]Easterbrook (1983, p. 292).

[25]Easterbrook (1983, p. 292).

[26]Stigler (1970, p. 526).

[27]Dau-Schmidt (1984, p. 87).

[28]Posner (1980a, p. 73).

10.2.3 Administrative Versus Criminal Penalties

Economists have long advocated that when deterrence could be achieved in the same way through those types of sanctions, fines would be preferred to imprisonment penalties.[29] The straightforward economic reason is that a prison sanction leads to substantial costs for society whereas fines still can shift funds from the perpetrator to society. The question, however, arises of whether the fine should necessarily be collected via a criminal procedure. The costs of an administrative procedure, through which fines are imposed, are substantially lower than the imposition of fines by means of criminal procedure.[30] It can hence be concluded that in principle, administrative law is more desirable when the monetary sanctions (including the administrative fines) will be effective.[31] The second issue is that in most legal systems the criminal proceedings are more accurate. The reason for this is that the investigations are conducted by professional lawyers[32] and the sanction is imposed by an impartial judge.[33] The criminal procedure may thus have a higher accuracy and better reduced error costs.[34] Administrative proceedings are less costly, but the error costs can be higher. Therefore, administrative fines should be applied to cases where the deterrence goal can be achieved by relatively modest sanctions.[35] However, imprisonment, which would obviously lead to much higher error costs, should not be imposed through an administrative procedure.

Gary Becker's model is developed according to several assumptions. One of these assumptions is obviously that agencies examining potential violations and prosecutors bringing cases to court work in the public interest in order to serve the goal of optimal deterrence. Wils further argues that there are also several conditions that will have to be met in order to make the specific sanction of imprisonment an effective instrument to deter hardcore cartels.[36] The first condition is that sanctions are imposed through a system with a dedicated investigator and prosecutor. The second condition is that the investigation process must be provided with sufficient power. The third condition is that judges or juries are willing to convict and the fourth condition is that the opinion that cartels deserve severe (criminal) punishment must be supported both publicly and politically.[37]

---

[29]Posner (1980b) and Polinsky and Shavell (1979) and Polinsky and Shavell (1991) and Polinsky and Shavell (1993).

[30]Faure (2009, p. 324).

[31]Polinsky and Shavell (1979) and Shavell (1985).

[32]Faure (2009, p. 325).

[33]Van den Bergh and Faure (2011, p. 65).

[34]Faure et al. (2009, pp. 173–176).

[35]Faure (2009, p. 326).

[36]Wils (2005, p. 39).

[37]Wils (2005, p. 39).

10.2.4 Under Enforcement of Antitrust Sanctions

Economic theory has proved that antitrust sanctions are to be set sufficient high in order to deter monopolistic behaviour, and public policy makers have indeed significantly increased antitrust sanctions in the past decades. Nonetheless, empirical studies show that the optimal deterrence has not been reached and the ever-increased sanction has not changed the incentives and behaviour of firms and individuals. In the survey among 1203 antitrust lawyers and practitioners, Sokol found that 44% of the respondents reported that the increased antitrust sanctions did not have significant impact—the enforcement is "the same as the present".[38] By studying the deterrence effect on 2321 business trading firms after cartel conduct was criminalized by the Australian Parliament and the Australian Competition and Consumer Commission (ACCC) in July 2009, Parker and Nielsen showed that the very serious sanctions, including criminal penalties, corporate fines and private action for damages, have little impact on the compliance management, and there was no correlation between the "fear" of being punished and the change of compliance performance.[39] Their study claims that the reaction of corporate behaviour and compliance management towards the increased penalty is more complicated than simply assuming that business people will change their behaviour because they are afraid of being punished.[40]

Those empirical findings showed the limitations of economic theories on deterrence and the arguments of increasing antitrust sanctions to the maximum level to achieve deterrence. In addition to other legal explanations for the under-deterrence of cartel criminal sanctions,[41] organizational studies have provided alternative analytical framework by arguing that antitrust enforcement should be improved through improving the internal mechanisms of the firms and adjusting their compliance decisions.[42] Behavioural studies suggest that individuals' perceived detection should be

---

[38]Sokol (2012, p. 211).

[39]Parker and Nielsen (2011).

[40]In another empirical study, Parker shows that business people in Australia tend to "rationalize away" the deterrence effect, for both people do not know antitrust law and those who know it well, they never believe that cartel criminalization will be applied to them personally, either because there is no connection between themselves and the law, or because they have the confidence and capacity to avoid being sanctioned. Parker (2013).

[41]For example, Buccirossi and Spagnolo argue that underdeterrence may come from the restrictions on antitrust fine ceilings imposed on cartels set by EU legislation. Such a ceiling requirement may be due to the consideration of preventing firms from bankruptcy. *See* Buccirossi and Spagnolo (2007) and Wils (2007); Peter Whelan argues that deterrence can only be achieved when there is "moral wrongfulness" for cartel activities. Whelan (2013); Stucke made a similar claim: "[t]there is no consensus on the morality of antitrust offenses." Stucke (2006).

[42]For an analysis of those internal compliance mechanisms and their effect on firm behaviour see Oded (2012).

analyzed from a psychological perspective—as Harry Kissinger once said, "deterrence is above all a psychological problem".[43] Prison penalty usually has a deterrent effect as it will never be reimbursed by the corporate employer.[44]

10.2.5 Towards an Optimal Antitrust Sanction

Given the under-enforcement of competition law, the current debate on antitrust sanctions is centered on three solutions: increase fines to a sufficiently high level to achieve deterrence;[45] to introduce criminal liabilities; to induce individual liabilities on managers and executives[46] and to identify the individual who is liable for cartel type conduct[47] in order to achieve an optimal enforcement.

In recent years, cartel activities have been made a felony in many jurisdictions, and the criminal sanctions have been increased to a rather severe level. In the US, price fixing made a felony in 1987 and courts could impose fines up to double of the harm of illegal profits (the greater of the two).[48] After the Antitrust Improvements Act were passed in 1990, the maximum corporate criminal fine has increased from USD one million to ten million, and the maximum individual fine has risen from USD 100,000 to USD 350,000, up to the maximum range of monetary penalty in the US Sentencing Guidelines.[49] In 2004, the Antitrust Criminal Penalty Enhancement and Reform Act 2004 increased the corporate fine from USD 10 million to USD 100 million; maximum individual imprisonment sentence from 3 to 10 years; maximum individual fine from USD 350,000 to USD 1 million. In the early 1970s, the average individual imprisonment sentence was 44 days.[50] This number increased to 247 days in the 1990s and during the 2005–2007, the average term of incarceration

---

[43]Harry Kissinger made this claim in explaining war and international relations ("Deterrence is above all a psychological problem. The assessment of risks on which it depends becomes less and less precise in the face of weapons of unprecedented novelty and destructiveness. A bluff taken seriously is more useful than a serious threat interpreted as a bluff". cited by Michael G. Mullen, Admiral, U.S. Navy, "It's time for a New Deterrence Model', *Joint Forces Quarterly*, 4th Quarter 2008, 2); *see also* Carroll who published his experiments and criticized the economic models of crime: "He or she is not viewed as the 'economic person' making exhaustive and complex calculations leading to an optimal choice. Rather, it is the 'psychological person', who makes a few simple and concrete examinations of his or her opportunities and makes guesses that can be far short of optimal." Carroll (1978, p. 1513).

[44]Barnett (2009) Criminalization of Cartel Conduct—the Changing Landscape.

[45]For example, Werden argues that the optimal cartel fine should be as high as 200% of the annual turnover. Werden (2009, p. 19).

[46]Werden (2013, pp. 191–194) and Cronin (2013).

[47]Ginsburg and Wright (2010); Markham pointed out the importance of corporate governance in deterring cartel. Markham (2013) and Massey (2012, p. 153).

[48]Connor (2006, p. 208).

[49]Robinson (1991, p. 651).

[50]Gallo et al. (1985), pp. 122–123.

prosecuted by the Antitrust Division of the US DOJ was 703 days.[51] From 1990 till 2010, 367 individuals were sentenced to criminal sanctions, which counted for 510 years imprisonment in total, 338 Individuals were sentenced to prison from 1990 to 2009.[52] The total annual prison days increased from 3313 in the 1990s to 31, 391 in 2007.[53] In the 1990s, 37% of the defendants sentenced to prison, while in 2009, 80% of the individuals violated the antitrust law were sent to prison.[54] Legislations on cartel criminalization have also been considered or adopted in Australia, Brazil, Canada, Chile, the Czech Republic, Iceland, Indonesia, Israel, Greece, Japan, Korea, Mexico, the Netherlands, New Zealand, Norway, Russia, South Africa, Thailand and Zambia.[55] In countries where cartel activities are criminalized, it is clear that legislators and prosecutors are influenced by the economic analysis of crime represented by Gary Becker's model and its deterrence story.[56] An efficient deterrence could be achieved when the potential perpetrator could internalize the social cost of crime, and legal sanctions should be set higher than the private benefits of the offender, which is calculated as the probability of being detected multiplied with the severity of the sanctioning.[57] When it is costly to raise the detection rate the sanction on illegal activities should be set at the maximum level to offset the decreased expected price, and such mechanisms include imposing higher fines or imprisonment sanctions.

Meanwhile, it has been advocated that individuals engaged in cartelistic activities should be given criminal liabilities, as the threat of imposing prison sentences would provide maximum deterrence and deter business people from participating in price fixing.[58] Boards of directors should take responsibility for antitrust compliance, and directors or officers bear the duty of supervising the implementation of compliance requirements, and once an individual employee fails to fulfill the requirement, it is reasonable to impose sanctions on individuals.[59] Even so, the prison sentences would not achieve optimal deterrence unless the magnitude of sentencing has been dramatically increased, as Connor and Lande's empirical studies of 75 cartels shows

---

[51] Werden (2009, p. 22).

[52] Antitrust Division, US Department of Justice, Ten Year Workload Statistics Report 12 (2012), http://www.justice.gov/atr/public/workload-statistics.pdf; In Europe, the EU Commission has significantly increased cartel fines to make it "quasi-criminal". For the details for cartel fines, see www.europa.eu.int/competition/cartels/statistics, Over half of EU Member States have made cartel activities criminal, *see* Girardet (2010), pp. 286–287.

[53] Hammond (2008).

[54] Hammond (2010).

[55] *see* Shaffer (2015) and Hammond (2010).

[56] The deterrence argument is rooted in the utilitarian theory, which indicates the goal of imposing punishment, as a form of suffering which reduces the utility of individuals, is to prevent future crime. *See* Beccaria (1767) and Bentham (1789). This to some extent contrasts with the legal theory where criminal law is viewed as aiming at punishing morally unacceptable acts, and the goals of criminal law include retribution, rehabilitation, incapacitation and education. Dau-Schmidt (1984, p. 87).

[57] Schwartz (1979, p. 1076).

[58] Ginsburg and Wright (2010, pp. 5–6).

[59] Ginsburg and Wright (2010, p 18).

that the deterrence effects of the sanctions combined, that is, the measured total monetary amount of corporate and individual fines, private damage compensation, restitution payment, incarceration, amounted only 9–21% of the total value of optimal sanctions. The current level of cartel penalties should be increased by at least five times to protect consumers and cartel victims.[60]

10.3 Choice of Sanctions in the AML

10.3.1 Administrative Sanctions

The current enforcement pattern of the AML strongly relies on administrative enforcement powers and administrative penalties. Article 46 of the AML[61] stipulates that three types of sanctions may be imposed by antitrust enforcement authorities when monopoly agreements are reached and implemented: to discontinue the violation, confiscate the illegal gain and imposing administrative fines of between 1 and 10% of the sales revenue in the previous year. If the monopoly agreement has not been implemented, a fine of less than RMB 500,000 should be imposed. The 2020 draft revision of the AML has significantly increased the fine on business enterprises (RMB 500,000) to RMB 50 million, and increased the fine on industrial associations (RMB 500,000) to RMB 5 million. Article 47 of the AML stipulates that the penalty for the abuse of the dominant position is also an administrative fine of between 1% and a maximum of 10% of the sales revenue in the previous year. Criminal liabilities specifically targeting antitrust violations are not found in the AML. From 2008 until 2015, among the 190 cases investigated by the NDRC and local branches, including 154 on horizontal monopoly agreements, 21 on vertical agreements and 7 on abuse of dominant position, only 8 cases were sanctioned by confiscating illegal gains; and among the 101 cases investigated by SAIC and its local branches, including 87 on horizontal monopoly agreements, 14 on abuse of dominant position, 20 of them

---

[60] Connor and Lande (2011).

[61] Article 46 of the AML: In case there exists a monopolistic agreement and is implemented by the undertakings in violation of this law, the anti-monopoly authorities shall order the undertakings to cease such act, the illegal gains shall be confiscated, and a fine between 1% and 10% of the turnover from the previous year shall be imposed; If the monopolistic agreement has not been implemented, a fine below RMB 500,000 shall be imposed. If the undertakings report actively the circumstance of their monopoly agreement to the antimonopoly authorities and provide important evidences, the antimonopoly authorities shall reduce or remit the fines according to own judgement. In case the associations of operators organize undertakings of the industry to reach monopoly agreement in violation of this law, the anti-monopoly authorities shall impose a fine below RMB 500,000; and if the circumstances are serious, the social organization register administrative department may rescind its registration.

were sanctioned by confiscation of illegal gains.[62] From August 2008 until the end of 2014, the SAIC has investigated 43 cases, and the NDRC has investigated 339 entities, among them 33 were foreign entities. Also, the NDRC has published 70 penalty decisions on the website, and 50 of them were on domestic entities, with an average fine of 2.2% of annual revenue; and 20 of them were on foreign entities, with an average fine of 4% of annual revenue.[63] Article 48 imposes penalties on concentrations that the anti-monopoly authority will "order it to cease doing so, to dispose of shares or assets, transfer the business or take other necessary measures to restore the market situation before the concentration within a time limit, and may impose a fine of less than RMB 500,000." In Article 55 of the 2020 draft revision of the AML, the fine of less than RMB 500,000 in Article 47 has been revised to a fine of less than 10% of the previous year's sales revenue.[64] The director of the anti-monopoly bureau at SAMR explained in an interview in 2019 that the base of fines should be set as the annual sales for all products in the previous year.[65]

Since 2014, MOFCOM has intensified the enforcement of Article 48 by imposing fines on transactions that failed to be notified, and announced a public "name and shame" measure for non-filers.[66] In December 2014, MOFCOM imposed a fine of 300,000 RMB on Unigroup for failing to notify before the acquisition of RDA Micro-electronics.[67] Already in 2016, MOFCOM has imposed the largest fines on the merging parties when MOFCOM found that the parties ignored the notification requirement intentionally and have violated the requirements the second time in less than a year. Bombardier Transportation Sweden was fined RMB 400,000 during its proposed joint venture with New United Group.[68] In August 2017, MOFCOM had published 17 decisions, and the first case on foreign-to-foreign transaction that was

---

[62] Lin (2016), Report on the Administrative Enforcement of Anti-monopoly Law in China (2008–2015), cited by Jet Deng and Yannis Katsoulacos, Antitrust Sanctioning in China: How can the NDRC Guidelines be Further Improved.

[63] Wang (2015).

[64] Article 55 of the 2020 draft revision of the AML: If the concentration of business operators has one of the following circumstances, the anti-monopoly law enforcement agency shall impose a fine of less than 10% of the previous year's sales: (1) Centralization shall be made without notification; (2) The implementation of concentration without approval after the declaration; (3) Decisions in violation of additional restrictive conditions; (4) Implementation of concentration in violation of a decision prohibiting concentration of business operators. In addition to the provisions of the preceding paragraph, antitrust enforcement agencies may order the suspension of concentration, add restrictive conditions that reduce the adverse effects of concentration on competition, and order to continue to perform the obligations in the additional restrictive conditions or change the additional restrictive conditions., Ordering the disposal of shares or assets within a time limit, transferring business within a time limit, and taking other necessary relief measures to restore the state before the concentration.

[65] Liu et al. (2020).

[66] Deng and Huang (2018).

[67] Administrative Penalties on Unigroup Corp. Ltd for Failing to Notify its Acquisition of RDA.

[68] China Antitrust Review 2016, Davis Polk & Wardwell LLP, Client Memorandum, at p. 3 available at https://www.davispolk.com/publications/china-antitrust-review-2016/.

not notified was Canon's acquisition of Toshiba Medical Systems. In 2018, MOFCOM imposed fines on 15 transactions and most of the cases were given fines of between RMB 150,000 to 200, 000, while two cases received fines of RMB 400, 000.[69] When the acquisition took several stages, MOFCOM held that each step should be found as mutually dependent and the parties should notify prior to the first step. In Meinian Onehealth's acquisition of Ciming, the merging parties only notified at the final stage. MOFCOM held that various stages of the acquisition were mutually dependent and had the same ultimate purpose. Meinian Onehealth was fined RMB 300,000 for violating the notification requirement.[70] MOFCOM also imposed fines on merging parties that failed to comply with their commitments. On December 8, 2014, MOFCOM published the decision that imposed a total fine of RMB 600,000 on Western Digital, for its conduct of violating Part 4(1) of the 2012 Conditional Clearance, by removing the department of Viviti/HGST and all employees were transferred to Western Digital without obtaining permission from MOFCOM. The 2012 Clearance required Viviti to maintain the business as a separated, independent entity.[71] On July 20, 2018, SAMR imposed a fine of RMB 300,000 on Paper Excellence BV, for its failure to notify the acquisition of Eldorado Brasil Celulose S.A.[72] Up to April 2018, 46 firms were publicly named, shamed and fined, and 28 of them were domestic firms, including SOEs.[73] It is reported that the fine will increase to a maximum of RMB 5 million.[74] The Article 55 of the 2020 draft revision of the AML has revised the fine of RMB 500,000 to up to 10% of the sales revenue in the previous year. According to Liu et al., since 2019, the SAMR has been more strict on cases that failed to notify and in 2019 the SAMR has imposed fines on 17 cases in total for failure to notify.[75]

NDRC provisional rules on Regulating the Authority of Price-related Administrative Penalties provided general conditions on determine fines. SAIC issued the Provisions on Determining the Illegal Gains in Cases with Administrative Penalties. When calculating the administrative fines imposed on horizontal agreements by NDRC, SAIC, Price Bureau and their local branches from 2008 till 2017, NDRC (on average RMB 227,123,078.80) DRC (on average RMB 36,940,193.33) and Price Bureau (on average RMB 37,088,799.90) are the leading enforcement agencies who

[69]Zhan et al. (2018, p. 6).

[70]China Competition Bulletin, Edition 47, June 2017, at p. 3.

[71]Administrative Penalties on Western Digital for Violating the Antimonopoly Law and MOFCOM Announcement [2012] No. 9 Regarding the Conditional Approval of the Acquisition of Hitachi Global Storage Technologies by Western Digital Corp.

[72]Update on Establishment of Single Antitrust Agency in China, October 24, 2018, Davis Polk Client Memorandum p. 3 available at https://www.davispolk.com/files/2018-10-24_china_consolidates_antitrust_powers_into_single_agency.pdf.

[73]Deng and Huang (2018).

[74]Antitrust in Asia, the Business Impact of Fast-Evolving Competition Laws, October 2017, Freshfields Bruckhaus Deringer, at p. 24, available at https://www.freshfields.com/49f98e/globalassets/our-thinking/campaigns/antitrust-in-asia/06304_pg_act_asia-guide_aw_interactive_v3.pdf.

[75]Liu et al. (et al. 2020).

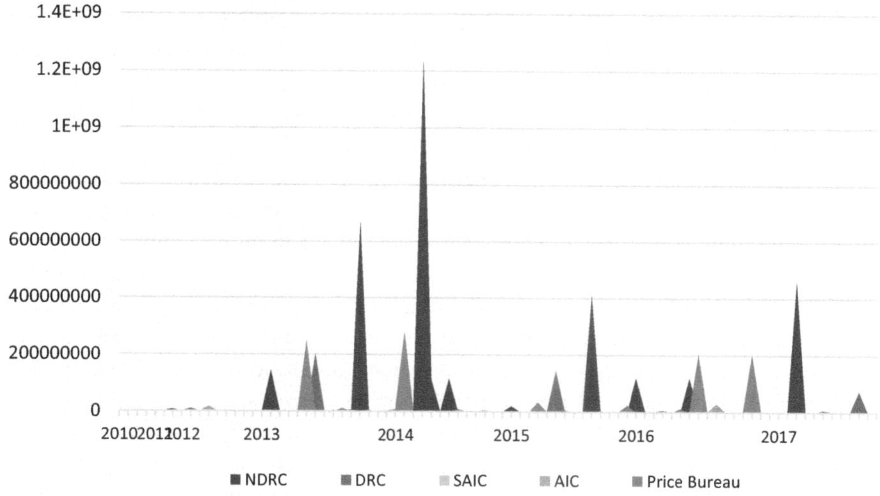

Chart 10.1 Amount of Administrative Fines imposed on Horizontal Agreements (2007–2018)

issue administrative fines. SAIC has imposed the smallest amount (on average RMB 587,400.00) (Chart. 10.1).

10.3.2 Criminal Sanctions

Criminal liability is only mentioned in Article 52 of the AML. A fine of RMB 20,000 to 100,000 for an individual or RMB 200,000 to RMB 1,000,000 for a business entity will be imposed on those who fail to cooperate with the investigation. Criminal liabilities specifically targeting antitrust violations are not found in the AML. Articles 52 and 54 have mentioned criminal sanctions for parties who do not provide proper evidence during the investigation, as well as for investigators who abuse their power during the investigation. Article 52 stipulates the penalty for providing fraudulent information. If during the process of antitrust inspection and investigation, "business operators refuse to provide related materials and information, provide fraudulent materials or information, conceal, destroy or remove evidence, or refuse or obstruct the investigation in other ways, the anti-monopoly authority shall order them to make rectification", a fine will be imposed on individuals of less than RMB 20,000, less than RMB 200,000 on entities. In serious situations, the anti-monopoly authority may impose a fine of RMB 20, 000 up to RMB 100,000 on individuals, and a fine of RMB 200,000 up to RMB1 million on entities. The level of fines stipulated in this article has been significantly increased in Article 59 of the 2020 draft revision of the

AML.[76] Moreover, where a crime is committed, the relevant business operators will assume criminal liability. However, the article concerned does not precisely define what exactly is meant by a 'crime'. The use for the word crime in this context is remarkable since the violations of the AML are not criminalized but only subject to administrative fines. In the 2020 draft revision of the AML, Article 57 adds criminal liabilities for business operators that conduct monopolistic behavior.

According to Clarke,[77] there are other reasons why antitrust criminalization may fail. One of the most important factors that should be taken into account considering the criminalization of cartel conduct is whether it has been supported by public opinion.[78] Compared with traditional crimes, the economic harm caused by cartel conduct normally attracts less emotional and moral response from the public,[79] especially in jurisdictions which do not have a well-established competition culture. Clarke points out that the lack of public awareness of the serious harm caused by cartel conduct leads to a weak political will to make the change towards antitrust criminalization.[80] However, the recent trend of criminalizing cartel agreements in many jurisdictions is seen as a top-down approach, that is, imposing criminal sanctions is more driven by the pressure from transnational cartel enforcement, rather than the bottom-up process which is led by widespread public opinion.[81] There are other circumstances that the public perception on criminalizing cartel conduct is led by the opinions from legal experts.[82] If the process of criminalizing the Anti-monopoly Law in China is driven by the transnational enforcement interests, the success of antitrust criminalization depends on the extent to which the professional opinion is aligned with such interests from abroad. Given the particular situation of government agencies and the judiciary in China, a shift of powers to the judiciary (which would be the consequence of criminalization) may at this moment not be indicated. As Wang has argued that the reasons for introducing criminal liabilities in China may not be convincing as criminalizing cartel behavior will impose substantial costs on judicial

[76] Article 59 of the 2020 draft revision of the AML: In cases when individuals refuse to provide relevant materials or information, or provide false materials or information, or conceals, destroys, or transfers evidence, or threatens personal safety when enforcement agencies review and investigate the case, the enforcement agency shall order it to make corrections. Administrative agencies and organizations authorized by laws and regulations with the function of managing public affairs may make recommendations to the relevant higher authorities and supervisory agencies in the above-mentioned situations that a fine of less than 1% of annual sales may be imposed on operators. If it is difficult to calculate the sales revenue, a fine of less than RMB 5 million shall be imposed. Individuals may be fined from RMB 200,000 to RMB 1 million. In cases of individuals or operators constitute a crime, they will take criminal liabilities.

[77] Clarke (2012, p. 77).

[78] Clarke (2012, p. 77) and Stucke (2006) and Parker (2006, p. 598).

[79] Clarke (2012, p. 77).

[80] Clarke (2012, p. 78).

[81] Harding (2006).

[82] Harding (2006) To better understand cartel conduct as a crime indeed requires certain economic and legal expertise. As Stucke held, "it may be that few people in society, if asked about price-fixing, would graph in their minds a triangle representing the deadweight welfare loss" Stucke (2006, p. 495).

resources, and criminal enforcement may not improve the enforcement effects given the role that administrative agencies play in the AML.[83] Thus, rather than moving from criminalization, there are possibilities of improving the current administrative enforcement, and to improve the two main factors in the Becker Model (p and S) by increasing the level of administrative fines and strengthening the role of courts in private enforcement, and in this way to increase the costs of antitrust violations.

10.4 An Analysis of Choice of Sanctions in Chinese Antitrust

The Becker Models shows that the legal sanction is set at the optimal level when potential infringers could internalize the external harm of the violation, thus those "inefficient violations"—when social harm exceeds the benefits could be deterred. As argued above the expected sanction for a potential violator consists of the probability (p) of being apprehended and convicted and then a sanction (S) imposed. Hence, the expected sanction for the potential offender consists of the outcome of the sanction multiplied by the probability. There are substantial possibilities to increase both the p and the S within the current Chinese model of administrative enforcement of antitrust law. To increase the probability and severity of sanctions, the role of courts should not be neglected. On the one side, courts are less affected by the pressure from interest groups in specific industries because courts' jurisdiction is much broader. Meanwhile, to achieve the optimal enforcement of competition law, the benefits of private enforcement is substantial. Private enforcement could facilitate the efficient allocation of public resources and thus provide more enforcement resources to complement public enforcement; private enforcement could monitor the public enforcement agencies and prevent shirking; also the strategies invented in private litigation and settlements could be applied by public regulators.[84]

During the last twelve years, the enforcement of the AML in China has been highly reliant on public enforcement and the sanctions imposed on antitrust violators are mainly administrative fines. The economic analysis of optimal legal sanctions developed by Gary Becker shows that offenders should fully internalize the social costs, and criminal sanctions may have to be imposed in order to sufficiently deter future infringements. In recent years, these models were reinvestigated by utilizing insights offered by behavioural law and economics, and these scholars examine the situation in particular when the assumption of rationality does not hold. The economic analysis presented in this chapter did not have the normative goal of providing the final answer to the question of whether criminalization of antitrust violations in China was indicated. The goal of the analysis presented here, was to show the conditions under which criminalization may work as they predicted from the economic literature. The economic arguments for judicial capacity will be discussed in the

[83] Wang (2020, p. 20).

[84] Stephenson (2005, p. 107).

next chapter, and the behavioral law and economics literature analyzed in Chap. 12 further provide valuable refinements of traditional models especially as far as the behaviour of offenders and regulators is concerned. The policy maker in China may benefit from these findings from economic theory in order to further improve both the substance and the enforcement of its antitrust law.

10.5 Conclusions

Economic analysis of antitrust sanctions is based on the theory of deterrence. When the deterrence effect is calculated upon the probability of detection, multiplied by the level of sanctions, economists have agreed that increasing the severity of sanctions will be more effective and less costly, and when deterrence could be achieved in the same way, fines would be preferred to imprisonment. The empirical findings on testing the economic theories of deterrence showed that corporate behaviour has not been affected by antitrust sanctions, and the current antitrust fines cannot achieve the optimal level to deter as theoretically predicted. The AML relies predominantly on administrative fines, and Articles 46–47 stipulate that the penalty for monopolistic behaviour is an administrative fine of from 1% up to a maximum of 10% of the sales revenue in the previous year. Although cartel criminalization has become a global trend, criminalizing monopolistic conduct would be ineffective when case error is substantial and the judiciary capacity is under-developed. The next chapter will discuss the role of courts under the AML and will further discuss enforcement issue of the competition cases.

References

Avio, K. L. (1998). The economics of prisons. *European Journal of Law and Economics, 6,* 143–175.

Barnett, B. A. (2009). Criminalization of cartel conduct—the changing landscape. Joint Federal Court of Australia/Law Council of Australia (Business Law Section) Workshop. Available at http://www.justice.gov/atr/criminalization-cartel-conduct-changing-landscape.ett.

Buccirossi, P., & Spagnolo, G. (2007). Optimal Fines in the Era of Whistleblowers—Should Price Fixers Still Go to Prison? In V. Goshal & J. Stennek (Eds.), *The political economy of antitrust.* Amsterdam: Elsevier.

Becker, G. S. (1968). Crime and punishment: An economic approach. *Journal of Political Economy, 76*(2), 169–217.

Bentham, J. (1789) *An introduction to the principles of morals and legislation*, Oxford: Claredon Press.

Beccaria. (1767). *Essay on crimes and punishment.*

Bowles, R., Faure, M. G., & Garoupa, N. (2008). The scope of criminal law and criminal sanctions: An economic view and policy implications. *Journal of Law and Society, 35*(3), 389–416.

Carroll, J. (1978). A psychological approach to deterrence: The evaluation of crime opportunities. *Journal of Personality and Social Psychology, 36*(12), 1512–1520.

Clarke, D. C. (2003). China's legal system and the WTO: Prospects for compliance. *Washington University Global Studies Law Review, 2,* 97–120.

Clarke, J. (2012). The increasing criminalization of economic law—a competition law perspective. *Journal of Financial Crime, 19*(1), 76–98.
Coffee, J. C. (1980). Corporate crime and punishment: A non-Chicago view of the economics of criminal sanctions. *American Criminal Law Review*, 419–476.
Cook, P. J. (1980). Research in criminal deterrence: lying the groundwork for the second decade. *Crime and Justice, 2*, 211–268.
Connor, J. M. (2006). Effectiveness of antitrust sanctions on modern international cartels. *Journal of Industry, Competition and Trade, 6*, 195–223.
Connor, J. M., & Lande, R. H. (2011). Optimal cartel deterrence: an empirical comparison of sanctions to overcharges. Available at: http://works.bepress.com/robert_lande/6/.
Cronin, Z. A. (2013). The competitor's dilemma tailoring antitrust sanctions to white-collar priorities in the fight against cartels. *Fordham International Law Journal, 36*(6), 1683–1732.
Deng, F., & Huang, C. (2018, August). A ten-year review of merger enforcement in China. *The Antitrust Source*. Available at http://www.antitrustsource.com.
Dau-Schmidt, K. G. (1984). Sentencing antitrust offenders: reconciling economic theory with legal theory. *William Mitchell Law Review, 9*(1), 75–100.
Easterbrook, F. H. (1983). Criminal procedure as a market system. *The Journal of Legal Studies, 12*(2), 289–332.
Faure, M. G. (2000). Compensation of non-pecuniary loss: an economic perspective. In U. Magnus, & J. Spier (Eds.) *European Tort Law*, Liber Amicorum for Helmut Koziol, Frankfurt am Main: Peter Lang, 143–159.
Faure, M. G. (2009). Environmental Crimes. In N. Garoupa (Ed.), *Criminal law and economics* (Vol. 3). Cheltenham: Edward Elgar.
Faure, M. G., Ogus, A., & Philipsen, N. (2009). Curbing consumer financial losses: The economics of regulatory enforcement. *Law and Policy, 31*(2), 161–191.
Fels, A., Wang, X., Ng, W., & Emch, A. (Eds.) *China Competition Bulletin*, A Publication of the Competition Law & Economics Network at Melbourne Law School, University of Melbourne, Edition 47, June 2017.
Ginsburg, D. H., & Wright, J. D. (2010). Antitrust sanctions. *Competition Policy International, 6*(2), 3–39.
Gallo, J. C., Craycraft, J. L., & Bush, S. C. (1985). Guess who came to dinner: an empirical study of federal antitrust enforcement for the period 1963–1984. *Review of Industrial Organization, 2*, 106–130.
Girardet, P. (2010). "What if Uncle Sam Wants You?": principles and recent practice concerning US extradition requests in cartel cases. *Journal of European Competition Law and Practice, 1*, 286–287.
Harding, C. (2006). Business collusion as a criminological phenomenon: Exploring the global criminalization of business cartels. *Critical Criminology*, 181–205.
Hammond, S. D. (2008). Recent Developments, Trends, and Milestones in the Antitrust Division's Criminal Enforcement Program, presented at the 56th Annual Spring Meeting of the ABA Section of Antitrust Law, March 26, 2008.
Hammond, S.D. (2010). The Evolution of Criminal Antitrust Enforcement over the Last Two Decades, Presented by the ABA Criminal Section and the ABA Center for Continuing Legal Education, at the 24th Annual National Institute on White Collar Crime, February 25, 2010.
Liu, C., Li, A., Bi, Y., Liu, S., Hong, L., & Liu, J. (2020). China's anti-monopoly law enters its second decade. King & Wood Mallesons on February 20, 2020, available at https://www.chinalawinsight.com/2020/02/articles/antitrust/chinas-anti-monopoly-law-enters-its-second-decade/#_ftn18.
King, D. (2010). Criminalization of cartel behavior, Ministry of Economic Development Occasional Paper 10/01.
Lin, W. (2016). Report on the Administrative Enforcement of Anti-monopoly Law in China (2008–2015).
Markham, J. W., Jr. (2013). The failure of corporate governance standards and antitrust compliance. *South Dakota Law Review, 58*(3), 499–542.

Massey, P. (2012). Criminalising competition law offenses—a review of Irish experience. *New Journal of European Criminal Law, 3*(2), 154–174.
Oded, S. (2012). Inducing Corporate Proactive Compliance: liability controls & corporate monitors, Doctoral Thesis at Erasmus University Rotterdam, 30 March 2012.
Parker, C., & Nielsen, V. L. (2011). Deterrence and the impact of calculative thinking on business compliance with competition and consumer regulation. *The Antitrust Bulletin, 56*(2), 377–426.
Parker, C. (2006). The "compliance" trap: The moral message in responsive regulatory enforcement. *Law and Society Review, 40*(3), 591–622.
Parker, C. (2013). The war on cartels and the social meaning of deterrence. *Regulation and Governance, 7,* 174–194.
Posner, R. A. (1980a). Retribution and related concepts of punishment. *The Journal of Legal Studies, 9*(1), 71–92.
Posner, R. A. (1980b). Optimal sentences for white collar criminals. *American Criminal Law Review*, 400–418.
Polinsky, A. M., & Shavell, S. (1979). The optimal trade-off between the probability and the magnitude of fines. *American Economic Review*, 880–891.
Polinsky, A. M., & Shavell, S. (1991). A Note on optimal fines when wealth varies among individuals. *American Economic Review, 81,* 618–621.
Polinsky, A. M., & Shavell, S. (1993). Should employees be subject to fines and imprisonment given the existence of corporate liability? *International Review of Law and Economics, 13,* 239–257.
Robinson, C. K. (1991). Developments in criminal antitrust enforcement. *Antitrust Law Journal, 60*(2), 649–656.
Shaffer, G. C. (2015). Nathaniel H. Nesbitt, and Spencer Weber Waller, Criminalizing Cartels: A Global trend?, in Arlen Duke, John Duns and Brendan Sweeney (Eds.), *Research Handbook on Comparative Competition Law*, Edgar Elgar 2015.
Schwartz, W. F. (1979). An overview of the economics of antitrust enforcement. *Georgetown Law Journal, 68,* 1075–1102.
Shavell, S. (1985). Criminal law and the optimal use of non-monetary sanctions as a deterrent. *Columbia Law Review, 85,* 1232–1262.
Shavell, S. (1993). The optimal structure of law enforcement. *The Journal of Law and Economics, 36,* 255–288.
Shavell, S. (2004). *Foundations of economic analysis of law*. Cambridge: Harvard University Press.
Stigler, G. J. (1970). The optimum enforcement of laws. *Journal of Political Economy, 78*(3), 526–536.
Stephenson, M. C. (2005). Public regulation of private enforcement: The case for expanding the role of administrative agencies. *Virginia Law Review, 91*(1), 93–173.
Stucke, M. E. (2006). Morality and antitrust. *Columbia Business Law Review, 3*, 443–547.
Sokol, D. (2012). Cartels, corporate compliance, and what practitioners really think about enforcement. *Antitrust Law Journal, 78,* 201–239.
Van den Bergh, R., & Faure, M. G. (2011). Critical issues in the enforcement of the anti-monopoly law in China: A law and economics perspective. In M. Faure & X. Zhang (Eds.), *Competition policy and regulation* (pp. 54–75). Cheltenham: Edward Elgar.
Wang, X. (2020). Reflections on the revision of China's antimonopoly law(我国《反垄断法》修订的几点思考). *Law Review* (法学评论) 2, 11–21.
Wang, E. X. (2015). An overview of China's antitrust enforcement, Charles River Associates, May 2015, available at https://china.ucsd.edu/_files/np-2015/Panel%204%20-%20WANG_Elizabeth.pdf.
Werden. (2009). Sanctioning cartel activity: Let the punishment fit the crime. *European Competition Journal, 5*(1), 19–36.
Whelan, P. (2013). Artel criminalization and the challenge of "moral wrongfulness". *Oxford Journal of Legal Studies*, 1–27.
Werden, G. J. (2013). Cartel deterrence through criminal enforcement: a rejoinder to Lande and Davis. *The Antitrust Bulletin, 58,* 191–194.

Wils, W. P. J. (2005). Is Criminalization of EU competition law the answer? In K. J. Cseres, M. P. Schinkel, & F. O. W. Vogelaar (Eds.), *Remedies and sanctions in competition policy: Economic and legal implications of the tendency to criminalize antitrust enforcement in the EU member states*. Cheltenham: Edward Elgar.

Wils, W. (2007). The European Commission's 2006 guidelines on antitrust fines: a legal and economic analysis. *World Competition* 30.

Zhan, H., Song, Y., & Yang, Z. (2018). A new era comes—highlights of the anti-monopoly law of China in 2018, Anjie Law Firm.

Chapter 11
Enforcement of Competition Law—Role of the Courts and Economic Experts

Abstract Agency public enforcement and private actions before the courts are the two complementing channels to cure market failure. Most antitrust jurisdictions rely on specialized antitrust agencies because it is believed that generalist courts do not have relevant expertise. When agencies are equipped with personnel having knowledge and expertise in economics, they investigate competition cases by applying such knowledge. At the same time, agencies with a top-down organization hierarchy may also suffer from public choice problems, and when the pressure from interest groups prevails, a court system should be built upon to enforce competition law through a more balanced system. Solely relying on the regulatory agencies to investigate competition cases, neglecting the fact that the goals of regulators may not be aligned with the goals of competition. The advantage for a court, but not agency, to enforce the law is that courts are restrained from regulatory capture, as defined in the public choice theory. The main challenge for courts to deal with complex economic antitrust cases is the lack of specific expertise, and such limitation could be remedied with the help of economic experts. This chapter discusses the economic complexity of the competition cases, the problem of specialization for courts versus agencies, and the role of experts. It will positively review the current development of private enforcement of the AML, and the potential role of expert witnesses.

11.1 Introduction

There is no doubt that antitrust cases are getting economically sophisticated. On the one hand, economic analysis has been widely acknowledged around the world by antitrust agencies,[1] and courts,[2] as well as private litigants. Antitrust enforcement agencies paid particular attention to the use of economic models. Antitrust lawyers and business practitioners take part in seminars and conferences sponsored by

---

[1] See f*or example*, Neven and De Coninck (2010).

[2] For example, Federal Judicial Center published Reference Manual on Scientific Evidence in 2000. The first two chapters of the Reference Guide in this manual are Reference Guide on Statistics and Reference Guide on Multiple Regression. Baker and Rubinfeld (1999, p. 387).

J. Ma, *Competition Law in China*,
https://doi.org/10.1007/978-981-15-5105-5_11

economists to study economic techniques.[3] The trend of moving towards economic analysis of competition law has been welcomed by academic scholars—to put it into the words of Friedman, the economic reasoning would make the antitrust analysis more "scientific".[4] On the other hand, whereas the increasing use of economic models in antitrust cases opened the market for economic consultancy,[5] for both agency and judicial decision makers it becomes an unavoidable burden to deal with sophisticated economic models. It is particularly challenging for generalist judges, for the reason that unlike antitrust enforcement agencies which have devoted significant investment to increase the ratio of economist professionals,[6] and are able to conduct econometric analysis themselves; sophisticated economic analysis of antitrust cases is often beyond the knowledge and experience of generalist judges.

There are two types of economic evidence that judges have to encounter. One type is the economic analysis of cases conducted by competition authority, and the other is the economic proof provided by private litigants. Judges may not be able to "re-do" the economic evidence that is provided by the competition agency.[7] In particular, judges are reluctant to examine how the regression was operated as well as how the parameters have been applied in the econometric models.[8] For private parities, judges are often under pressure to make quick decisions by interpreting the often conflicting economic evidence that is provided by agencies, parties or expert witness.[9] This raises some issues, such as whether an expert witness is objective and reliable. Moreover, both parties would engage in "expert shopping" in order to

---

[3]Botteman (2006 p. 71).

[4]Friedman (1953, pp 3–4) and *see also* Weller (1997, pp. 871–935).

[5]Neven claimed that the demand for economic consultancy in Europe has dramatically increased since the 1990s, especially after the promulgation of the EC Merger Regulation. Neven (2006, p. 748).

[6]Both in the US and EU, the ratio of economists to lawyer at the competition enforcement agencies has increased significantly. In the EU, the Chief Competition Economist at the Directorate-General Competition (DG COMP) was appointed in 2003. Until 2005, among over 700 officials working at (DG COMP), 200 of them have an economics or business background, and about 20 of them hold a Ph.D. degree in economics. In 2005, 10 specialized economists who have a Ph.D. degree in industrial organization were hired by this office either as a permanent EU official, or as a temporary agent. *See* Roeller (2005, p. 16). Thus, as Neven argued, the number of professionals with an economic background working at the competition agency is comparable with those working in the economic consultancy firms. However, the economic resources that are devoted to case analysis are still unbalanced between private parties and the competition agency. *See* Neven (2006, p. 752, p. 781). In the US, the enforcement agencies are well-equipped with both professionals of PhD economists, but also antitrust lawyers who have a solid understanding of economic reasoning. *See* Baker and Bresnahan (2006, p. 28).

[7]For example in the EU, Botteman claimed that "There are very few instances where the CFI and the ECJ have been confronted with econometric analyses carried out by the Commission or by experts acting on behalf of the notifying parties or other third parties." Botteman (2006 p. 73, p. 85).

[8]Botteman (2006, p. 86).

[9]Back to 1948 Judge Prettyman pointed out that "The tribunal does the best it can to decipher the truth from the resultant welter. Nothing could be sillier." Prettyman, 'Needed: New Trial Technique: Suggestions for the Trial of Complicated Cases', 34 ABA J 766, 770 (1948) cited by Massel (1962, p. 48).

provide the most sophisticated economic models, which significantly increases the litigation cost. Given the limited capacity of interpreting the economic language, the power of judicial review becomes rather limited. The limited judicial capacity for assessing economic evidence has been named by Frank Easterbrook as the "limits of antitrust".[10]

It is not a new topic to discuss the allocation of enforcement power between agency and courts. For over a century, law and economics scholars have developed a rich 'law enforcement' literature studying whether administrative or judicial enforcement could achieve an efficient outcome. Traditional law and economics scholars approach this question by providing a list of criteria, such as the enforcement cost, how much money is being spent on building prison, collecting fines, or hiring judges and police; the enforcement error, that is who is more likely to make fewer mistake in making decisions. Traditional law and economics literature also suggest that judges are more likely to be impartial, and objective; whereas agency officials are at the risk of regulatory capture, although they also enjoy the advantage of being flexible in implementing the law and policies. The issue of allocating enforcement power between agency and courts becomes more complex because legal problems today are becoming more sophisticated. Experts are often involved to help judges and agency officials to understand technical, specialized and complicated issues related to the case. It is therefore worthwhile to reexamine the criteria on law enforcement and in particular to investigate whether it is the agency officials or the general judges who are best equipped to make decisions based on the expert input that has been provided internally or externally. It is relevant to enrich the scholarly debate on administrative and judicial power allocation; it is also relevant to respond to the political debate on which institutional design is better for achieving the enforcement goals, and how to improve the performance of the regulatory agencies and specialized courts in expert-involved cases.[11] The comparison would have implications for the recent debate of whether enforcement competence should be shifted from courts to agencies, which expertise in a certain field of law and policy should be assured,[12] and whether enforcement power should be initially delegated to agencies or courts when a particular law or policy needs to be implemented.[13]

---

[10] Baker and Bresnahan (2006, p. 29).

[11] It has been both an academic and a political concern to improve the performance of regulatory agencies by improving the institutional and organizational designs. For example, the study of competition agencies: Wright and Diveley (2012, pp. 1–22).

[12] Kovacic (1997, p. 920).

[13] This is named by Wright and Diveley "Expertise Hypothesis", *see* Wright and Diveley (2012 p. 5). Note that the legislative debate on delegating enforcement power to agencies or courts has lasted for centuries. Back to 1887 when the Interstate Commerce Act was promulgated, one of the most debated issues was whether this Act should be enforced by courts or agencies. *See* Stephenson (2006, p. 1039). *see also* Gilligan et al. (1989, pp. 35, 47–49). In the US, the legislative debate on allocating powers on the interpretation of statutes also refers to the Chevron doctrine and its exceptions, which defines when administrative agencies are empowered to interpret the statute. *See* Stephenson (2006, p. 1041).

As discussed in Chap. 9, most jurisdictions rely on administrative agencies to deal with antitrust cases. Agency public enforcement and private actions before the courts are the two complementing channels to cure market failure.[14] Most antitrust jurisdictions rely on specialized antitrust agencies because it is believed that generalist courts do not have relevant expertise. When agencies are equipped with personnel having knowledge and expertise in economics, they investigate competition cases by applying such knowledge. At the same time, agencies with a top-down organization hierarchy may also suffer from public choice problems, and when the pressure from interest groups prevails, a court system should be built upon to enforce competition law through a more balanced system. Solely relying on the regulatory agencies to investigate competition cases, neglecting the fact that the goals of regulators may not be aligned with the goals of competition. The advantage for a court, but not agency, to enforce the law is that courts are restrained from regulatory capture, as defined in the public choice theory. The main challenge for courts to deal with complex economic antitrust cases is the lack of specific expertise, and such limitation could be remedied with the help of economic experts. This chapter discusses the economic complexity of the competition cases, the problem of specialization for courts versus agencies, and the role of experts. It will positively review the current development of private enforcement of the AML, and the potential role of expert witnesses. It tends to argue that judges tend to avoid doing complex economic analysis, and rely on relatively easy models in their daily work. Moreover, it discusses the behaviour bias of juries and expert witness, whom the judges rely on in their decision-making process. It is not true that economist experts can always provide non-biased, useful help. This and the next chapter of this book provide preliminary thought on how to mitigate this bias, such as improving the training program of judges, as well as formulating expert groups.

11.2 Economic Complexity of the Competition Cases

Economic analysis has become the main substance of competition cases, and it would be impossible to discuss a competition case without knowing economics. Economic analysis has been widely acknowledged around the world by antitrust agencies,[15] courts,[16] as well as private litigants.[17] Not only does a competition law class look like

[14]Dogan and Lamley (2008, p. 15).

[15]See f*or example*, Neven and De Coninck.

[16]For example, Federal Judicial Center published Reference Manual on Scientific Evidence in 2000. The first two chapters of the 'reference guide' in this manual are 'reference guide on Statistics' and 'reference guide on Multiple Regression'. Baker and Rubinfeld (1999, p. 387).

[17]As Baye and Wright put it: "The battle of the experts has become a standard, and critical battle in the antitrust litigation wars." Baye and Wright (2011, p. 5).

an economics class,[18] but competition agency and lawyers are economic specialists, even the court decisions read like "short treatises on microeconomic analysis."[19]

Competition enforcement agencies have progressively paid increased attention to the use of economic models. Competition lawyers and business practitioners regularly take part in seminars and conferences sponsored by economists to study economic techniques.[20] The increasing use of economic analysis has been welcomed by academic scholars, who argued that competition enforcement should be considered in a "scientific" and "technocratic"[21] way, being less influenced by political and other non-economic concerns.[22] At the same time, competition cases also become increasingly complex because of the advances of modern economic theories and techniques. Whereas the increasing use of economic models in antitrust cases opened the market for economic consultancy,[23] dealing with sophisticated economic models imposes unavoidable burden on competition enforcers.

Competition cases can be litigated at courts either by private parties, or as a follow-up of the public enforcement.[24] Judges are expected to review the economic analysis conducted by a competition authority, or the economic proof provided by private litigants. In theory, judges are expected to apply general rules to find judicial facts by analyzing the economic evidence. This expectation, however, may not be realistic in practice. For example, the empirical study by Baye and Wright shows that the more economically complex an antitrust case is, the more likely it is that the federal court's judge's decision is appealed.[25] Moreover, the impact of cognitive science on the behaviour of judges should be taken into account when analyzing complex, often conflicting economic expert testimony, which contains both sophisticated economic theory, and technical econometric models including demand estimation, critical loss analysis, and effects of vertical restraints. The situation becomes more challenging when experts are subject to cognitive biases as well.[26]

Since antitrust authorities in many jurisdictions have proposed the development of private enforcement of antitrust law,[27] judges are expected to take up the challenge of making decisions on antitrust disputes. By taking the recent discussion of

---

[18]Farber and McDonnell (2005, p. 620). Discussions of antitrust often focus on economics, leaving many students with the feeling that they have mistakenly wandered into an economics class rather than a law class. .

[19]Easterbrook (1984, p. 57).

[20]Botteman (2006, p. 71).

[21]Crane (2008, p. 1159).

[22]Recalling the century-long debate on economic versus non-economic goals of antitrust law. *see also* Sokol (2015, p. 1247).

[23]Neven claimed that the demand for economic consultancy in Europe has dramatically increased since the 1990s, especially after the promulgation of the EC Merger Regulation. Neven (2006, p. 748).

[24]Lianos (2009, p. 6).

[25]Baye and Wright (2011, p. 5).

[26]Faure and Visscher (2011, p. 385).

[27]For example, Schreiber (2010).

behavioral law and economics into account, it becomes doubtful to impose increasing responsibilities on judges for deciding economic complex antitrust cases.

11.3 Economic Experts at the Agency Versus Court

The definition of 'expert' may contain two aspects: on the one hand, the individual has to demonstrate a consistent capability and performance in a specific field or domain, and possesses superior knowledge as well as the ability to communicate the knowledge to others. On the other hand, the expert has to be recognized publicly, either by other experts or by an acknowledged institution to be thus countable.[28] In the US, expert testimony is defined as specific knowledge and expertise that is beyond the comprehension of an ordinary person and Federal Rule of Evidence 702 made it clear that an expert witness testimony would only be required when it is beyond the "common knowledge of the average layman".[29] The expert is expected to provide assistance in truth finding by giving explanations, drawing inferences and conclusions, based on the known facts as well as her or his professional knowledge.[30]

11.3.1 Economic Experts at the Agency

In 1938, Landis made the classic argument that administrative agencies are superior in providing expertise in regulatory decision making.[31] Information is collected at a cheaper cost, and regulatory expertise will be developed if agencies are structured based on specialized functions. However, the argument for developing expert agencies often ignores the fact that agency officials are bureaucrats who often do not have sophisticated, technical training either.[32] They are not different from general judges when they start their career at the agency. Experts could provide technical support and can be hired internally and externally to produce expert input when policy documents are issued, or cases need to be decided.

When agencies are in need of experts, agency proceedings do not have to go through the court-room testimony, and evidence rules are not applied.[33] An agency may select experts according to the different needs on specific qualities and expertise that is required.[34] Agency officials may have more knowledge on the technical issue

[28]Petroski (2013, p. 108).
[29]Baker (1992).
[30]Baker (1992, pp. 331–332).
[31]Landis (1938), The Administrative Process.
[32]Wright and Diveley (2012, p. 5).
[33]Lettow (1986, p. 8).
[34]Lettow (1986, p. 8).

than a general judge when making the choice of selecting an expert.[35] Experts provide testimony before an agency in the format of submitting a report or a presentation, whereas expert testimony before a court must be provided in the format which fits into cross-examination.[36] In agency proceedings, experts are invited to provide new data, information on technical issues and are allowed to present the entire story on that issue. Both sides of the views are often investigated when "follow-up" studies are conducted by other experts.[37] In this way, criticisms are included in these expert reports, and the invited experts do not need to argue for one side. The most important difference in the selection of experts in agency and court proceedings lies in the fact that experts before the agency take the responsibility of developing studies on the issue, and experts can work in a team to provide a more comprehensive study.[38] However, experts before a court often work individually, and they must take a stand on the issue by working with the clients.

There was also evidence showing that staff working at administrative agencies are experts themselves. They either obtain the knowledge of a particular industry by doing repeated work, or have received training even before they have entered the entry-level position as an industry regulatory.[39] Therefore, they may develop a deep knowledge, as well as a personal and professional network which may enhance their connection within the industry.[40] In this sense, experts before agencies could encounter less risk of principal-agent problems between judges and expert witnesses.[41]

11.3.2 Economic Experts at the Court

Many scholars have argued that it is a challenging task for general judges to deal with antitrust cases, given the specific requirement of understanding complex economic evidence. As mentioned above, the empirical study by Baye and Wright shows that the more economic complex an antitrust case is, the more likely the federal court's judge's decision is appealed.[42] In their study, the appeal rate for cases with economic complexity is about 10% higher than the general cases.[43] This finding is consistent with other empirical studies on judges' performance in patent law cases. The

---

[35]Lettow (1986, p. 8).

[36]Lettow (1986, p. 9).

[37]Lettow (1986, p. 9).

[38]Lettow (1986, p. 9).

[39]Macey (1992, p. 103).

[40]Macey (1992, p. 103).

[41]Note the "epistemic deference" problem: there is an epistemic asymmetry between judges and experts. *See* Brewer (1998).

[42]Baye and Wright (2011, p. 5).

[43]Baye and Wright (2011), p. 6.

empirical studies by Moore,[44] Chu,[45] Wagner and Petherbridge[46] show that the more technical the case it, the more likely it is that the decisions by district court have been reversed by the Federal Circuit.

Tomlin and Cooper's research shows that 48% of the judges in the US state courts were not "adequately prepared" to assess complex, diverse expert testimony.[47] When judges are in need of support from experts, unlike agencies which can hire experts as part of their decision making team, general judges often take evidence provided by expert witness. However, expert witnesses have been widely criticized as the expert input of sophisticated cases, and these critics include the conflict role and mission between an expert witness (as a private profiter) and judges, the misleading use of expert witness by lawyers, the biased information provided by the expert witness, and the low level of trust in expert testimony. Posner has clearly expressed his worry of relying on an expert witness when dealing with technical questions.[48]

11.3.3 Comparing Experts at the Agency Versus Courts

There is, however, rather limited empirical evidence comparing the performance of administrative agencies and courts in making and implementing law and policies. As mentioned in Chap. 9 of this book, Wright and Diveley investigated 718 antitrust cases from 1976 until 2010 decided by the federal district court judges and FTC Commissioners, and showed that case decisions by the FTC Commissioners are more likely to be appealed and reversed than cases decided by generalist judges.[49] Their research challenges the conventional view that agencies outperform general judges in economic complex cases, and they expressed doubt that the claim for a higher level of regulatory discretion lacked sufficient empirical support.[50] In the US, empirical evidence showed that from the 1940 s till the 1990 s, in about 70% of the time, the Court supported the position of the administrative agencies, although the success rate of agencies may vary.[51] In administrative agency cases, courts are willing to examine whether the agency complied with procedural rules rather than substantive policies in the case.[52] As economic regulators, courts are less affected by the pressure from interest groups in specific industries because courts' jurisdiction is much broader.

---

[44]Moore (2001).

[45]Chu (2001, pp. 1075–1164).

[46]Wagner and Petherbridge (2004 , pp. 1105–1180).

[47]Tomlin and Cooper (2006).

[48]Posner (2001, p. 277). ("By having technical experts present evidence at trial that the judge and jury is expected somehow to assimilate.").

[49]Wright and Diveley (2012, p. 13).

[50]Wright and Diveley (2012, p. 22).

[51]Crowley (1987, pp. 266–267) and Humphries and Songer (1999, p. 209).

[52]Crowley (1987, pp. 265–83) and Sheehan (1990, pp. 875–85).

11.4 Party Versus Court Appointed Experts

An individual is called as an expert when he/she can demonstrate superior ability and performance for a specific task, or possess specific knowledge and have the ability to communicate the knowledge in a specific field to others; thus because of their superior knowledge, skills, and information commanded, they are recognized, and counted as an expert by peers or institutions.[53] Expert opinions may not achieve absolute "neutrality", as his/her views that are drawn from a particular research design and the interpretation of the data, may have been affected by the prevailing culture as well as personal attitudes in the social context.[54] Scientific observations and experiments cannot be fully "independent" as broader external checks and applicable social norms may have influence on the objectivity and reliability of their results.[55]

The neutrality problem is strengthened when expert witnesses are subject to selection bias, affiliation bias, and compensation bias.[56] When litigants cherry-pick the experts out of the pool of qualified experts in that subject, and select one of them who could provide favourable opinions, that person represents perhaps only 1 in over 1000 in the pool of the experts. The unrepresentative opinions in the case are thus exaggerated in the courtroom and serve as the selection bias.[57] When experts are coached and prepared by the litigant's attorney, they may easily be partisan biased, and may suffer from the cognitive anchor, observer effects, confirmatory bias that are exploited by the litigant attorney. The affiliation bias may explain how expert witnesses are assigned to be a partisan member after interacting with the party lawyers and failing to assess the fair and accurate value of the facts.[58] Lawyers can also influence experts through the anchor technique to make experts stick to an even unrelated number when, for example, estimating the value of damages. Experts may also be subject to confirmatory bias to selectively choose information that supports their opinions.[59] Moreover, expert opinions may be shaped by the arrangement of their compensation and the fee structure, and pre-trial meetings may influence experts to provide biased, partisan opinions.[60]

11.4.1 Party Appointed Experts

For private parties, judges are often under pressure to make quick decisions by interpreting the often conflicting economic evidence that is provided by agencies,

---

[53]Petroski (2013, p. 108).
[54]Deason(1998, p. 101).
[55]Deason (1998, p. 102).
[56]Robertson (2010 p. 184).
[57]Robertson (2010, p. 185).
[58]Robertson (2010, p. 187).
[59]Robertson (2010, p. 186).
[60]Robertson (2010, p. 188).

parties or expert witness. This raises some issues, such as whether an expert witness is objective and reliable. Moreover, both parties would engage in "expert shopping" in order to provide the most sophisticated economic models, which significantly increases the litigation cost. Given the limited capacity of interpreting the economic language, the power of judicial review becomes rather limited.

Lawyers are incentivized to look for experts who can provide arguments to support their position. Once economists agree to behave as advocates, both parties therefore are engaged in "expert shopping", or "battle of the experts",[61] and such "competition for experts" would dramatically increase the litigation costs. Economics is an objective science by nature, as Friedman said, "in precisely the same way as any of the physical sciences".[62] In scientific reasoning, making assumptions can be fundamental to assess the validity and reliability.[63] In the field such as geometry, conclusions change dramatically when a different assumption is made.[64] Economic analysis of antitrust cases often starts from data collection. It seems that experienced economists are in particular talented at discovering the relevant information from published or unpublished resources.[65] The fragmented, often limited data, however, can be used to explain the connection between one or more factors with others by going through a process called "inferences". Therefore, the data is assembled to provide an explanation of the relationships between factors in a market place.[66] For economists, choosing assumption is of crucial importance for building models and conducting data analysis.[67] Economic analysis may lead in different directions based on their beliefs of the robustness of the market.[68] The importance of building models based on assumptions leads to the indeterminacy nature of economic discipline. Economists may develop various elaborate models under different assumptions and the purpose of this scientific research is to better understand the function of the market and economy.

The role and mission of economists as researchers, however, are different from those of lawyers, who are engaged in the adversarial trial system and hold a duty of being persuasive. First of all, the efforts and energy that economist experts devote to an antitrust case are often not the result of a fruitful contribution to economic knowledge, since the data set collected and used for litigation is often considered as confidential information and secrecy is required.[69] The primary pay-off of serving as

[61] Van Dusen (1962, pp. 498, 500).

[62] Friedman (1953, p. 4).

[63] Weller (1997, p. 888).

[64] Weller (1997, p. 888).

[65] Areeda (1988, p. 1033).

[66] Areeda (1988, p. 1033).

[67] As Stigler put it: "The apparatus of economics is very flexible: without breaking the rules of the profession—by being illogical or even by denying the validity of the traditional theory—a sufficient clear person can reach any conclusion he wishes on any real problem (in contrast to formal problems)." Stigler (1965, p. 63).

[68] Fox (1986, p. 579).

[69] Mandel (1999, p. 118).

expert witness could only be evaluated in monetary terms, but not the research values. Secondly, to serve as an expert witness, economists are required to 'take a stand' and to focus on one side of the argument, among many of the alternative assumptions. Being engaged in an adversarial trial system, attorneys have to select the 'best-fit' expert with whom they could foresee the success of winning the case. Therefore, the selection of antitrust economists will often be "polarized".[70] The plaintiff may choose an economic expert who could provide evidence based on the assumption of a robust private power, whereas the defendant may choose a different economic expert who could argue for the success of a free market.[71] To a lawyer, the value of an economist expert is not about how a sophisticated and precise model could explain a social phenomenon, but about how such a model could be applied to win the argument for their clients. Therefore, a 'selection' of experts means a 'selection' of arguments. The "expert shopping" problem indicates the inconsistency of the mission and roles of economist experts versus attorney in antitrust litigation. This inconsistency problem could cause a significant negative effect of choosing to be an expert witness: economists may become 'locked-into' their testimonies.[72] Being hired by attorneys and sticking to a one-sided position, economists may ruin their academic reputation once the biased or flawed view is attacked.[73]

Many judges, and also juries are aware of the 'selection' problem between attorneys and experts, or as Judge Posner defined, "the problem of partisanship",[74] and have explicitly expressed their distrust of expert witnesses.[75] The conflict of missions between economic experts and judges also indicates the long evolution of how economic analysis could be incorporated into antitrust judicial decision making.[76] Above all, the assumptions that economists make, and based on which the data analysis could follow, are nevertheless over-simplified.[77] One clear example is that the welfare of consumers is often calculated through the proxy of consumer surplus, which indicates that consumers are better off through lower prices.[78] Factors that are not quantifiable, such as consumer preferences, are often excluded. The choice of economic proxy, the development of dynamic models and the methodology of calculating economic factors often lead to a continuous debate among economists themselves. The unsolved issue of how non-economic, unquantifiable factors could be incorporated into economic models, made economists become involved in a century-long discussion regarding whether antitrust law should only pursue the goal of economic

---

[70] Fox (1986, p. 580).

[71] Fox (1986, p. 580).

[72] Mandel (1999, p. 119).

[73] Mandel (1999, p. 119).

[74] Posner (1999, p. 1477) and Posner (1999, p. 91).

[75] Areeda (1988, p. 1033) and Harrison (2001, p. 256).

[76] One of the major debated issues in implementing the competition policy in Europe is to what extent economic analysis should be used, and what role economists should play in the antitrust decision making. *See* Roeller (2005, p. 13).

[77] Fox (1986, p. 581).

[78] Fox (1986, p. 581).

efficiency. The issue of how a trade-off between efficiency and non-economic values, such as protection of freedom, equal opportunity, and fairness could be made will be left to judges who must translate the language of economic analysis into legal rules.[79]

Legal rules must be clear, short-run effect based, and purpose oriented. Legal rules must be developed in a clear and simple way in order to reduce the administrative costs of the legal system and to provide guidance to judges and firms.[80] The standard that courts applied when admitting expert testimony was a "general acceptance" standard set by *Frye v. United States.*[81] In 1993, the *Daubert v. Merrill Dow Pharmaceuticals, Inc.*[82] decision made by the Supreme Court increased the standard for expert testimony to be accepted. The Supreme Court referred to the Federal Rules of Evidence 702,[83] and made clear that to be admissible in the federal court, the scientific evidence must be "relevant", and "reliable". Scientific evidence that fails to meet such a standard will be excluded.

11.4.2 Courts Appointed Experts

In the US, Federal Rule of Evidence (FRE) 706 granted judges discretion to select experts as witness. Court-appointed experts help judges understand the testimony provided by party experts, and their investigations, experiments and analysis may provide external information, and therefore test and evaluate the reliability of the party experts' testimony and resolve the conflicts between the party experts.[84] In reality, judges may not have sufficient resources to search and select experts in specific fields, and may not have time to communicate with experts on the facts of the case when experts write reports and prepare for testimony and cross-examination.[85] Judges may also be unwilling to appoint experts who may impede judicial objectivity, and thus increase the risk of reversal on appeal.[86] Thus, judges often make the selection based on their personal contacts through an informal process, or rely on

[79]Fox (1986, p. 585).

[80]Baker and Bresnahan (2006, p. 3).

[81]Frye v. United States, 293 F. 1013, 1014 (D.C. Cir. 1923) ("while courts will go a long way in admitting expert testimony deduced from a well-recognized scientific principle or discovery, the thing from which the deduction I made must be sufficiently established to have gained general acceptance in the particular field in which it belongs.").

[82]Daubert v. Merrell Dow Pharms., Inc, 509 U.S. 579 (1993) ("It is the trial judge's responsibility to ensure that any and all scientific testimony or evidence admitted is not only relevant, but reliable.").

[83]The Federal Rules of Evidence—Rule 702: If scientific, technical, or other specialized knowledge will assist the trier of fact to understand the evidence or to determine a fact in issue, a witness qualified as an expert by knowledge, skill, experience, training, or education, may testify hereto in the form of an opinion or otherwise.

[84]Deason (1998, at pp. 84–86).

[85]Robertson (2010, p. 200).

[86]Lee (1988, p. 480).

their recommendations on experts or consulting their private opinions before the trial.[87]

The inconsistency of the mission and roles between economist experts and attorneys may give rise to the problem that experts are often manipulated by attorneys who have obtained a dominant position in the litigation process.[88] The empirical study by Anthony Champagne et al. shows that the opinions of expert witness are likely to be influenced by attorneys.[89] Attorneys may strategically choose experts to provide the type of testimony that they want. It was argued that experts are selected by appearance, personality and status, but not based on the quality of their testimony.[90] This selection bias could be explained by Judge Posner's argument that in the market of antitrust litigation, the nature of expert business is to achieve a favourable result for clients, and experts is not paid based on the quality, and accuracy of the testimony, but on the extent to which it could contribute to a favourable outcome.[91] Dishonest, inaccurate, even misleading information that the experts may provide could not be easily discovered,[92] and therefore market failure may occur when experts are not subject to ethic rules or other types of self-regulation as when they are engaging in academic activities.

Considering that the goal of being persuasive in the adversarial system, and suffering from the deficits (deficiencies) of detecting dishonest and inaccurate testimony will be highly costly, an important question arises as to how in reality the experts are selected. This question should be investigated through the perspective of what kind of expert would be welcomed by juries. There is much evidence to show that juries are biased and distracted by the presentation and appearance of experts. First of all, an expert with high institutional authority is more likely to be selected compared with those who are less well-known. For example, many have been aware that Nobel Prize winner Robert Lucas has provided a testimony for a price-fixing class action suit.[93] Richard Schmalensee, who holds the title of the dean of MIT's Sloan School and a member of President Bush's Council of Economic Advisers, was selected to be an expert witness for the Microsoft case.[94] The range of hourly compensation could well explain the differences of expert's authority.[95] Many jurors believe that those with high authority deserve a premium and such an investment should be made by litigants.[96] For the jurors, institutional authority seems to be a proxy to evaluate the

---

[87]Deason (1998, p. 76).

[88]Harrison (2001, p. 260).

[89]Champagne et al. (1992, p. 5).

[90]Harrison (2001, p. 260).

[91]Posner (1999, p. 1540) and Harrison (2001, p. 267).

[92]Harrison (2001, p. 268).

[93]Mandel (1999, p. 116).

[94]Mandel (1999, p. 116).

[95]Harrison (2001, p. 269).

[96]Shuman et al. (1994, pp. 193, 200).

qualification and the intellectual competence of the experts, as those who regularly publish in prestigious journals may have higher ethical standards.[97]

11.5 The Role of the Court in the AML

11.5.1 Private Actions

In Article 50 of the Anti-monopoly Law in China, litigants should bear the burden of proof.[98] After the Supreme People's Court issued the Provisions on Several Issues Concerning the Application of Law in the Trial of Civil Dispute Cases Arising from Monopolistic Conduct in 2012,[99] it has been specified that in the burden of proof has to be shared in monopolistic agreement and abuse of market dominant position cases. When the alleged monopolistic conduct is a monopolistic agreement as described in Article 13.1 (1)-(5) of the AML, the defendant shall assume the burden to prove that the agreement does not have the effect of excluding or restricting competition.[100] When the alleged monopolistic conduct is an abuse of dominant market position as described in Article 17.1 of the AML, the plaintiff shall assume the burden to prove that the defendant has a dominant position in the relevant market and has abused its dominant market position.[101] The Interpretation did not explain the burden of proof for vertical cases, and thus the Civil Litigation Law's rule will apply. According to Articles 1 and 2 of the Judicial Interpretation, both stand-alone and follow-on cases could be brought for damage actions.[102] Individuals, businesses or organizations directly or indirectly harmed by anti-competitive behaviour are qualified to bring the lawsuit. Articles 3, 4 and 5 stipulate the first-instance damage actions which fall within the jurisdiction of the intellectual property tribunal of intermediate courts.[103] Article 6 clarified that the proceedings with the same subject matter at the same court could be combined into one set. Joint actions, but not collective actions or class actions, are permitted.[104] In cases involving monopolistic conduct by public utilities,

---

[97] Harrison (2001, p. 270).

[98] Article 50 of the AML: The business operators that carry out the monopolistic conduct and cause damages to others shall bear the civil liability according to law.

[99] Zuigao Renmin Fayuan Guanyu Shenli Yin Longduan Xingwei Yinfa De Minshi Jiufen Anjian Yingyong Falyu Ruogan Wenti De Guiding (最高人民法院关于审理因垄断行为引发的民事纠纷案件应用法律若干问题的规定) [Provisions of the Supreme People's Court on Several Issues Concerning the Application of Law in the Trial of Civil Dispute Cases Arising from Monopolistic Conduct], Interpretation No. 5 [2012] of the Supreme People's Court, issued by the Supreme People's Court on May 3 2012 and effective on June 1 2012.

[100] Article 7 of the Provision, id.

[101] Article 8 of the Provision, id.

[102] Articles 1–2 of the Provision, id.

[103] Articles 3, 4 to 5 of the Provision, id.

[104] Article 6 of the Provision, id.

the Provision made clear in Article 9 that the court may presume the defendant obtained a dominant position unless there is evidence showing to the contrary.

During the five years after the AML entered into force in 2008, 172 antitrust cases were accepted and among them 71 cases were filed in the fifth year. The majority of the cases were on abuse of dominant position and vertical constraint, but they were mainly dismissed by court or settled at a small amount of compensation, and no follow-on action has been reported.[105] The number of cases filed and accepted by courts increased dramatically in the recent seven years. In 2013, 71 cases were accepted and 69 of them were concluded. By May 2014, 188 cases were accepted and 172 of them were concluded.[106] By the end of 2017, 700 private civil cases were accepted in total and among them 90% were on abuse of dominant position, and 630 of the cases have been closed.[107] In 2019, 41 civil cases were adjudicated and published. Among them, 2 decisions were made by the Supreme Court, 21 cases were adjudicated by courts in Beijing, and 24 were cases were on abuse of dominant position and 12 cases related to monopoly agreements.[108] Under the current legal framework of private antitrust litigation in China, an individual victim may face some challenges in bringing the lawsuit in front of the intermediate courts at the provincial level, and competition cases are usually ruled at the intellectual property tribunals.

Article 7 of the 2012 Judicial Interpretation imposes the burden of proving monopoly agreements, the suffered losses and causality on the plaintiff and requires the defendant to prove that the agreement does not have anti-competitive effects.[109] Individual claimants have difficulty in accessing market information, calculating market share and damage loss due to anti-competitive practice. Meanwhile, with time and capacity constraints and limited support from experienced experts and economists, courts also face the challenge of collecting evidence and such pressure will be ultimately transferred to the plaintiff; thus antitrust litigation in China becomes a tactic for companies with resources, leaving individual victims with ever increased barriers to justice.[110]

In August 2014, the Jiangsu High Court dismissed the abuse of dominance (imposing discriminatory conditions) in an oil transport case against Taizhou Petroleum and Chemical Corporation, Yangzi Petrochemical Corporation and Sinopec. The first instance, the Nanjing Intermediate Court dismissed the claim for not having provided sufficient evidence. The Jiangsu High People' Court defined the relevant market and concluded that the defendant did not hold a dominant position.[111]

In December 2015, a handicapped telecoms user named Yang Zhiyong, sued China Telecom for abusing its dominant position and charging high prices to handicapped people by packaging broadband access and other services. The Shanghai Intermediate

---

[105] Hou (2015, p. 1).

[106] Zhan and Tan (2015).

[107] Zhan et al. (2018).

[108] Liu et al. (2020).

[109] Zhan and Tan (2015).

[110] Hou (2015, p. 8) and Zhan and Tan (2015).

[111] China Competition Bulletin, Edition 35, January/February 2015, at p. 7.

People's Court dismissed the case and the Shanghai High People's Court upheld the first-instance judgement. The High People's Court held that Yang Zhiyong could have other choices on network services in his neighborhood, and based on China Telecom's fee policy there was a lack of evidence to prove that China Telecom had the capacity to control prices and hold dominant position.[112] This case clearly shows that individual victims bear a high burden of proof and obtaining sufficient evidence of the defendant's abusive act is an institutional barrier for private antitrust litigation.

In May 2016, the Supreme People's Court overturned the judgement by Shaanxi High People's Court judgement. The plaintiff, Wu Xiaoqin claimed that Shaanxi Broadcast & TV Network Intermediary (Group) Co Ltd sold basic cable television services in addition to premium cable television services, which lead to a price increase of RMB 5/month. The Shaanxi High People's Court dismissed Wu's claims, because the Court found that although the Shaanxi Broadcast held a dominant position, it offered the two types of services separately and it should not be considered as bundling. The Supreme People's Court ruled in favour of Wu by admitting Shaanxi Broadcast & TV Network held a dominant position. It was ordered to pay back RMB 15 to Wu.[113]

In June 2016, a distributor of Panasonic of factory automation control products, Shanghai Rijing Electric, sued Panasonic and two other distributors for implementing a horizontal agreement on market sharing. The Shanghai No.1 Intermediate People's Court dismissed the case because the plaintiff did not provide evidence on the agreement. The court provided two economic reasons, one is that the relationship between Panasonic and its distributors is not horizontal, but vertical. The other is that the restrictions imposed on vertical relationships may not have anti-competitive effects.[114]

In August 2016, the Beijing High People's Court dismissed the first follow-on damage claims. The plaintiff, Mr Tian Junwei claimed damage compensation of RMB 10.44 from his purchase of Abbott infant formula at Carrefour store, after the NDRC imposed fines on Abbott in August 2013 for engaging in RPM. Both the Beijing Intellectual Property Court and the Beijing High People's Court dismissed the claim. The Beijing High People's Court ruled that the plaintiff failed to provide evidence on the monopoly agreement between Abbott and Carrefour, and the NDRC's decision could not prove that the Abbott's unlawful pricing conduct was related to Carrefour store.[115]

In 2017, a Shenzhen Lawyer Xu Shuqing brought a lawsuit against Tencent for abuse of dominant position at the Shenzhen Intermediate People's Court and appealed to Guangdong High People's Court. Xu created a type of emotion indicator for Wechat, a social media mobile application run by Tencent and it was rejected by Wechat. Xu claimed that Tencent has abused its dominant position and imposed unreasonable and discriminatory conditions on selecting emotions. Tencent argued

---

[112]China Competition Bulletin 2016, Edition 40, January/February, at p. 16.

[113]China Competition Bulletin, Edition 44, September/October 2016, at p. 3.

[114]China Competition Bulletin, Edition 44, September/ October 2016, at p. 3.

[115]China Competition Bulletin, Edition 45, November/December 2016, at p. 8.

that Xu had failed to define the relevant market, and the emotion indicator was advertised on his "ask a lawyer" service. The Shenzhen Intermediate People's Court ruled that Xu could not prove the definition of relevant market, or if there were alternatives for distributing his creation of emotions. The court did not provide further analysis and the High court dismissed the appeal.[116]

Up to 2015, no other report had been made on whether guilty pleas in agency investigations would be accepted by courts and no follow-on action had been taken.[117] Up to February 2017, no judicial review case had been filed on the decisions made by NDRC, SAIC, and MOFCOM.[118] In 2016, among 20 adjudicated cases in Chinese courts nationwide, in only 1 case did the plaintiff prevail, and in 6 cases the courts raised objections to jurisdiction, and the plaintiff withdrew claims in 6 cases.[119] At provincial level, courts both at the local level and the intermediate level ruled in favour of the competition agency cases, including the administrative litigation brought by the concrete horizontal agreement in Jiangsu Province in 2014,[120] the vehicle inspection companies cartel case in Shaanxi province in 2016,[121] the seven accounting firms' appeal in 2017.[122] Even though collective action mechanism has been considered to be an effective mean to resolve the information problem to spur private litigation, it may not be desirable for China.

11.5.2 Judicial Capacity

In the Supreme People's Court Notice on Intellectual Property Courts Jurisdictional Matters, Article 3 stipulates that first instance cases of anti-monopoly civil disputes fall within the jurisdiction of the Intellectual Property Court in Beijing, Shanghai and Guangzhou. In July 2016, the Supreme Court issued Opinions of the Supreme Court on Promotion of the "Three in One" for the Trial of Civil, Administrative, and

---

[116]China Competition Bulletin, Edition 47, June 2017, at p. 7.

[117]Hou (2015, p. 7).

[118]Zhao and He Jing (2017, p. 1179).

[119]Ren (2017, p. 11).

[120]Yuangao Nanjing Jiangong Jituan Youxian Gongsi Hunningtu Fengongsi Yu Beigao Jiangsusheng Wujiaju Wujia Xingzheng Chufa Xingwei Yian De Xingzheng Caidingshu (原告南京建工集团有限公司混凝土分公司与被告江苏省物价局物价行政处罚行为一案的行政裁定书) [Administrative Ruling of Plaintiff Nanjing Construction Engineering Group Co., Ltd. Concrete Branch and Defendant Jiangsu Price Bureau] September 24, 2014 available at http://wenshu.court.gov.cn/.

[121]陕西:30家机动车检测机构垄断涨价被罚570余万元(Shaanxi: 30 motor vehicle inspection agencies fined 5.7 million yuan for charging monopoly price) *Xinhuanews*, April 13 2016, available at http://finance.sina.com.cn/roll/2016-04-13/doc-ifxriqqv5567588.shtml (accessed 30.03.2020).

[122]临沂25家会计师事务所垄断协议案(Monopoly agreement case of 25 accounting firms in Linyi) Shandong Administration for Market Regulation official website August 20, 2019, available at http://amr.shandong.gov.cn/art/2019/8/20/art_88466_6978770.html (accessed 15.03.2020).

Criminal cases Involving Intellectual Property Rights in Courts Nationwide.[123] The Opinion clarified that antitrust cases are included in the IP civil disputes. Antitrust disputes are tried at IP courts or tribunals in China, and the Supreme People's Court issued the Provisions on Intellectual Property Tribunal on January 1, 2019. According to this provision, starting from January 2019, competition cases will be directly heard by the IP Tribunal of the Supreme People's Court, and the newly established IP tribunal has 1 Chief Judge, 3 Deputy Chief Judges and 23 Judges.[124]

Courts tend to avoid the conflicts with agencies when analysis of anti-competitive effects is required in competition cases. In 2015, the Ji'an Salt Company appealed the administrative penalty decision imposed by the Ji'an AIC at the Ji'an Intermediate People's Court. Ji'an AIC imposed a fine of RMB 160,000 on Ji'an Salt Company for bundling the sale of table salt with low-sodium salt and rock salt. On April 24, 2015, the Court dismissed the appeal. Before it filed the administrative lawsuit at the Intermediate People's Court, Ji'an Salt Company filed the administrative reconsideration with the Ji'an Municipal Government, and this decision affirmed the decision by Ji'an AIC. The Company first filed the lawsuit before the Ji'an District People's Court, and the district court upheld the AIC's decision; in addition, the court found that the Company violated Article 6 of the Anti-Unfair Competition Law. Overall, both the district court and the intermediate court upheld AIC's decision.[125] Similarly, in May 2016, among the 25 accounting firms who received administrative penalty decision issued by Shandong AIC in breach of Article 13 of the AML, 7 of them applied for administrative reconsideration before SAIC, and appealed before the Lixia District People's Court in Jinan. The court dismissed the proceedings on August 11, 2016 and concluded that the evidence was "valid", the application of law was "appropriate" and "in accordance with proper procedures".[126] One firm challenged the SAIC administrative reconsideration decision and appealed to the Xicheng District People's Court in Beijing, then appealed to the Beijing Intermediate People's Court. The Intermediate People's Court focused on two aspects, one is whether the Shandong AIC had determined the facts accurately, and secondly whether the law had been applied properly. The court found that the agreement restricted the entry of other business operators and had negative anti-competitive effects. The court upheld Shandong AIC's decision, the SAIC's administrative reconsideration decision, and dismissed the appeals.[127]

---

[123] Zuigao Renmin Fayuan Guanyu Zai Quanguo Fayuan Tuijin Zhishi Chanquan Minshi Xingzheng He Xingshi Anjian Shenpan Sanheyi Gongzuo de Yijian (最高人民法院关于在全国法院推进知识产权民事、行政和刑事案件审判"三合一"工作的意见) [Opinions of the Supreme People's Court on Promoting the "Three in One" Trial of Civil, Administrative and Criminal Cases Involving Intellectual Property Rights in Courts Nationwide] issued on July 5, 2016 and effective on July 5, 2016.

[124] Zhan, Song and Yang (2018, p. 4).

[125] China Competition Bulletin, Edition 38, July/August 2015, at p. 3.

[126] China Competition Bulletin, Edition 43, July/August 2016, at p. 4.

[127] China Competition Bulletin, Edition 47, June 2017, at p. 6.

In May 2013, two plaintiffs alleged that three taxi operators abused dominant position by preventing self-employed taxi drivers from freely choosing taxi companies. The plaintiff's claims were rejected at the Xi'an Intermediate People's Court and the Shaanxi High People's Court, and both ruled that the taxi operators did not hold a dominant position. The plaintiffs applied for the Supreme People's Court's retrial. On March 17, 2016, the Supreme People's Court dismissed the application because it found that the evidence to prove the operator held a dominant position and engaged in exclusive dealing was insufficient.[128]

Checks and balances on the agency's decisions at the central and local level are provided externally through the judicial enforcement of administrative law. Parties have the formal right to defend their position through filing an administrative litigation or applying for administrative reconsideration, although research shows that appeals against the administrative penalty decision by local agencies have been extremely rare, and no appeal against SAIC or NDRC has been reported.[129] Companies are reluctant to appeal because the administrative decision is often made after meetings and negotiations between the respondent and the agency, or because of the fear of retribution.[130] The under-development of antitrust judicial review can also be explained by the low confidence of Chinese judges dealing with competition law and economics, and judges tend to trust administrative agencies for their expertise in assessing anti-competitive effects.[131] For example, on August 22, 2016, The Beijing High People's Court dismissed the first follow-on damages antitrust case, after the NDRC issued the penalty decision against Abbott and other infant formula producers for RPM. Both the Beijing Intellectual Property Court at the first instance and the Beijing High People's Court claimed that the plaintiff failed to submit sufficient evidence.[132] In a most recent case, on May 31, 2017, the Beijing Intermediate People's Court dismissed the appeals against the Shandong Province AIC's decision on fining seven accounting firms for their monopolistic agreements.[133]

When comparing the capacity of enforcing competition law by agency or courts in China, the public choice theory assumes that enforcing agencies and the judiciary are all working together in the public interest to deter antitrust violations. If the judges are willing to serve public interest, the choice between criminalizing antitrust law and imposing administrative fines depends on whether the judges or the administrative regulators have more specialized expertise in dealing with antitrust cases. Generally speaking, judges are more trusted given the fact that they are more independent and obtain superior information about the cases. In contrast, the public choice analysis becomes more relevant if there is evidence showing that judges are rather pursuing their private interests, or judicial decisions are influenced by legislatures at a superior

---

[128]China Competition Bulletin, Edition 41, March/April 2016, at p. 5.

[129]Zhang (2015).

[130]US Chamber of Commerce (2014).

[131]Zhang (2011).

[132]China Competition Bulletin, edition 45, November/December 2016.

[133]China Competition Bulletin, edition 47, June 2017.

level and by external political pressures. In this case, the level of transparency and accuracy of court opinions and decisions remains low.

The under-development of private enforcement in China could be explained from the perspective of legal culture and legal tradition. According to Winston, in contrast to the rule of law the Chinese legal tradition follows the rule by law, and law is perceived as amoral, and the function of the law is to strengthen state control.[134] This understanding empowers the ruler to interpret the law, which results in the situation that the ruler enjoys the status 'above-the-law'.[135] For example, it has been argued that in many East Asian countries economic development is the most important political goal, and the concern of facilitating economic reform even overrides individual rights.[136] Another reason is the under-developed judicial capacity, and judges are not yet qualified to deal with the complicated antitrust cases. It has been argued that the courts in China are relatively weak and its judges are not qualified enough to handle complex cases.[137] This situation has been dramatically improved after the state judicial examination in 2002 and the enactment of the Civil Servant Law in 2005.[138] However, it may remain a challenging task to train judges to do complex economic analysis on competition cases.

11.5.3 Role of Economic Experts

Article 13 of the Working Rules for the Anti-monopoly Committee of the State Council as follows: "For scientific consultation on significant issues, the Anti-monopoly Committee shall organize consulting panels consisted of experts in law and economics and other concerned persons. Members of the consulting panel shall be recommended by a member agency of the committee. It shall be the duty of the committee to prescribe the specific method to select and appoint members of the consulting panel." After the enactment of the AML, an Expert Advisory Board was established and it is composed of 21 experts including law and economics professionals and specialists in industries.[139] The Board has prevailing influence on formulating the provisions and guidelines of the AML, and has organized the annual international conference called competition policy forum. On March 20, 2019, the third session of the State Council Anti-Monopoly Committee Expert Advisory Board completed its election and was formally established. The current expert advisory board is composed of 17 experts, and Lang Sheng, the former deputy director of the Standing Committee of the National People's Congress Legal and Industrial Commission is the chair of the board, and Zhao Xiaoguang, the former deputy director of the State

[134] Winston (2005, p. 313).
[135] Li (2011, p. 6) and Winston (2005, p. 314).
[136] Tay (2007) and Killion (2004, p. 511).
[137] Clarke (2003, p. 108).
[138] Michelson and Li (2012, p. 4).
[139] Ohlhausen (2013).

Post Bureau is the deputy board chair.[140] The expert group have visited Shanghai, Zhejiang, Guangdong and other places to discuss enforcement issues of the fair competition review system at the local level with officials and business representatives, and drafted investigation reports and proposals for the revision of the AML and the fair competition review system. The expert group have also participated in international conferences and seminars on fair competition review and Internet platform enterprise competition compliance evaluation index.[141] In daily case analysis, MOFCOM has invited external economic experts when evaluating the market shares and concentration level, and the price effects by learning the economic tools and methods. Economic analysis has been taken into account in NDRC's investigation of Qualcomm, and SAIC's investigation of Tetra Pak. Economic experts' testimony has also been included for example in the *Huawei v. Samsung* decision by the Shenzhen Intermediate People's Court, and the *Qihoo 360 v. Tencent* decision by the Supreme Court.[142]

11.6 Conclusions

Agency public enforcement and private actions before the courts are the two complementing channels to cure market failure. Most antitrust jurisdictions rely on specialized antitrust agencies because it is believed that generalist courts do not have relevant expertise. When agencies are equipped with personnel having knowledge and expertise in economics, they investigate competition cases by applying such knowledge. At the same time, agencies with a top-down organization hierarchy may also suffer from public choice problems. Competition agencies may abuse their structural and institutional advantages of the organization.[143] Regulatory gaming may occur once market entry, standard setting or sustaining a dominant position is made through government approval.[144] When the pressure from interest groups prevails, a court system should be built upon to enforce competition law through a more balanced system. Solely relying on the regulatory agencies to investigate competition cases, neglecting the fact that the goals of regulators may not be aligned with the goals of competition. The advantage for a court, but not agency, to enforce the law is that courts are restrained from regulatory capture, as defined in the public choice theory. The main challenge for courts to deal with complex economic antitrust cases is the lack of specific expertise, and such limitation could be remedied with the help of economic experts.

---

140 回眸2019:反垄断与公平竞争(Looking Back on 2019: Antitrust and Fair Competition)SAMR Development and Research Center, January 19, 2020, available at https://www.imsilkroad.com/news/p/398809.html?from=singlemessage&isappinstalled=0.

141 Looking Back on 2019: Antitrust and Fair Competition, id.

142 Fei Deng et al (2018, pp. 2, 10, 11).

143 Dogan and Lamley (2008, p. 2).

144 Dogan and Lamley (2008, p. 3).

This chapter compared the decision-making capacity between agencies and courts when experts are involved to provide technical and specialized suggestions. Experts before agencies may have less risk of principal-agent problems as it is at the court. Economic expert witness appointed by parties may be biased and manipulated by attorneys and those appointed by courts may suffer from the selection problem. In the case of private enforcement of the AML, the appeals against the administrative penalty decisions made by SAIC, NDRC, SAMR and their local branches are extremely rare and in most cases courts ruled in favour of the competition agency. The empirical findings suggested that administrative enforcement is still dominant in the enforcement of the AML. Although public choice arguments are relevant for improving private enforcement, a judicial review system on administrative decisions and follow-on actions of antitrust cases are not yet established due to institutional and cultural obstacles.

References

Areeda, P. (1988). Always a borrower: Law and other disciplines. *Duke Law Journal, 1988*(5), 1029–1043.

Baker, T. E. (1992). The impropriety of expert witness testimony on the law. *Kansas Law Review, 40,* 325–364.

Baker, J. B., & Rubinfeld, D. L. (1999). Empirical methods in antitrust litigation: review and critique. *American Law and Economics Review, 1*(1), 386–435.

Baker, J. B., & Bresnahan, T. F. (2006). Economic evidence in antitrust: defining markets and measuring market power, John M. Olin Program in Law and Economics, *Stanford Law School Working Paper No. 328*, available at http://ssrn.com/abstract=931225.

Baye, M. R., & Wright, J. D. (2011). Is antitrust too complicated for generalist judges? The impact of economic complexity and judicial training on appeals. *Journal of Law and Economics, 54*(1), 1–24.

Botteman, Y. (2006). Mergers, standard of proof and expert economic evidence. *Journal of Competition Law and Economics, 2*(1), 71–100.

Brewer, S. (1998). Scientific expert testimony and intellectual due processes. *Yale Law Journal, 107,* 1535–1681.

Crane, D. A. (2008). Technocracy and antitrust. *Texas Law Review, 86,* 1159–1221.

Chu, C. A. (2001). Empirical analysis of the federal circuit's claim construction trends. *Berkeley Technology Law Journal, 16,* 1075–1164.

Champagne A et al. (1992). Expert witness in the court: an empirical examination. *Judicature Journal*, 76

Crowley, D. W. (1987). Judicial review of administrative agencies: does the type of agency matter? *The Western Political Quarterly, 40*(2), 265–283.

Damien, J. N., & De Coninck, R., Best practices on the submission of economic evidence and data collection, DG Competition, European Commission, Office of the Chief Economist

Deng, F. (2018). Roundtable on Antitrust Developments in China Ten Years On, the antitrust source, August 2018

Deason, E. E. (1998). Court-appointed expert witnesses: scientific positivism meets bias and deference. *Oregon Law Review, 77,* 59–156.

Dogan, S. L., & Lamley, M. A. (2008) Antitrust law and regulatory gaming. John M. Olin Program in Law and Economics, Stanford Law School Working Paper No. 367.

Easterbrook, F. H. (1984). Foreword: The court and the economic system. *Harvard Law Review, 98*(4), 4–60.

Farber, D. A., & McDonnell, B. H. (2005). "Is there a text in this class?" the conflict between textualism and antitrust. *Contemporary Legal Issues, 14,* 619–668.

Faure, M., & Visscher, L. (2011). The role of experts in assessing damages—A law and economics account. *European Journal of Risk Regulation*, 376–396.

Fels. A., Wang, X., Ng, W., & Emch, A. (Eds.) *China Competition Bulletin*, A Publication of the Competition Law & Economics Network at Melbourne Law School, University of Melbourne, Edition 40, January/February 2016.

Fels, A., Wang, X., Ng, W., & Emch, A. (Eds.) *China Competition Bulletin*, A Publication of the Competition Law & Economics Network at Melbourne Law School, University of Melbourne, Edition 41, March/April 2016.

Fels, A., Wang, X., Ng, W., & Emch, A. (Eds.) *China Competition Bulletin*, A Publication of the Competition Law & Economics Network at Melbourne Law School, University of Melbourne, Edition 44, September/October 2016.

Fels, A., Wang, X., Ng, W., & Emch, A. (eds.) *China Competition Bulletin*, A Publication of the Competition Law & Economics Network at Melbourne Law School, University of Melbourne, Edition 45, November/December 2016.

Fels, A., Wang, X., Ng, W., & Emch, A. (Eds.) *China Competition Bulletin*, A Publication of the Competition Law & Economics Network at Melbourne Law School, University of Melbourne, Edition 47, June 2017.

Friedman, M. (1953). Essay on the methodology of positive economics, in *Essays in Positive Economics*, University of Chicago Press.

Fox, E. M. (1986). The politics of law and economics in judicial decision making: antitrust as a window. *New York University Law Review, 61,* 554–588.

Gilligan, T. W., et al. (1989). Regulation and the theory of legislative choice: the interstate commerce act of 1887. *Journal of Law and Economics, 32,* 47–49.

Harrison, J. L. (2001). Reconceptualizing the expert witness: social costs, current controls and proposed responses. *Yale Journal on Regulation, 18,* 253–314.

Humphries, M. A., & Songer, D. R. (1999). Law and politics in judicial oversight of federal administrative agencies. *The Journal of Politics, 61*(1), 207–220.

Hou, J. A. (2015) Is Chinese private antitrust litigation ready to take off? Zelle Hofmann Voelbel & Mason LLP, Competition Policy International 2015, available at https://dev.competitionpolicyinternational.com/is-chinese-private-antitrust-litigation-ready-to-take-off/.

Kovacic, W. E. (1997). The quality of appointments and the capability of the Federal Trade Commission. *Administrative Law Review, 49,* 915–962.

Landis, J. M. (1938). *The administrative process*. Yale University Press.

Lettow, C. F. (1986). Strategic choices in the selection of expert witness. *Natural Resources & Environment, 2*(2), 6–9.

Lee, T. V. (1988). Court-appointed experts and judicial reluctance: A proposal to amend Rule 706 of the federal rules of evidence. *Yale Law & Policy Review, 6*(2), 480–503.

Lianos, I. (2009). "Judging" economists. Economic Expertise in Competition Law Litigation—A European View, *CLES Working Paper Series 1/2009.*

Liu, .C, Li, A., Bi, Y., Liu, S., Hong, L., & Liu, J. (2020). China's anti-monopoly law enters its second decade. King & Wood Mallesons on February 20, 2020, available at https://www.chinalawinsight.com/2020/02/articles/antitrust/chinas-anti-monopoly-law-enters-its-second-decade/#_ftn18.

Macey, J. R. (1992). Organizational design and political control of administrative agencies. *Journal of Law Economics and Organization, 8*(1), 93–110.

Massel, M. S. (1962). Economic analysis in judicial antitrust decisions. *ABA Antitrust Section, 20,* 46–61.

Mandel, M. J. (1999). Going for the gold: Economists as expert witness. *Journal of Economic Perspectives, 13*(2), 113–120.

Moore, K. A. (2001). Are district court judges equipped to resolve patent cases? *Harvard Journal of Law and Technology, 15,* 1–39.
Neven, D. J. (2006). Competition economics and antitrust in Europe. *Economic Policy, 21*(48), 742–791.
Neven, D. J., & De Coninck, R. (2010). Best practices on the submission of economic evidence and data collection, DG Competition of European Commission Staff Working Paper, available at https://ec.europa.eu/competition/antitrust/legislation/best_practices_submission_en.pdf.
Ohlhausen, M. K. (2013). Illuminating the Story of China's Anti-monopoly Law, the antitrust source October 2013.
Posner, R. A. (2001). Antitrust law, 2nd edition Chicago University Press.
Posner, R. A. (1999a). An economic approach to the law of evidence. *Stanford Law Review, 51,* 1477–1546.
Posner, R. A. (1999). The law and economics of the economic expert witness. *Journal of Economic Perspectives*, 91–100
Prettyman. (1948). Needed: New trial technique: suggestions for the trial of complicated cases. *American Bar Association Journal, 34*(9), 766–660.
Petroski, K. (2013). Texts versus testimony: Rethinking legal uses of non-legal expertise. *University of Hawaii Law Review, 35*(1), 81–128.
Ren, Q. (2017). Anti-monopoly litigation in China: a review for the year of 2016. Competition Policy International Asian Column, March 27, 2017 available at https://www.competitionpolicyinternational.com/anti-monopoly-litigation-in-china-a-review-for-the-year-of-2016/.
Roeller, L. H. (2005). Economic analysis and competition policy enforcement in Europe, In: P. A. G. Van Bergeijk, E. Kloosterhuis (Eds.), *Modelling European Mergers: Theory, Competition Policy and Case Studies*, Edward Elgar 2005, pp. 13–27.
Rubinfeld, D. L. (1985). Econometrics in the courtroom. *Columbia Law Review, 85*(5), 1048–1097.
Robertson, C. T. (2010). Blind expertise. *New York University Law Review, 85*(1), 174–257.
Sheehan, R. S. (1990). Administrative agencies and the court: A reexamination of the impact of agency type on decisional outcomes. *Western Political Quarterly, 43*(December), 875–885.
Schreiber, T. (2010). Private antitrust litigation in the European Union. *The International Lawyer, 44*(4), 1157–1172.
Shuman, D. W., Whitaker, E., & Champagne, A. (1994). An empirical examination of the use of expert witnesses in the courts—Part II: a three city survey. *Jurimetrics Journal, 34,* 193–208.
Stephenson, M. C. (2005). Public regulation of private enforcement: the case for expanding the role of administrative agencies. *Virginia Law Re view, 91*(1), 93–173.
Stephenson, M. C. (2006). Legislative allocation of delegated power: uncertainty, risk, and the choice between agencies and courts. *Harvard Law Review, 119*(4), 1035–1070.
Sokol, D. D. (2015). Tensions between antitrust and industrial policy. *George Mason Law Review, 22*(5), 1247–1268.
Stigler, G. J. (1965). *Essays in the history of economics.* University of Chicago Press
Tomlin, J. T., & Cooper, D. (2006). When should judges appoint experts?: A law and economics perspective. Bepress Legal Series working Paper 1699, available at https://law.bepress.com/expresso/eps/1699.
US Chamber of Commerce. (2014). *Competing Interests in China's Competition Law Enforcement: China's Anti-monopoly Law Application and the Role of Industrial Policy* available at https://www.uschamber.com/sites/default/files/aml_final_090814_final_locked.pdf.
Van Dusen. (1962). A United States district judge's view of the impartial medical expert system, 32 F.R.D.
Wright, J. D., & Diveley, A. M. (2012) Do expert agencies outperform generalist judges? Some preliminary evidence from the Federal Trade Commission. *Journal of Antitrust Enforcement,* 1–22
Weller, C. D. (1997). Antitrust economics as science after Daubert. *Antitrust Bulletin, 42,* 871–935.

Wagner, P., & Petherbridge, L. (2004). Is the federal circuit succeeding? An empirical assessment of judicial performance. *University of Pennsylvania Law Review, 152,* 1105–1180.

Zhao, B., & He, J. (2017). How China's enforcement agencies and courts are shaping antitrust policies on vertical restraints. *George Mason Law Review, 24,* 1171–1212.

Zhan, H., Song, Y., & Yang, Z. (2018) A new era comes-highlights of the anti-monopoly law of China in 2018, Anjie Law Firm, available at http://www.anjielaw.com/en/uploads/soft/190201/1-1Z2011P205.pdf.

Zhan, H., & Tan, W. (2015). Private antitrust enforcement in China. Anjie Law Firm June 30, 2015, available at http://en.anjielaw.com/publications_detail/newsId=303.html.

Zhang, A. H. (2011). The enforcement of the anti-monopoly law in China: An institutional design perspective. *The Antitrust Bulletin, 56*, 631–663.

Zhang, A. H. (2015). Taming the Chinese leviathan: Is antitrust regulation a false hope? *Stanford Journal of International Law, 51*, 195–228.

Chapter 12
The Enforcement of Competition Law—A Behavioral Law and Economics Perspective

Abstract The choice of enforcement instruments in competition law has become a major debate around the world. In recent years, many competition authorities commentators have argued for a more "mixed" approach in antitrust enforcement, acknowledging that three enforcement instruments—private, administrative and criminal enforcement—are not substitutes to each other, but rather compliments, and should be better coordinated based on the strengths and weaknesses of each mechanism. This chapter address the insights of this issue by incorporating the recent development of behavioral economics and examine to what extent those insights lead to a different optimal mix of enforcement instruments. Behavioral findings can explain the ineffectiveness of some of the existing mechanisms and allow to provide more balanced criteria for determining the optimal mix of instruments in antitrust enforcement. This chapter discusses the optimal mix of enforcement instruments from the perspective of public and private enforcers. The findings of behavioral studies provided a more nuanced criteria when assessing the pros and cons of each instrument, and may be relevant to explain some of the reasons why the enforcement mechanisms become ineffective.

12.1 Introduction

In the previous chapters, law and economics theories have been applied to discuss the mix of public and private enforcement, the choice on sanctions, and the role of agency versus courts in antitrust enforcement. It made clear that when administrative agencies are the dominant antitrust player to enforce competition law, the biggest concern is building up the capacities of the agency. Administrative fines are generally superior to criminal sanctions, but the effectiveness of the law enforcement could be strengthened through criminal penalties. Introducing criminal law brings in the concern of defining moral wrongfulness, and confiscating illegal gains might be the alternative if cartel criminalization lacks prerequisites. In this chapter, the 'mix' of enforcement instruments is reexamined by taking the recent development of behavioural economics into account.

J. Ma, *Competition Law in China*,
https://doi.org/10.1007/978-981-15-5105-5_12

The Becker Model is developed based on the rationality assumption. Several limitations of applying the Rational Choice Theory in the implementation of legal rules have been mentioned by behavioural law and economics scholars.[1] Behavioural psychologists,[2] economists[3] and social scientists[4] have devoted significant efforts to the study of the heuristic biases in an individual's decision making process, which indicate the tendency of deviating from the rational choice models that classic Law and Economics literature relies on. Among these findings, there were some cognitive biases that have attracted attention from lawyers and legal scholars,[5] and have been addressed in the context of the behavioural analysis of law.[6]

Herbert Simon developed the concept of 'bounded rationality',[7] which indicates that a human being's behaviour may deviate from the classic economic models due to limited intellectual skills. According to Korobkin and Ulen, bounded rationality in decision making is justified by two reasons. The first reason is that such decisions are made to specially meet aspirations.[8] The decision that makes the actor feel satisfied may be different from the decision that maximizes the actor's utility. The second reason is the use of heuristics,[9] which makes the assumption of maximizing expected utility fail. The behavioural economics theory indicates that due to the high cost of processing information, as well as the cognitive limitations of human beings, actors often do not conduct complex cost-benefit analysis when they make decisions. Instead, people engage in a process of 'satisficing', meaning that in their decisions people do not choose the option that maximizes their utility, but rather choose one that satisfies their aspirations.[10]

The findings of the behavioural law and economics literature have been applied to criminal law. It is, for example, held that the criminals are in a specific group with extreme risk preferences, and people in different groups may perceive the severity of punishment differently.[11] It is also held that as a consequence of a number of heuristics and biases, in reality the severity of punishment is often weakened.[12] Behavioural

[1] Korobkin and Ulen (2000, p. 1067), McAdams and Ulen (2009).

[2] Kahneman et al. (1982); For a summary of the research findings by Tversky and Kahneman, see Kahneman (2003, pp. 1449–1475); research by other psychologists, see for example, Evans (1984, p. 451).

[3] For example, Babcock and Loewenstein (1997, p. 109), Benartzi and Thaler (1995, pp. 73–92), Camerer and Hogarth (1999, pp. 7–42).

[4] For example, Fiske and Taylor (1991), Weinstein (1980, p. 806).

[5] The selection of these biases are based on Langevoort (1998, pp. 1503–1506), Faure (2008).

[6] Rachlinski claimed that the methods that behavioural law and economics uses rely on the concepts that Tversky and Kahneman developed, such as endowment effect, framing, anchoring and hindsight bias. *See also* Korobkin and Ulen (2000).

[7] Simon (1957), Simon (1955, p. 99).

[8] Korobkin and Ulen (2000, p. 1075).

[9] Korobkin and Ulen (2000, p. 1076).

[10] Simon (1979, p. 503).

[11] Robinson and Darley (2004, p. 193), Baron and Kennedy (1998).

[12] McAdams and Ulen (2009).

theory has also been applied to antitrust,[13] although it is also debated and some have argued that behavioural antitrust is "not ready for the main stage".[14]

12.2 Behavioural Economics

Behavioural economists and cognitive psychologists argue that people have limited brainpower to calculate the utility pay-off of their conduct. Rather, they often engage in a process of "satisficing", in which process a target is chosen to meet their aspirations. Herbert Simon defined it as "bounded rationality".[15] These cognitive biases were mainly discovered by a series of experiments conducted by both psychologists and economists. For example, Tversky and Kahneman defined the anchoring effects that a randomly chosen starting point will influence the estimates.[16] Anchor effects suggest that individuals do not easily make adjustments. Anchoring will, for example, be very important in the behaviour of judges in relation to the sanction that has been claimed by the prosecutor and that will hence function as an "anchor" from which it may become difficult to deviate.

Daniel Kahneman and Aversky proposed their prospect theory,[17] and suggested that people value losses more than the gains. This loss aversion bias[18] leads to the framing effects,[19] meaning that an individual's decisions are affected by how future losses and gains are framed. Due to the reason that there is an asymmetry between the losses and gains, people suffer more utility loss to give up an object than the amount to acquire it, in other words, people are less willing to give up the things that they own, and this bias is named as the endowment effect.[20] The compelling experiments conducted by Kahneman, Knetsch and Thaler[21] show that the sellers who own the decorated mug value the product much more highly than the potential buyers. The mug is considered to be a loss for the sellers but a gain for the buyers. The endowment effect shows that it is more difficult for the owner to give up a product in exchange for money. In the experiment conducted by Knetsch, about 90%

---

[13]Reeves and Stucke (2011, p. 1542), Stucke (2007).

[14]Van den Bergh (2013).

[15]Simon (1979, p. 493).

[16]Anchoring effects: a randomly chosen starting point that will influence the estimates. See Tversky and Kahneman (1974). Tversky and Kahneman (1974).

[17]Prospect theory: people value losses more than the gains (Kahneman and Tversky 1979, p. 263).

[18]Loss aversion: there is an asymmetry between the losses and gains, people suffer more utility loss to give up an object than the amount to acquire it. This effect may affect decision making process in many domains of policy issues. See examples provided by Samuelson and Zeckhauser (1988, pp. 7–59).

[19]Framing: individual's decisions are affected by how future losses and gains are framed. Kahneman and Tversky (1984, p. 343).

[20]Kahneman et al. 1990, p. 1325; Knetsch 1989, pp. 1277–1284; Kahneman et al. 1990, pp. 1325–1348.

[21]Kahneman et al. (1990).

of the participants are unwilling to trade the gift they have received as compensation for answering a questionnaire.[22] In recent years, many researchers were engaged to investigate the difference between people's willingness to accept (WTA) in exchange to give up something they own and people's willingness to pay (WTP) to obtain it. Most results have confirmed the existence of loss aversion,[23] and this effect may affect the decision-making process in many domains of policy issues.[24]

Samuelson and Zeckhauser extended the discussion on endowment effect to situations where even the framing of gains and losses is absent. They argue that people tend to retain the status quo.[25] For example, people tend to maintain the current or previous decision, such as choosing the products of same brands, or staying in the same job[26]; also, few people would like to switch to Dvorak keyboards from QWERTY keyboard, although it was more efficient to use.[27] Another example was that after the earthquake in Tokyo in 1923, most people preferred to put up tents in places where their houses were located, and the policy plan of redesigning the city was unable to be implemented.[28] Fischhoff's experiments have found that people are likely to increase the likelihood of an event's occurrence after knowing that it happened.[29] Hindsight bias refers to overestimating the likelihood of an event after learning that it did occur.[30] Psychologists have found that hindsight biases could be observed in various situations, such as surgeons evaluating surgical cases, among medical diagnosis, in voters' election predictions.[31]

In addition, representative effects refer to ignoring the actual statistical information and making a biased judgment between the reality and its appearance. Egocentric bias refers to over-estimating one's own abilities and the tendency of interpreting information favourably towards oneself. Individuals tend to show a strong bias when assessing their capacity compared with others, which leads to a result of selective optimism and over-confidence. Psychologists' research shows that overconfidence exists when people consider their own activities and their futures.[32]

Unrealistic optimism may lead to under-estimation of the probability that unpleasant events will happen to one-self.[33] Moreover, self-serving judgments exist in both

---

[22] Knetsch (1989, pp. 1277–1284).

[23] For an overview of these experiments, *see* Tversky and Kahneman (1991, pp. 1055–1056), Novemsky and Kahneman (2005, pp. 119–120).

[24] See examples provided by Samuelson and Zeckhauser (1988, pp. 7–59).

[25] Samuelson and Zeckhauser (1988).

[26] Samuelson and Zeckhauser (1988, p. 8).

[27] Camerer and Kunreuther (1989, p. 577).

[28] Camerer and Kunreuther (1989, p. 577).

[29] Fischhoff (1975, pp. 288–299).

[30] Hindsight bias: People are likely to over-estimate the likelihood of an event's occurrence after knowing it happened (Fischhoff 1975). Kamin and Rachlinski (1995, p. 91); Korobkin and Ulen (2000, pp. 1095–1100).

[31] Kamin and Rachlinski (1995, p. 91).

[32] Weinstein (1980, pp. 806–820), Taylor and Brown (1988, pp. 193–210).

[33] Jolls (1998, pp. 1658–1663), Sunstein (1997, pp. 1182–1184).

bargaining and non-bargaining situations.[34] For example, the well-known research by Ola Svenson shows that around ninety percent of drivers believe that their driving capacity is above the average.[35] Jolls concluded that most results showed that people believe their chances of encountering negative outcomes are significantly lower than average.[36] Viscusi and Magat's research show that ninety-seven percent of interviewed consumers believe that they are better than average in avoiding accidents.[37] In Baker and Emery's study, none of the respondents replied that they would encounter a risk of divorce, although they estimated that the divorce rate in the US at that time was about fifty percent.[38] In the experiment conducted by Hastorf and Cantril in 1954,[39] students from Princeton and Dartmouth were asked to count the number of infractions during a football game. The result showed that the opponents counted more infractions than the supporters for each team, and this result could be considered to be evidence of self-serving bias in the real world.

Tversky and Kahneman refers availability heuristic to a type of bias that people are likely to make a judgment on the frequency of an event base on how 'available' this type of event is, in order words, how easily they could imagine the occurrence of such an event.[40] For example, Combs and Slovic found that media reporting has a causal influence on people's perception of deaths. People tend to believe that deaths are more likely caused by reported disasters and homicide, but not events like diabetes and breast cancer.[41]

Here is the list of examples of heuristic biases:

- Anchoring effects: a randomly chosen starting point that will influence the estimates.
- Prospect theory: people value losses more than the gains.
- Loss aversion: there is an asymmetry between the losses and gains, people suffer more utility loss to give up an object than the amount to acquire it.
- Framing: individual's decisions are affected by how future losses and gains are framed.
- Endowment effect: people give a higher value to the things that they have obtained and are less willing to give up the things that they own.
- Representativeness: people tend to make a judgement on whether an item belongs to a category or a group based on judging whether its characteristics belong to that group.[42]

---

[34] Babcock et al. (1997, p. 915); for an overview of these psychological research on overconfidence, *see* Camerer and Lovallo (1999, p. 306, footnote 1).

[35] Svenson (1981, pp. 143–148).

[36] Jolls (1998, p. 1659).

[37] Viscusi and Magat (1987).

[38] Baker and Emery (1993, p. 439).

[39] Hastorf and Cantril (1954, pp. 129–134).

[40] Tversky and Kahneman (1973).

[41] Combs and Slovic (1974, pp. 837–849).

[42] Tversky and Kahneman, pp. 92–93, Sunstein (1997, pp. 1188–1189), Hanson and Kysar (1999, p. 630).

- Egocentric bias: Egocentric bias refers to over-estimating one's own abilities and the tendency of interpreting information favourable towards oneself. Individuals tend to show a strong bias when assessing their own capacity compared with others, which leads to selective optimism and overconfidence.[43]
- Availability heuristic: people are likely to make judgments on the frequency of an event based on how available this type of event is, and how easily they could imagine the occurrence of such an event.[44]
- Status Quo bias: the status quo will be taken as the reference point when people make choices and choose alternatives. People have a high tendency of adhering to the status quo.[45]
- Extremeness Aversion: people are likely to avoid extreme answers. People tend to change to choose a modest answer when a third, extreme option is added.[46]

12.3 Behavioural Biases of Public Agencies

12.3.1 Selection Bias and Myopia

Behavioural public choice theory argues that by sitting in the position between voters and political overseers, administrative agencies may have to make decisions to meet the needs of both sides. The problem is, however, that the preferences of both the voters and the politicians may be biased.[47] Since voters are exposed to the availability bias, the performance of administrative agencies and their political oversees is often evaluated through policy output or used political resources, and the outcome of the policy is often neglected.[48] Voters are likely to prefer the policy that makes them "feel good", and may have difficulties in evaluating the real costs, benefits, and quality of the public policy.[49] When responding to the request of voters, "appearance" to take action would matter a lot for politicians to be reelected, although such actions may

---

[43]Psychologists' research shows that over-confidence exists when people consider their own activities and their futures. *See* Weinstein(1980), Taylor and Brown(1988). Unrealistic optimism may lead to under-estimation of the probability that unpleasant events will happen to one self. *See* Jolls (1998, pp. 1658–1663), Sunstein (1997, pp. 1182–1184).

[44]Tversky and Kahneman (1973, p. 207).

[45]Samuelson and Zeckhauser (1988, p. 7).

[46]Simonson and Tversky (1992, pp. 281, 290).

[47]Cooper and Kovacic (2012a, p. 784), Lucas Jr. and Tasic (2015, p. 217) ("voters and politicians do not evaluate policies globally by considering all angles, including the interrelationships among policies. Instead, their analyses are subject to pervasive framing, salience, and vividness effects."); *See also* Hirschleifer (2008, p. 856).

[48]Cooper and Kovacic (2012a, p. 784).

[49]Cowen (2005, p. 445) ("All voters will be excessively attracted to policies that make citizens "feel good about themselves". Individuals on all sides of the political spectrum will be unwilling to confront difficult trade-offs"). Lucas Jr. and Tasic (2015, p. 218).

not be the welfare-increasing decisions for a society, especially in the long run.[50] As a consequence administrative agencies have on the one hand to deal with cognitive biases of their own, but on the other hand they are also confronted with *additional* biases coming from voter myopia and biases of their political overseers, which may increase the risk of sub-optimal decision making.

This may also have relevance in the enforcement of competition law. Agency regulators may have a strong selection bias when responding to competition cases. The bias of "appear to take action" may make agency regulators prefer to enforce the "big" case, since big cases could not only give them favourable political payoff,[51] but also attract maximum public attention within a short run, which is named as the "salience effect" by cognitive psychologist. Agencies are likely to prefer to issue "tough" decisions towards big companies, in order to gain publicity rather than to work on less significant cases, even when those would have an impact on changing the legal doctrine.[52] High-profile cases against industry giants such as GM, IBM, Microsoft, Intel, Google often receive dramatic publicity.[53]

The selection bias of agencies also reflects the weakness of the administrative enforcement system, that is, public regulators are likely to be short-run thinkers and may suffer from the bias of myopia. Very often the performance of public regulators is assessed based on yearly, or monthly targets, and psychologists have found that such an evaluation mechanism would lead to short-run thinking.[54] Since there is no uniform, consistent and internationally accepted standard to evaluate the quality of competition agencies' work,[55] agencies tend to initiate "high profile" investigations, or to increase the quantity of the cases, instead of making welfare increasing long-term decisions.[56] The ex-post evaluation of case decisions is often ignored, and agencies prefer to move on and to take actions to investigate the next case, because an *ex-post* assessment may discredit the presumptions on which the initial intervention was based. Also, since the number of decisions is often the indicator of an agency's performance in the international comparison, competition authorities are likely to

[50] Anthony Patt and Richard Zeckhauser found that "take action"—such as cleaning up a polluted resource, is more favourable to the public than inaction—for example preserving the source, because taking action is easier to be visualized. *See* Patt and Zeckhauser (2000, p. 45); *see also* Lucas Jr. and Tasic (2015, p. 230).

[51] Coate et al. (1995).

[52] Muris (2005, p. 166) ("For an agency like the FTC, the most attention is paid publicly to the prosecution of cases, preferably "big" ones, or to the launching of "tough" regulations, while non litigation activities that have a major impact on public policy or less obviously significant cases and rules that do not tackle large players, but that alter doctrine in important ways, are usually overlooked.").

[53] Sokol (2012a, p. 701).

[54] Camerer found that when New York taxi drivers set daily income targets, they will stop working once the target is met Camerer et al. (1997).

[55] Kovacic et al. (2011).

[56] Kovacic (2009, pp. 903, 922–923).

focus on increasing the quantity of the cases in order to have a higher rank when compared with authorities in other regions.[57]

12.3.2 *Expert Bias and Overconfidence*

Traditional law and economics scholars argue that dealing with complex cases is often beyond the capacity of judges,[58] and administrative agencies are particularly superior because especially in the US and the EU, competition authorities are well-equipped with professionals, usually both PhD holding economists and antitrust lawyers who have a solid understanding of the economic reasoning. In the US, empirical evidence showed that from the 1940s till the 1990s, in about 70% of the time, the Court has supported the position of the administrative agencies, although the success rate of agencies may vary.[59] In administrative agency cases, courts are willing to examine whether the agency complied with procedural rules rather than substantive policies in the case.[60] Nonetheless, in times when agencies are still devoting efforts to increasing their investment to recruit more professionals, what has often been neglected is the fact that the solutions provided by experts are not always socially optimal, because experts themselves suffer from an over-confidence bias. Leonid Rozenblit and Frank Keil developed a study to test the effect of over-confidence bias when people deal with complex problems.[61] They used a phrase "illusion of explanatory depth" to describe that the over-confidence effect is the worst when people are asked a question to explain complex phenomena, compared with other questions such as the knowledge of facts, explaining the procedure issue, or reproducing a narrative story. Their study indicates that, even for experts, their capacity to explain causations or make predictions may be limited, and such capacity advantage may even become an "illusion".[62] Kruger and Dunning found that people are often over-confident about what they do not know and tend to develop a superficial understanding of the subjects to show their competence.[63] Although the story that regulators are facing "unknown unknowns"[64]

[57] For example, the competition authority in Russia has a strong bias on merely increasing the number of case decisions. *See* Paneiakh and Novikov (2014).

[58] The judicial capacity restraint of assessing economic evidence has been named by Frank Easterbrook as the "limits of antitrust", details see Chap. 11 of this book.

[59] Crowley (1987, pp. 266–267), Humphries and Songer (1999, p. 209).

[60] Crowley (1987), Sheehan (1990, pp. 875–85).

[61] Rozenblit and Keil (2002).

[62] *See also* Tasic (2009, p. 428).

[63] Kruger and Dunning (1999, p. 1121).

[64] Tasic (2009, p. 430).

is not new,[65] what cognitive psychologists have found is that the over-confidence bias of experts in a competition agency deserves more attention. In particular since there is little competition among regulators,[66] it becomes difficult for regulators to hear counterarguments and to correct the over-confidence bias by themselves.

12.3.3 Anchoring and Coherence Effects

Experimental research shows that a confirmation bias may occur when the outcome of the situation becomes ambiguous. Once individuals have reached their own judgement, they may ignore new evidence or may distort the interpretation of new evidence which will contradict their initial judgement.[67] A competition regulator may read evidence selectively in order to support their pre-existing policy preferences,[68] and such psychological phenomenon is named as the "coherence effect".[69] It refers to the mental process when analyzing evidence and arguments of a case. If there is an emerging conclusion, individuals tend to selectively choose arguments to strengthen the conclusion and filter out conflicting views. The emerging conclusion accelerates the analyzing process by spotting the favourable evidence and arguments, as they are more "coherent" with the conclusion.[70] In the 1960s and 1970s, the decisions on non-price vertical restraints reflected FTC's reluctance of changing the antitrust policy in order to respond to the new development of economics.[71]

Anchoring effect refers to the tendency of making decisions based on a chosen starting point. In administrative enforcement, political leaders at the agency have a strong tendency of discrediting their predecessor's work, and choosing their own anchor when the new political term starts. It is often claimed that it was a "bad situation" when they arrived at the office, although the quality of previous work is often not evaluated.[72]

---

[65] Also in the area of tort law when assessing damages there is substantial evidence of bias in the judgement of experts. For an overview *see* Faure and Visscher (2011, p. 376).

[66] Friedman argues that the crucial difference between public and private actors is that there is no similar market competition among regulators. *See* Friedman (2009, p. 127).

[67] Cooper and Kovacic (2012b, p. 47).

[68] Cooper and Kovacic (2012a, b, pp. 47, 791) ("Once a regulator takes a position on a particular policy, she will want to filter future matters in a way that supports her initial wisdom").

[69] Simon (2004), Simon and Scurich (2011, p. 711).

[70] Simon and Scurich (2011, p. 711).

[71] Cooper and Kovacic (2012a, p. 788).

[72] Kovacic (2015, p. 257).

12.3.4 *The Behaviour of Regulatee*

Classic public choice theory claims that regulators often fail to promote public interest and are likely to be incentivized by expanding their own political power and influence.[73] Given the fact that agency and industries are in a relatively close relationship, bureaucrats are likely to be captured by interest groups. The discovery of myopia, coherence effect and anchoring effect has important implications when assessing the effects of the industry lobby at the agency. Firstly, lobbying at the regulatory agency might become more complex because firms can alter their strategies in order to "frame" the thinking process of the Commissioner. Secondly, once interest groups have succeeded in "framing" the regulator's thinking or the public opinions, it becomes difficult to make public actors change their impressions. Because after the antirust agencies have developed their initial view of the market or business practices, it is often psychologically challenging for them to accept counter- arguments or to change the initial anchor, and the biased views on industry or market can exist for a long time.[74]

12.3.5 *Implications*

The implications of the behavioural findings on the regulators are that administrative enforcement may not be effective if agencies are not able to develop mechanisms to correct their biases and errors. Cooper and Kovacic were sceptical about the effectiveness of the learning effect at a competition agency, which is usually applied to correct biased decisions of private actors, because public regulators rarely receive prompt feedback on their decisions. Unlike in the market where firms could be punished through a repeated transaction if their decisions are erroneous, there is often a long time lag between the policy decision and the learning of policy implementation.[75] Even though decisions made by public agencies are wrong, it is doubtful whether such mistakes would be corrected or punished. Therefore, the crucial issue to reduce the negative effect of the biased decisions made by agencies is to provide immediate feedback to policy makers. Since reviewing agencies' work through the bureaucratic channel would be "more biased",[76] one possible solution is to provide external observers' peer-review, such as review by public consultancy, journalists,

---

[73]In antitrust law, *see* Shugart II (1995, pp. 7–8) ("Legislative and policy decisions in the realm of antitrust are shaped not by some ideal conception of the public interest, but rather by the interaction between well-organized private interest groups seeking protection from the forces of competition and politicians and other government officials seeking to maximize their own personal welfare.").

[74]Cooper and Kovacic (2012a, p. 791).

[75]Cooper and Kovacic (2012b, p. 50).

[76]The biased decisions of regulators may come directly from the biased preferences of their political overseers. Some argues that politicians are more biased than regulators. Choi and Pritchard (2003, p. 38) ("Politicians themselves may face their own behavioural biases, and there is no reason to think that the politicians' biases are any less than those facing regulators") Lucas Jr. and Tasic (2015,

public interest organizations, trade associations, or international organizations such as the OECD and UNCTAD.[77] Another mechanism is to develop a more extensive judicial review,[78] because the pressure being reviewed by someone unknown would make regulators more careful with counter-arguments when they prepare the written record, and in this way their expert over-confidence bias might be reduced.[79]

12.4 The Behaviour of Private Litigants

Empirical evidence indicates that private enforcement can generate substantial benefits to society, not only by stimulating deterrence, but also by providing compensation through victims,[80] However, law and economics scholars have indicated that private damage actions should be encouraged with caution because it often leads to over enforcement when plaintiffs' attorneys pursue private interests by bringing frivolous lawsuits. In the US, mechanisms such as treble damages and the attorney's fee have incentivized plaintiffs to sue, even when the filed cases can hardly provide full compensation or deter any violators.[81]

Traditional law and economics scholarship addresses this failure from the principal-agent problem between attorneys and litigants. Also the costs involved in class actions as well as the availability of treble damages and contingency fees for lawyers are blamed for this over-enforcement. However, it has also been claimed that criticisms on the private litigation system do not have a strong empirical support. The behavioural literature addresses this issue based on the self-serving bias of litigants, and on the fact that decisions to litigate or settle depend on the expectations and confidence of the parties that they will win the case.

12.4.1 The Behaviour of Litigants

The starting point of the analysis is that both plaintiff and defendants are subject to "self-serving bias" when predicting the likelihood of success,[82] and both parties are overconfident about the trial outcome. Experiments showed that plaintiffs tend

p. 203) ("Because political actors have little incentive to behave rationally, irrationality is common in politics, and it has a substantial negative effect on the law").

[77] Kovacic et al. (2011, p. 40), Hyman and Kovacic, p. 2172).

[78] Seidenfeld (2002, p. 486).

[79] Choi and Pritchard (2003, p. 38).

[80] Joshua Davis and Robert Lande found that the benefits of private enforcement were substantial. In the 60 largest successful private US antitrust cases since 1990, private action has recovered USD 33.8 to 35.8 billion for victims of anti-competitive conduct. *See* Davis and Lande (2013, p. 1272).

[81] For a summary of the criticisms on private enforcement of the US Antitrust Law, *See* Lande and Davis (2008, pp. 883–887).

[82] Roth and Murnighan (1982, p. 1123).

to have a higher level of confidence,[83] and such a positive attitude often makes it more difficult to settle the case.[84] After reviewing most of the experiments which were designed to test the expectations of plaintiffs and defendants, Babcock and Lowenstein concluded that the plaintiff's expectations concerning the amount to be awarded by the judge are approximately twice as high as the expectations of the defendant.[85] Their own experiment also confirmed this conclusion, that is, the existence of self-serving bias leads to the result that plaintiffs hold higher expectations than defendants.[86]

Moreover, plaintiffs and defendants' bias of predicting the trial outcome also depends on how ambiguous the information is, and how information will be interpreted.[87] Lowenstein and Moore's experiment showed that settlement could only be facilitated when there is no other possibility to interpret the information differently. As soon as there is a slight degree of ambiguity in the interpretation of the information, each party has a strong tendency to interpret it in a self-biasing way, and settling the case becomes difficult because of the divergent expectations.[88] When the predictions of trial outcomes are significantly different between two parties, it is highly likely that they will end up in a costly dispute.[89] Moreover, according to their experiments, the relationship between self-serving bias and impasse of civil litigation was causal[90] and proportional,[91] that is, the larger the differences of the self-serving biases are, the less likely it is that the case will be settled. When information becomes clearer and the uncertainty of the trial outcome is mitigated, such as imposing a damage cap, the self-serving bias could be reduced and in this way, a settlement could be facilitated.[92]

Cognitive psychologists tend to explain the behaviour of frivolous litigation by understanding the "psychological barriers" of litigants to settle out of court.[93] The prospect theory developed by Kahneman and Tversky showed that individuals are risk averse towards moderate-to-high probability gains, as well as towards low probability losses; at the same time, people become risk lovers towards moderate-to-high probability losses and towards low-probability gains.[94] Given the fact that plaintiffs view settlement and trial as gains, and plaintiffs view settlement and trial as losses, if

---

[83]Babcock et al. (1995a, p. 1337).

[84]Loewenstein et al. (1992); Note that theorists may reach a similar conclusion. For example, Bourjade et al. (2009) argued that "It should be the violators who settle and the innocent firms that refuse." Bourjade et al. (2009, p. 372).

[85]Babcock et al. (1997, p. 915).

[86]Babcock et al. (1997, p. 914).

[87]Dunning et al. (1989, p. 1082).

[88]Loewenstein and Moore (2004, pp. 37, 38).

[89]Babcock et al. (1997, p. 915).

[90]Babcock et al. (1995a, b, p. 1337).

[91]Loewenstein et al. (1992, p. 135).

[92]Babcock and Pogarsky (1999, p. 341).

[93]Korobkin and Guthrie (1994, pp. 109–110).

[94]Kahneman and Tversky (1979, p. 263), Tversky and Kahneman (1992, p. 297).

both parties view winning the case are a moderate-to-high probability event, plaintiffs are more likely to behave as a risk averse person, and choose to settle the case, but defendants will choose to go to trial. On the other hand, if both parties view winning the case as a low-probability event, plaintiffs are likely to go to trial and defendants will prefer to settle.[95] Therefore, it is often the innocent firms which insist to a trial at court to prove their innocence, and the violators are often immune from punishment and able to settle out of the court. Thus, behavioural findings tend to show that the self-serving bias in information interpretation could explain what motivates private parties to sue, and how such behaviour would lead to over or under deterrence of private litigation.

Plaintiff and defendants choose to settle the case or to go to trial based on their perception of the likelihood of success. However, they might under-estimate or over-estimate such a probability given their self-serving biases. In the early 1980s, experimental economists applied the self-serving biases to explain their results of the bargaining games.[96] The seminal work conducted by Babcock and Loewenstein in the 1990s has proven that self-serving biases cause litigation impasses, that is, when plaintiffs are more positive towards the outcomes of the trail than defendants, due to the reason of self-serving biases, it is less likely that the case will be settled.[97] Lowenstein and Moore's experiment showed that settlement could only be facilitated when there is no other interpretation of the information presented to plaintiff and defendants. As soon as there is a slight degree of ambiguity in the interpretation of the information, each party has a strong tendency to interpret the information in a self-biasing way, and settling the case becomes difficult because of the divergency of expectations.[98]

Babcock and Loewenstein have reviewed most of the experiments which are designed to test the expectations of plaintiffs and defendants.[99] It was shown that a plaintiff's expectation of the amount awarded by the judge is about twice that of the defendant.[100] Their own experiment confirmed this finding and they concluded that the existence of self-serving biases leads the plaintiffs hold higher expectations than defendants.[101] When the predictions of trial outcomes are significantly different between two parties, it is highly likely that they will be involved in a costly

[95] This is named as the Framing Theory of Litigation, Guthrie (2000, pp. 167–168). For details, *see* Rachlinski (1996, p. 113), Korobkin and Guthrie (1997, p. 77), Babcock et al. (1995b, p. 289), Korobkin and Guthrie (1994, p. 107).

[96] Roth and Murnighan (1982, p. 1123).

[97] Loewenstein et al. (1992, pp. 135–159); Note that theorists may reach a similar conclusion. For example, Bourjade et al. argued that "It should be the violators who settle and the innocent firms that refuse." *See* Bourjade et al. (2009, p. 372).

[98] Loewenstein and Moore (2004, pp. 37, 38).

[99] Babcock and Loewenstein (1997, p. 109).

[100] Babcock et al. (1997, pp. 913, 915).

[101] Babcock et al. (1997, p. 914).

dispute.[102] Moreover, according to their experiments, the relationship between self-serving biases and the impasse of civil litigation was causal[103] and proportional,[104] that is, the larger the self-serving biases are, the less likely that the case has been settled. Lillard and Viscusi's results showed that the defendants' settlement offer will be positively affected by the higher trial awards, and such awards would not influence the plaintiff's request; meanwhile, the plaintiff's incentive to sue would be positively correlated with the higher possibility of winning at trial.[105]

The empirical test of competition cases showed similar results. Perloff and Rubinfeld's research showed that cartel cases and cases of refusals to deal have low settlement rates, and they admitted that it could be explained by the optimistic prediction of the plaintiffs on the likelihood of receiving damage compensations. Meanwhile, the settlement rates were the lowest when the plaintiff was an employee, a licensee, or a dealer; the settlement rates reached the highest when the plaintiff was a close competitor, a supplier or a buyer. The settlement rate increased from 54.5 to 90.9% when plaintiffs were large firms.[106]

12.4.2 Implications

An important implication of the literature is that the expectations of the trial outcome could affect the risk attitude of plaintiffs and defendants. Those diverging expectations could explain the existence of often excessive and sometimes non meritorious private damage actions. Debiasing techniques, such as information disclosure, could be developed to mitigate the self-serving bias in interpreting ambiguous information.[107] Moreover, Babcock and Loewensten claimed that merely informing private actors about their own hindsight bias would not be enough, because they may consider that they are immune to those biases.[108] Research by Sloan et al. and Nisbett et al. shows that it is more effective to ensure that the information provided to people is concrete.[109] Guthrie argued that more "vivid information" should be provided, such as the chances of their losses,[110] and Slovic and Fischhoff supported this, arguing that explaining why a certain event happened to the subject could effectively reduce hindsight bias.[111]

---

[102]Babcock et al. (1997, p. 915).

[103]Babcock et al. (1995a, pp. 1337–1343).

[104]Loewenstein et al. (1992, p. 135).

[105]Lillard and Viscusi (1990).

[106]Rubinfeld, p. 176.

[107]For a summary of the literature, *see* Babcock et al. (1997, p. 916).

[108]Babcock et al. (1997, p. 921).

[109]Nisbett et al. (1976, pp. 107–116).

[110]Guthrie (2000, p. 210).

[111]Slovic and Fishhoff (1977, p. 544).

Another debiasing mechanism is to show the subject more clear and concrete information on the opposite side of their arguments. Research by Koriat et al.[112] and Lord et al.[113] has found that neglecting counterarguments was one of the driving reasons for the over-confidence biases. Babcock et al. tested this finding in their experiment, and found that the self-serving bias could indeed be reduced when actors can "consciously" consider the opposite evidence of their reasoning, that is, the weaknesses in their case.[114] Thus, it might be useful to arrange pretrial meetings to inform both parties of the counter-arguments. According to Babcock et al., pretrial conferences and meetings could be considered to be a low cost debiasing technique.

Summarizing, the behavioural literature does confirm insights from the law and economics concerning private enforcement that frivolous and in some cases non-meritorious suits could be brought. That is not as such an argument against private enforcement of antitrust, but just a reason to use debiasing techniques, such as information disclosure in order to reduce the over-confidence bias.

12.5 Behavioural of Criminals

Behavioural scientists have criticized criminal law on the basis that it could not have the effect of influencing individuals' behaviour, simply because the "transmission of influence" from the criminal doctrine to a particular conduct is much more complex than the standard economic analysis assumes.[115] The prerequisites for reaching a deterrence effect, such as that the punishment must be delivered immediately and with aggressive intensity, are often lacking. Managers tend to become overconfident when the de facto detection rates become very low. Sociologists conducted a series of studies to show how the perception of punishment could be influenced by the experience of peers,[116] and such perception could be updated after individuals have gained their own experience.[117] This finding could be proved by the study by Connor and Lande[118] who showed that managers estimated the probability of being caught by talking to other mangers. Moreover, the severity of the punishment could hardly be measured by the duration of the sentence because they are not in a linear relationship.[119] The experiment on animals showed a strong "adaptation to intensity" effect and shows that for criminals the ever increasing punishment would have little effect

[112]Koriat et al. (1980).

[113]Lord et al. (1984, p. 1231).

[114]Babcock et al. (1997, p. 913).

[115]Robinson and Darley (2004, p. 174).

[116]Cook (1980).

[117]Matsueda et al. (2006, p. 950).

[118]Connor and Lande (2012).

[119]Robinson and Darley (2004, p. 187).

since criminals get used to it.[120] Daniel Kahneman's research shows that the duration of the negative experience does not have a significant impact on the remembered pain of such experience.[121] This result indicates that what matters most in setting the severity of the punishment is not the duration of the prison term; instead, it is the intensity of the negative experience.[122] These findings provide valuable insights for the design of punishment especially for the recidivists.

12.6 Behavioural of Judges

The research by Englich, Mussweiler and Strack confirms the anchoring effects in judicial decisions and shows that the sentencing decisions of legal experts are heavily influenced by sentencing anchors. The research by Danziger et al. shows that in the contentious rulings, judges tend to make decisions to maintain the status quo, and this tendency could be overcome by taking a break or eating a meal. Empirical tests conducted by Guthrie, Rachlinski and Wistrich showed that the decision making process of the judges was influenced by five cognitive biases: anchoring, framing effects, hindsight bias, representativeness and egocentric bias. Their study shows that judges are unaware of their cognitive illusions and make decisions by relying on heuristics, which results in systematic errors in their judgments.[123]

12.7 Comparing Behavioral Biases

One implication of the just discussed psychological literature is that one can doubt the effectiveness of the traditional remedy to increase the severity of punishment in the case of more severe crime (more particularly the length of the present term). There is no direct link between the length of the punishment and an expected change in behaviour. Moreover, within the context of criminalizing cartels, the psychological literature shows that this may have little effect if there is no alternative mechanism to ensure that corporations adjust their behaviour. Cognitive psychology found that the change of behaviour relies on reinforcement, in particular reinforcing good behavior. Extreme punishment may have a counter-effect and should be avoided. Behaviour findings support the argument of building a compliance culture and internal compliance programs in firms. The surveys and interviews with business managers and

---

[120] Robinson and Darley (2004, p. 186); The adaptation effect is named by Brickman and Campbell as 'Hedonic treadmill' *See* Brickman and Campbell (1971, p. 287).

[121] Kahneman (1999, p. 4), Redelmeier and Kahneman (1996, p. 3).

[122] In particular, it is important to increase the maximum intensity and the end intensity of the painful experience. However, the punishment with high intensity, short duration and with the most intensive, painful punishment at the end is usually defined as 'torture' (Robinson and Darley 2004, pp. 190–191).

[123] Guthrie et al. (2001, p. 784).

practitioners showed that criminal doctrines could hardly reach the deterrence goal and attention needs to be paid to the corporations' compliance culture and their internal organizations.[124] Behavioural literature could well support those arguments.

Private actors refer to those who interact in the market place- victims, consumers, firms, competitors, and lawyers. Public actors often distinguish themselves from private actors, for the reasons that they are expected to pursue public interest, not private interest; also, they are not a "lay person", and often considered as "experts" or "professionals" in one field. Moreover, they do not work in a market with repeated transactions and do not receive reciprocal reactions and feedbacks. Research on the behaviour of public actors points to three potential problems which may to some extent explain government failure. The first is related to the behavioural agent theory, which indicates that public actors are subject to the same type of cognitive bases as individuals in the market place. The second is behavioural political economy or behavioral public choice theory,[125] which suggests that public actors are exposed to individual cognitive biases, plus additional political biases because of their social status. The third issue is that since public actors do not interact with competitors through repeated market transactions, they are less likely to correct irrational decisions through a learning effect.

12.7.1 Behavioural Agent Theory

Behavioural agent theory argues that public enforcers including regulators, judges and prosecutors, are the same as individuals in the society and are subject to cognitive biases as anyone else.[126] Both victims and enforcers are individuals, and are subject to the same type of cognitive biases.[127] The research by Englich, Mussweiler and Strack confirms the anchoring effects in judicial decisions and shows that the sentencing decisions of legal experts are heavily influenced by sentencing anchors.[128] Empirical tests conducted by Guthrie, Rachlinski and Wistrich showed that the decision making process of the judges was influenced by five cognitive biases: anchoring, framing effects, hindsight bias, representativeness and egocentric bias. Their study show that judges are unaware of their cognitive illusions and make decisions by relying on heuristics, which results in systematic errors in their judgments.[129] Rachlinski and Farina shows that representativeness, availability bias and loss aversions are applicable to Congress, the courts, regulators, and executives, which may lead to

---

[124]Sokol (2012b, p. 203).

[125]Lucas Jr. and Tasic (2015, pp. 199–264), Berggren (2012, p. 199).

[126]Tasic (2009, p. 423).

[127]For example, Cass Sunstein said "For every bias identified for individuals, there is an accompanying bias in the public sphere." Sunstein (2014, p. 102), Liaison and Zeckhauser raised this point earlier (1998, p. 7).

[128]Englich et al. (2006, pp. 188–200).

[129]Guthrie et al. (2001, p. 784).

the wrong match of problems and solutions.[130] Timur Kuran and Cass Sunstein argued that regulators are subject to availability bias and may over-estimate the salient events. This leads to the self-reinforcing cycles of excessive risk regulation.[131] David Hirshleifer proved that financial regulators are exposed to salience effects, over-confidence, xenophobia and scape-goating effects.[132]

12.7.2 Behavioural Political Economy Theory

The second argument is that public actors may make undesirable policies when they are motivated by public choice incentives and at the same time subject to behavioural biases, so public actors are more likely to be exposed to errors than individuals in private decision making settings.[133] In political decision making, public regulators have to respond to the (often irrational) preferences of the voters, and they distinguish themselves from lay-people because they are exposed to additional biases, both as an individual and an elected political official.[134] Whereas public choice theory claims that bureaucrats may fail to represent the interest of voters, behaviouralists may argue that regulatory distortion and inefficiency may just come from the fact that public agents represent the irrational, and often biased preferences of voters.[135] Viscusi pointed out that regulators may make decisions that deviate from social welfare maximizing goals due to their cognitive mistakes in risk assessment.[136] Viscusi explained that such bias may either come from individuals' misconception, or it is influenced by political factors such as the motivation of being selected by voters.[137] Behavioural political economy theory tends to argue that individuals in the political arena are more likely to be affected by cognitive bias than those in the marketplace, for the reason that political actors make decisions that do not affect themselves directly, and bureaucrats are significantly influenced by the biases of voters and politicians.[138] Another important reason is that the time lag in providing feedback for public regulators is much longer than in the market, so the learning effect becomes weaker.[139]

[130] Rachlinski and Farina (2002, p. 549).
[131] Kuran and Sunstein (1999, p. 683).
[132] Hirshleifer (2008, p. 856).
[133] Viscusi and Gayer (2015, p. 978).
[134] Rachlinski and Farina (2002).
[135] Caplan (2007).
[136] Viscusi (1995, pp. 50–54).
[137] Viscusi and Hamilton (1999, pp. 1010, 1025).
[138] Lucas Jr. and Tasic (2015, p. 4).
[139] Schnellenbach and Schubert (2015, pp. 395, 396).

12.8 Compare Debiasing Strategies

12.8.1 Learning Effects

In economic theory, it was claimed that by taking repeated actions, individuals could learn from their mistakes and learn to make utility maximizing decisions. In a market with repeat players, the one who under- or over-estimate risks would be driven out of the market. Irrational decisions will be corrected and after learning from their own mistakes, repeat players can place their decisions back to rational choice models.

Although the behavioural antitrust literature has criticized such assumptions and claimed that in reality firms often deviate from strict rationality and learning might be difficult[140]; compared with public actors, firms are more likely to be incentivized by the market mechanism to make profit maximizing decisions,[141] and to develop strategies to combat the heuristic biases and their bounded rationality.[142] Under the pressure of engaging in repeated, competitive market transactions, it is relatively easier for consumers, firms and lawyers to learn from their mistakes,[143] to reduce errors,[144] because irrational decisions might be punished by the market itself.[145] The learning effect in the market place could hardly occur in the political arena because public actors face less pressure from competitors and the biased decisions are seldom corrected through a tit-for-tat game. Also, public policy makers often receive late, or even no feedback for their decisions. Compared with economic proxies such as price, profit, and output in the market, indicators for the outcome of public policies are largely lacking; therefore measuring, evaluating and providing feedback for public regulators becomes difficult and less practical.[146]

12.8.2 Mitigating Errors

For private parties, judges are often under pressure to make quick decisions by interpreting the often conflicting economic evidence that is provided by agencies, parties or expert witness.[147]

---

[140] Tor (2013, p. 6).

[141] Van den Bergh (2013, p. 211).

[142] Reeves and Stucke (2011, p. 1542).

[143] List (2004, p. 615).

[144] Glaeser (2006, pp. 140–141, 144–146).

[145] Rubin (1998, pp. 1705, 1715), Stucke (2007, p. 515).

[146] Cooper and Kovacic (2012a, p. 792).

[147] Back to 1948 Judge Prettyman pointed out that "The tribunal does the best it can to decipher the truth from the resultant welter. Nothing could be sillier." Prettyman, 'Needed: New Trial Technique: Suggestions for the Trial of Complicated Cases', 34 ABA J 766, 770 (1948) cited by Massel (1962, p. 48).

A recent study by Epstein, Landes and Posner shows that the extent to which judges disagree with each other primarily depends on workload. If the workload is light, the majority of the judge panel are not likely to be interrupted by dissent, because it will not take them too much effort to try to rebut and to persuade the public that the majority is correct. In their research, it is clear that the Supreme Court has a much higher dissent rate (62%), where only 8 to 10 majority opinions are written every year, than in the courts of appeals (2.6%), where a mean of 54 opinions are written by court of appeals judges.[148] Their arguments could be proved by a recent survey conducted by the Dutch Association for the Judiciary (*Nederlandse Vereniging poor Rechtspraak*), which shows that 73% of the judges and prosecutors who responded, admitted that they "sometimes" or "often" compromised because of the "too high" workload.[149] Given the work pressure and the time limits, it is a common practice that only the chair-person will read the entire case files, and the other two judges sitting in the judge panel will make decisions based on the case summaries or memo.[150] It shows the strong tendency to compliance when people are facing workload pressure. This finding could be proved by the recent studies on circuit court judges in the US. Huang's research shows that lower court decisions are less likely to be reversed by circuit court judges when the workload is high.[151] This evidence recalled the earlier studies on social environmental psychology which shows that group members tend to conform with others when the group is working under stress. Group members are willing to give up their efforts of contributing their own inputs; instead, complying with the order given by the central authority. Meanwhile, the group leader also becomes more receptive to the information provided by group members.[152] This implies the tendency of individuals to shift responsibility to their peers and those in a superior hierarchy in stressful situations.[153]

12.9 Towards an Optimal Enforcement

This chapter has discussed the consequences of the behavioural literature for the choice of optimal instruments to enforce competition law. To some extent the heuristic biases may affect both public as well as private actors. However, the specific conditions under which the biases occur may indicate a preference either for private or public enforcement. One general finding so far is that biases may affect all of the instruments concerned. The crucial question is therefore whether under particular circumstances specific biases can be expected to be stronger with one actor rather

[148] Epstein et al. (2011, pp. 104, 106).

[149] Fruytier et al. (2013, p. 46), Holvast and Doornbos (2015, p. 50).

[150] Holvast and Doombos (2015, p. 58).

[151] Huang (2011, p. 1116).

[152] Driskell and Salas (1991, p. 474).

[153] Klein (1976).

than with the other, thus leading to a preference for a particular enforcement instrument; another consequence of the literature is that the effectiveness of enforcement instruments could be improved by taken into account the cognitive problems, thus aiming at this so-called debiasing.

Whereas law and economics literature focuses on the costs of the enforcement mechanism, cognitive psychology shifted the perspective to the behaviour of public versus private actors. Traditional law and economics arguments start from the analysis of market failure and government failure, and behavioural literature could contribute by adding the analysis of *behavioural* market failure and *behavioural* government failure, referring to the additional error costs when individuals perform sub optimally because of the limited cognitive functions of the brain.[154] When comparing the effectiveness of public or private enforcement instruments, behavioural studies showed that public actors are more likely to be exposed to cognitive errors, because regulators often have to respond to the often biased, irrational preferences of both the voters and the political overseers. Economic theories have already indicated that the decision making mechanisms by private parties are superior to the public ones because private decisions are more likely to be accurate,[155] cognitive psychology provided evidence to reinforce this argument.[156] Moreover, it was argued that private actors are both more incentivized and more likely to develop strategies to learn from their mistakes and identify the cognitive biases that they have experienced. Public actors, however, have less incentive to behave rationally and their mistakes are less likely to be identified because they do not receive prompt feedback as it is the case in the market place. If economists argue that bureaucrats often lack the incentive to correct the failure of the market decision-making,[157] behavioural economists would say that they also lack the incentive to correct their own failure. While public choice theory indicates that the undesirable outcome of public policies may come from the rational maximization behaviour of regulatory agents, behavioural theory claims that such inefficiency may be considered the result of irrationality. When public policy fails, the costs are often externalized to the public, and the individual decision maker do not take responsibility.[158]

In the economic model of law enforcement, law and economic scholars argued that public enforcement would be superior to private enforcement to achieve the deterrence goal, because public enforcers enjoy the advantage of setting the right level

---

[154]Behavioural market failure could be considered as an extension of market failure, *see* Bar-Gill (2002). ("The behavioral market failure, with its emphasis on misperception and bias, is a direct extension of the imperfect information problem.") Oren Bar-Gill, *Competition and Consumer Protection: A Behavioral Economics Account*, in Swedish Competition Authority, the Pros and Cons of Consumer Protection, December 19, 2011, available at http://papers.ssrn.com/sol3/papers.cfm?abstract_id=1974499. For the relationship between behavioural government failure and public choice theory, *see* Rachlinsky and Farina (2002).

[155]Schumpeter (1942), Buchanan and Tullock (1962, Chap. 4).

[156]Glaeser (2006), p.133.

[157]Mueller (2003).

[158]Lucas Jr. and Tasic (2015, p. 259).

of sanctions and detection efforts.[159] This argument, however, may be challenged when behaviour literature shows that public actors suffer from myopia, salience effect, and selection bias. In addition, the problems that public actors are facing are more complex,[160] and often require a comprehensive trade-off, in which situation individuals are more likely to be exposed to biases. Even though regulators are often the experts of the industry, they might be biased by, and over-confident about their experience. A consequence of this literature is that public enforcement can in some cases not lead to deterrence because of the less-desirable performance of public actors, due to their irrational behaviour. If public actors are more likely than private ones to be subject to biases the policy maker should be careful with an increasing use of public enforcement instruments, and debiasing mechanisms must be developed to provide feedback to let regulators learn from their errors and mistakes.

Another aspect when comparing public and private enforcement is the availability of information, as it is often claimed that private enforcement has more information, or in Shavell's words, private parties "enjoy an inherent advantage in knowledge",[161] and public regulators have to spend more on screening and detecting.[162] Behavioural literature pointed out that the advantage of information may be reduced when private parties suffer from a self-serving bias in interpreting information. To develop an effective system for private litigation, debasing mechanisms could be developed to reduce the self-serving bias of private litigants.

This leads to two conclusions. When there is evidence that cognitive biases of public actors are stronger than those of private litigants, the traditional law and economics argument in favour of public enforcement may be weakened and an additional argument supporting private enforcement would be present. However, this argument strongly relies on evidence that the cognitive problems are stronger with public than with private actors. A second conclusion is that to the extent that there is evidence of cognitive problems, debiasing tools could be developed. It may be relatively easier to debias private actors than public actors (given the fact that the latter are also under pressure from their political superiors) this may constitute yet another argument in favour of private enforcement where debiasing (for example through information disclosure) may be able to remedy problems like the overconfidence bias. Problems with public actors (like for example the self-serving bias) may, however, be much more difficult to remedy.

12.10 Conclusions

The tradition law and economics literature has developed criteria to assess the pros and cons of different instruments in the enforcement of competition policy. On the

---

[159] Polinsky (1980, p. 110).

[160] Lucas Jr. and Tasic (2015, p. 259).

[161] Shavell (1984, p. 357).

[162] Segal and Winston (2007, p. 206).

basis of the finding that each instrument (private, administrative or criminal) has particular weaknesses the law and economics literature has advocated the use of a so-called optimal mix of instruments. Although to an important extent the findings of this literature have also been employed by competition authorities, empirical evidence on the effectiveness of the enforcement mix still seems to show serious under-deterrence. For example: administrative authorities often only select particular highbrow cases, which are not necessarily those which would be the most important ones from a public interest perspective; private enforcement often suffers from collective action problems resulting in a lack of incentives to bring a suit, or to the reverse problem of frivolous and unmeritorious lawsuits; and the criminal sanctions do not seem to be able to lead to the necessary behavioural changes, for example, a better compliance with competition law.

This chapter analyzed the findings of cognitive psychology which provide additional explanations for the failure of the current enforcement mix in competition policy. The psychological literature therefore can have an important added value by showing why individual or public actors, in a different way than the traditional models expected, did not always react to the behavioural incentives provided through the different enforcement instruments as predicted by the economic models. That explanatory power of the behavioural literature already has an important added value. The behavioural literature also shows that within the choice between the three enforcement instruments (private, administrative and criminal) the prevalence of particular cognitive biases may be one of the criteria to choose for one (for example private enforcement) rather than the other (for example public). Finally, the behavioural literature equally indicates that although biases may lead to suboptimal outcomes there are remedies which the policymaker can employ, leading to a debiasing and thus increasing the effectiveness of particular policy instruments. The behavioural literature therefore can enable the policymaker to better understand why a particular mix of enforcement mechanisms may not be as effective as was predicted in the literature. Moreover, the behavioural literature can equally provide indications on how the effectiveness of enforcement instruments could be increased by employing debiasing techniques.

References

Babcock, L., & Loewenstein, G. (1997). Explaining bargaining impasse: The role of self-serving biases. *Journal of Economic Perspective, 11,* 109–126.

Babcock, L., & Pogarsky, G. (1999). Damage caps and settlement: A behavioral approach. *The Journal of Legal Studies, 28,* 341–370.

Babcock, L., Loewenstein, G., Issacharoff, S., & Camerer, C. (1995a). Biased judgements of fairness in bargaining. *American Economic Review, 85,* 1337–1343.

Babcock, L., Farber, H. S., Fobian, C., & Shafir, E. (1995b). Forming beliefs about adjudicated outcomes: Perceptions of risk and reservation values. *International Review of Law and Economics, 15*(3), 289–303.

Babcock, L., Loewenstein, G., & Issacharoff, S. (1997). Creating convergence: Debiasing biased litigants. *Law and Social Inquiry, 22*(4), 401–413.

Baker, L. A., & Emery, R. E. (1993). When every relationship is above average: Perceptions and expectations of divorce at the time of marriage. *Law and Human Behavior, 17*, 439–450.

Bar-Gill, O. (2011). Competition and consumer protection: A behavioral economics account. In *Swedish competition authority, the pros and cons of consumer protection* (Vol. 1, pp. 4–5). http://papers.ssrn.com/sol3/papers.cfm?abstract_id=1974499.

Baron, S., & Kennedy, L. W. (1998). Deterrence and homeless male street youths. *Canadian Journal of Criminology, 40*(1), 27–60.

Benartzi, S., & Thaler, R. H. (1995). Myopic loss aversion and the equity premium puzzle. *Quarterly Journal of Economics, 110*(1), 73–92.

Berggren, N. (2012). The time for behavioral political economy? An analysis of articles in behavioral economics. *Review of Austrian Economics, 25*, 199–221.

Bourjade, S., Rey, P., & Seabright, P. (2009). Private antitrust enforcement in the presence of pre-trial bargaining. *Journal of Industrial Economics, 57*(3), 372–409.

Brickman, P., & Campbell, D. (1971). Hedonic relativism and planning the good society. In M. H. Appley (Ed.), *Adaptation-level theory: A symposium* (pp. 287–302).

Buchanan, J. M., & Tullock, G. (1962). *The calculus of consent: Logical foundations of constitutional democracy*. Ann Arbor: University of Michigan Press. Chapter 4.

Camerer, C. F., & Hogarth, R. M. (1999). The effect of financial incentives. *Journal of Risk and Uncertainty, 19*, 7–42.

Camerer, C. F., & Kunreuther, H. (1989). Decision processes for low probability events: Policy implications. *Journal of Policy Analysis and Management, 8*(4), 565–592.

Camerer, C., & Lovallo, D. (1999). Overconfidence and excess entry: An experimental approach. *The American Economic Review, 89*(1), 306–318.

Camerer, C., Babcock, L., Loewenstein, G., & Thaler, R. H. (1997). Labor supply of New York City cabdrivers: One day at a time. *Quarterly Journal of Economics, 112*, 407–441.

Caplan, B. (2007). *The myth of the rational voter: Why democracies choose bad policies*. Princeton: Princeton University Press.

Choi, S. J., & Pritchard, A. C. (2003). Behavioral economics and the SEC. *Stanford Law Review, 56*(1), 1–73.

Coate, M. B., Higgins, R. S., & McChesney, F. S. (1995). Bureaucracy and politics in FTC merger challenges. In F. S. McChesney & W. F. Shughart II (Eds.), *The causes and consequences of antitrust: The public-choice perspective*.

Combs, B., & Slovic, P. (1974). Causes of death: Biased newspaper coverage and biased judgements. *Journalism Quarterly, 56*, 837–849.

Connor, J. M., & Lande, R. H. (2012). Cartels as rational business strategy: New data demonstrates that crime pays. *Cardozo Law Review, 34*, 427–490.

Cook, P. (1980). Research in criminal deterrence: Laying the groundwork for the second decade. In N. Morris & M. Tonry (Eds.), *Crime and justice: An annual review of research* (Vol. 2). Chicago: University of Chicago Press.

Cooper, J. C., & Kovacic, W. E. (2012a). Behavioral economics and its meaning for antitrust agency decision making. *Journal of Law, Economics and Policy, 8*(4), 779–800.

Cooper, J. C., & Kovacic, W. E. (2012b). Behavioral economics: Implications for regulatory behavior. *Journal of Regulatory Economics, 41*, 41–58.

Cowen, T. (2005). Self-deception as the root of political failure. *Public Choice, 124*(3), 437–451.

Crowley, D. W. (1987). Judicial review of administrative agencies: Does the type of agency matter? *The Western Political Quarterly, 40*(2)/*31*(June), 265–283.

Davis, J. P., & Lande, R. H. (2013). Toward an empirical and theoretical assessment of private antitrust enforcement. *Seattle University Law Review, 36,* 1269–1335.

Driskell, J. E., & Salas, E. (1991). Group decision making under stress. *Journal of Applied Psychology, 76*(3), 473–478.

Dunning, D., Meyerowitz, J. A., & Holzberg, A. D. (1989). Ambiguity and self-evaluation: The role of idiosyncratic trait definitions in self-serving assessments of ability. *Journal of Personality and Social Psychology, 57*(6), 1082–1090.

Englich, B., Mussweiler, T., & Strack, F. (2006). Playing dice with criminal sentences: The influence of irrelevant anchors on experts' judicial decision making. *Personality and Social Psychology Bulletin, 32,* 188–200.

Epstein, L., Landes, W. M., & Posner, R. A. (2011). Why (and when) judges dissent: A theoretical and empirical analysis. *Journal of Legal Analysis, 3*(1), 101–137.

Evans, J. St. B. T. (1984). Heuristic and analytic processes in reasoning. *British Journal of Psychology, 75*(4), 451–468.

Faure, M. (2008). Calabresi and behavioral tort law and economics. *Erasmus Law Review, 4,* 75–102.

Faure, M. G., & Visscher, L. (2011). The role of experts in assessing damages—A law and economics account. *European Journal of Risk Regulation, 3,* 376–396.

Fischhoff, B. (1975). Hindsight & foresight: The effect of outcome knowledge on judgment under uncertainty. *Journal of Experimental Psychology: Human Perception and Performance, 1,* 288–299.

Fiske, S. T., & Taylor, S. E. (1991). *Social cognition* (2nd ed.). New York: McGraw-Hill.

Friedman, J. (2009). A crisis of politics, not economics: Complexity, ignorance, and regulatory failure. *Critical Review, 21.*

Fruytier, B. G. M., Dikkers, J., Keesen, M., Janssen, J., van den Berg, I., Valeton, N., & Schouteten, R. L. J. (2013). *Werkdruk bewezen. Eindrapport werkdrukonderzoek rechterlijke macht.* Utrecht/Nijmegen: Hogeschool Utrecht/Radboud Universiteit Nijmegen. External research report. Retrieved from https://repository.ubn.ru.nl/handle/2066/126420.

Glaeser, E. L. (2006). Paternalism and psychology. *University of Chicago Law Review, 73,* 133–156.

Guthrie, C. (2000). Framing frivolous litigation: a psychological theory. *The University of Chicago Law Review, 67*(1), 163–215.

Guthrie, C., Rachlinski, J. J., & Wistrich, A. J. (2001). Inside the judicial mind. *Cornell Law Review, 86*(4), 777–830.

Hanson, J. D., & Kysar, D. A. (1999). Taking behavioralism seriously: The problem of market manipulation. *NYU Law Review, 74,* 630–749.

Hastorf, A., & Cantril, H. (1954). They saw a game: A case study. *Journal of Abnormal and Social Psychology, 49*(1), 129–134.

Hirshleifer, D. A. (2008). Psychological bias as a driver of financial regulation. *European Financial Management, 14*(5), 856–874.

Holvast, N. L., & Doornbos, N. (2015). Exit, voice, and loyalty within the judiciary: Judges' responses to new managerialism in the Netherlands. *Utrecht Law Review, 11*(2), 49–63.

Huang, B. I. (2011). Lightened Scrutiny. *Harvard Law Review, 124*(5), 1109–1152.

Humphries, M. A., & Songer, D. R. (1999). Law and politics in judicial oversight of federal administrative agencies. *The Journal of Politics, 61*(1), 207–220.

Hyman, D., & Kovacic, W. (2013). Institutional design, agency life cycle, and the goals of competition law. *Fordham Law Review, 81*(5), 2163–2174.

Jolls, C. (1998). Behavioral economic analysis of redistributive legal rules. *Vanderbilt Law Review, 51,* 1658–1663.

Kahneman, D. (1999). Objective happiness. In D. Kahneman, E. Deiner, & N. Schwartz (Eds.), *Well-being: The foundations of hedonic psychology.* New York: Russell Sage Foundation.

Kahneman, D. (2003). Maps of bounded rationality: Psychology for behavioral economics. *The American Economic Review, 93*(5), 1449–1475.

Kahneman, D., & Tversky, A. (1979). Prospect theory: An analysis of decision under risk. *Econometrica, 47*(2), 263–291.
Kahneman, D., & Tversky, A. (1984). Choices, values and frames. *American Psychologist, 39,* 341–350.
Kahneman, D., Slovic, P., & Tversky, A. (Eds.). (1982). *Judgment under uncertainty: Heuristics and biases*. Cambridge University Press.
Kahneman, D., Knetsch, J. L., & Thaler, R. (1990). Experimental tests of the endowment effect and the Coase theorem. *Journal of Political Economy, 98,* 1325–1348.
Kamin, K. A., & Rachlinski, J. J. (1995). Ex post ≠ ex ante: Determining liability in hindsight. *Law and Human Behavior, 19*(1), 89–104.
Klein, A. L. (1976). Changes in leadership appraisal as a function of the stress of a simulated panic situation. *Journal of Personality and Social Psychology, 34,* 1143–1154.
Knetsch, J. L. (1989). The endowment effect and evidence of nonreversible indifference curves. *American Economic Review, LXXIX,* 1277–1284.
Koriat, A., Lichtenstein, S., & Fischhoff, B. (1980). Reasons for confidence. *Journal of Experimental Psychology: Human Learning and Memory, 6*(2), 107–118.
Korobkin, R., & Guthrie, C. (1994). Psychological barriers to litigation settlement: An experimental approach. *Michigan Law Review, 93,* 107–192.
Korobkin, R., & Guthrie, C. (1997). Psychology, economics and settlement: A new look at the role of the lawyer. *Texas Law Review, 76,* 77–121.
Korobkin, R. B., & Ulen, T. S. (2000). Law and behavioral science: Removing the rationality assumption from law and economics. *California Law Review, 88*(4), 1051–1144.
Kovacic, W. (2009). Rating the competition agencies: What constitutes good performance? *George Mason Law Review, 16,* 903–926.
Kovacic, W. (2015). Creating a respected brand: How regulatory agencies signal quality. *George Mason Law Review, 22,* 237–258.
Kovacic, W. E., Hollman, H. M., & Patricia, G. (2011). How does your competition agency measure up? *European Competition Journal, 7,* 25–45.
Kruger, J., & Dunning, D. (1999). Unskilled and unaware of it: How difficulties in recognizing one's own incompetence lead to inflated self-Assessments. *Journal of Personality and Social Psychology, 77*(6), 1121–1134.
Kuran, T., & Sunstein, C. R. (1999). Availability cascades and risk regulation. *Stanford Law Review, 51*(4), 683–768.
Lande, R. H., & Davis, J. P. (2008). Benefits from private antitrust enforcement: An analysis of forty cases. *University of San Francisco Law Review, 42,* 879–918.
Langevoort. (1998). Behavioral theories of judgment and decision making in legal scholarship: A literature review. *Vanderbilt Law Review, 51,* 1499–1540.
Liaison, D. I., & Zeckhauser, R. (1998). Amos Tversky and the ascent of behavioral economics. *Journal of Risk and Uncertainty, 16*(1), 7–47.
Lillard, L. A., & Viscusi, W. K. (1990). *The bargaining structure of the litigation process.*
List, J. A. (2004). Neoclassical theory versus prospect theory: Evidence from the marketplace. *Econometrica, 72*(2), 615–625.
Loewenstein, G., & Moore, D. A. (2004). When ignorance is bliss: Information exchange and inefficiency in bargaining. *The Journal of Legal Studies, 33,* 37–58.
Loewenstein, G., Issacharoff, S., Camerer, C., & Babcock, L. (1992). Self-serving assessments of fairness and pretrial bargaining. *Journal of Legal Studies, 22,* 135–159.
Lord, C., Lepper, M., & Preston, E. (1984). Considering the opposite, a corrective strategy for social judgment. *Journal of Personality and Social Psychology, 47*(6), 1231–1243.
Lucas, G. M., Jr., & Tasic, S. (2015). Behavioral public choice and the law. *West Virginia Law Review, 118,* 199–264.
Massel, M. S. (1962). Economic Analysis in Judicial Antitrust Decisions. *ABA Antitrust Section, 20,* 46–61.

Matsueda, R., Kreager, D., & Huizinga, D. (2006). Deterring delinquents: A rational choice model of theft and violence. *American Sociological Review, 71*(1), 95–122.

McAdams, R. H., & Ulen, T. S. (2009). Behavioral criminal law and economics. In Garoupa, N. (Ed.), *Criminal law and economics*. Edward Elgar. Chapter 18.

Mueller, D. C. (2003). *Public choice III*. Cambridge: Cambridge University Press.

Muris, T. J. (2005). Principles for a successful competition agency. *The University of Chicago Law Review, 72*(1), 165–187.

Nisbett, R. E., Borgida, E., Crandall, R., & Reed, H. (1976). Popular induction: Information is not always informative. In Carroll, J. & Payne, J. (Eds.), *Cognition and social behavior*. Hillsdale, NJ: Lawrence Erlbaum Associates. Reprinted in Kahneman, D., Slovic, P., & Tversky, A. (Eds.). (1982). *Judgment under uncertainty: Heuristics and biases*. Cambridge University Press.

Novemsky, N., & Kahneman, D. (2005). The boundaries of loss aversion. *Journal of Marketing Research, 42*(2), 119–128.

Paneiakh, E. L., & Novikov, V. V. (2014). Izlishne podozritel'noe vedomstvo: posledstviia «palochnoi» sistemy dlia raboty Federal'noi antimonopol'noi sluzhby, in Russian [Overly suspicious Office: Consequences "cane" system for the Federal Antimonopoly Service]. Series "Policy Paper on Law Enforcement". The Institute for the Rule of Law, European University, St. Petersburg, Internet address: http://www.enforce.spb.ru/images/analit_zapiski/Web_IRL_2014_02_PolicyMemo_EllaPaneyakh_Novikov_FAS_bur_expansion.pdf.

Patt, A., & Zeckhauser, R. (2000). Action bias and environmental decisions. *Journal of Risk and Uncertainty, 21*, 45–72.

Polinsky, M. (1980). Private versus public enforcement of fines. *Journal of Legal Studies, 9*(1), 105–127.

Prettyman. (1948). Needed: new trial technique: Suggestions for the trial of complicated cases. *American Bar Association Journal, 34*(9), 766–660.

Rachlinski, J. J. (1996). Gains, losses and the psychology of litigation. *Southern California Law Review, 70*, 113–186.

Rachlinski, J. J., & Farina, C. F. (2002). Cognitive psychology and optimal government design. *Cornell Law Review, 87*(2), 549–615.

Redelmeier, D., & Kahneman, D. (1996). 'Patients' memories of painful medical treatments: Real time and retrospective evaluations of two minimally invasive procedures. *Pain, 116*, 3–8.

Reeves, A., & Stucke, M. (2011). Behavioral antitrust. *Indiana Law Journal, 86*, 1527–1586.

Robinson, P. H., & Darley, J. M. (2004). Does criminal law deter? A behavioral science investigation. *Oxford Journal of Legal Studies, 24*(2), 173–205.

Roth, A. E., & Murnighan, E. (1982). The role of information in bargaining: An experimental study. *Econometrica, 50*, 1123–1142.

Rozenblit, L., & Keil, F. (2002). The misunderstood limits of folk science: An illusion of explanatory depth. *Cognitive Science, 26*, 521–562.

Rubin, E. L. (1998). Putting rational actors in their place: Economics and phenomenology symposium: the legal implications of psychology: Human behavior, behavioral economics, and the law. *Vanderbilt Law Review, 51*(6), 1705–1728.

Rubinfeld, D. L. Antitrust settlements. In Blair, R. D., Sokol, D. D. (Eds.), *The Oxford handbook of international antitrust economics* (pp. 172–186).

Samuelson, W., & Zeckhauser, R. (1988). Status quo bias in decision making. *Journal of Risk and Uncertainty, 1*(1), 7–59.

Schnellenbach, J., & Schubert, C. (2015). Behavioral political economy: A survey. *European Journal of Political Economy, 40*.

Schumpeter, J. A. (1942). *Capitalism, socialism and democracy*. London: Routledge.

Segal, I., & Winston, M. D. (2007). Public vs private enforcement of antitrust law: A survey. *European Competition Law Review, 28*, 323–332.

Seidenfeld, M. (2002). Cognitive loafing, social conformity, and judicial review of agency rulemaking. *Cornell Law Review, 87*(2), 486–548.

Shavell, S. (1984). Liability for harm versus regulation of safety. *Journal of Legal Studies, 13,* 357–374.

Sheehan, R. S. (1990). Administrative agencies and the court: A reexamination of the impact of agency type on decisional outcomes. *Western Political Quarterly, 43*(December), 875–85.

Shugart II, W. F. (1995). Public choice theory and antitrust policy. In McChesney, F. S. & Shughart II, W. F. (Eds.), *The causes and consequences of antitrust: The public-choice perspective*. University of Chicago Press.

Simon, H. A. (1955). A behavioral model of rational choice. *Quarterly Journal of Economics, 69,* 99–118.

Simon, H. A. (1957). Rational choice and the structure of the environment. In *Models of man: social and rational*. New York: Wiley.

Simon, H. A. (1979). Rational decision making in business organizations. *American Economic Review, 69*(4), 493–513.

Simon, D. (2004). The third view of the black box: Cognitive coherence in legal decision making. *The University of Chicago Law Review, 71*(2), 511–586.

Simon, D., & Scurich, N. (2011). Lay judgments of judicial decision making. *Journal of Empirical Legal Studies, 8*(4), 709–727.

Simonson, I., & Tversky, A. (1992). Choice in context: Tradeoff contrasts and extremeness aversion. *Journal of Marketing Research, 29*(3), 281–295.

Slovic, P., & Fishhoff, B. (1977). On the psychology of experimental surprises. *Journal of Experimental Psychology: Human Perception and Performance, 3,* 544–551.

Sokol, D. (2012a). The strategic use of public and private litigation in antitrust. *Southern California Law Review, 85,* 689–732.

Sokol, D. (2012b). Cartels, corporate compliance, and what practitioners really think about enforcement. *Antitrust Law Journal, 78,* 201–240.

Stucke, M. E. (2007). Behavioral economics at the gate: Antitrust in the twenty-First century. *Loyola University Chicago Law Journal, 38,* 513–591.

Sunstein, C. (1997). Behavioral analysis of law. *University of Chicago Law Review, 64,* 1175–1196.

Sunstein, C. R. (2014). *Why nudge? The politics of libertarian paternalism.* Yale University Press.

Svenson, O. (1981). Are we all less risky and more skillful than our fellow drivers? *Acta Psychologica, 47*(2), 143–148.

Tasic, S. (2009). The illusion of regulatory competence. *Critical Review, 21*(4), 423–436.

Taylor, S. E., & Brown, J. D. (1988). Illusion and well-being: A social psychological perspective on mental health. *Psychological Bulletin, 103*(2), 193–210.

Tor, A. (2013). The market, the firm, and behavioral antitrust. In *Oxford handbook on behavioral economics and the law*. Retrieved from http://ssrn.com/abstract=2293733.

Tversky, A., & Kahneman, D. (1982). Judgements of and by representatives. In Kahneman, D., Slovic, P., & Tversky, A. (Eds.), *Judgement under uncertainty: Heuristics and biases*. Cambridge University Press.

Tversky, A., & Kahneman, D. (1973). Availability: A heuristic for judging frequency and probability. *Cognitive Psychology, 4,* 207–232.

Tversky, A., & Kahneman, D. (1974). Judgment under uncertainty: Heuristics and biases. *Science, 185,* 1124–1131.

Tversky, A., & Kahneman, D. (1991). Loss aversion in riskless choice: A reference-dependent model. *The Quarterly Journal of Economics, 106*(4), 1039–1061.

Tversky, A., & Kahneman, D. (1992). Advances in prospect theory: Cumulative representation of uncertainty. *Journal of Risk and Uncertainty, 5,* 297–323.

Van den Bergh, R. (2013). Behavioral antitrust: Not ready for the main stage. *Journal of Competition Law and Economics, 9*(1), 203–229.

Viscusi, W. K. (1995). Carcinogen regulation: risk characteristics and biases in policy decisions. *American Economic Review* (Papers and Proceedings), *85*(2), 50–54.

Viscusi, W. K., & Gayer, T. (2015). Behavioral public choice: The behavioral paradox of government policy. *Harvard Journal of Law and Public Policy, 38,* 973–1007.

Viscusi, W. K., & Hamilton, J. T. (1999). Are risk regulators rational? Evidence from hazardous waste cleanup decisions. *The American Economic Review, 89*(4), 1010–1027.

Viscusi, W. K., & Magat, W. A. (1987). *Learning about risk: Consumer and worker responses to hazard information*. Harvard University Press.

Weinstein, N. D. (1980). Unrealistic optimism about future life events. *Journal of Personality and Social Psychology, 39*(5), 806–820.

Chapter 13
Extraterritorial Effects of Chinese Competition Law: A Comparative View on Merger Policy

Abstract Differences in the assessment standards and notification procedures of merger policy across jurisdictions impose substantial transaction costs on international business and commerce. In this chapter, the issue of the internationalization of merger policy will be discussed by focusing on the extraterritorial applications, conflicts, and solutions provided by three important antitrust jurisdictions—the US, EU and China. Empirical studies on merger decisions in the US, EU and China show that such differences may come from the higher, or lower standard in the analysis of merger effects, and the different priorities of competition goals by the antitrust authority. An international convergence in merger policy may face challenges because jurisdictions may easily incorporate non-economic goals, such as protecting domestic enterprises, when making decisions on transnational mergers. Since the EU and the US proposed two distinct approaches on the internationalization of competition policy, and after the initiatives on creating a global antitrust legal framework failed, today's antitrust world relies on bilateral agreements and multilateral cooperation through transnational networks. Technical assistance, experts' working groups, and the use of "best practice" recommendations provide useful resources for antitrust agencies' to enhance mutual learning. A global convergence in merger policy, although it is difficult from the view of agreeing on one single text of global antitrust law, might be gradually achieved through the efforts by antitrust agencies across jurisdictions by improving their capacity, applying similar analytical tools, and harmonizing assessment procedure rules.

13.1 Introduction

The development of international commerce and the wave of global mergers raise the debate of merger policies in jurisdictions with antitrust laws. At the same time, compared with other competition issues, merger policy has a significant global impact. Mergers between multinational companies are required to notify competition authorities in several jurisdictions.[1] It may impose compliance costs on businesses if merger

[1] Niels and Kate (2004, p. 1).

J. Ma, *Competition Law in China*,
https://doi.org/10.1007/978-981-15-5105-5_13

rules are implemented differently in each country due to different concerns of policy goals; furthermore, the divergences and conflicts between merger control policies may constrain future economic growth, increase transaction costs and the uncertainty of multinational business.[2]

In the past decade, both public and private actors have been involved in developing competition policy in the context of globalization. International organizations and non-governmental networks are established to facilitate the convergence in substantial and procedural rules of merger policy. This chapter is to address the issue of the internationalization of merger policy by focusing on the extraterritorial applications, conflicts, and solutions provided by the US, EU, and China. It will first compare merger policies in the three antitrust jurisdictions and discuss how empirical evidence could show the differences in the merger decisions. It will also analyze how different understandings of merger policy, in particular, the pursuit of competition goals, would give rise to conflicts in a global merger review. Following this discussion, the chapter aims at presenting the current solutions proposed towards the internationalization of merger review, including bilateral and multilateral agreements, harmonization of merger rules and the cooperation between regulators.

13.2 Extraterritorial Enforcement and Conflict of Merger Regulation

13.2.1 US Antitrust Law

In the US, Section 7 of the Clayton Act states that the acquisition which 'may be substantially to lessen competition, or to tend to create a monopoly', should not be allowed. This text was formulated indicates that mergers will be assessed ex ante.[3] The anti-competitive effects can be assessed by comparing the market structure before and after the merger.

The extraterritorial enforcement of the Sherman Act follows the 'intended effects test', which was first developed by Judge Learned Hand at the Second Circuit in *Alcoa* case 1945.[4] When non-US firms reached cartel agreements in other countries, for example, in Switzerland, but have an 'intended effect' within the United States—where the products are sold, the US antitrust laws will hold jurisdiction on the foreign conduct. The central question to be asked is not where the cartel agreement was made, but whether such an agreement has effects on the US market. Since then, 'intended effects tests' have been widely applied by US courts and enforcement agencies, although courts had different opinions upon measuring the severity of the effects and

[2]Hunt (2007).

[3]Blair and Haynes (2011, p. 505).

[4]148 F. 2d 416 (2d Cir. 1945).

how to define the meaning of "intent".[5] In *Continental Ore Co. v. Union Carbide & Carbon Corp.*, the Supreme Court held that "a conspiracy to monopolize or restrain the domestic or foreign commerce of the United States is not outside the reach of the Sherman Act just because part of the conduct complained of occurs in foreign countries."[6]

This principle was further reinforced in Supreme Court judgment in *Hartford Fire Insurance Co. v. California*,[7] where British reinsurers conspired with US partners to influence the American commercial insurance market.[8] The Supreme Court held that "It is well established by now that the Sherman Act applied to foreign conduct that was meant to produce and did in fact produce some substantial effect in the United States."[9] "True conflict" means that the party cannot comply with both domestic law and foreign laws simultaneously. In this case, it was made clear that the principle of comity will not be incorporated because the defendant could have complied with the US law without violating the British law.[10]

13.2.2 EU Competition Law

Articles 101 and 102 of the EU Competition Law do not provide clear provisions on extraterritorial applications, however, extraterritorial enforcement of the EU Competition law was made possible by going through three stages in case law. Before the 1988 *Wood Pulp* case, the European Commission first established the 'economic entity doctrine', referring to how the location where the undertaking operates will be relevant for the application of the EU Competition Law,[11] and later the 'implementation doctrine' was applied. It clarifies that the place where the entity 'implements' their cartel decisions will be addressed by the extraterritorial application of the EU Competition Law.[12] Under the *Wood Pulp* case, the EU Competition can be applied when non-EU forms 'implement' cartel agreements within the EU market. In the *Gencor* judgment, EU Competition Law has jurisdiction as long as the proposed merger

[5]Mcneil (1998, p. 433).

[6]Continental Ore Co. v. Union Carbide & Carbon Corp. 370 U.S. 690, 704 (1962).

[7]509 US 764 (1993) 773; 799; 796–797.

[8]McNeill (1998, p. 426).

[9]Hartford Fire Ins. Co. v. California, 509 U.S. 764 (1993).

[10]Guzman (1998, p. 1508).

[11]*see* judgements in Imperial Chemical Industries Limited v Commission (Dyestuffs); and Case 6/72, Europemballage Corporation and Continental Can Company Inc v. Commission, [1973] E.C. R. 219, p. 15.

[12]Geradin et al. (2008, pp. 3–4) *see* judgement in Woodpulp European Court of Justice, Joined Cases 89, 104, 114, 116, 117 and 125 to 129/85. A. Ahlström Osakeyhtiö and others v Commission [1988] E.C.R. 5193.

has "immediate, reasonably foreseeable, and substantial effect" in the community,[13] even if the merger is between non-EU firms.[14]

The aim of these principles established by EU case law is to "catch" those illegal cartel violators located outside the jurisdiction of the community.[15] The 'economic entity doctrine' will be applied to price fixing subsidiaries even when their decisions are made by non-EC parent companies. The 'implementation doctrine' and the 'effects doctrine' both originate from the 'territoriality principle', which was established to deal with illegal cartels that are not located in the Community, but have their decisions "implemented" or have an "effect" on the trade or consumer welfare of the European Community.[16]

13.2.3 Conflicts of Regulatory Regimes

In the US, since the "effects test" was established in *Alcoa*, price fixer outside the US territory but selling products in the US will be reached by the "long arm" of the Sherman Act. Similarly, since the *Wood Pulp* case, the EU Competition Commission implicitly referred to the "effects doctrine" in order to catch the price fixing cartels which have anti-competitive effects on the Commission dimension. In *Gencor v. Commission*,[17] the Court of First Instance (CFI) adopted the "effects doctrine" in deciding whether EC Merger Regulation could be applied to enterprises established outside the territory of the European Community.[18] The US model of utilizing an "effects test" has raised very active criticisms and rejections from international counterparts, "blocking statutes" were promulgated to strengthen their counter-balance power to the extraterritoriality of the US law. For example, some argued that the use of "effects doctrine" in the EU may seem to be a consequence in order to counterbalance their enforcement power in the transnational antitrust practice.[19] The Australian Cartels Act states that it applies to "cartels conducted abroad but affecting the domestic market".[20] Countries such as Canada, Australia, Republic of the Philippines, Japan and Korea even invoked discovery blocking statutes and judgment blocking statutes to reject the enforcement of US court judgments.[21]

In a merger review, the conflict of antitrust enforcement was a consequence of the differences in regulatory control in different jurisdictions. Competition authorities may apply different criteria, procedure or standards in anticompetitive assessment,

---

[13] *see* Case T-102/96, Gencor v. Commission, [1999] E.C.R. II-753, para. 90, Court of First Instance.

[14] Geradin et al. (2008, p. 4).

[15] Geradin et al. (2008, pp. 4–6).

[16] Geradin et al. (2008, pp. 4–6).

[17] Case T-102/96, Gencor Ltd. v. EC Commission, 1999 E.C.R. II-753, [1999] 4 CMLR 971.

[18] George et al. (2004, p. 571).

[19] Calvani (2005, p. 1130).

[20] The Australian Trade Practice Act of 1974.

[21] Chang (1993, pp. 295–320).

therefore international companies may face different judgment and decisions, such as receiving a substantial fine in one country, but receive approval or settlement in another country.[22] In the Boeing-McDonnell Douglas case in 1997,[23] the merger was opposed by the EU Commission after receiving approval from the US counterpart. Similarly, in the GE-Honeywell case in 2001, the European Commission blocked the merger without considering the reactions from the US regulators.[24] In the Microsoft, Inc case in 2004,[25] Microsoft received 497 million Euro fines by the Commission but was settled in the US.

13.2.4 A Perspective from Competition Goals

As many have argued, the differences in the merger decisions between the US and the EU may come from the different competition goals that the antitrust jurisdiction strives to pursue.[26] By reviewing the decisions in the *Virgin/British Airways* and the *GE/Honeywell* cases, commentators argued that in general the US antitrust authority seems to be less interventionist.[27] Cento Veljanovski provided the data that in 2000, the probability of intervention by the EU Commission was about ten times higher than the US authority, and it was about nine times more likely to block a merger.[28] One of the explanations which have been widely agreed was that this difference was due to the lack of consensus regarding the ultimate aim of antitrust law.[29] The US antitrust law has developed for over a century and since the mid-1980s, the antitrust policy in the US has been framed under the strong influence of the Chicago School. In contrast, the European approach has a strong focus on the concept of dominance, and therefore tends to follow a legalistic approach.[30] In the EU, if a firm holds a dominant position, its effects on competition in the given market, or in another market (through 'leveraging the market power') must be treated with caution.[31] The concerns of preventing the abuse of dominant position and protecting the competition

[22]Boeing and McDoell case; F. Hoffman-Larouche Ltd. Empagran S.A., 124 S. Ct. 2359(2004); Intel Corp. Advanced Micro Devices, Inc., 542 U.S., 124 S. Ct. 2466(2004).

[23]Case IV/M. 877, Boeing/McDonnell Douglas v. Commission, 1997 O.J. (C 372) 17.

[24]Case M. 2220 General Electric/Honeywell, Commission Decision of July 3, 2001; Commission Decision 2004/134/EC of 3 July 2001 Declaring a Concentration (merger) between General Electric Co. and Honeywell International, Inc. Incompatible with the Common Market and the EEA Agreement, 2004 O.J. (L48) 1.

[25]Case T-201/04, Microsoft Corp. v. Commission; Press Release, European Commission, Commission Gives Microsoft Last Opportunity to Comment before Concluding its Antitrust Probe (August 6, 2003), Ref. No. IP/03/1150.

[26]Van den Bergh and Camesasca (2006), Van den Bergh (2006), Faure and Zhang (2011).

[27]Niels and Kate (2004, p. 7).

[28]Veljanovski (2004, p. 156).

[29]Stevens (2002, pp. 284–285).

[30]Niels and Kate (2004, p. 11).

[31]Niels and Kate (2004, p. 13).

process reflected the influence of Ordoliberalism.[32] Seeing the different decisions for *GE/Honeywell* as well as *Boeing/McDonnell Douglas* made by the antitrust authority in the US and the EU, some commentators criticized the EU approach as being to 'protect competitors'.[33] The divergent views on competition goals may bring difficulties in harmonizing antitrust practice among jurisdictions,[34] which would add transaction costs for global business operators, and impose deterrence effects on the efficiency-enhancing mergers.[35]

13.3 The Internationalization of Competition Law: Cooperation and Convergence

The United States and the European Union hold two different positions on the internationalization of competition rules. The EU approach focuses on the development of an international institutional framework, such as international organizations or treaties, through diplomatic efforts, under which national sovereignty is respected, and states act in their own interest. The EU approach expects the international community to take the EU competition law as the main source of influence, and international cooperation could be promoted through harmonization. In contrast, the US approach is against establishing international competition rules; rather, international cooperation could be facilitated through horizontal coordination between national government officials, as well as the extraterritorial application of national laws.[36] These two positions became more integrated in the process of internationalization of competition law,[37] and international regimes are developed into two main categories: one is bilateral agreements signed between national governments, and the other is multilateral agreements functioning under international organizations and transnational networks.

13.3.1 Bilateral Agreements

The most effective antitrust cooperation on enforcement is the bilateral agreements signed between competition agencies. These agreements are non-binding "soft law" aiming at promoting cooperation on the exchange of information and performing duties of notification and consultation. It is not mandatory, however, for each party to

[32] Schmitz (2002, p. 338).

[33] Kolasky (2004, p. 30), Boeder (2000, pp. 142–143), Karacan (2004, p. 234).

[34] Schnell (2004, p. 253).

[35] Kolasky (2002, p. 547).

[36] Maher (2002, p. 113), Waller (1996, p. 1111).

[37] Maher (2002, p. 113).

take action or to change the substances of their national laws.[38] The goal of bilateral agreements is to remind both parties to take into account of the consequences of their competition decisions, in particular to compare the "relative significance" of the cartel activities on one party's jurisdiction with the effect on the other's territory. This consideration is also often written under the "comity principle"[39] If positive comity is incorporated in the bilateral agreements, the party has to respond to the request of the other state by invoking domestic competition law when anti-competitive conduct in its jurisdiction has a negative effect on the other state[40] Positive comity is an effective mechanism to control transboundary business when it has anti-competitive effects but is located outside the jurisdiction of domestic law. Therefore, signing bilateral agreements with positive comity could be a useful tool when the extraterritorial application of domestic competition law is weak.[41] In addition, bilateral agreements serve as a tool to facilitate antitrust cooperation by encouraging states to exchange information and evidence in antitrust investigations. These requirements, however, are not mandatory and do not provide detailed guidelines on how both agencies and courts can release confidential information, evidence and testimony in antitrust proceedings. In *United States v. Baker Hughes, Inc*[42] and *Hartford Fire Ins. Co.,*[43] the US courts made clear that courts cannot challenge the exercise of jurisdiction if enforcement agencies (Department of Justice or the Federal Trade Commission) have taken the position of positive comity.[44]

The US and EU signed a bilateral agreement on competition cooperation in 1991,[45] and this agreement was reinforced in 1998.[46] Bilateral agreements have also been signed between US and its trading partners: Canada,[47] Australia, Brazil, Germany, Israel, Japan[48] and Mexico.[49] Positive comity was incorporated in the bilateral agreements between the EU and Israel, Brazil, Japan, and Canada.[50] More than forty

---

[38]Matsushita (2002, p. 468).

[39]Geradin et al. (2008, p. 8).

[40]Matsushita (2002, p. 470).

[41]Matsushita (2002, p. 470).

[42]United States v. Baker Hughes, Inc., 731 F. Supp. 3.

[43]Hartford Fire Ins. Co. v. California, 113 S. Ct. 2891, 2909 (1993).

[44]Pitofsky et al. (1995, p. 396).

[45]Agreement between the Government of the United States of America and the Commission of the European Communities Regarding the Application of their Competition Laws, September 23, 1991; O.J. L 95/47.

[46]Agreement Between the Government of the United States of America and the European Communities on the Application of Positive Comity Principles in the Enforcement of Their Competition Laws, June 3–4, 1998 (entered into force June 4, 1998); O.J. L. 173/28.

[47]Agreement between the Government of the United States of America and the Government of Canada Regarding the Application of Their Competition and Deceptive marketing Practices Laws, August 3, 1995.

[48]Agreement between the Government of the United States of America and the Government of Japan Concerning Cooperation on Anti-competitive Activities, October 7, 1999.

[49]www.usdoj.gov/atr/public/international/docs/.

[50]Epstein (2002, p. 359).

mutual assistance treaties have been signed under the 1994 American International Antitrust Enforcement Assistance Act, which could be counted as bilateral agreements on mutual assistance of enforcing competition laws, and such cooperation is often on a case-by-case basis.[51] Bilateral agreements between the US and the EU, the US and Canada, Australia and New Zealand[52] went one step further and were called "second-generation" cooperation, because the exchange of confidential information was allowed on reciprocity basis.[53] By 2015, China had signed antitrust cooperation agreements with Australia, Brazil, European Commission, Republic of Korea and the United Kingdom. India has cooperation agreements with the EU, US and Australia.[54]

Although bilateral agreements established rules on information exchange and notification, they did not clarify how both authorities and courts can cooperate at a substantial level in investigation proceedings, recognizing evidence, exchange of witness, and anti-competitive effects assessment. Also, since bilateral agreements are non-binding soft laws, it does not solve the conflicts in international antitrust cooperation when two nations have different standards in assessing anticompetitive effects. The state may refuse to take action when the conduct is exempted or approved in their national law.[55] A successful cooperation between two countries must be supported by harmonized competition rules in the substance or procedure of assessing anti-competitive effects across borders.

13.3.2 Transnational Networks and Multilateral Agreements

Shortly after the Second World War, the International Trade Organization (ITO) was proposed under the Havana Charter in order to establish a global competition legal framework.[56] ITO, together with the World Bank and the International Monetary Fund, was designed to build the post-war economic order.[57] This proposal, however, after receiving objections from the US, was replaced by the General Agreement on Tariffs and Trade (GATT) system under which competition issues were neglected.[58] In 1993, a working group called the Munich Group drafted a detailed antitrust code

---

[51] Maher (2002, p. 131).

[52] Closer Economic Relations—Trade Agreement, March 28, 1983; Nemeth (2006), 'Trade and Competition Policy Reforms', Acta Oeconomica, vol. 56, No. 4, at p. 450.

[53] Pitofsky et al. (1995, p. 401).

[54] Cejnar (2015, p. 371).

[55] Matsushita (2002, p. 471).

[56] Havana Charter for an International Trade Organization, March 24, 1948. Article 46 U.N. Doc. E/c/2/78.

[57] Waller (1997, pp. 347–350).

[58] Smitherman (2004, p. 834).

to be adopted by the WTO.[59] Their efforts of harmonizing international antitrust law was supported by Europe, but rejected by US government officials.[60] In 1995, the EU proposed to incorporate a Working Group on the Interaction between Trade and Competition Policy within the WTO, and the principal task of this working group is to consider the possibility of harmonizing national competition rules.[61] The working group was created in 1996 during the WTO Ministerial Meeting in Singapore, with a core mission of identifying the trade and competition issues between Members that should be considered within the WTO framework.[62] In 2001 Doha Ministerial Declaration, it made clear that negotiations on the harmonization of competition issues should be held after the next WTO Ministerial Meeting. This proposal, however, failed because of the objection from the US, and was dropped in 2003 at the Fifth Ministerial Conference in Cancun.[63] In 2004, the Decision by the General Council of the WTO stated that Doha Work Program should not include issues on the "interaction between trade and competition policy".[64] Thus, initiatives on establishing a global antitrust legal framework failed and there is no harmonized international competition rule until today.[65]

In 1967 and 1973, responding to the GATT's concern on the US extraterritorial application of its antitrust law, the Organization for Economic Cooperation and Development (OECD) established the Competition Law and Policy Committee (CLPC), and issued its first recommendation on competition.[66] To promote information sharing and cooperation in enforcement between antitrust agencies, as well as legal harmonization of competition rules, since 1967, OECD has issued several recommendations, asking members to notify other states with important interests in their antitrust investigation, coordinate in procedures and exchange information.[67] The most relevant documents related to discussions on issues of antitrust harmonization are the Recommendation of the Council for Cooperation between Member Countries in Areas of Potential Conflicts between Competition and Trade Policies, adopted in 1986, and the Recommendation of the Council Concerning Effective Action Against Hard Cartels adopted in 1998.[68] Also, members are encouraged to sign agreements

---

59 International Antitrust Code Working Group, Draft International Code as a GATT-MTO-Plurilateral Trade Agreement, July 10, 1993.

60 Waller (1997, p. 347).

61 Damtoft and Flangan (2009, p. 142).

62 Singapore Ministerial Declaration, December 13, 1996. http://www.wto.org/english/thewto_e/minist_e/min96_e/wtodec_e.htm.

63 Damtoft and Flanagan (2009, p. 142).

64 Doha Ministerial Declaration, November 14, 2001. http://www.wto.org/english/thewto_e/minist_e/min01_e/mindecl_e.htm.

65 Geradin (2009, p. 195).

66 Organization for Economic Cooperation and Development, Council Recommendation Concerning Cooperation between Member Countries on Restrictive Business Practices Affecting International Trade (October 5, 1957).

67 Smitherman (2004, p. 839).

68 Lanucara (2002, p. 442).

between themselves based on recommendations.[69] These recommendations helped antitrust agencies among OECD member countries to cooperate and to learn from the "best practices", although these recommendations are non-binding and strict compliance is not required.[70]

For UN Members, antitrust issues were negotiated under the United National Conference on Trade and Development (UNCTAD). UNCTAD adopted the Set of Multilaterally Agreed Equitable Principles and Rules for the Control of Restrictive Business Practices in 1980,[71] aiming at building information exchange channels between states in the proceedings of detecting restrictive business conduct, and states were required to perform a duty of consultation during their investigation.[72] In addition, the recent development of Global Competition Forum, and the UNCTAD Intergovernmental Group of Experts on Competition Law and Policy, provide a useful forum for discussions among developing countries and developed economies.[73]

Within the EU, national authorities of the Member States cooperate on the forum of the European Competition Network (ECN); whereas outside the EU, since 2001 competition authorities have cooperated under the International Competition Network (ICN). Both transnational networks function as useful platforms for information sharing and the convergence in procedural and substantive issues.[74] ICN has its members from competition agencies over 104 countries around the globe, and 96 percent of them utilize the materials provided by ICN in their daily investigation.[75] Competition agencies refer the ICN best practice guides in merger review, the investigations of cartel, dominant position and assessing unilateral conduct. Non-governmental stakeholders, including practitioners, organizations, academics, both lawyers and economists are encouraged to participate in various Working Groups, and to work with antitrust agencies in the process of promoting convergence in substantive and procedural laws.[76] The Merger Working Group of ICN was established to promote the adoption of best practices in order to enhance the effectiveness of merger review in each jurisdictions, to facilitate convergence in procedural and substantive rules, and to reduce the costs of public and private actors in multi-jurisdictional merger reviews. The main activities of Merger Groups include projects on revising recommended practices, investigating techniques for merger view, and to promote and implement the working group's work product. The Guiding Principles and Recommended Practices for merger notification and review procedures have been adopted

---

[69]Organization for Economic Cooperation and Development: Revised Recommendation of the Council Concerning Cooperation between Member Countries on Anti-competitive Practices Affecting International Trade July 27–28 1995.

[70]Sokol (2007, p. 47).

[71]U.N. Doc. TD/RBP/Conf./10 (1980).

[72]Basedow (2000, p. 1043).

[73]Maher (2002, p. 122).

[74]Smitherman (2004, p. 840).

[75]ICN Factsheet and Key Messages, International Competition Network (2009). http://www.internationalcompetitionnetwork.org/uploads/library/doc608.pdf.

[76]Sokol, 'Limiting Anti-Competitive Government Interventions that Benefit Special Interests', http://papers.ssrn.com/sol3/papers.cfm?abstract_id=1463462, p. 30.

by ICN memberships and those agencies are invited to participate in ICN Working group meetings and Annual Conferences.

13.3.3 Harmonization

Conflicts in international antitrust enforcement would hardly be mitigated if national authorities apply different criteria, procedure, and standards in competition assessment. It is possible that antitrust cases are legal under one country's legislation but illegal in another country. National competition authorities and regulators are not empowered to investigate even if there are bilateral agreements and comity provisions do apply. It has been argued that, many international conflicts, such as *Wood Pulp, Laker Airways, Hartford Fire Insurance case*, are the clear example showing the result of different treatment of anti-competitive practice.[77]

It is not a new topic to discuss the possibility of harmonizing competition rules and to set a common standard among jurisdictions. On the one hand, Member States adopt competition laws by following the same model of the EU competition law during the EU Enlargement in 2004,[78] differences in merger regulation in the EU and US tend to become smaller today[79]; on the other hand, conflicts in applying the standard of anti-competitive effects still remain. To lower the costs for firms doing transnational business, some have advocated the convergence on a single, uniformed international antitrust law; or, if "perfect convergence" is not feasible, the substance of national competition laws should at least be to some extent harmonized,[80] or set minimum standards[81]; some others have argued for common notification procedures.[82] For example, the basic requirements in merger control, including the process of collecting data, the waiting periods and deadlines in the pre-merger notification process, do not have significant differences, and have the potential for harmonization across jurisdictions.[83]

The discussion of harmonizing international competition law focuses on two issues: one way of harmonization refers to the mutual agreement on a minimal level of international law in order to implement the same law in all countries. The other way is to have essential harmonization, with mutually agreed differences. One of the most important advantage of harmonizing international competition policy is reducing legal uncertainty. The costs of researching, learning competition laws in other jurisdictions, as well as adopting relevant business strategies are substantially high. By reducing legal uncertainty, harmonizing international competition law is

[77]Klodt (2001).

[78]Calvani (2005, p. 1136).

[79]Calvani (2005, p. 1136).

[80]Shenefield (2004, p. 386).

[81]Basedow (2000, p. 48).

[82]Kovacic (2003, p. 310).

[83]Gerber (2002, p. 293).

advocated for the reason of reducing transaction costs, and information costs, and in this way sustains cross-border business activities.

13.3.4 International Regulators

The strong reliance on administrative enforcement of merger policy makes it important to discuss how national regulators could cooperate at international level. Although various information sharing mechanisms have been developed for decades,[84] cooperation in the substance of antitrust agencies remains difficult. It may be valid to argue that the weak cooperation between antitrust agencies contributes to the low capacity of antitrust institutions in developing countries. Substantial efforts were devoted to organize workshops and courses to train regulators in countries which have weak experience in antitrust law. In the developed world, regulators sit in the working group on a routine basis and try to reach a harmonized regulatory guidelines and standards. For example, the EU and the US signed a document on bilateral cooperation on merger review, which is called the "Best Practices" document. This document is the result of the Merger Working Group, and the group's goal is to provide "a set of best practices on cooperation in reviewing mergers that require approval on both sides of the Atlantic with a view to enhancing the good relationship developed over the last decade."[85]

For antitrust agencies in developing countries, learning from the "best practices" from experienced agencies might be helpful to improve their capacity and the quality of their decisions. For antitrust enforcers, their decision-making power is often politically bounded, and their rule-making authority is strongly associated with the national governments, which makes it institutionally difficult to propose a truly independent international antitrust agency with its own rules and enforcement policies[86] Thus, antitrust technical assistance is provided through the "short term interventions" and "long term advisors" program. These programs offers opportunities for young antitrust agencies to receive help by exchanging experts, for example, allowing an economists from the FTC to work at the antitrust agency in Mexico for a year.[87] In this way, enforcement agencies in developing countries could seek help from more experienced agencies, and improve their capacities through mutual learning.

---

[84] In October 1994, the US Congress adopted the International Antitrust enforcement Assistance Act. (Pub. L. 103438, 108 Stat. 4597) Attorney General and the FTC cooperate with antitrust agencies in other countries.

[85] Press Release, European Commission Competition Directorate General, EU and US Issue Best Practices Concerning Bilateral Cooperation in Merger Cases, October 30, 2002.

[86] Guzman (2004, p. 366).

[87] Sokol (2009b, p. 1088).

13.4 Practices in China

Competition agencies (NDRC, SAIC and MOFCOM) have separately signed bilateral MOUs with antitrust enforcement agencies in Korea, Japan, Australia, Russia, the US and the EU. In May 2004, the Directorate General for Competition of the European Commission and MOFCOM signed the Terms of Reference of the EU-China Competition Policy Dialogue, which becomes a permanent mechanism for consultation on competition issues between the EU and China.[88] In bilateral cooperation between China and other antitrust jurisdictions, antitrust agencies exchange information on the enforcement of competition law and the updates of competition policy, regulation and guidelines. For example, in the MOU between China and the US, it made clear that the information exchanged include the updates of antitrust policy and enforcement, the inquiry on the suggestions of competition enforcement and policy, comments on competition laws, policy, regulation and guidelines, and the updates on the responses among enterprises, government agencies and the social public to competition issues.[89]

In October 2015, the MOFCOM and the European Commission's Directorate-General for Competition have signed up the Practical Guidance for Cooperation on Reviewing Merger Cases, which aims at strengthening cooperation and coordination on reviewing mergers.[90] Article 5 states that for merger cases that are under review both in China and the EU, competition enforcement agencies maintain communication on the merger review procedure and substance of defining the relevant market, theories of damages, assessment of competitive effects and designs on remedies during the merger control investigation (from accepting the file until making decisions on the investigation).[91] Article 7 of the Guidance states that both enforcement agencies may coordinate on the information required for merger parties and the third party, including exchanging the draft documents of inquiry.[92] This practical guidance has been updated to the Practical Guidance for Cooperation on Reviewing Merger Cases signed on May 7, 2019 between the European Commission Directorate-General for

[88]https://competitioncooperation.eu/zh/eu-asia-competition-policy-cooperation/.

[89]Zhongmei Gongtong Qianshu Fantuolasi He Fanlongduan Hezuo Liangjie Beiwanglu (中美共同签署反托拉斯和反垄断合作谅解备忘录) [China and US signed antitrust and antimonopoly cooperation memorandum], July 27 2011, available at http://www.gov.cn/gzdt/2011-07/27/content_1914969.htm. The memorandum states that the cooperation between competition agencies in China and the US include (1) to inform the important developments in competition policies and antitrust enforcement; (2) to strengthen the enforcement capacity through competition policy and legal activities; (3) to exchange antitrust enforcement experience according to actual needs; (4) to comment on the revision of antitrust laws and related supporting legislative documents; (5) to exchange views on multilateral competition laws and policies; (6) to exchange experiences in improving public awareness of competition policy.

[90]Practical Guidance for Cooperation on Reviewing Merger Cases between Directorate-General for Competition of European Commission and Ministry of Commerce of P.R.China, available at https://ec.europa.eu/competition/international/bilateral/practical_guidance_mofcom_en.pdf.

[91]Article 5 of the Practical Guidance, id.

[92]Article 7 of the Practical Guidance, id.

Competition and SAMR.[93] On the same date, both parties have also signed the Practical Guidance for Cooperation on Investigating Anti-monopoly Cases.[94] In the Memorandum of Understanding on a Dialogue in the Area of State Aid Control Regime and the Fair Competition Review System signed between the SAMR and the Directorate-General for Competition of the European Commission in April 2019, Article 3 explicitly listed the information that could be exchanged.[95] The bilateral agreements signed between competition agencies in China and the European Commission are valuable to enhance the collaboration and knowledge sharing during the investigation of competition cases. However, the limitation of such cooperation on information exchange is that when the information is relevant to national interest, both agencies are empowered to make the information confidential and do not exchange that sensitive information.[96]

13.5 Conclusions

Differences in substantial and procedural rules of merger policy may impose compliance costs on international business corporations. Empirical studies on merger decisions in the US, the EU and China showed that such differences come from the higher, or lower standard in the analysis of the merger effects, as well as the different priorities of competition goals by the antitrust authority. An international convergence in merger policy face challenges because jurisdictions may easily incorporate non-economic goals, such as protecting domestic enterprises, when making decisions on transnational mergers. Since the EU and the US proposed two distinct approaches on the internationalization of competition policy, and after the initiatives on creating a global antitrust legal framework failed, today's antitrust world relies on bilateral

---

[93] Practical Guidance for Cooperation on Reviewing Merger Cases between Directorate-General for Competition of European Commission and the State Administration for Market Regulation of P.R. of China, available at https://ec.europa.eu/competition/international/bilateral/practical_guidance_merger.pdf.

[94] Practical Guidance for Cooperation on Investigating Anti-monopoly Cases between the Directorate-General for Competition of European Commission and the State Administration for Market Regulation of P.R. of China, available at https://ec.europa.eu/competition/international/bilateral/practical_guidance_antimonopoly.pdf.

[95] Memorandum of Understanding on a Dialogue in the Area of State Aid Control Regime and the Fair Competition Review System between the SAMR and the Directorate-General for Competition of the European Commission, available at https://ec.europa.eu/competition/international/bilateral/mou_china_2019.pdf.

[96] For example, Article 3.2 of the Memorandum of Understanding on Cooperation in the area of Anti0monopoly Law between the Directorate-General for Competition of the European Commission and the NDRC and the SAIC stated: "No Side is required to communicate information to the other if such communication is prohibited by the laws or regulations of the Side possessing the information or would be incompatible with the interests of that Side in the application of its laws." Available at https://ec.europa.eu/competition/international/bilateral/mou_china_en.pdf.

agreements and multilateral cooperation through transnational networks. Technical assistance, experts' working groups, and the use of "best practice" recommendations provide useful resources for antitrust agencies' to enhance mutual learning. A global convergence in merger policy may be gradually achieved through the efforts by antitrust agencies across jurisdictions that improve their capacity, applying similar analytical tools, and harmonizing assessment procedure rules.

References

Basedow, J. (2000). International antitrust: From extraterritorial application to harmonization. *Louisiana Law Review, 60,* 1037–1052.

Blair, R. D., & Haynes, J. S. (2011). The efficiencies defense in the 2010 horizontal merger guidelines. *Review of Industrial Organization, 39,* 57–68.

Boeder, T. L. (2000). The Boeing-McDonnell Douglas merger. In Evenett, S. J., Lehmann, A., & Steil, B. (Eds.), *Antitrust goes global: what future for transatlantic cooperation*? Brookings Institution Press and Chatham House.

Calvani, T. (2005). Conflict, cooperation, and convergence in international competition. *Antitrust Law Journal, 72*(3), 1127–1146.

Cejnar, L. (2015). The International dimension of competition law. *International Trade & Business Law Review, 18,* 360–375.

Chang, S. W. (1993). Extraterritorial application of US antitrust laws to other pacific countries: Proposed bilateral agreements for resolving international conflicts within the pacific community. *Hastings International and Comparative Law Review, 16,* 295–320.

Damtoft, R. W., & Flangan, R. (2009). The development of international networks in antitrust. *The International Lawyer, 43*(1), 137–150.

Epstein, J. (2002). The other side of harmony: Can trade and competition laws work together in the international market place? *American University International Law Review, 17,* 343–368.

Faure, M., & Zhang, X. (2011). *Competition policy and regulation, recent developments in China, the US and Europe*. Edward Elgar.

Fox, E. M. (2003). International antitrust and the Doha Dome. *Virginia Journal of International Law, 43,* 911–932.

George, B. C., Dymally, L. V., & Lacey, K. A. (2004). Increasing extraterritorial intrusion of European union authority into US business mergers and competition practices: US multinational business underestimate the strength of the European Commission from GE-Honeywell to Microsoft. *Connecticut Journal of International Law, 19*(3), 571–617.

Geradin, D. (2009). The perils of antitrust proliferation: The globalization of antitrust and the risks of overregulation of competitive behavior. *Chicago Journal of International Law, 10*(1), 189–211.

Geradin, D., Reysen, M., & Henry, D. (2008). Extraterritoriality, comity and cooperation in EC Competition Law. Retrieved from https://ssrn.com/abstract=1175003.

Gerber, D. J. (2002). Competition law. *The American Journal of Comparative Law, 50*. Supplement: American Law in a Time of Global Interdependence: U.S. National Reports to the 16th International Congress of Comparative Law (Autumn, 2002), 263–296.

Guzman, A. T. (1998). Is international antitrust possible? *New York University Law Review, 73,* 1501–1548.

Guzman, A. (2004). The case for international antitrust. *Berkeley Journal of International Law, 22,* 355–374.

Hunt, W. A. (2007). Business implications of divergences in multi-jurisdictional merger review by international competition enforcement agencies. *Northwestern Journal of International Law and Business, 28,* 147–170.

Karacan, P. (2004). Differences in merger analysis between the United States and the European Union, highlighted in the context of the Boeing/McDonnell Douglas and GE/Honeywell mergers. *The Transnational Lawyer, 17,* 209–258.

Klodt, H. (2001). Conflicts and conflict resolution in international anti-trust: Do we need international competition rules? *World Economy, 24*(7), 877–888.

Kolasky, W. J. (2002). Conglomerate mergers and range effects: It is a long way from Chicago to Brussels. *George Mason Law Review, 10,* 533–550.

Kolasky, W. J. (2004). What is competition? A comparison of US and European Perspectives. *The Antitrust Bulletin, 49,* 29–54.

Kovacic, W. E. (2003). Extraterritoriality, institutions, and convergence in international competition policy. *Proceedings of the Annual Meeting (American Society of International Law), 97,* 309–312.

Lanucara, L. (2002). The globalization of antitrust enforcement: Governance issues and legal responses. *Indiana Journal of Global Legal Studies, 9*(2), 433–459.

Maher, I. (2002). Competition law in the international domain: Networks as a new form of governance. *Journal of Law and Society, 29*(1), 111–136.

Matsushita, M. (2002). International cooperation in the enforcement of competition policy. *Washington University Global Studies Law Review, 1,* 463–475.

McNeill, J. (1998). Comment extraterritorial antitrust jurisdiction: Continuing the confusion in policy, law and jurisdiction. *California Western International Law Journal, 28,* 426–458.

Nemeth, A. (2006). Trade and competition policy reforms. *Acta Oecon, 56*(4), 449–453.

Niels, G., & Kate, A. (2004). Introduction: Antitrust in the US and the EU—Converging or diverging paths. *Antitrust Bulletin, 49,* 1–28.

Pitofsky, R., Rill, J. F., Wood, D. P., Ehlermann, C. D., & Lipsky, A. (1995). The challenge of international regulatory competition: Trade and competition policy. *Proceedings of the Annual Meeting (American Society of International Law), 89,* 395–408.

Schmitz, S. (2002). How dare they? European merger control and the European Commission's blocking of the General Electric/Honeywell merger. *University of Pennsylvania Journal of International Economic Law, 23*(2), 325–384.

Schnell, D. K. (2004). All bundled up: bringing the failed GE/Honeywell merger in from the cold. *Cornell International Law Journal, 37,* 217–262.

Shenefield, J. (2004). Coherence or confusion: The future of the global antitrust conversation. *Antitrust Bulletin, 49,* 385–434.

Smitherman, C. W. (2004). The future of global competition governance: Lessons from the transatlantic. *American University International Law Review, 19,* 769–881.

Sokol, D. D. (2007). Monopolists without borders: The institutional challenge of international antitrust in a global gilded age. *Berkeley Business Law Journal, 4*(1), 36–123.

Sokol, D. D. (2009a). Limiting anti-Competitive government interventions that benefit special interests. *George Mason Law Review, 17,* 119–189.

Sokol, D. D. (2009b). The future of international antitrust and improving antitrust capacity. *Northwestern University Law Review, 103,* 1081–1096.

Stevens, S. (2002). The increased aggression of the EC Commission in extraterritorial enforcement of the merger regulation and its impact on transatlantic cooperation in antitrust. *Syracuse Journal of International Law and Commerce, 29,* 263–302.

Van den Bergh, R. (2006). The economics of competition policy and the draft of the Chinese competition law. In Eger, T., Faure, M. G., & Zhang, N. (Eds.), *Economic analysis of law in China.* Edward Elgar.

Van den Bergh, R., & Camesasca, P. D. (2006). *European competition law and economics—A comparative perspective*. Thomson/Sweet & Maxwell.
Veljanovski, C. (2004). EC merger policy after GE/Honeywell and Airtours. *The Antitrust Bulletin, 49,* 153–194.
Waller, S. W. (1996). National laws and international markets: Strategies of cooperation and harmonization in the enforcement of competition law. *Cardozo Law Review, 18,* 1111–1128.
Waller, S. W. (1997). The internationalization of antitrust enforcement. *Boston University Law Review, 77,* 343–404.

Chapter 14
Conclusions

The Anti-monopoly Law of China (the AML) was promulgated in 2007 and came into force in August 2008. The AML has incorporated both economic and non-economic goals, and industrial policy concerns are considered to be predominant. The role of State-owned enterprises and the issue of administrative monopolies has to be understood in the context of market reform and the developments of national industrial policy. The AML followed a clear bureaucratic enforcement, and since May 2018, the State Administration for Market Regulation (SAMR) has become the enforcement agency of the AML.

The AML has experienced a 13 years long legislative debate. The earliest rule of protecting competition was adopted in October 1980. In September 1987, the State Council promulgated administrative regulation on price control, and the Price Law was effective in May 1998. In 1993, the Anti-unfair Competition law was promulgated and it was revised in November 2017. The AML is composed of 57 articles in 8 chapters. Chapter 1 provides general provisions, and Chap. 2 (Articles 13–16) deals with monopoly agreements. Chapter 3 (Articles 17–19) covers the abuse of dominant position, and Chap. 4 (Articles 20–31) focuses on concentrations. Chapter 5 (Articles 32–37) deals with administrative monopolies, and Chap. 6 is about investigative procedure (Articles 38–45) and Chap. 7 (Articles 46–54) is about legal liabilities and the last chapter is supplementary provisions.

14.1 The AML at the Twelfth Year

After twelve years of experience, China has become one of the major antitrust jurisdictions in the world, and studying its particular features, rather than treating Chinese competition law as a mere legal transplantation, deserves efforts from academics and practitioners. In this book, it has been argued that competition law in China has a predominant feature of incorporating industrial policy in competition case decisions, and administrative enforcement has been predominant in the investigations of monopoly agreement, abuse of dominant position and concentrations. From a

J. Ma, *Competition Law in China*,
https://doi.org/10.1007/978-981-15-5105-5_14

positive aspect, Chaps. 2 and 3 of this book provide an overview on these characteristics, and Chaps. 4–8 analyze the substances of the law. Chapters 9–13 discuss how administrative enforcement of the law could be understood from a law and economics perspective. The 12 year of enforcement of competition law has shown that a comprehensive legal framework has already been established, and the guidelines and provisions implemented by three agencies have specified the details in substantive and procedural law. The enforcement action has been significantly improved and the Chinese antitrust regime is clearly standing between the antitrust giants.

14.2 A Competition System Mixed with Industrial Policy

The goals of competition raised a century-long debate in the US and EU. While the US Antitrust Law focuses on total welfare and consumer welfare, the EU Competition Law has experienced a policy change from non-economic goals, in particular market integration goal, to consumer welfare. Chinese competition law incorporates multiple goals, as the Article 1 of the AML text states goals of preventing and restraining monopolistic behaviour, protecting fair competition, increasing economic efficiency, protecting consumer interest and social public interest, protecting a healthy development of socialist market economy. The revised version of the AML in 2020 adds one more goal of protecting innovation.[1] With unclear hierarchy of the multiple goals, incorporating various economic and non-economic considerations may encounter the challenge of mixing competition law with industrial policy and other types of social policy. Separating industrial policy from competition law will not be easy. It is institutionally combined, historically evolved and path-dependent.

Nonetheless, a policy change has emerged since the establishment of a fair competition review system. In March 2015, the State Council published the Several Opinions of the CPC Central Committee and the State Council on Deepening the Reform of Systems and Mechanisms to Accelerate the Implementation of Innovation-driven Development Strategies, in which it made clear that competition policy and industrial policy share the same goal of improving market innovation. The Opinion states that market competition has the fundamental role to stimulate innovation and create a fair, open and transparent market environment. Since May 2016, the State Council has initiated the reform to establish a fair competition review system to coordinate competition policy and industrial policy. The Opinions of the State Council on Establishing A Fair Competition Examination System in the Building of the Market System states that the core of the market reform is to make the market play a *decisive* role in the allocation of resources. Regulations at ministerial and provisional level have been implemented to require administrative agencies conduct

[1] In the revised version, the Article 1 of the AML lists six goals: to prevent and restrain monopolistic behaviour, to protect fair competition, to encourage innovation, improve economic efficiency, protect consumer interest and social public interest, to promote a healthy development of socialist market economy.

a fair competition review when developing rules, policies and regulatory documents for economic activities. In the 2020 draft revision of the AML, Article 4 mentioned that the fundamental function of competition policy will be strengthened by the State. Article 9 was added and explicitly states that the State establishes and implements a fair competition review system, regulates government administrative actions, and prevents the introduction of policies and measures that exclude or restrict competition. If the fair competition review system could be implemented, competition policy and industrial policy could be coordinated, and different types of enterprises, including SOEs, private and foreign enterprises would be treated equally within the legal framework of competition law.[2] The fair competition review system could further prevent administrative monopolies as it prohibits abusive behaviour by administrative agency's ex-ante, as Article 42 of the 2020 draft revision of the AML requires administrative agencies to conduct a fair competition review when formulating regulations that involve market-driven economic activities. The case study in Chaps. 6 and 8 of this book shows that competition enforcement on cases related to abusive dominant position has been significantly improved after the fair competition review system is introduced.

The central argument of this book is that, industrial policy still plays an important role in the formulation and enforcement of competition law in China, and the real focus of the issue is the reliance on administrative and regulatory pattern in the enforcement of the law. During the first years of antitrust enforcement in China, it has been criticized that incorporating non-economic goals in competition law would raise the concerns of economic nationalism and protectionism.[3] Focusing on industrial policy would give favourable treatments to domestic or State-owned companies but become more strict on foreign and private companies.[4] This argument may not hold today. As the EU Competition Commissioner Neelie Kroes claimed in 2007 that the protectionist goal was "old fashioned" for an industrial policy,[5] competition policy in China at its 12th year enforcement can no longer be criticized for protecting competitors. The State Council Notice on Issuing the Plan for Market Regulation During the 13th Five-Year Plan Period stated that competition policy has the function of regulating market order, protecting fair competition, encouraging market innovation, strengthening institutional reform, improve market efficiency and social benefits. In many ways, competition policy in China is expected to play a fundamental and decisive role in developing a socialist market economy, and a fair and modernized view on the administrative model is to be developed to improve the effectiveness of the AML in the new decade.

---

[2] Wang (2020, p. 13).

[3] Davis (2010), Wei (2011).

[4] Davis (2010).

[5] Kroes (2007).

14.3 Economic Analysis on Case Decisions

When a law and economics analysis is applied to examine the case decisions of the AML, it tends to draw a conclusion that economic arguments are playing an increasingly important role in case analysis. However, the enforcement agencies, in particular administrative agencies, tend to 'select' certain arguments to support their decisions without taking a full picture of detailed economic analysis. In published decisions, it is often observed that the agency listed a few economic elements to support their decisions, without mentioning the counter-arguments and does not provide supportive evidence or a more careful pro-and anti-competitive evaluation. In vertical restraints, pro-competitive arguments include solving principal-agent coordination problem and preventing free-riding, improving distribution network and encouraging distributors make specific investment.

In the RPM cases published by administrative agencies, although economic reasonings were mentioned briefly in the decision, those reasonings are mainly in the aspect of anti-competitive effects. The pro-competitive arguments are not mentioned, and a detailed pro and counter-arguments was missing. Efficiency gains were not taken as exemptions that could grant the firms a reduction of fines. While courts ruled that it is not sufficient to prove the agreement has been implemented, but also the agreement has effects to prevent and restrict competition, the price bureau, NDRC and DRC tends to rely on the same methodology of horizontal agreements, which prohibits agreements with price-fixing terms. The court ruled that it is important to prove whether the agreement has effects on preventing and restricting competition, and the factors to be taken into account include whether the relevant market is competitive, whether the market power of the defendant is strong, the intent of the defendant to enforce RPM, the competition effects of RPM. In the *Ruibang/Johnson & Johnson* case decided by the court, although both pro- and anti-competitive effects were analyzed, the pro-competitive effects were considered irrelevant. In the Wuliangye, Maotai, and other RPM cases published by enforcement agencies, the economic analysis of pro and anticompetitive effects was very brief and evidence to prove anti-competitive effects was not mentioned.

In *Qihoo 360 versus Tencent* case, the Supreme People's Court rejected the SSNIP test and refused to analyze Tencent's market power through calculating price elasticity as the increase in price to the platform which it does not require users to pay has a different business model change than traditional business service. It showed that the SSNIP test has its limitations in market dominance cases when the parties operate in the online market. In the 2020 draft revision of the AML, Article 21 (Article 19 of the AML) adds that to determine internet operators have a dominant market position, factors such as network effects, economies of scale, lock-in effects, and the ability to master and process related data should be considered. Article 11 of the SAMR Interim Provisions on Prohibiting Abuse of Dominant Market Positions also mentioned that in determining market dominance for business operators in the industry of Internet or other new economic formats, factors such as competition characteristics, business models, number of users, network effects, locking effects, technical features, market innovation, capacity of mastering and handling relevant data, the business operator's market force in the relevant market could be taken into account.

In the new era of antitrust enforcement, economic knowledge and methods are essential in the analysis of cases in the industry of internet. The AML is to be revised to incorporate economic factors in the assessment of anti-competitive effects. Economic analysis is also valuable to analyse the institutional design and the costs and benefits of enforcement instruments that are to be applied in the investigation of monopolistic agreements, abuse of dominant position and concentrations. Competition regulators in China are therefore encouraged to study economic theory and empirical methods in order to improve the accuracy and consistency of their decisions.

14.4 Enforcement of the Law

The AML in China relies on administrative enforcement and administrative penalties. Three enforcement agencies: SAIC, NDRC and MOFCOM have been responsible for price and non-price related monopolistic conduct and concentrations and only in the 10th year of the enforcement three agencies have been merged into one, the SAMR. The separation of enforcement power has been criticized for a lack of efficiency, creating inconsistency and legal uncertainty, whereas combining the agencies into one single authority may also generate concerns of the danger of abuse monopolistic enforcement power and reducing the benefits of regulatory competition. When discussing the institutional design of the competitive system, it is also argued that a "mix" of enforcement institutions should be introduced. Part III of the book examined the pros and cons of the current enforcement regime of the AML from a law and economics perspective, and proposed that focusing on the improvement of the organization structure and capacity building of the competition agency would be more realistic in practice. Introducing additional instruments, such as criminal liabilities should take the side effects of legal transplantation into account.

Chapter 9 of this book summarized the criteria that are frequently used for designing a well-functioning agency, and suggested methods for building agency capacity, such as training professional agency staff, improving the organization of the agency, and improving the leadership of the agency. Chapter 10 discussed the economic analysis of antitrust sanctions and compared the pros and cons of administrative versus criminal penalties under the Becker Model. It suggested that instead of shifting the enforcement power to the judiciary, it may be more practical to increase the cost of antitrust violations through administrative fines. Chapter 11 of this book compares the enforcement capacity of agencies and courts in handling economic complex antitrust cases. Specialized antitrust agencies are equipped with personnel having knowledge and expertise, while may also suffer from public choice problems. Courts are restrained from regulatory capture, but general judges are not able to conduct sophisticated economic analysis themselves. Chapter 11 compared the decision-making capacity between agencies and courts when experts are involved to provide technical and specialized suggestions. Experts before agencies may have less risk of principal-agent problems as it is on the court. An economic expert witness appointed by the parties may be biased and manipulated by attorneys and those appointed by the courts may suffer from the selection problem. Empirical findings suggested that the appeals against the administrative penalty decisions made by SAIC, NDRC, SAMR and their local branches are extremely rare and in most cases courts ruled in favour of the competition agency. Although public choice arguments are relevant for improving private enforcement, a judicial review system on administrative decisions and follow-on actions of antitrust cases are not yet established and an administrative enforcement is still dominant. Chapter 12 of the book analyzed the enforcement issue from the perspective of behavioral law and economics. Behavioural law and economics could provide experimental evidences on the extent to which law and economics analysis should be amended when individuals are not perfectly rational.

14.5 Towards Antitrust Internationalization

When jurisdictions pursuing different goals, the conflict of antitrust enforcement may emerge in developed and developing countries. Competition authorities may apply different criteria, procedure or standards in competition assessment, therefore international companies may face different judgment and decisions. As discussed in Chap. 13, the US and EU hold two different positions on internationalization of competition rules. While the EU approach focuses on the developing of an international institutional framework, the US approach relies on the coordination between national government officials, and the exterritorial application of national laws. Four mechanisms have been developed in the internationalization of competition law: the establishment of international competition organizations, transnational networks and multilateral agreements, implementing bilateral agreements and harmonizing the substance and procedures of competition law, and strengthening the international cooperation between regulators. Competition agencies in China have separately signed MOU with antitrust jurisdictions in North America, Europe and Asia, which states that information on the enforcement of competition law and updates of competition policy, regulation and guidelines will be exchanged. Nonetheless, the limitation of such cooperation is that both agencies will make the information confidential when it is relevant to national interest. Chapter 13 of this book shows that to enhance international cooperation and mutual learning, mechanisms such as introducing technical assistance, organizing experts' working groups and applying the "best practice" recommendations could provide be adopted. It is also a positive trend that economic theories, analytical tools and empirical methods are widely applied, and a convergence of international competition law could be observed when competition law and policy system across jurisdictions are modernized and a minimum standard could be adopted in the analysis and assessment of competition effects.

14.6 Future Research

This book summarized the legislative history, policy goals, substantive and procedural law and enforcement issues of the AML from 2008 till early 2020. It explained the institutional framework of the competition law and policy in China and introduced the policy reform made by competition agencies during the first decade of competition enforcement in China. Since the establishment of the SAMR in 2018, the AML has entered its second decade, and there are a few issues that are valuable for future research.

The first issue is the enforcement of competition policy under the legal framework of the fair competition review. Article 9 of the 2020 draft revision of the AML has incorporated the fair competition review system, proposed by the State Council in 2016. Administrative agencies at central and local levels are expected to review business-related regulations and policies and to re-examine existing market regulations to ensure the consistency of industrial policy and competition policy. It is expected that the fair competition review system would significantly strengthen the enforcement power of the AML on preventing administrative monopolies, and detailed implementing rules and self-review policies are to be followed to explore the impact of the fair competition review system on legal and economic institutions in China.

The second issue is the reform of substantive and procedural law by the SAMR. Since its establishment, the SAMR has unified several provisions and regulations issued by the SAIC and NDRC, and has promulgated new provisions to integrate various existing regulations on the substantive and procedural law of monopoly agreements, abuse of dominant position and merger review. It also is reported that the SAMR has strengthened its enforcement efforts in the AML, not only the 2020 draft revision has significantly increased the level of administrative fines for anti-monopoly violations, but also a 30% increase in the antitrust cases filed and investigated has been observed in 2018.[6] This book has briefly introduced the contents of the new regulation and it is important to study the policy change that made by SAMR and to understand how the new provisions are implemented.

The third issue is the challenge of understanding competition cases in the Internet and e-commerce industries. The 2020 draft revision of the AML added the goal of "encouraging innovation" in Article 1, which indicates the new enforcement priority of competition cases in Internet sectors in the digital economy.[7] As discussed in Chap. 6 of this book, when the SSNIP test is not applicable in non-price markets, network externalities, lock-in effects, economies of scale and the ability to master and process related data in multi-sided online markets have to be carefully analysed.

---

[6]China to Take Tougher Antitrust Efforts, Says Latest Draft on Anti-monopoly Law, CGTN, January 2, 2020, available at https://news.cgtn.com/news/2020-01-02/China-to-take-tougher-antitrust-efforts-MVNpH6Ubwk/index.html.

[7]China Seeks More Aggressive Antitrust Enforcement as It Proposes Amendments to the Anti-monopoly Law, Freshfields Bruckhaus Deringer, January 9, 2020, available at http://knowledge.freshfields.com/en/Global/r/4056/china_seeks_more_aggressive_antitrust_enforcement_as_it.

Enforcement agencies and courts have to develop economic capacity in analysing antitrust cases involving high-tech and intellectual property rights issues. Competition cases on monopolistic agreements, merger reviews and private litigation in the Internet and data-related sectors also emerged in the last decade, and those cases are to be explored and studied in detail in the future research.

References

Davis, B. (2010). China's anti-monopoly law: Protectionism or a great leap forward? *Boston College International and Comparative Review, 33,* 305–321.

Kroes, N. (2007). Speech: Industrial policy and competition law and policy. *Fordham International Law Journal, 30,* 1401–1412.

Wang, X. (2020). Reflections on the revision of China's antimonopoly law (我国《反垄断法》修订的几点思考). *Law Review* (法学评论) (2), 11–21.

Wei, D. (2011). China's anti-monopoly law and its merger enforcement: Convergence and flexibility. *Journal of International Economic Law, 14*(4), 807–844.

The manufacturer's authorised representative in the EU is Springer Nature Customer Service Centre GmbH, Europaplatz 3, 69115 Heidelberg, Germany. If you have any concerns regarding our products, please contact ProductSafety@springernature.com

Printed and bound by CPI Group (UK) Ltd, Croydon, CR0 4YY
25/09/2026
02222903-0008